Hawaii The Big Island Revealed
The Ultimate Guidebook

4th Edition

Andrew Doughty

WIZARD
PUBLICATIONS
INC

Hawaii The Big Island Revealed
The Ultimate Guidebook; 4th Edition

Published by Wizard Publications, Inc.
Post Office Box 991
Lihuʻe, Hawaiʻi 96766–0991

ISBN-13:   978-0-9717279-4-6   4106
ISBN-10:   0-9717279-4-5
Library of Congress Control Number 2005924272
Printed in China

Cataloging-in-Publication Data

Doughty, Andrew
    Hawaii the Big Island revealed : the ultimate guidebook / Andrew Doughty. – 4th ed.
Lihue, HI : Wizard Publications, Inc., 2006
        308 p.: col. illus., col. photos, col. maps; 21 cm.
        Includes index.
        Summary : a complete traveler's reference to the island of Hawaii, with full color
photos, maps, directions, and candid advice by an author who resides in Hawaii.
        ISBN 978-0-9717279-4-6
        ISBN 0-9717279-4-5
        LCCN 2005924272

        1. Hawaii Island (Hawaii) – Guidebooks. 2. Hawaii Island (Hawaii) – Description
and travel. I. Title.

DU 622
919.69__dc21

All photographs (except cover & page 16) taken by Andrew Doughty and Leona Boyd.
Cartography by Andrew Doughty.
All artwork and illustrations by Andrew Doughty and Lisa Pollak.

Past and present lava flow information for maps was graciously provided by an over-worked and under-appreciated United States Geological Survey, the silent partner to all mapmakers. Keep up the good work!

Cover imagery courtesy of NASA. Original raw imagery has been computer modified by Wizard Publications, Inc., and the resulting photograph is copyrighted by Wizard.

Pages 2–3: Kilauea's Puʻu ʻOʻo vent up close.

We welcome any comments, questions, criticisms or contributions you may have, and have incorporated some of your suggestions into this edition. Please send to the address above or e-mail us at **aloha@wizardpub.com**.

Check out our Web site at **www.wizardpub.com** for up-to-the-minute changes.

To Harry and Mary
Their love of travel lives on…

CONTENTS

CONTENTS

VOLCANO SIGHTS
85

HILO & PUNA SIGHTS
106

HAMAKUA & WAIMEA SIGHTS
123

SADDLE ROAD SIGHTS
138

BEACHES
147

ACTIVITIES
176

("Activities" continued...)

CONTENTS

ACTIVITIES
(Continued)
176

ADVENTURES
225

ISLAND DINING
240

WHERE TO STAY
278

The Big Island has it all. Nowhere else in the world will you find the diversity available here. Pristine rain forests, lava deserts, world-class beaches, snow-covered mountains, an active volcano, dazzling sunsets and just about every activity you can think of. The island is huge—about the size of Connecticut. Navigating your way through this maze of opportunity can be daunting.

Most travel publishers send a writer or writers to a given location for a few weeks to become "experts" and to compile information for guidebooks. To our knowledge, we at Wizard Publications are the only ones who actually *live* our books.

We hike the trails, ride the boats, eat in the restaurants, explore the reefs and do the things we write about. It takes us one to two *years*, full time, to do a first edition book, and we visit places *anonymously*. We marvel at writers who can do it all in a couple weeks staying in a hotel. Wow, they must be *really* fast. Our method, though it takes much longer, gives us the ability to tell it like it is in a way no one else can. We put in many long hours, and doing all these activities is a burdensome grind. But we do it all for you—only for you. (Feel free to gag at this point.)

We have found many special places that people born and raised here didn't even know about because that's *all we do*—explore the island. Visitors will find the book as valuable as having a friend living on the island.

We recognize the effort people go through to visit the Big Island, and our goal is to expose you to as many options as possible so you can decide what you want to see and do. We took great pains to structure this book in such a way that it will be fun, easy reading and loaded with useful information. This book is not a bland regurgitation of the facts arranged in textbook fashion. We feel strongly that guidebooks should present their information so that you don't have to read through every single page every time you want to find something. If you are here on vacation, your time is extremely precious. You don't want to spend all your time flipping through a book looking for what you want. You want to be able to locate *what* you want, *when* you want it. You want to be able to access a comprehensive index, a thorough table of contents, and refer to high quality maps that were designed with you in mind. You want to know which helicopter, SCUBA, boat tour or lu'au is the best on the island. You want to find special hidden gems most people overlook. You want to be shown those things that will make this vacation the best of your life.

A quick look at this book will reveal features never before used in a guidebook. Let's start with the maps. They are more detailed than any other maps you will find, and yet they omit extraneous information that can sometimes make a chore out of reading a map. We know that people in unfamiliar territory sometimes have a hard time determining where they are on a map, so we included landmarks. Most notable among these are mile markers. At every mile on main roads, the government has erected numbered markers to tell you where you are. We are the first to put these markers on a map so you can use them as reference points. In addition, we repeatedly drove or walked every inch of every road on the maps. This is important because *many* of the roads represented on existing maps have been shifted, moved or eliminated, making "current" maps obsolete. Where needed, we've drawn legal public beach access in yellow, so you'll *know* when you are legally entitled to cross someone's land. Most guidebooks have the infuriating habit of mentioning a particular place or sight, but *fail to mention how to get there!* You won't find that in our book. We tell you exactly how to find the hidden gems and use our own special maps to guide you.

One of the things unique to this book is the acceptance of change. We produce brand new editions of our books every two years or so, but in the intervening time we are constantly incorporating changes into the text nearly every time we do a new printing. We also post these changes on our Web site. This allows us to make some modifications throughout the life of each edition. We don't have the luxury of making every change that happens on a weekly basis, but it does give us more flexibility than if we only acknowledged changes every two years.

As you read this book, you will also notice that we are very candid in assessing businesses. Unlike some other guidebooks that send out questionnaires asking businesses to *rate themselves* (gee, they *all* say they're good), we've had *personal* contact with the businesses listed in this book. One of the dirty little secrets about guidebook writers is that they often make cozy little deals for good reviews. Well, you won't find that here. We accept no payment for our reviews, we make no deals with businesses for saying nice things, and there are *no advertisements* in our book. What we've seen and experienced is what you get. If we gush over a certain company, it comes from personal experience. If we rail against a business, it is for the same reason. All businesses mentioned in this book are here by *our* choosing. None have had any input into what we say, and we have not received a single cent from any of them for their inclusion. (In fact, there are some that would probably pay to be left out, given our comments.) We always approach businesses as anonymous travelers. This ensures that we are treated the same as you. What you get is our opinion on how they operate. Nothing more, nothing less.

Sometimes our candor gets us into trouble. For instance, this book used to be the only guidebook sold at the Visitor Center in Hawai'i Volcanoes National Park. After undergoing a rigorous multi-month review process by government bureaucrats, this book was deemed "the most accurate book we've ever seen for the Big Island." They even wanted to sell our *Kaua'i* book there, a first at the park, because they liked the way we thoroughly researched things. But thoroughness cuts both ways. When those same bureaucrats later realized that we had revealed a secret but *public* trail (previously unknown to the general public) that led to the erupting Pu'u 'O'o vent through a beautiful forest, they stopped selling this book and fumed over the loss of control to the vent. (The trail is outside the park and therefore outside the control of the bureaucrats.) It's not the first time this book has been pulled from shelves for being too honest, and it won't be the last.

This book is intended to bring you independence in exploring the Big Island. We don't want to waste any of your precious time by giving you bad advice or bad directions. We want you to experience the best that the island has to offer. Our objective in writing this book is to give you the tools and information necessary to have the greatest Hawaiian experience possible.

We hope we succeeded.

Andrew Doughty
Kailua-Kona, Hawai'i

Brand new liquid land flows in a scene as primordial as the island's birth.

As with people, volcanic islands have a life cycle. They emerge from their sea floor womb to be greeted by the warmth of the sun. They grow, mature and eventually die before sinking forever beneath the sea.

HOW IT BEGAN

Sometime around 70 million years ago a cataclysmic rupture occurred in the Earth's mantle, deep below the crust. A hot spot of liquid rock blasted through the Pacific plate like a giant cutting torch, forcing magma to the surface off the coast of Russia, forming the Emperor Seamounts. As the tectonic plate moved slowly over this hot spot, this torch cut a long scar along the plate, piling up mountains of rock, producing island after island. The oldest of these islands to have survived is Kure. Once a massive island with its own unique ecosystem, only its ghost remains in the form of a fringing coral reef, called an atoll.

As soon as the islands were born, a conspiracy of elements proceeded to dismantle them. Ocean waves unmercifully battered the fragile and fractured rock. Abundant rain, especially on the northeastern sides of the mountains, easily carved up the rock surface, seeking faults in the rock and forming rivers and streams. In forming these channels, the water carried away the rock and soil, robbing the islands of their very essence. Additionally, the weight of the islands ensured their doom. Lava flows on top of other lava, and the union of these flows is always weak. This lava also contains countless air pockets and is criss-crossed with hollow lava tubes, making it inherently unstable. As these massive amounts of rock accumulated, their bases were crushed under the weight of subsequent lava flows, causing their summits to sink back into the sea.

What we call the Hawaiian Islands are simply the latest creation from this island-making machine. Someday they will disappear, existing as nothing more than footnotes in the Earth's turbulent geologic history.

Kaua'i and Ni'ihau are the oldest of the eight major islands. Lush and deeply eroded, the last of Kaua'i's fires died with its volcano a million years ago. O'ahu, Moloka'i, Lana'i, Kaho'olawe—their growing days are over, as well. Maui is in its twilight days as a growing island. After growing vigorously, Hawaiian volca-

noes usually go to sleep for a million years or so before sputtering back to life for one last fling. Maui's volcano Haleakala has entered its final stage and last erupted around 1790.

The latest and newest star in this island chain is Hawai'i. Born less than a million years ago, this youngster is still vigorously growing. Though none of its five volcano mountains is considered truly dead, these days Mauna Loa and Kilauea are doing most of the work of making the Big Island bigger. Mauna Loa, the most massive mountain on Earth, consists of 10,000 *cubic miles* of rock. Quieter of the two active volcanoes, it last erupted in 1984. Kilauea is the most boisterous of the volcanoes and is the most active volcano on the planet. Kilauea's most recent eruption began in 1983 and was still going strong as we went to press. Up and coming onto the world stage is Lo'ihi. This new volcano is still 3,200 feet below the ocean's surface, 20 miles off the southeastern

The wonder of creation can still be seen at night at Kilauea Volcano.

In regions of the island blessed with abundant rains, verdant growth carpets the landscape.

coast of the island. Yet in a geologic heartbeat, the Hawaiian islands will be richer with its ascension, sometime in the next 100,000 years.

These virgin islands were barren at birth. Consisting only of volcanic rock, the first life forms to appreciate these new islands were marine creatures. Fish, mammals and microscopic animals discovered this new underwater haven and made homes for themselves. Coral polyps attached themselves to the lava rock and succeeding generations built upon these, creating what would become a coral reef.

Meanwhile, on land, seeds carried by the winds were struggling to colonize the rocky land, eking out a living and breaking down the lava rock. Storms brought the occasional bird, hopelessly blown off course. The lucky ones found the islands. The even luckier ones arrived with mates or had fertilized eggs when they got here. Other animals, stranded on a piece of floating debris, washed ashore against all odds and went on to colonize the islands. These introductions of new species were rare events. It took an extraordinary set of circumstances for a new species to actually make it to the islands. Single specimens were destined to live out their lives in lonely solitude. On average, a new species was successfully deposited here only once every 20,000 years.

When a volcanic island is old, it is a sandy sliver, devoid of mountains. When it's middle aged, it can be a lush wonderland, a haven for anything green, like Kaua'i. And when it is young, it is dynamic and unpredictable, like the Big Island of Hawai'i. Of all the Hawaiian Islands, none offers a larger range of climates and landscapes than the Big Island. The first people to discover Hawai'i's treasures must have been humbled at their good fortune.

THE FIRST SETTLERS

Sometime around the fourth or fifth century AD a large double-hulled voyaging canoe, held together with flexible sennit lashings and propelled by sails made of woven pandanus, slid onto the sand on the Big Island of Hawai'i. These first intrepid adventurers, only a few dozen or so, encountered an island chain of unimaginable beauty.

The ancient Polynesians were exceptional navigators. These stones, at the navigational heiau near Mahukona, were aligned to point the way to other Hawaiian islands, Tahiti and other far away places.

They had left their home in the Marquesas Islands, 2,500 miles away, for reasons we will never know. Some say it was because of war, overpopulation, drought, or just a sense of adventure. Whatever their reasons, these initial settlers took a big chance and surely must have been highly motivated. They left their homes and searched for a new world to colonize. Doubtless, most of the first groups perished at sea. The Hawaiian Islands are the most isolated island chain in the world, and there was no way for them to know that there were islands in these waters. (Though some speculate that they were led here by the golden plover—see box on facing page.)

Those settlers who did arrive brought with them food staples from home: taro, breadfruit, pigs, dogs and several types of fowl. This was a pivotal decision. These first settlers found a land that contained almost no edible plants. With no land mammals other than the Hawaiian bat, the first settlers subsisted on fish until their crops matured. From then on, they lived on fish and taro. Although we asso-

ciate throw-net fishing with Hawai'i, this practice was introduced by Japanese immigrants much later. The ancient Hawaiians used fishhooks and spears, for the most part, or drove fish into a net already placed in the water. They also had domesticated animals, which were used as ritual foods or reserved for chiefs.

Little is known about the initial culture. Archaeologists believe that a second wave of colonists, probably from Tahiti, may have subdued these initial inhabitants around 1000 AD Some may have resisted and fled into the forest, creating the legend of the Menehune.

Today, Menehune are always referred to as being small in stature. Initially referring to their social stature, the legend evolved to mean that they were physically short and lived in the woods away from the Hawaiians. (The Hawaiians avoided the woods when possible, fearing that they held evil spirits, and instead stayed on the coastal plains.) The Menehune were purported to build fabulous structures, always in one night. Their numbers were said to be vast, as many as

500,000. It is interesting to note that in a census taken of Kaua'i in around 1800, 65 people from a remote valley identified themselves as Menehune.

The second wave probably swept over the island from the south, pushing the first inhabitants ever-north. On a tiny island north of Kaua'i, archeologists have found carvings, clearly not Hawaiian, that closely resemble Marquesan carvings, probably left by the doomed exiles.

This second culture was far more aggressive and developed into a highly class-conscious society. The culture was governed by chiefs, called Ali'i, who established a long list of taboos called kapu. These kapu were designed to keep order, and the penalty for breaking one was usually death by strangulation, club or fire. If the violation was serious enough, the guilty party's entire family might also be killed. It was kapu, for instance, for your shadow to fall across the shadow of the Ali'i. It was kapu to interrupt the chief if he was speaking. It was kapu to prepare men's food in the same container used for women's food. It was kapu for women to eat pork or bananas. It was kapu for men and women to eat together. It was kapu not to observe the days designated to the gods. Certain areas were kapu for fishing if they became depleted, allowing the area to replenish itself.

While harsh by our standards today, this system kept the order. Most Ali'i were sensitive to the disturbance their presence caused and often ventured outside only at night, or a scout was sent ahead to warn people that an Ali'i was on his way. All commoners were required to pay tribute to the Ali'i in the form of food and other items. Human sacrifices were common, and war among rival chiefs the norm.

By the 1700s, the Hawaiians had lost all contact with Tahiti, and the Tahitians had lost all memory of Hawai'i. Hawaiian canoes had evolved into fishing and inter-island canoes and were no longer capable of long ocean voyages. The Hawaiians had forgotten how to explore the world.

Hawai'i's First Tour Guide?

Given the remoteness of the Hawaiian Islands relative to the rest of Polynesia (or anywhere else for that matter), you'll be forgiven for wondering how the first settlers found these islands in the first place. Many

scientists think it might have been this little guy here. Called the kolea, or golden plover, this tiny bird flies over 2,500 miles nonstop to Alaska every year for the summer, returning to Hawai'i after mating. Some of these birds continue past Hawai'i and fly another 2,500 miles to Samoa and other South Pacific islands. The early Polynesians surely must have noticed this commute and concluded that there must be land in the direction that the bird was heading. They never would have dreamed that the birds leaving the South Pacific were heading to a land 5,000 miles away, and that Hawai'i was merely a stop in between, where the lazier birds wintered.

OUTSIDE WORLD DISCOVERS HAWAI'I

In January 1778 an event occurred that would forever change Hawai'i. Captain James Cook, who usually had a genius for predicting where to find islands, stumbled upon Hawai'i. He had not expected the islands to be here. He was on his way to Alaska on his third great voyage of discovery, this time to search for the Northwest Passage linking the Atlantic and Pacific Oceans. Cook approached the shores of Waimea, Kaua'i, at night on January 19, 1778. The next morning Kaua'i's inhabitants awoke to a wondrous sight and thought they were being visited by gods. Rushing out to greet their visitors, the Kauaians were fascinated by what they saw: pointy-headed beings (the British wore tri-cornered hats) breathing fire (smoking pipes) and possessing a death-dealing instrument identified as a water squirter (guns). The amount of iron on the ship was incredible. (They had seen iron before in the form of nails on driftwood but never knew where it originated.)

It's hard to believe that the Big Island will eventually look like this oldest Hawaiian Island, Kure Atoll. One day its last ghostly remains will sink forever beneath the sea.

Cook left Kaua'i and briefly explored Ni'ihau before heading north for his mission on February 2, 1778. When Cook returned to the islands in November after failing to find the Northwest Passage, he visited the Big Island of Hawai'i.

The Hawaiians had probably seen white men before. Local legend indicates that strange white people washed ashore at Ke'ei Beach sometime around the 1520s and integrated into society. This coincides with Spanish records of two ships lost in this part of the world in 1528. But a few weird-looking stragglers couldn't compare to the arrival of Cook's great ships and instruments.

Despite some recent rewriting of history, all evidence indicates that Cook, unlike some other exploring sea captains of his era, was a thoroughly decent man. Individuals need to be evaluated in the context of their time. Cook knew that his mere presence would have a profound impact on the cultures he encountered, but he also knew that change for these cultures was inevitable, with or without him. He tried, unsuccessfully, to keep the men known to be infected with venereal diseases from mixing with local women, and he frequently flogged infected men who tried to sneak ashore at night. He was greatly distressed when a party he sent to Ni'ihau was forced to stay overnight due to high surf, knowing that his men might transmit diseases to the women (which they did).

Cook arrived on the Big Island at a time of much upheaval. The mo'i, or king, of the Big Island had been badly spanked during an earlier attempt to invade Maui and was now looting and raising hell throughout the islands as retribution. Cook's arrival and his physical appearance (he was 6 feet, 4 inches) assured that the Hawaiians would assume him to be

The Day the Gods Cried...

At the south end of Alii Drive in Kona, just before it dead ends, there is a lava road leading toward the ocean. This field of lava and an area around the point called Kuamo'o have an extraordinary past. Here occurred an event that forever changed a people. For it was here that the Hawaiians abolished their ancient religion one day in 1820.

The Hawaiian religion was based on the kapu system. A myriad of laws were maintained, with death being the usual punishment for violation. The Hawaiians believed that rigid enforcement for a single violation was necessary, or else the gods would punish the whole community in the form of earthquakes, tsunamis, lava flows and famine. When Captain Cook came, he and his men were unaware of the many laws and inadvertently violated many of them. When natural punishments failed to materialize, many Hawaiians concluded that the gods would not enforce the laws. Since many found the kapu laws burdensome and oppressive, there was pressure to abolish them. While King Kamehameha I was alive, however, none dared challenge the kapu system. Almost as soon as he died, King Kamehameha II, pressured by his stepmother Ka'ahumanu, decided to put an end to the kapu system and destroy the temples around the island. This was before any missionaries ever came to these islands.

It was decided that the action would be consecrated by the simple act of having the king eat with women in public in November 1819. This had heretofore been kapu, and the penalty for breaking this law was death. In breaking this kapu in public, Kamehameha II declared an end to the old ways. One of his cousins, Kekuaokalani, was to be king of the spiritual world and challenged him. The ferocious battle took place near here in early 1820. His cousin was hit by Kamehameha II's forces, and the man's grieving wife ran to his side as he fell. She cried out, begging that her wounded husband's life be spared. Instead she and her husband were summarily executed on the spot, with her body falling on top of his. The Hawaiian religion, as a dominant force, died with them on that bloody day. If you look to the south, you can see what look like terraces cut into the side of the mountain. These are the graves of the many hundreds who died in that very battle.

Today there is a resurgence of the Hawaiian religion. Hawaiians are grappling with their role in the world and are reaching back to their roots. The religion that seemingly died on that raw lava field is being reborn in the hearts of some contemporary Hawaiians.

the god Lono. Lono was responsible for fertility of the land. Every year the ruling chiefs and their war god Ku went into abeyance, removing their power so that Lono could return to the land and make it fertile again, bringing back the spring rains. During this time all public works stopped and the land was left alone. At the end of this *Makahiki* season man would again seize the land from Lono so he could grow crops and otherwise make a living upon it. Cook arrived at the beginning of the Makahiki, and the Hawaiians naturally thought *he* was the god Lono, coming to make the land fertile. Cook even sailed into Keala-kekua Bay, *exactly* where legend said Lono would arrive.

The Hawaiians went to great lengths to please their "god." All manner of supplies were made available. Eventually, they became suspicious of the visitors. If they were gods, why did they accept Hawaiian women? And if they were gods, why did one of them die?

Cook left at the right time. The British had used up the Hawaiians' hospitality (not to mention their supplies). But shortly after leaving the Big Island, the ship broke a mast, making it necessary to return to Kealakekua Bay for repairs. As they sailed back into the bay, the Hawaiians were nowhere to be seen. A chief had declared the area kapu to help replenish it. When Cook finally found the Hawaiians, they were polite but wary. Why are you back? Didn't we please you enough already? What do you want now?

As repair of the mast went along, things began to get tense. Eventually the Hawaiians stole a British rowboat (for the nails), and the normally calm Cook blew his cork. On the morning of February 14, 1779, he went ashore to trick the chief into coming aboard his ship where he would detain him until the rowboat was returned. As Cook and the chief were heading to the water, the chief's wife begged the chief not to go. By now tens of thousands of Hawaiians were crowding around Cook, and he ordered a retreat. A shot was heard from the other side of the bay and someone shouted that the Englishmen had killed an important chief. A shielded warrior with a dagger came at Cook, who fired his pistol (loaded with non-lethal small shot). The shield stopped the small shot, and the Hawaiians were emboldened. Other shots were fired. Standing in knee-deep water, Cook turned to call for a cease-fire and was struck in the head from behind with a club, then stabbed. Dozens of other Hawaiians pounced on him, stabbing his body repeatedly. The greatest explorer the world had ever known was dead at age 50 in a petty skirmish over a stolen rowboat.

When things calmed down, the Hawaiians were horrified that they had killed a man they had earlier presumed to be a god. See page 70 to see what finally happened to Cook's body.

KAMEHAMEHA THE GREAT

The most powerful and influential king in Hawaiian history lived during the time of Captain Cook and was born on this island sometime around 1758. Until his rule, the Hawaiian chain had never been ruled by a single person. He was the first to "unite" (i.e., conquer) all the islands.

Kamehameha was an extraordinary man by any standard. He possessed herculean strength, a brilliant mind, and boundless ambition. He was marked for death before he was even born. When Kamehameha's mother was pregnant with him, she developed a strange and overpowering craving—she wanted to *eat* the eyeball of a chief. The king of the Big Island, mindful of the rumor that the unborn child's real father was his bitter enemy, the king of Maui, asked his advisors to interpret. Their conclusion was unanimous: The child would grow to be a rebel, a killer of chiefs. The king decided that the child must die as soon as he was born, but the baby was instead whisked away to a remote part of Waipi'o Valley to be raised.

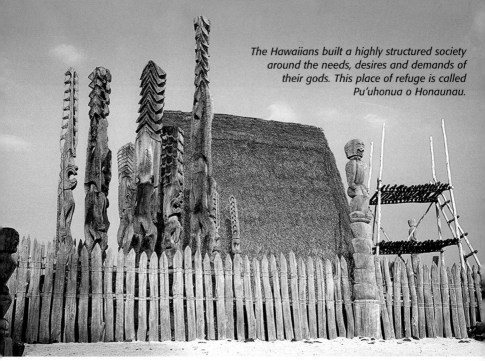

The Hawaiians built a highly structured society around the needs, desires and demands of their gods. This place of refuge is called Pu'uhonua o Honaunau.

In ancient Hawaiian society, your role in life was governed by the class you were born into. The Hawaiians believed that breeding among family members produced superior offspring (except for the genetic misfortunates who were killed at birth), and the highest chiefs came from brother/sister combinations. Kamehameha was not of the highest class (his parents were merely cousins), so his future as a chief would not come easily.

As a young man, Kamehameha was impressed by his experience with Captain Cook. He was among the small group that stayed overnight on Cook's ship during Cook's first pass of Maui. (Kamehameha was on Maui valiantly fighting a battle in which his side was getting badly whooped.) Kamehameha recognized that his world had forever changed, and he shrewdly used the knowledge and technology of westerners to his own advantage.

Kamehameha participated in numerous battles. Many of them were lost (by his side), but he learned from his mistakes and developed into a cunning tactician.

When he finally consolidated his rule over the Big Island (by luring his enemy to be the inaugural sacrifice at the Pu'ukohola Heiau near Kawaihae), he fixed his sights on the entire chain. In 1795 his large company of troops, armed with some western armaments and advisors, swept across Maui, Moloka'i, Lana'i and O'ahu. After some delays with the last of the holdouts, Kaua'i, their king finally acquiesced to the inevitable, and Kamehameha became the first ruler of all the islands. He spent his final years governing the islands peacefully from his capital at Kailua Bay and died in 1819.

MODERN HAWAI'I

During the 19th century, Hawai'i's character changed dramatically. Businessmen from all over the world came here to exploit Hawai'i's sandalwood, whales, land and people. Hawai'i's leaders, for their part, actively participated in these ventures and took a piece of much of the action for themselves. Workers were brought in from many parts of the world, changing the racial makeup of the islands. Government corruption became the order of the day, and everyone seemed to be profiting, except the Hawaiian commoner. By the time Queen Lili'uokalani lost her throne to a group of American businessmen in 1893, Hawai'i had become directionless, barely resembling the Hawai'i Captain Cook had encountered the previous century. The kapu system had been abolished by the Hawaiians shortly after the death of Kamehameha the Great. The "Great Mahele," begun in 1848, had changed the relationship Hawaiians had with the land. Large tracts of land were sold by the Hawaiian government to royalty, government officials, commoners and foreigners, effectively stripping many Hawaiians of the land they had lived on for generations.

The United States recognized the Republic of Hawai'i in 1894 with Sanford Dole as its president. It was later annexed and became an official territory in 1900. During the 19th and 20th centuries, sugar established itself as king. Pineapple was also a major crop in the islands, with the island of Lana'i being purchased in its entirety for the purpose of growing pineapples. As the 20th century rolled on, Hawaiian sugar and pineapple workers found themselves in a lofty position—they became the highest paid workers for these crops in the world. As land prices rose and competition from other parts of the world increased, sugar and pineapple became less and less profitable. Today, these crops no longer hold the position they once had. The "pineapple island" of Lana'i has shifted away from pineapple growing and is looking toward luxury tourism. The sugar industry is now dead on the Big Island, and sugar lands are being converted to other purposes while the workers move into other vocations, often tourist-related.

The story of Hawai'i is not a story of good versus evil. Nearly everyone shares in the blame for what happened to the Hawaiian people and their culture. Westerners certainly saw Hawai'i as a potential bonanza and easily exploitable. They knew what buttons to push and pushed them well. But the Hawaiians, for their part, were in a state of flux. The mere appearance of westerners seemed to reveal a discontent, or at least a weakness, in their system that had been lingering just below the surface. In fact, in 1794, a mere 16 years after first encountering westerners and under no military duress from the West, Kamehameha the Great *volunteered* to cede his island over to Great Britain. He was hungry for western arms so he could defeat his neighbor island opponents. He even declared that, as of that day, they were no longer people of Hawai'i, but rather people of Britain. (Britain declined the offer.) And in 1819, immediately after the death of the strong-willed Kamehameha, the Hawaiians, of their own accord, overthrew their own religion, dumped the kapu system and denied their gods. This was *before* any western missionaries ever came to Hawai'i.

Nonetheless, Hawai'i today is once again seeking guidance from her heritage. The echoes of the past seem to be getting louder with time, rather than diminishing. Interest in the Hawaiian language and culture is at a level not seen in many decades. All who live here are very aware of the issues and the complexities involved, but there is little agreement about where it will lead. As a result, you will be exposed to a more "Hawaiian" Hawai'i than those who might have visited the state a decade ago. This is an interesting time in Hawai'i. Enjoy it as observers, and savor the flavor of Hawai'i.

Going with the flow—Big Island style.

In order to get to the islands, you've got to fly here. While this may sound painfully obvious, many people spend time trying to find an ocean cruise to the Islands. There are no regular cruises between Hawai'i and the mainland.

GETTING HERE

When planning your trip, a travel agent can be helpful. Their commission has been paid directly by the travel industry, though that may change in the future. The Internet is a great source for companies selling travel packages. If you don't want to or can't go through these sources, there are large wholesalers that can get you airfare, hotel and a rental car, often cheaper than you can get airfare on your own. **Pleasant Holidays** (800) 242–9244 is one of the more well-known providers of complete package tours.

They are re-nowned for their impossibly low rates. We've always been amazed that you can sometimes get round trip airfare from the mainland, a hotel, and car for a week for as low as $700 per person, depending on where you fly from and where you stay. That's a small price to pay for your little piece of paradise. Also, **Cheap Tickets** (800) 377–1000 usually lives up to its name.

If you arrange airline tickets and hotel reservations yourself, you can often count on paying top dollar for each facet of your trip. The prices listed in the WHERE TO STAY chapter reflect the RACK rates, meaning the published rates before any discounts. Rates can be significantly lower if you go through a wholesaler.

When you pick your travel source, shop around—the differences can be dramatic. A good source can make the difference between affording a *one-week* vacation and a *two-week* vacation. It's not always a straightforward process; there is an art to it. Look in the Sunday travel section of your local newspaper—the bigger the paper, the better, or check on-line versions of major papers.

Flight schedules change all the time, but United and others often have *direct* flights to Kona from the mainland. Not having to cool your heels while changing planes on O'ahu is a *big* plus because inter-island flights aren't quite as simple and painless (or cheap) as they used to be. Flight attendants zip up and down the aisles hurling juice at you for the short, inter-island flight. If you fly to the Big Island from Honolulu, either into Kona (where most arrive) or Hilo, sit on the left side (seats with an "A") coming in (right side going out) for superb views of several other islands. When flying to O'ahu from the mainland, seats on the left side have the best views. Inter-island flights are done by Aloha (800–367–5250), Hawaiian (800–367–5320), Go! (888–435–9462) and Island Air (800–652–6541).

WHAT TO BRING

This list may assist you in planning what to bring. Obviously you won't bring everything on the list, but it might make you think of a few things you may otherwise overlook:
- Waterproof sunblock (SPF 15 or higher)
- Two bathing suits
- Shoes—flip-flops, trashable sneakers, reef shoes, hiking shoes
- Mask, snorkel and fins
- Camera with lots of film or a digital
- Extra batteries (which can be hard to find in remote places) for that camera
- Warm clothes (for Mauna Kea or other high-altitude activities) and junk clothes for bikes, etc.
- Fanny pack—also called waist pack,

to carry all your various vacation accouterments; waterproof ones are convenient for snorkeling
- Flashlight if you like caves or for the lava field at night if there's a surface flow
- Mosquito repellent for some hikes (*Lotions*—not liquids—with DEET seem to work the longest)
- Light rain jacket
- Shorts and other cool cotton clothing
- Cheap, simple backpack—you don't need to go backpacking to use one; a 10-minute trek to a secluded beach is much easier if you bring a simple pack
- Hat or cap for sun protection

GETTING AROUND
Rental Cars

Rental car prices in Hawai'i *can be* (but aren't always) cheaper than almost anywhere else in the country, and the competition is ferocious. Nearly every visitor to the Big Island gets around in a rental car, and for good reason—it's a *big* island. Fortunately, none have mileage charges.

At Kona Airport, rental cars can easily be obtained from the booths across the street from the Main Terminal. It's a good idea to reserve your car in advance since companies can run out of cars during peak times.

Many hotels, condos and rental agents offer excellent room/car packages. Find out from your hotel or travel agent if one is available. You can rent a car in Hilo and return it to Kona (or vice versa). There's usually an extra fee of about $50–$100 (depending on the company and car).

Below is a list of rental car companies. The local area code is 808. Some have desks at various hotels.

Alamo	**(800) 327–9633**
	Kona: 329–8896
	Hilo: 961–3343

Avis	**(800) 321–3712**
	Kona: 327–3000
	Hilo: 935–1290
Budget	**(800) 527–0700**
	Kona: 329–8511
	Hilo: 935–6878
Dollar	**(800) 800–4000**
	Kona & Hilo:
	(866) 434–2226
Enterprise	**(800) 736–8222**
	Kona: 331–2509
	Hilo: 934–0359
Harper	**(800) 852–9993**
	Kona & Hilo: 969–1478
Hertz	**(800) 654–3011**
	Kona: 329–3566
	Hilo: 935–2896
National	**(800) 227–7368**
	Kona: 329–1674
	Hilo: 935–0891
Thrifty	**(800) 367–5238**
	Kona: (877) 283–0898

If you are between the ages of 21 and 25, **Alamo** and **Dollar** are your best bets. You'll pay about $20–$25 extra for the crime of being young and reckless, but at least you won't have to take the bus. If you're under 21—rent a bike or moped or take the bus.

4-Wheel Drive

We *strongly* believe that the best vehicle for the island is a 4-wheel drive vehicle. They come closed (like an Explorer or a Trooper) or open (like a Wrangler). They are more expensive, but there are several roads, beaches and sights that you can't visit without 4WD. Even the short paved road into Waipi'o Valley requires the low gear offered in 4WD. Saddle Road (described on page 138) is contractually off limits to most cars. That means that if you drive it, the insurance you take out with the rental company is void, so you or your insurance company back home would have to eat it. 4WDs rented at **Harper** go without this restriction. (Though Harper prices are *much, much* higher and we've been told by readers that they can be picky during their post-rental inspection.) Different companies have different restrictions, but from a *practical* standpoint, 4WD is the way to go. The drawbacks to *open* JEEPS are more wind and

4WDs can unlock some of the Big Island's more secluded beaches, such as this empty black sand beach at Road to the Sea.

heat and no trunk. Closed 4WDs are best. Expect to pay up to $30–$80 per day for the privilege of cheating the road builders. For some reason, they usually cost much more in Kona than Hilo.

Motorcycles & Scooters

If you really want to ham it up, you can try renting a HOG. *(Disclaimer*—Wizard Publications will not be held liable for bad puns.) **Kona Harley-Davidson** (326–9887) rents Harleys for $125 per day. **DJ's Rentals** (329–1700) in Kona rents Harleys ($120–$135 per day for sportsters, $145 for soft tails) and mopeds for $45. (Mopeds are only useful around Kailua town.)

Motor Homes

The Big Island is the only Hawaiian island where staying in an RV is a viable alternative to hotels. (Ironically, in New Zealand the biggest RV brand is Maui brand, but in real life, Maui doesn't *have* any RVs.) With so much territory to cover and good roads leading to so many places, the RV life might be for you, especially if you're traveling with kids.

Some things to consider:

Motor homes are a relatively new concept here, and you won't find any RV parks or facilities that you might be used to on the mainland.

Beach parks and campgrounds are your best bet for parking. Technically you're supposed to get camping permits to stay at most of them. The best places are Namakani Paio (967–7321) at Volcanoes National Park (it's free) and Kapaʻa Beach Park in North Kohala (though bees are sometimes a problem there). Spencer Beach Park is also good. There are no campgrounds near Kona that we can recommend, but remember, you can park anywhere. See CAMPING on page 179 for more on campsites.

These things don't carry as much waste as you may think, so finding places to empty it will be an ongoing consideration. You can only dump it in Hilo or Kona. Try to use the bathroom facilities at the campgrounds whenever possible.

Harper (800–852–9993) does a pretty good job fixing you up. Their 22-footers are not huge, but they're comfortable. It's not as easy to arrange as a rental car, so do it in advance. You'll need an RV rider from your own insurance. It's $186 per day (plus $200 fee per rental from Kona). If you'd like to pay *way more* than that amount, **Island RV** (334–0464) will separate you from $300 each day.

A Few Driving Tips

Gasoline is *obscenely* expensive here. You may want to have some FedExed to you from home to save money. (OK, maybe not *that* expensive.) Kona is said to have the highest gas prices in the United States (about 15¢ higher than expensive Hilo). Whether that's true or not, prepare to get hammered at the pump. If you're in the Kohala resort area, there's a station off the road to the Waikoloa Resorts at the 76 mile marker. The cheapest gas on the east side of the island is in Hilo or Pahoa, south of Hilo. The cheapest on the *whole island* is in Kona at Costco (but you have to be a Costco member). It's marked on the map on page 165 and not far from the Kona Airport. Many companies charge a top-off fee due to the airport's distance to town, so fill it to the top.

Seat belt and **Child Restraint** use is required by law, and the police will pull you over for this alone. Wide open roads and frequently changing speed limits make it easy to accidentally speed here. Police usually cruise in their own private, unmarked vehicles, so you won't see them coming. We're not supposed to tell you this, but local protocol dictates that you flash your headlights for a couple of miles when you pass a police car to warn drivers coming the other way. So if you see someone flashing their lights at you, you'd better check your speed.

It's best not to leave anything valuable in your car. There are teenagers here who pass the time by breaking into cars. Hapuna Beach and several Hilo waterfalls are notorious for car break-ins. When we park at a beach or waterfall, or any other place frequented by visitors, we take all valuables with us, leave the windows up, and leave the doors unlocked. (Just in case someone is curious enough about the in-side to smash a window.) There are plenty of stories about someone walking 100 feet to a waterfall in Hilo, coming back to their car, and finding that their brand new video camera has walked away. And don't be gullible enough to think that trunks are safe. Someone who sees you put something in your trunk can probably get at it faster than you can with your key.

Kailua-Kona possesses the dry town syndrome: At the first drop of rain, many Kona drivers become vehicularly uncoordinated, driving like a drunken cat on ice, so beware of this.

Traffic has increased *a lot* in the past few years and you should expect to get stuck in it, especially in Kona. Just remember that it could be worse—you could be in traffic back home *and on your way to work*.

Buses

Our main island bus is called **Hele-On** (961–8744). It was designed for local use, so it doesn't go to all the places that visitors want to go. However, it does go between Hilo and Kona and they do take luggage (for an extra fee). Call them for a schedule and rates. There are also bus tours from **Roberts Hawai'i** (329–1688) and **Jack's** (329–2555).

GETTING MARRIED ON THE BIG ISLAND

A beautiful beach at sunset; many couples dream of such a background for their special day. 'Anaeho'omalu Beach, pictured on page 43, is one of the more popular spots for sunset weddings. The Big Island offers an almost unlimited selection of wedding, reception and honeymoon possibilities. Although you can set everything up yourself using the Internet and e-mail, it's usually easier and *sometimes* less expensive to use a professional who can assist you. Almost all of the major resorts have wedding coordinators who can offer suggestions. Alternatively, we've listed a couple of other companies, *outside* of the resorts, that can assist you in your arrangements.

Paradise Weddings Hawaii
    (800) 428–5844 or (808) 883–9067
Anderson Portraits Hawaii
    (866) 832–8626

Expect to pay around $550 for a minimal wedding package (officiant, flowers, photography and video). Resorts generally charge a hefty fee to use their grounds whether you are a guest or not. All beaches are public but it won't be a *private* ceremony. Consider renting a private home or an entire B&B in which to hold the ceremony and reception. See our Web site at www.wizardpub.com for links and wedding license requirements.

WEATHER

The weather on the Big Island is more diverse than any island or other comparably sized chunk of land *in the world*. You name it, we got it. According to the

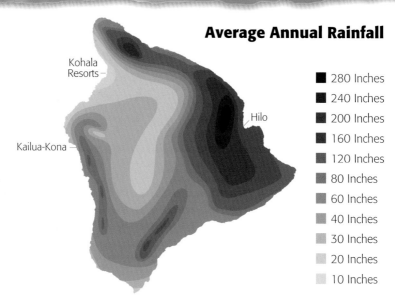

Average Annual Rainfall

Kohala Resorts

Hilo

Kailua-Kona

- 280 Inches
- 240 Inches
- 200 Inches
- 160 Inches
- 120 Inches
- 80 Inches
- 60 Inches
- 40 Inches
- 30 Inches
- 20 Inches
- 10 Inches

Köppen Climate Classification System (which is probably *your* favorite system too, right?), the Big Island has 10 of the 15 types of climatic zones in the world. (Not *climactic* zones, which we accidentally printed in a previous edition. Boy, people were *really* anxious to find one of *those*!) Only Cold Continental Climate categories are absent. Here we've got tropical, monsoonal, desert and even *periglacial* climates, among others. So no matter what kind of weather you like, we are sure to have it here. As you ascend the slopes of the volcanoes, you lose about 3 degrees for every thousand feet. Call 961–5582 for a recording of today's forecast.

Kailua-Kona has weather that can best be described as eternal springtime. Quite simply, it's almost always warm and wonderful. The average high and low in February (the coldest month) is 80° and 64°, whereas the high and low in August (the warmest month) is 87° and 69°. Humidity is usually between 50% and 80%. The temperature change between night and day is greater than the temperature change between winter and summer, so it

could easily be said that nighttime is the winter of the Big Island. Balmy wraparound onshore breezes usually keep it comfortable. The exception is during Kona winds (so named because they come from the Kona direction, rather than out of the northeast as is usually the case). Kona winds occur about 5%–10% of the time and bring stillness or warm air to Kona, creating uncomfortably humid conditions. Normal conditions in Kona and Kohala mean clear mornings with afternoon clouds created by thermal heating, so morning is usually better for activities such as air tours. During the summer, evening showers often occur as warm moist air is cooled, squeezing rain out of the humidity. Because it is totally protected from the trade winds by Hualalai, Kona is the only place in the state that gets most of its rainfall in the summer afternoons and evenings. The higher up the mountain, the more rain you get.

Hilo's weather is almost always described with one word—*rain.* Hilo is the wettest city in the United States. Annual rainfall is rarely less than 100 inches, usually much more. But rain is not a constant here. Hilo has times of drought like anywhere else. (Like when rainfall was a *mere* 70 inches one year, triggering *rationing*.) Most of the rain falls at night. When daytime showers do occur, they are often intense but short lived. That said, rain or cloudiness *will* be a factor here. One of the reasons that Kailua-Kona is so much more popular than Hilo is that visitors like sunny weather, and Hilo can't compete in that area. Also, all that rain has to go somewhere, which is why the ocean off Hilo is not nearly as clear as Kona's runoff-free waters.

The Kohala resort area is the driest part of the island, with rainfall usually around 10 inches per year. Sunshine is almost assured (which is why it is so popular). The weather penalty here is the wind. As the lava fields heat up during the day, the air heats and rises. Air from the ocean rushes in to fill the void, creating strong afternoon convective breezes. The hotter, drier and sunnier it is that day, the breezier it may be that afternoon.

The general rule of thumb is that in wet areas like Hilo, most of the rain falls at night and early morning. Dry areas like Kona and Kohala get their rains in the late afternoon and early evenings.

Water temperatures range from 75° at its coldest in February to 82° at its warmest in September/October. It's colder in some areas where freshwater springs percolate from the ocean's floor and float to the top, forming a boundary called a *Ghyben-Herzberg lens*.

PLANNING YOUR TRIP

Visitors are usually unprepared for the sheer size and diversity of the Big Island. The island is over 4,000 square miles, and a circular trip around, on Highways 19 and 11, is a hefty 222 miles. During that drive you pass through dozens of

different terrains and climates. (And that doesn't even include Saddle Road, Lower Puna, any of North Kohala or scores of other places.) Put simply, this island is too big and too diverse to try to see in a few days. The graphic on page 29 will put it in perspective.

If you are on the island for three days or less, it's our recommendation that you don't try to see the whole island; you'll only end up touring Hawai'i's exotic blacktop. Pick a side. Since one of your days should be spent at the volcano, that leaves you with a scant two days to experience either Hilo's and Puna's beauty or the Kona side's diversity and activities.

Deciding which side of the island to spend the most time on is a difficult decision, but the numbers are definitely skewed. Most visitors spend most of their time on the western, or Kona, side. There are several reasons for this:

Kona Side

The Kona side has the sunshine. The climate in Kona is as perfect as weather gets, and the Kohala resort area has the highest number of sunny days of anywhere in the state. The Kona side also has *far* more activities available. This leads to another reason—the ocean. Since it's on the leeward side of the island, and because there are no permanent streams on the entire west side of the island (except for the one from Kona to Hilo that's filled with tax money), Kona has the calmest, clearest water in the state. Water sports such as swimming, snorkeling, SCUBA, fishing—you name it—are usually unmatched on the Kona side. This side also has the best beaches on the island, with some, such as Hapuna, consistently rated in the top five in the United States. (With a few notable exceptions, the Hilo side has poor beaches.) All this adds up to a traveler's delight, one of the reasons that the Kona side has such a high visitor repeat ratio.

But stand by for a shock when you fly into Kona Airport for the first time. Kona makes a *rotten* first impression on the uninitiated airborne visitor. Part of the airport sits atop a lava flow from 1801, and the first thing you think when you fly in over all that jet black lava is, "I came all this way for *this?*" Don't worry, it gets much better.

Hilo Side

On the other hand, the Kona side is short of what Hilo has in abundance— green. Whereas much of the Kona side is dominated by lava, Hilo is plant heaven. The weather usually comes from the northeast, so Hilo gets around 140 inches of rain per year. This is paradise for anything that grows. Hilo also has breathtaking waterfalls. You won't find *one* on the Kona side unless it's in the lobby of your hotel. Hilo's weather has created beautiful folds and buckles in the terrain. The unweathered Kona side lacks angles—it's mostly gentle slopes. Lastly, Hilo is *much* more convenient for exploring Kilauea volcano.

The Two Sides

The schism between the two sides of the island is wide and deep. Because the two sides are so different and the distances so large (for Hawai'i, that is), most people who live on the west side haven't been to Hilo or Kilauea volcano in years. Most Hilo residents haven't been to Kona in years. Both sides tend to playfully badmouth the other. The Kona side creates the tax base and the Hilo side, the center of county government, spends it (often on Hilo-oriented infrastructure). Hilo has lots of roads that few drive, while Kona drivers curse the traffic on their limited roads.

Suggested Itinerary

If you have a week on the Big Island, you might want to spend four to five days on the Kona side and two to three days in Hilo or Puna. The volcano itself can take one to two days, and you're better off exploring it from Hilo or Puna than from Kona. Hilo all but closes down on Sundays, with most business, even the few tourist-related ones, taking the day off.

GEOGRAPHY

The Big Island is made up of five volcanoes. (See map on the foldout back cover.) Kohala in the north is the oldest. Next came Mauna Kea, Hualalai, Mauna Loa, and finally Kilauea. None are truly dead, but only Mauna Loa and Kilauea make regular appearances, with an oc-

Only on the Big Island can you experience both conditions on the same day a few dozen miles apart.

casional walk-on by Hualalai. Nearly the size of Connecticut, all the other Hawaiian Islands could easily fit inside the Big Island's 4,000 square miles. And it's the only state in the union that gets bigger every year (thanks to Kilauea's land-making machine).

Gentle slopes are the trademark of this young island. It hasn't had time to develop the dramatic, razor-sharp ridges that older islands such as Kaua'i possess. The exception is the windward side of Kohala Mountain where erosion and fault collapses have created a series of dramatic valleys. Two of our mountains rise to over 13,000 feet. Mauna Kea, at 13,796 feet, is the tallest mountain in the world when measured from its base, eclipsing such also-rans as Mount Everest and K-2. Mauna Loa, though slightly shorter, is much broader, earning it the moniker as the *largest* mountain in the world. It contains a mind-numbing 10,000 cubic *miles* of rock.

Another of our mountains is not really a mountain at all. Kilauea, looking more like a gaping wound on Mauna Loa, is the undisputed volcano show-off of the planet. Hundreds of thousands of cubic yards of lava per day issue from its current outlet, Pu'u 'O'o, creating and repaving land on a daily basis.

All this adds up to an exciting and dynamic geographic location. Things change faster here than any place you will ever visit. There have been lots of times that we have gone to a certain beach or area only to find that it has changed beyond recognition. A new black sand beach shifts to another location. Trails become absorbed by a restless and vigorous Mother Nature. Whole roads get covered with lava. Island hopping in this state is like traveling through time. This is an exciting time in the life cycle of this particular island. Enjoy the

How Big is The Big Island of Hawai'i?

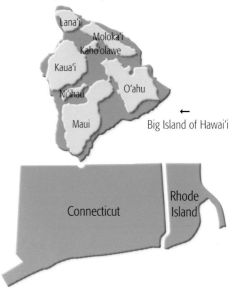

island in its youth, for like all youths, this, too, shall pass.

SO IS HAWAI'I AN ISLAND OR A STATE?

Both. This island, more than any other in this state, is a bit schizophrenic when it comes to names. This is the biggest island in the state, so it is commonly referred to as (brace yourself) *the Big Island.* Its Hawaiian name is *Hawai'i.* So far, so good. But the whole *state* is called Hawai'i. So you figure the capital must be here, right? Nope, Honolulu is on O'ahu. This must be where most of the people live, right? Uh-uh. O'ahu has 80% of the population. Well, this must be where Pearl Harbor is, correct? Wrong answer—it's on O'ahu, too. So why is the state named after *this* island? Because it's the *biggest* island, and this is where King Kamehameha the Great was from. It was he who brought all the islands under one rule for the first time. His first capital was here at Kailua (another naming headache—see below). When you do all that, you have some historical influence. In this book we will refer to this island as *the Big Island.* When we say Hawai'i, we mean the whole state. (Even my brother, when he came to visit the Big Island, called from Honolulu to have us pick him up, assuming it must be on the "main" island.) In short, *in Hawai'i* could be anywhere—*on Hawai'i* is on the Big Island.

I won't even get into the name confusion for the town of Waimea. (Or is it Kamuela? See page 133.) Let's tackle a more annoying naming problem. The main town on the west side is called **Kailua-Kona**, **Kona**, **Kailua** or sometimes **Kailua Town**. In the old days it was simply Kailua. Though there are also towns named Kailua on O'ahu and Maui, it didn't present much of a problem to anyone until the Post Office discovered these islands. In order to keep from messing up the mail *(don't say it!)* they decided to rename the town. (Technically, they renamed their post office, but the subtlety is lost on those who have to address mail.) Since this is the *kona* side of the island (kona being the name of the less common wind that comes from this direction), they cleverly named the Post Office *Kailua-Kona.* To complicate matters further, the builders of the airport here named it the *Kona Airport,* so people began to refer to a trip here as "going to Kona." All this leaves you with a quandary. What do you call this place? Well, in keeping with our editorial policy of taking gutsy stands, we'll call it Kailua-Kona...except when we call it Kona or Kailua Town. In fairness, that's because most who live here do the same.

HAZARDS
The Sun

The hazard that affects by far the most people (excluding the accommodations tax) is the sun. The Big Island, at 19°–20° latitude, receives sunlight more directly than anywhere on the mainland. (The more overhead the sunlight is, the less atmosphere it filters through.) If you want to enjoy your *entire* vacation, make sure that you wear a strong sunblock or cover up, even while snorkeling. We recommend a waterproof sunblock with at least an SPF of 15. Gels work best in the water, lotions on land. Try to avoid the sun between 11 a.m. and 2 p.m. when the sun's rays are particularly strong. If you are fair-skinned or unaccustomed to the sun and want to lay out, 15–20 minutes per side is all you should consider the first day. You can increase it a bit each day. *Beware of the fact that our ever-constant breezes will hide the symptoms of a burn until it's too late.* You might find that trying to get your tan as golden as possible isn't worth it. Tropical suntans are notoriously short lived, whereas you are sure to remember a burned vacation far longer. If, after all of our warnings, you *still* get burned, aloe vera gel works well to relieve the pain. Some come with lidocaine in them. Ask your hotel front desk if they have any aloe plants on the grounds. Peel the skin off a section and make several crisscross cuts in the meat, then rub the plant on your skin. *Oooo, it'll feel so good!*

Water Hazards

The most serious water hazard is the surf. Though more calm in the summer and on the west side, high surf can be found anywhere on the island at any time of the year. The sad fact is that more people drown in Hawai'i each year than anywhere else in the country. This isn't said to keep you from enjoying the ocean, but rather to instill in you a healthy respect for Hawaiian waters. See BEACHES for more information on this.

Ocean Critters

Hawaiian marine life, for the most part, is quite friendly. There are, however, a few notable exceptions. Below is a list of some critters that you should be aware of. This is not mentioned to frighten you out of the water. The odds are overwhelming that you won't have any trouble with any of the beasties listed below. But should you encounter one, this information should be of some help.

Sharks—Hawai'i does have sharks. They are mostly white-tipped reef sharks and the occasional hammerhead or tiger shark. Contrary to what most people think, sharks are in every ocean and don't pose the level of danger people attribute to them. In the past 25 years there have been only a handful of documented shark attacks off the Big Island, mostly tigers attacking surfers. Considering the number of people who swam in our waters during that time, you are more likely to choke to death on a bone at a lu'au than be attacked by a shark. If you do happen to come upon a shark, however, swim away slowly. This kind of movement doesn't interest them. *Don't* splash about rapidly. By doing this you are imitating a fish in distress, and you don't want to do that. The one kind of ocean water you want to avoid is murky water, such as that found near river mouths. These are not interesting to swim in anyway. Most shark attacks occur in murky water at dawn or dusk since sharks are basically cowards who like to sneak up on their prey. In general, don't go around worrying about sharks. *Any* animal can be threatening. (Even President Carter was once attacked by a rabbit.)

Portuguese Man-of-War—These are related to jellyfish but are unable to swim. They are instead propelled by a small sail and are at the mercy of the wind. Though small, they are capable of inflicting a painful sting. This occurs when the long, trailing tentacles are touched, triggering hundreds of thousands of spring-loaded stingers, called nematocysts, which inject venom. The resulting burning sensation is

usually very unpleasant but not fatal. Fortunately, the Portuguese Man-of-War is very uncommon on the west shore of the island. When they *do* come ashore, they usually do so in great numbers, jostled by a strong storm offshore. If you see them on the beach, don't go in the water. If you do get stung, immediately remove the tentacles with a gloved hand, stick or whatever is handy. Rinse thoroughly with salt or fresh water to remove any adhering nematocysts. Then apply ice for pain control. If the condition worsens, see a doctor. The old treatments of vinegar or baking soda are no longer recommended. The folk cure is urine, but you might look pretty silly applying it.

Sea Urchins—These are like living pin cushions. If you step on one or accidentally grab one, remove as much of the spine as possible with tweezers. See a physician if necessary.

Coral—Coral skeletons are very sharp and, since the skeleton is overlaid by millions of living coral polyps, a scrape can leave proteinaceous matter in the wound, causing infection. This is why coral cuts are frustratingly slow to heal. Immediate cleaning and disinfecting of coral cuts should speed up healing time. We don't have fire coral around the Big Island.

Sea Anemones—Related to the jellyfish, these also have stingers and are usually found attached to rocks or coral. It's best not to touch them with your bare hands. Treatment for a sting is similar to that for a Portuguese Man-of-War.

Bugs

Though devoid of the myriad of hideous buggies found in other parts of the world, there are a few evil critters brought here from elsewhere that you should know about. The worst are **centipedes**. They can get to be six or more inches long and are aggressive predators. They shouldn't be messed with. If you get stung, even by a baby, the pain can range from a bad bee sting to a bad gunshot wound. Some local doctors say the only cure is to stay drunk for three days. Others say to use meat tenderizer. **Scorpions** are present on the dry, western side of the island. Though not as nasty as the ones you see in the movies, a sting is unpleasant nonetheless. They're usually a couple inches across and mildly aggressive. **Cane spiders** are big, dark, and look horrifying, but they're not poisonous. (Though they seem to *think* they are. I've had *them* chase *me* across the room when *I* had the broom in my hand.) We *don't* have no-see-ums, those irritating sand fleas common in the South Pacific and Caribbean. (A Hawaiian voyaging canoe that traveled to and from Tahiti on a cultural mission several years ago unknowingly brought them back. The crew was forced into quarantine against their will where the tiny biting insects were discovered and exterminated. No-see-ums would have easily spread here and changed Hawai'i forever.)

Mosquitoes were unknown in the islands until the first stowaways arrived on Maui on the *Wellington* in 1826. Since then they have thrived. A good mosquito repellent containing DEET will come in handy, especially if you plan to go hiking. *Lotions* (not thin liquids) with DEET seem to work and stick best. Forget the guidebooks that tell you to take vitamin B12 to keep mosquitoes away; it just gives the little critters a healthier diet. If you find one dive bombing you at night in your room, turn on your overhead fan to help keep them away. Local residents and resorts often rely on genetically engineered plants such as Citrosa,

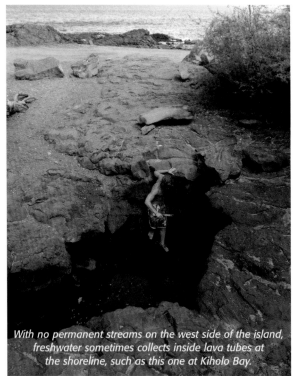
With no permanent streams on the west side of the island, freshwater sometimes collects inside lava tubes at the shoreline, such as this one at Kiholo Bay.

which irritates mosquitoes as much as they irritate us.

Bees and **yellow jackets** are more common on the drier west side of the island. Usually, the only way you'll get stung is if you run into one. If you rent a scooter, beware; one of us received his first bee sting while singing *Come Sail Away* on a motorcycle. A bee sting in the mouth can definitely ruin one of your precious vacation days.

There have been reports that some **fire ant** colonies have been spotted on the island, but we've never seen any.

Regarding **cockroaches**, there's good news and bad news. The bad news is that here, some are bigger than your thumb and can fly. The good news is that you probably won't see one. One of their predators is the **gecko**. This small, lizard-like creature makes a surprisingly loud chirp at night. They are cute and considered good luck in the Islands (probably because they eat mosquitoes and small roaches).

Leptospirosis is a bacteria that is found in some of Hawai'i's freshwater. It is transmitted from animal urine and can enter the body from open cuts, eyes and by drinking. Around 100 people a year in Hawai'i are diagnosed with the bacteria, which is treated with antibiotics if caught relatively early. You should avoid crossing streams such as Waipi'o with open cuts, and treat all water found in nature with treatment pills before drinking. (Most filters are ineffective for lepto.)

Though not a bug, one animal you are almost sure to see is the **mongoose**. Think of it as a stealth squirrel with mean-looking red eyes. Mongooses (no, not mongeese) are bold enough to take on cobras in their native India and were brought here to help control rats. Great idea, except mongooses are active during the day and rats work the night shift, so never the twain shall meet. It was a disas-

ter for local birds since mongooses love bird eggs. Kaua'i is the only major island to avoid the mongoose (and vice versa), and the difference between its bird population and the Big Island's is dramatic.

There are no **snakes** in Hawai'i (except for some reporters). There is concern that the brown tree snake *might* have made its way onto the islands from Guam. Although mostly harmless to humans, these snakes can spell extinction to native birds. Government officials aren't allowed to tell you this, but we will: If you ever see one anywhere in Hawai'i, please *kill it* and contact the Pest Hotline at (808) 586–7378. At the very least, call them immediately. The entire bird population of Hawai'i will be grateful.

Frogs

There are some irritating visitors that first arrived on the island a few years back and won't leave. (Well, besides the in-laws.) They're small tree frogs, called Coqui, that emit a whistle all night long. Cute at first, like a bird. But incessant and ultimately irritating. Most of the resorts do their best to deal with them, but there's a chance that some errant froggies may occasionally give you a long night. The Hilo side is froggier (I *swear* that's a real word) than Kona.

Vog

Vog is a mixture of water vapor, carbon dioxide and sulfur dioxide. Each day Kilauea belches 2,500 *tons* of sulphur dioxide. (Since the current eruption began, it has produced enough sulphur dioxide to fill a *half million* Goodyear blimps.) These gases react with sunlight, oxygen, dust particles and water in the air to form a mixture of sulfate aerosols, sulfuric acid and other oxidized sulfur compounds. Why should *you* care? Because our trade winds blow toward the southwest, carrying the vog from its source, down the coast where the winds wrap around Mauna Loa and head up the coast. Then daytime onshore breezes and nighttime offshore breezes rake it back and forth across Kona. If you have a severe lung condition or are very asthmatic, you *may* experience discomfort. (When our asthmatic nephew visits us, he has no problems, for what it's worth.) Those who stay in Kohala and Hilo are usually free from vog. In all, it's probably less than the smog in most mainland cities, but we did want to alert you to one of the few negatives to living on an active volcano. Call 885–7143 for the vog index.

Dehydration

Bring and drink lots of water when you are out and about, especially when you are hiking. Dehydration sneaks up on people. By the time you are thirsty, you're already dehydrated. It's a good idea to take an insulated water jug with you in the car or one of those 1½ liter bottles of water. Our weather is almost certainly different than what you left behind, and you will probably find yourself thirstier than usual. Just fill it before you leave in the morning and *suck 'em up* (as we say here) all day.

Curses

Legend says that if you remove any lava from the island, bad luck will befall you. *Balderdash!* you say. Hey, we don't know if it's true or not. You don't have to be a believer, but we at Wizard Publications along with resorts and local post offices, get boxes of lava that come in all the time from visitors who brought a souvenir of lava home, only to have their house burn down, have their foot fall off or get audited by the IRS. Coincidence?

Maybe. But if you decide to do it anyway, remember... you've been warned.

Also, if the curse isn't enough to dissuade you, the TSA has written us asking us to inform you that they will *confiscate* any large lava rocks, coral or sand found in your luggage.

Grocery Stores

Definitely a hazard. Though restaurants on the Big Island are expensive, don't think you'll get off cheap in grocery stores. You'll certainly save money by cooking your own food, but you'll be amazed, appalled and offended by the prices you see here. If you are staying at a condo, savvy travelers should head over to Costco (334–0770) just north of Kona (shown on map on page 165) to stock up. If you're not a member of this national warehouse store, you *might* qualify for membership. (Call 800–774–2678 for info.) If so, the savings on food and everything else are incredible, especially for Hawai'i. Otherwise, ask around to see if any residents you are dealing with will let you go with them.

There are no large grocery stores in the Kohala resort area, but you'll find one 6 miles up Waikoloa Road (which is across from the 75 mile marker) in Waikoloa Village. They're easy to find in Kona and Hilo.

TRAVELING WITH CHILDREN

Should we have put this section under HAZARDS, too? The Hilton Waikoloa probably has the most extensive children's activity program. Their Camp Menehune (ages 5–12) is a youngster's dream. Several other Kohala resorts also try hard to cater to families. If your keiki (kid) is looking for an adventure, check out page 233 where we have a dandy adventure just for them. Though they don't actually *rent babies*, **All About Babies**

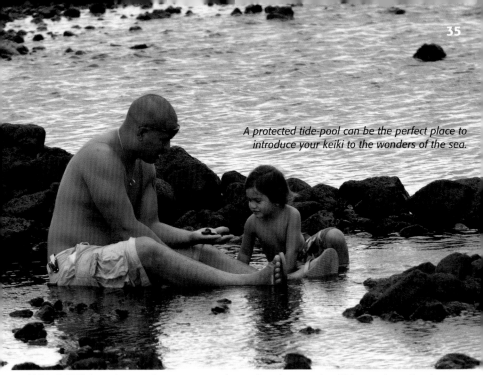

A protected tide-pool can be the perfect place to introduce your keiki to the wonders of the sea.

(883–3675) has the usual assortment of keiki paraphernalia for rent, such as car seats, strollers, cribs, bathtubs, etc.

For swimming, the beach in front of the King Kamehameha's Kona Beach Hotel or the tide-pools at the National Energy Lab in Kona, and Onekahakaha in Hilo are probably the safest on the island. (Check them out yourself to be sure.) We don't need to tell you that keikis and surf don't mix.

There's a great playground at **Higashihara Park** just south of Kona past the 115 mile marker. Another one is at the corner of Kuakini Hwy and Makala Blvd. at the north end of Kona, and **Waimea Park** in Waimea. See Waimea map.

If you want to eat at a nice restaurant but are afraid the little ones might get restless, we've noticed that many parents often eat at the Kona Inn, where the strip of grass between the restaurant and the shoreline serves as a convenient romping area for kids when they are finished. You can still keep an eye out for them so they don't wander too far.

Lastly, you should know that it's a big fine plus a mandatory safety class if your keiki isn't buckled up.

THE PEOPLE

There's no doubt about it, people really *are* friendlier in Hawai'i. You will notice that people are quick to smile and wave at you here. (Those of us who live in Hawai'i have to remember to pack our "mainland face" when we journey there. Otherwise, we get undesired responses when we smile or wave at complete strangers.) It probably comes down to a matter of happiness. People are happy here, and happy people are friendly people. Some people compare a trip to an outer island in Hawai'i to a trip back in time, when smiles weren't rare, and politeness was the order of the day.

Ethnic Breakdown

The Big Island has an ethnic mix that is as diversified as any you will find. Here, *everyone* is a minority; there are no majorities. The last census revealed the ethnic makeup below:

White	46,904
Asian	39,702
Hawaiian or Other Pacific Islander	16,724
Black	698
American Indian or Alaska Native	666
Other	1,695
Mixed or didn't respond	42,288
Total	**148,677**

Some Terms

A person of Hawaiian blood is Hawaiian. Only people of this race are called by this term. They are also called Kanaka Maoli, but only another Hawaiian can use this term. Anybody who was born here, regardless of race (except whites) is called a local. If you were born elsewhere but have lived here awhile, you are called a kama'aina. If you are white, you are a haole. It doesn't matter if you have been here a day or your family has been here for over a century—you will always be a haole. The term comes from the time when westerners first encountered these islands. Its precise meaning has been lost, but it is thought to refer to people with no background (since westerners could not chant the kanaenae of their ancestors).

The continental United States is called the Mainland. If you are here and are returning, you are not "going back to the states" (we *are* a state). When somebody leaves the island, they are off-island.

Hawaiian Time

One aspect of Hawaiian culture you may have heard of is Hawaiian Time. The stereotype is that everyone in Hawai'i moves just a little bit slower than on the mainland. Supposedly, we are more laid-back and don't let things get to us as easily as people on the mainland. This is the stereotype... OK, it's *not* a stereotype. It's real. Hopefully, during your visit, you will notice that this feeling infects *you* as well.

You may find yourself letting another driver cut in front of you in circumstances that would incur your wrath back home. You may find yourself willing to wait for a red light without feeling like you're going to explode. The whole reason for coming to Hawai'i is to experience beauty and a sense of peace, so let it happen. If someone else is moving a bit more slowly than you want, just go with it.

Shaka

One gesture you will see often and should not be offended by is the *shaka* sign. This is done by extending the pinkie and thumb while curling the three middle fingers. Sometimes visitors think it is some kind of local gesture indicating *up yours* or some similarly unfriendly message. Actually, it is a friendly act used as a sign of greeting or just to say *Hey*. Its origin is thought to date back to the 1930s. A guard at the Kahuku Sugar Plantation on O'ahu used to patrol the plantation railroad to keep local kids from stealing cane from the slow moving trains. This guard had lost his middle fingers in an accident and his manner of waving off the youths became well known. Kids began to warn other kids that he was around by waving their hands in a way that looked like the guard's, and the custom took off.

THE HAWAIIAN LANGUAGE

The Hawaiian language is a beautiful, gentle and melodic language that flows smoothly off the tongue. Just the sounds of the words conjure up trees gently blowing in the breeze and the sound of the surf. Most Polynesian languages share the same roots, and many have common words. Today, Hawaiian is spoken *as an everyday language* only on the privately owned island of Ni'ihau. Visitors are often intimidated by Hawaiian. With a few ground rules you will come to realize that pronunciation is not as hard as you might think.

When missionaries discovered that the Hawaiians had no written language, they sat down and created an alphabet. This Hawaiian alphabet has only twelve letters. Five vowels; A, E, I, O and U as well as seven consonants; H, K, L, M, N, P and W. The consonants are pronounced just as they are in English with the exception of W. It is often pronounced as a V if it is in the middle of a word and comes after an E or I. Vowels are pronounced as follows:

A—pronounced as in *Ah* if stressed, or *above* if not stressed.
E—pronounced as in *say* if stressed, or *dent* if not stressed.
I—pronounced as in *bee*.
O—pronounced as in *nose*.
U—pronounced as in *stew*.

If you examine long Hawaiian words, you will see that most have repeating syllables, making it easier to remember and pronounce.

One thing you will notice in this book are glottal stops. These are represented by an upside-down apostrophe ʻ and are meant to convey a hard stop in the pronunciation. So if we are talking about the type of lava called ʻaʻa, it is pronounced as two separate As.

Another feature you will encounter are diphthongs, where two letters glide together. They are ae, ai, ao, au, ei, eu, oi, and ou. Unlike many English diphthongs, the second vowel is always pronounced. One word you will read in this book, referring to Hawaiian temples, is *heiau* (hey-ee-ow). The e and i flow together as a single sound, then the a and u flow together as a single sound. The ee sound binds the two sounds, making the whole word flow together.

Let's take a word that might seem impossible to pronounce. When you see how easy this word is, the rest will seem like a snap. The Hawaiʻi State Fish used to be the humuhumunukunukuapuaʻa. At first glance it seems like a nightmare. But if you read the word slowly, it is pronounced just like it looks and isn't nearly as horrifying as it appears. Try it. Humu (hoo-moo) is pronounced twice. Nuku (noo-koo) is pronounced twice. A (ah) is pronounced once. Pu (poo) is pronounced once. Aʻa (ah-ah) is the ah sound pronounced twice, the glottal stop indicating a hard stop between sounds. Now you can try it again.

Humuhumunukunukuapuaʻa. Now, wasn't that easy? OK, so it's not easy, but it's not impossible either.

Below are some words that you might hear during your visit.

ʻAina (eye-nah)—Land.

Akamai (ah-kah-MY)—Wise or shrewd.

Aliʻi (ah-LEE-ee)—A Hawaiian chief; a member of the chiefly class.

Aloha (ah-LOW-ha)—Hello, goodbye or a feeling or the spirit of love, affection or kindness.

Hala (hah-la)—Pandanus tree.

Hale (hah-leh)—House or building.

Hana (ha-nah)—Work.

Hana hou (ha-nah-HO)—To do again.

Haole (how-leh)—Originally foreigner, now means Caucasian.

Heiau (hey-ee-ow)—Hawaiian temple.

Hula (hoo-lah)—The story-telling dance of Hawaiʻi.

Imu (ee-moo)—An underground oven.

ʻIniki (ee-nee-key)—Sharp and piercing wind (as in Hurricane ʻIniki).

Kahuna (kah-HOO-na)—A priest or minister; someone who is an expert in a profession.

Kai (kigh)—The sea.

Kalua (KAH-loo-ah)—Cooking food underground.

Kamaʻaina (kah-ma-EYE-na)—Long-time Hawaiʻi resident.

Kane (kah-neh)—Boy or man.
Kapu (kah-poo)—Forbidden, taboo; keep out.
Keiki (kay-key)—Child or children.
Kokua (koh-koo-ah)—Help.
Kona (koh-NAH)—Leeward side of the island; wind blowing from the south, southwest direction.
Kuleana (koo-leh-AH-nah)—Concern, responsibility or jurisdiction.
Lanai (lah-NIGH)—Porch, veranda, patio.
Lani (lah-nee)—Sky or heaven.
Lei (lay)—Necklace of flowers, shells or feathers. The lehua blossom lei is the lei of the Big Island.
Liliko'i (lee-lee-koy)—Passion fruit.
Limu (lee-moo)—Edible seaweed.
Lomi (low-mee)—To rub or massage; lomi salmon is raw salmon rubbed with salt and spices.
Lu'au (loo-ow)—Hawaiian feast; literally means taro leaves.
Mahalo (mah-hah-low)—Thank you.
Makai (mah-kigh)—Toward the sea.
Malihini (mah-lee-hee-nee)—A newcomer, visitor or guest.
Mauka (mow-ka)—Toward the mountain.
Moana (moh-ah-nah)—Ocean.
Mo'o (moh-oh)—Lizard.
Nani (nah-nee)—Beautiful, pretty.
Nui (new-ee)—Big, important, great.
'Ohana (oh-hah-nah)—Family.
'Ono (oh-no)—Delicious, the best.
'Okole (oh-koh-leh)—Derrière.
Pakalolo (pah-kah-low-low)—Marijuana.
Pali (pah-lee)—A cliff.
Paniolo (pah-nee-OH-low)—Hawaiian cowboy.
Pau (pow)—Finish, end; *pau hana* means quitting time from work.
Poi (poy)—Pounded kalo (taro) root that forms a paste.
Pono (poh-no)—Goodness, excellence, correct, proper.
Pua (poo-ah)—Flower.

Pupu (poo-poo)—Appetizer, snacks or finger food.
Puka (poo-ka)—Hole.
Wahine (vah-hee-neh)—Woman.
Wai (why)—Fresh water.
Wikiwiki (wee-kee-wee-kee)—To hurry up, very quick.

Quick Pidgin Lesson

Hawaiian pidgin is fun to listen to. It's like ear candy. It's colorful, rhythmic and sways in the wind. Below is a list of some of the words and phrases you might hear on your visit. It's tempting to read some of these and try to use them. If you do, the odds are you will simply look foolish. These words and phrases are used in certain ways and with certain inflections. People who have spent years living in the islands still feel uncomfortable using them. Thick pidgin can be incomprehensible to the untrained ear (that's the idea). If you are someplace and hear two people engaged in a discussion in pidgin, stop and eavesdrop a bit. You won't forget it.

Pidgin Words & Phrases

An' den—And then? So?
Any kine—Anything; any kind.
Ass right—That's right.
Ass wy—That's why.
Beef—Fight.
Brah—Bruddah; friend; brother.
Brok' da mouf—Delicious.
Buggah—That's the one; it is difficult.
Bus laugh—To laugh out loud.
Bus nose—How one reacts to a bad smell.
Chicken skin kine—Something that gives you goose bumps.
Choke—Plenty; lots.
Cockaroach—Steal; rip off.
Da kine—A noun or verb used in place of whatever the speaker wishes. Heard constantly.
Fo Days—plenty; "He got hair fo days."

Geevum—Go for it! Give 'em hell!

Grind—To eat.

Grinds—Food.

Hold ass—A close call when driving your new car.

How you figga?—How do you figure that? It makes no sense.

Howzit?—How is it going? How are you? Also, Howzit o wot?

I owe you money or wot?—What to say when someone is staring at you.

Make house—Make yourself at home.

Make plate—Grab some food.

Mek ass—Make a fool of yourself.

Mo' bettah—This is better.

Moke—A large, tough local male. (Don't say it unless you *like beef*.)

No can—Cannot; I cannot do it.

No make li dat—Stop doing that.

No, yeah?—No, or is "no" correct?

'Okole squeezer—Something that suddenly frightens you ('okole meaning derrière).

O wot?—Or what?

Pau hana—Quit work. (A time of daily, intense celebration in the islands.)

Poi dog—A mutt.

Shahkbait—Shark bait, meaning pale, untanned people.

Shaka—Great! All right!

Shredding—Riding a gnarly wave.

Sleepahs—Flip flops, thongs, zoris.

Stink eye—Dirty looks; facial expression denoting displeasure.

Suck rocks—Buzz off, or pound sand.

Talk stink—Speak bad about somebody.

Talk story—Shooting the breeze; to rap.

Tanks eh?—Thank you.

Tita—A female moke. Same *beef* results.

Yeah?—Used at the end of sentences.

MUSIC

Hawaiian music is far more diverse than most people think. Many people picture Hawaiian music as someone twanging away on an 'ukulele with his voice slipping and sliding all over the place like he has an ice cube down his back. In reality, the music here can be outstanding. There is the melodic sound of the more

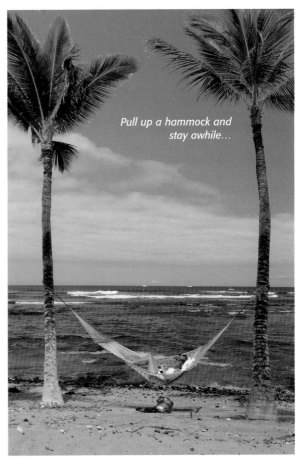

Pull up a hammock and stay awhile...

This photo has absolutely nothing to do with the basics. We just thought it was cool.

traditional music. There are young local bands putting out modern music with a Hawaiian beat. There is even Hawaiian reggae. *Hawaiian Style Band*, the late *Israel Kamakawiwo'ole* (known locally as Bruddah Iz) and *Bruddah Waltah* are excellent examples. Even if you don't always agree with all of the messages in the songs, there's no denying the talent of these groups. If you get a chance, stop by **Mele Kai** (329–1454) in Kona at Ka'ahumanu Plaza. They have a good selection of Hawaiian music. **Borders Books** (331–1668) in Kona or in Hilo (933–1410) also has a good selection.

THE HULA

The hula evolved as a means of worship, later becoming a forum for telling a story with chants (called mele), hands and body movement. It can be fascinating to watch. When most people think of the hula, they picture a woman in a grass skirt swinging her hips to the beat of an 'ukulele. But in reality there are two types of hula. The modern hula, or hula 'auana, uses musical instruments and vocals to augment the dancer. It came about after westerners first encountered the islands. Missionaries found the hula distasteful, and the old style was driven underground. The modern type came about as a form of entertainment and was practiced in places where missionaries had no influence. Ancient Hawaiians didn't even use grass skirts. They were later brought by Gilbert Islanders.

The old style of hula is called hula 'olapa or hula kahiko. It consists of chants and is accompanied by percussion only and takes years of training. It can be exciting to watch as performers work together in a synchronous harmony. Both men and women participate, with women's hula being softer (though no less disciplined) and men's hula being more active. This type of hula is physically demanding, requiring strong concentration. Keiki (children's) hula can be charming to watch as well.

The world's best gather each year for a week starting the first Thursday after Easter Sunday for the **Merrie Monarch**

Festival (named after the 19th-century king credited with reviving the hula). Tickets are often hard to come by if you wait too long. Call (808) 935–9168 *right* after New Years Day if you want to be assured of getting a seat. Otherwise, check it out on TV. It will utterly dazzle you.

A NOTE ON PERSONAL RESPONSIBILITY

In past editions we've had the sad task of removing places that you can no longer visit. The reason, universally cited, is *liability*. Although Hawai'i has a statute indemnifying landowners, the mere threat is often enough to get something closed. Because we, more than any other publication, have exposed heretofore unknown attractions, we feel the need to pass this along.

Please remember that this isn't Disneyland—it's nature. Mother Nature is hard, slippery, sharp and unpredictable. If you go exploring and get into trouble, whether it's your ego that's bruised or something more tangible, please remember that neither the state, the private land owner nor this publication *told* you to go. You *chose* to explore, which is what life, and this book, are all about. And if you complain to or threaten someone controlling land, they'll rarely fix the problem you identified. They'll simply close it...and it will be gone for good.

MISCELLANEOUS INFORMATION

It is customary here for *everyone* to remove their shoes upon entering someone's house (sometimes their office).

If you are going to spend any time at the beach, woven bamboo beach mats can be found all over the island for $2–$3. Some roll up, some can be folded. The sand comes off these easier than it comes off towels.

It's a good idea to get your photos developed here. That's because developers are more familiar with the colors. (Just try to get a black or green sand beach to look right from a mainland developer, and you'll see what I mean.) If you don't want to pay retail-retail, try Costco, Wal-Mart or Longs. Most have a cheap one-hour service and are surprisingly good. Most will redo the photos to make the color right.

Around the island you'll see signs saying VISITOR INFORMATION, VOLCANO UPDATE or something similar. Allow me to translate. That's usually code for WE WANT TO SELL YOU SOMETHING.

The area code for the state is 808. Daylight Savings isn't observed here.

If you wear sunglasses, *polarized* lenses are highly recommended. Not only are our colors more vivid here, but the lower latitudes of Hawai'i make polarized lenses particularly effective.

If you want to arrange a lei greeting for you or your honey when you disembark the airplane, Greeters of Hawai'i (800) 366–8559 can make the arrangements for around $25. Nice way to kick off a romantic trip, huh?

A WORD ABOUT DRIVING TOURS

The Big Island is, to use the scientific term, *one big bugga*. With this in mind, we have decided to describe the various parts of the island in a series of tours. You're not being pigeonholed into seeing the island in this order, but we had to organize the regions in some fashion, and this seemed the logical way to do it rather than a scattershot description. You can take these tours from any place you are staying, but we have described most of them (except the Hilo tour and the Hamakua/Waimea tour) on the assumption that you are starting from the west (Kona) side because the majority of Big Island visitors do just that. The Hamakua/Waimea section is described from the Hilo side first because it is convenient to see it that way after traveling to Hilo via Saddle Road.

Nearly every guidebook divides the Big Island and its sights by districts. (See graphic on fold-out back map.) While this land division made perfect sense to the ancients who divvied up the island among themselves, it is not real helpful to the modern traveler who cruises the island by car. So we have divided the island up in a way that makes more sense to today's visitor. It takes into account where most people stay and how they drive. Look at the inside *front* cover to see how we have divided the island and on what pages we describe the sights.

Most main roads have mile markers erected every mile. Since Hawai'i is mostly void of other identification signs, these little green signs can be a big help in knowing where you are at a given time. Therefore, we have placed them on the maps represented as a number inside a small box 16. We will often describe a certain feature or unmarked road as being, "⁴/₁₀ miles past the 22 mile mark." We hope this helps.

For directions, locals usually describe things as being on the **mauka** side of the highway (meaning toward the mountains) or **makai** (toward the ocean).

Beaches, activities and adventures are mentioned briefly, but described in detail in their own separate sections.

BOOKS

There is an astonishing variety of books available about Hawai'i and the Big Island. Everything from history, legends, geology, children's stories and just plain ol' novels. **Borders Books** at Henry Street and Highway 11 in Kona (331–1668) and in Hilo at the Waiakea Center on Highway 11 (933–1410) have dazzling selections. Walk in and lose yourself in Hawai'i's rich-

ness. **Basically Books** on Kamehameha in Hilo (961–0144) also has a superb collection of Hawaii titles. They also have the best selection of topographic maps on the island. A good resource.

THE INTERNET

Our Web site, **www.wizardpub.com** has recent changes, links to cool sites and the latest satellite weather shots and more. We also show our own aerial photos of nearly every place to stay, so you'll know if oceanfront *really* means oceanfront. It also has links to every company listed in the book that has a site—both those we like and those we recommend against. For the record, we don't charge a cent for links (it would be a conflict of interest), and there are no advertisements on the site. (Well...except for our own books, of course.) We could have listed all of the Web addresses in the book, but it seemed pretty mean to make you type in all of those URL addresses. We also have a calendar of upcoming events.

If you're on-island and need Web access (to check your mail, etc.), most of the big resorts have business services available for around $20 an hour. **Kona Business Center** (329–0006) in Kona has Internet access for $8 per hour. **Lava Java** in Kona (see ISLAND DINING) has Web access and good cinnamon rolls—what a combo! Lots of other places around Kona offer Internet access including the UPS Store, Mail Boxes, and Epitopia.

If you brought your computer...shame on you, you're on vacation. Anyway, **Turquoise Technologies** (331–0897) can set you up with a temporary local dial up account for $10 set-up fee plus a $20 per month. If you have Wi-Fi, **Kona Brewing Co.** and a gathering area at the Kona Coast Shopping Center have free hi-speed Wi-Fi.

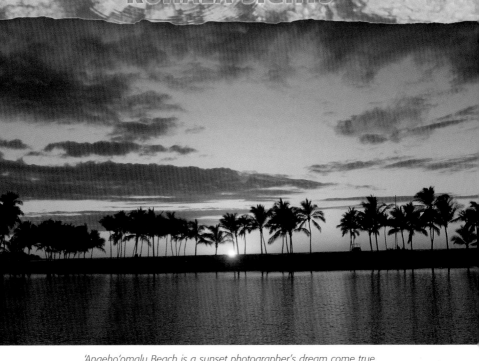

'Anaeho'omalu Beach is a sunset photographer's dream come true.

Kohala is the oldest volcano on the island, having last sputtered 60,000 years ago. It contains lush forest, dry lava desert, windswept grassy plains and outrageous beaches. Some of the most expensive resorts on the island are along the Kohala Coast.

This is a large, diverse area to cover in one section, but because of the way the island's resorts are distributed and the roads are laid out, most will see this area in a circular driving tour, so that's how we'll describe it. We're going to start as you leave Kona (see map) heading up Hwy 190. If you're staying in Kohala, you can come up Waikoloa Village Road and pick up the description on Hwy 190 heading north. If staying in Hilo, pick it up from Waimea.

UP HIGHWAY 190 FROM KAILUA-KONA

As you leave Kona, you'll take Palani Road, which becomes Mamalahoa Highway (190) heading north. (See map on 45 or page 60.) From near sea level, you will be heading up to 3,564 feet then down again into Hawi, so gas up on that cheap *(ha!)* Kona gasoline.

Leaving Kailua-Kona, it's hard to believe that just above the town is a beautiful fern and 'ohi'a cloud forest steeped in fog and moss. Weather here is determined by altitude because the mountain literally creates its own rain through convection. You can see it by taking Kaloko Road just south of the 34 mile marker. Follow it for 7 miles as it winds upward into another world. Just before

DIVERSION ALERT!

the end of the road, turn left and it will dead end at 5,000 feet with expansive views (clouds permitting) of Kona below. Morning is best for this drive; don't ride your brakes on the way down.

As you leave Kona, you'll get some good views down the coast. Keep an eye out for renegade peacocks (which sound like cats being tortured) from the Makalei Golf Course around the 32 mile marker.

The highway bisects several channels and tubes in the lava between the 28 and 26 mile markers. Rivers of molten stone coursed down the mountain here during the 1800 Hualalai lava flow. If you look down the coast, you'll get an idea of the scale of a "typical" lava flow.

By the 19 mile marker you have passed from Hualalai Mountain to the slopes of Mauna Loa. Proof is in the form of a lava flow here that ran for 30 miles in 1859 all the way to Kiholo Bay, destroying Kamehameha's fishpond (see BEACHES). If clouds are absent, you may see the top of Mauna Kea and its many dome-enclosed telescopes ahead and on your right.

As you continue, you'll notice cactus scattered about, and trees appear again. Parker Ranch starts at the 14 mile marker, part of a colossal 175,000 acre cattle ranch.

At the 11 mile marker is the road through Waikoloa Village, which leads down to the Kohala mega-resorts. It's marked by a giant obelisk erected by Waikoloa Land Co. in a fit of psychedelic creativity. Waikoloa Village is a relatively new and stark community. Due to its location, on the leeward side of the saddle between Mauna Loa and Mauna Kea, it's usually pretty windy. *(So consistently windy that when the wind stops, the cows fall down.)* If you are staying at a mega-resort in Kohala, you'll want to know that there is a fairly large grocery store here.

Still on Hwy 190 between the 5 and 2 mile markers off to your right (up mauka) there's a large hill, called Holoholoku. Everyone has seen the famous WWII photo and statue of the scene where Marines on Iwo Jima raised the American flag over Mt. Suribachi. Possibly the most dramatic WWII photo ever taken, it puts a lump in your throat every time you see it. What you don't know is that those very guys practiced storming the hill right there on Holoholoku because it was thought to be similar to Suribachi in size and shape.

As you approach the town of Waimea (Kamuela), you may decide to check it out now. Since this is the crossroads between the east and west sides of the island, we could have included it here or in the section on Hamakua. After careful analysis of driving patterns, accommodation indexes and topography…we flipped a coin and put it in the HAMAKUA section. Waimea has an incredibly colorful history

North Kohala

Often 4WD from here → — 'Upolu Airport

Kamehameha Birth Site — Mo'okini Heiau

Hawi

Kohala Club Hotel

Kapa'au

N *W* *E* *S*

Lighthouse
20°14.777'
155°46.284'

Kapa'a Beach Park

270 18 19 20 21 21

Kohala Village Inn

22

21

250

Kynnersley

23 24

Kapanai'a Bay
Keokea Beach Pa

25 26

27 **270**

28

Navigational Heiau

15

19

Mahukona Beach Park

18

Kohala Ditch

Waikama Falls (2nd) 28

Pololu Beach

Lapakahi State Historical Park

14

17

16

17

Akoni Pule Highway

Detailed map on page 231 →

Pololu Trail

Pololu Valley

Honokane Nui Valley

13

12

15

Kohala is the oldest surviving Big Island volcano. The mountain last erupted 60,000 years ago and is considered "extinct," but will probably cough back to life in a million years or less for a last gasp at island-making before it is pronounced truly dead. Haleakala on Maui is now in that final phase. Diamond Head on O'ahu is the product of its volcano's last gasp phase.

11

14

13

10

Kohala Mountain Road

Kohala Mountain

9

12

8

11

7

10

6

0   2 MILES

9

Road Crest at 3,564 feet

5

Crystal Cove

8

7

It's not hard to guess which is the wet windward side, and which is the dry leeward side.

4

⌣ Indicates Foot Trails
67 Roadside mile markers
⋯ Unpaved Roads

6

270

3

250 5

Pu'ukohola Heiau

Kawaihae

4

2 67

Spencer Beach Park

Mau'umae Beach

66 65 64 63 62 61 60 3

Waimea (Kamuela)
Detailed Map on page 135

56 Miles to Hilo

59 58

68

Kauna'oa (Mauna Kea) Beach

19

Kawaihae Road **19**

← Queen Ka'ahumanu Highway

Hapuna Beach

69

32 Miles to Kailua-Kona

36 miles To Kona

190

1

© 2006 Wizard Publications, Inc.

and is worth exploring. If you do it now, turn to page 133 before continuing on.

KOHALA MOUNTAIN ROAD

See map on facing page or on page 135 to get to Highway 250. (Left at the Chevron station.) You are traveling up the spine of the sleeping Kohala Volcano. (They say you shouldn't honk your horn or you may wake it up.) You're still on the dry leeward side and will crest at 3,564 feet before descending to the sea.

Around the 14 mile marker you'll start to see a huge mountain looming in front of you. That's not on this island; it's *Maui*, 30 miles across the sea. On clear days, the island of Maui seems to tower over the little town of Hawi even more than the Big Island's own volcanoes. Sometimes it looks gigantic, and sometimes it's less impressive. It's the same reason the moon always looks enormous when it's near a mountain horizon or through trees—it gives your brain some scale to compute its size. Maui looks biggest when you see it *with or through* something other than on the ocean's horizon.

NORTH SHORE OF KOHALA

Be sure to take the road to Hawi, not Kapa'au, near the 20 mile marker. As you pull into Hawi, you're greeted by a couple of old banyan trees on your right. You'll want to head right (east), but if you're hungry, *Bamboo Restaurant* on your left is your best bet. There you will also find *Gallery at Bamboo*, which has excellent wood carvings and silk paintings. Also consider stopping by *Tropical Dreams*. They have *outstanding* ice cream made here on the island. We unselfishly review it every time we are on the north shore, just to be thorough.

The sleepy little towns of *Hawi* and *Kapa'au* lie at this northernmost point of the island. Until the '70s, this was sugar country. When Kohala Sugar pulled out, this area was left high and dry. Rather than let their towns die, residents stuck it out, opening shops and other small businesses. Today, this area is enjoying a comeback of sorts. There are lots of artists who call this area home. A Japanese investment company bought most of Kohala Sugar's land assets (19,000 acres) in 1988 when land here was cheap and has *plans* for a resort at Mahukona, a restaurant at the end of the road overlooking Pololu Valley and more. But they've been *planning* for a long time. In the meantime, this is a quiet, peaceful community. It's said that the investor bought all this land after simply flying over it in a helicopter—without ever touching it!

Heading east, you come to the town of *Kapa'au*. On the mauka side of the highway in Kapa'au is a statue of *King Kamehameha the Great*. If it looks just like the famous one standing in front of the Judiciary building in Honolulu, that's because it's the same...sort of. When the Hawaiian Legislature commissioned the statue in 1878, it was cast in Paris and put on a ship. Unfortunately, the ship and its cargo were lost at sea near the Falkland Islands in the South Atlantic. Since they had shipping insurance, they used the money to order a new one. Meanwhile, the captain of the wrecked ship later spotted the "lost" statue standing in Port Stanley (somebody had salvaged it). He bought it for $500 and shipped it (this time successfully—must have FedExed it) to Hawai'i where its broken arm was repaired, and it was erected where you see it now. On King Kamehameha Day (June 11) the statue is piled high with leis and other decorations and is quite a sight to see. There are public restrooms here behind the building.

Continuing east, just before the 24 mile marker, is the road to **Kalahikiola Church**, built in 1855. Guidebooks usually tell you to stop by, check it out, and talk story with the caretaker or minister. Sounds sweet, but most of the times we've stopped by, it's been empty and locked. (Another myth shattered!)

If you're into lighthouses or want to see some raw coastline and have a 4WD vehicle, take a left ½ mile past the 24 mile marker onto Maulili (which is just after Old Halaula Mill Rd.). After ⅓ mile it becomes dirt. Turn right when it ends and the short paved section leads to a gate. After the gate (remember to close it behind you), the bumpy road leads to the **Kauhola Point Lighthouse**. This area is wild and undeveloped and sports nice views of the sea cliffs that wrap around the north shore. The area a few hundred yards to the right (east) is full of abandoned sugar equipment and cars. Many are actually embedded in the *side*

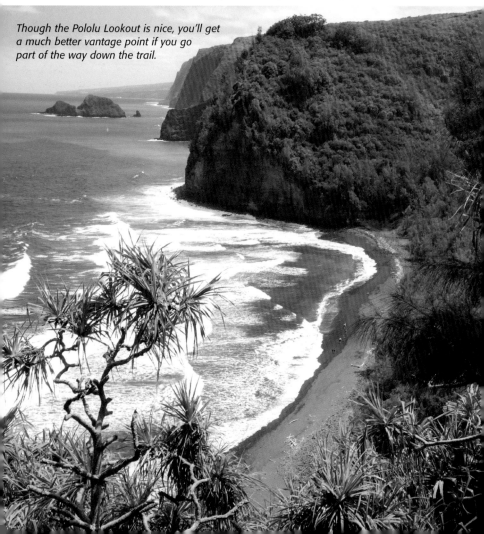

Though the Pololu Lookout is nice, you'll get a much better vantage point if you go part of the way down the trail.

of the cliff, evidence of the rapid pace of cliff erosion. Just a few decades ago the cars were buried in "stable" ground and the cliffs were farther out.

Back on the highway, look to your left just before the 25 mile marker. There is a large banyan tree with a nifty **tree house**. Wouldn't you have *loved* a tree house like that when you were a kid?

Though you're above the ocean and there are no navigable rivers, a popular activity here is **kayaking** in an unlikely place—the old Kohala Ditch. There are also ATV **tours** along the coastal cliffs, both described under ACTIVITIES.

POLOLU VALLEY

The end of the road is the **Pololu Valley Lookout**. This outstanding vista displays the raw, untamed side of the Big Island. (Unfortunately, the state sometimes lets the vegetation block out some of the view. The view's *much* nicer halfway down the trail mentioned below.) Nearly vertical cliffs are battered unmercifully by the winter north shore surf. Four hundred feet below is **Pololu Beach**, accessed via a 15–20 minute trail down through lush vegetation. (If you make it back *up* in 15 minutes, we're proud of you. It means you didn't stop once.) If it's been raining much, the trail may be slippery. At the bottom, in several spots, you'll find black sand dunes over 100 feet high, now mostly covered with vegetation. This type of black sand beach is formed as water constantly chips away at the lava river bed. Though the beach is not very swimmable (the surf and current are usually too violent), it's very picturesque and a nice place to observe Mother Nature's force. During the week you may have it nearly to yourself down there. Halfway down the trail is a small natural

A REAL GEM

platform that looks out over the beach—a good photo op. Be sure to leave the gate at the bottom as you found it—open or closed.

The beach is prettier from below than above. On the opposite side of the valley, a trail leads up the wall over to the next valley, called **Honokane Nui**. (See ADVENTURES.) These seven valleys, from Pololu to Waipi'o, are the only part of this new island that show much sign of erosion.

In ancient times Pololu Valley was a bountiful source for waterworn stones. Thousands of tons of stones have been hauled from here to build temples, houses, and other structures. The massive Pu'ukohola Heiau, 25 miles away at Kawaihae, was built from stones from this valley. A gigantic chain of people passed stones hand to hand all the way. If one was dropped, it was left where it lay (unless it was on his foot) to prevent the cadence from being interrupted. When you're ready, head back west past Hawi.

MO'OKINI HEIAU

Near the 20 mile marker is a sign saying simply "Upolu Airport." This road (unpaved past the airport) leads to the northernmost tip of the island and past two important sites. You head left when you reach the quiet 'Upolu Airport. The county does a *terrible* job maintaining the unpaved portion. If it's dry, you *may* make it the 1½ miles to the heiau described below. Otherwise, it's 4WD on at least *part* of the unpaved section and the last part might even scare 4-wheelers. Puddles last a *long time* here, and some of them are large enough to have nearly spawned their own unique ecosystem.

This area is dominated by the legacy of two influential men—an ancient priest named **Pa'ao** and **Kamehameha the Great**. Pa'ao is said to have arrived in the 11th or 12th century and changed the islands. He was born in Tahiti or on one of its neighbor islands. It is said that the islands were in a state of anarchy when Pa'ao arrived. He restructured society, introduced the concept of human sacrifice and brought other similar traditions. Here he built the Mo'okini Heiau, where countless people were put to death to please Pa'ao's hungry gods. You'll have to park at the gate and walk five minutes to the heiau.

Even before we knew the gory details about Mo'okini Heiau's history, the place gave us the heebie-jeebies. We aren't the only ones who have noticed that the area around the temple is filled with an eerie, ghostly lifelessness, and it's the only place on the island that we like to avoid (not counting the Department of Motor Vehicles). Used for human sacrifices, the area feels devoid of a soul. The quiet is not comforting, but rather an empty void. The walls of Mo'okini are extremely tall and thick—oral tradition says that some

of the rocks were passed by hand from Pololu Valley, 9 miles away. Just in front of the heiau is a large lava slab with a slight dip in it. In front of it is a raised stone. It takes little imagination to see that this slab was the *holehole* stone, where unfortunate victims were laid while the flesh was stripped from their bones. These bones were then used to make fishhooks and other objects. The number of Hawaiians sacrificed here ran into the tens of thousands.

You should give little weight to any descriptive signs at the heiau. In the past we've seen "official" signs making bizarre and inaccurate claims such as one that indicated "conclusive evidence" that the heiau was built around 300 AD. That's at least 700 years off. In fact, the people who arrived here in 300 AD came from the Marquesas Islands. They are the ones who were overwhelmed by the Tahitians who came with Pa'ao who built this temple and became the Hawaiians we know today.

Farther down the road is the **Kamehameha Akahi Aina Hanau Heiau**.

This is where Kamehameha the Great, who conquered all the islands, was said to have been born. (Actually, many think he was born nearby, but not right here.) Kamehameha means "the lonely one," which seems ironically fitting given the almost palpable loneliness this area of the island exudes.

After Kamehameha's birthplace you will come to an old Coast Guard LORAN station where you'll probably encounter boulders blocking the road. If so, retrace your route to the highway.

As you pass the tip of Kohala on 270, take note of how quickly you go from green to lots of dry scrub and an arid feel. That's the rain shadow effect, when the mountain causes it to rain more on one side than on the other.

There are a couple of places along this stretch to swim or snorkel—Kapa'a Beach Park and Mahukona, both described in BEACHES.

Near the 15 mile marker, look toward the ocean in the distance, and you can see stones sticking up in the air from a fascinating *navigational* heiau where the stones are aligned to point to other Hawaiian islands, Tahiti and more. You can walk to it from Mahukona. We recently took a GPS here and were able to verify that the stones really do align with Polynesian destinations. Pretty impressive.

By the way, Mahukona is also the name given to the Big Island's first and now-forgotten volcano, located offshore. This volcano started it all, but sank beneath the water less than half a million years ago.

On a clear day, you can't miss seeing Maui from here. But on *very* clear late afternoons, in addition to Maui's two mountains, you may see the islands of Lana'i, Kaho'olawe (in front of Lana'i from this angle) and Moloka'i between Lana'i and Maui. Look at the island chain map on

the back cover to orient yourself. Sunsets from this area can be superb.

LAPAKAHI STATE HISTORICAL PARK

At the 14 mile marker is Lapakahi State Historical Park, which consists of the remains of an old Hawaiian village. There is a trail running through the village, complete with markers noting interesting spots. Open 8 a.m. to 4 p.m., admission is free. This self-guided tour takes around 45 minutes, and the brochure does a reasonable job of explaining what you are seeing. Lapakahi is interesting at times and worthwhile for anyone interested in a taste of how the ancient Hawaiians may have lived in such an inhospitable place. That said, this is the worst run state park you'll find on the island. Although the staff might be nice, they convey some of the worst and most inaccurate information we've run across in any park in the state. An example: "This area was once lush rain forest until western man came along and cut it down, causing the rainfall to go from 100 inches to 10 inches annually." (In reality, this was originally a thin, rocky and scrubby *dryland* forest until *the Hawaiians* burned it down to plant crops after they discovered Hawai'i. This area is dry because it is, and always has been, in the rain shadow of Kohala Mountain.)

Also be careful if there's still a brochure box near the road entrance at Lapakahi. The first time we opened it, we got a handful of bees instead of a brochure.

One often overlooked aspect to Lapakahi is the fabulous water in Koai'e Cove (described in BEACHES). But don't expect to get the warmies from the staff, who seem to resent snorkelers here.

The highway between the 14 mile marker and Kawaihae (2 mile marker) is replete with dirt roads leading toward the ocean. You may be tempted to explore them, especially if you have 4WD. With that in mind, using a variety of vehicles and on foot, we traversed nearly every inch of all of them, including their branches (and we can cough up the dust-balls to prove it). The result? We can say with complete confidence that all of these roads are utterly wretched and lead to absolute squat. The entire coastline in this area is rocky and mostly unprotected. There are *no* beaches. It's pretty but not beautiful, and the land is harsh and unforgiving. (The real beauty of this area is underwater, with lots of extensive coral formations and ultra-clean water.) The only people who bother to make their way to the coast along this stretch are shoreline fishermen. So don't bother unless you have *way* too much time on your hands. The only exception is **Crystal Cove** near the 5 mile marker. The SCUBA is outstanding and fairly easy to access. (See SCUBA in ACTIVITIES.) Some local shoreline fishermen have driven pole holders into the lava in this area to practice shoreline fishing. I'm sure they won't mind if you borrow them. Otherwise, kiss off this area. It'll make you thirsty just *looking* at it.

KAWAIHAE

The tiny port town of Kawaihae has a few places to eat and shop and is the launching area for some fishing and SCUBA operations. Otherwise, there's not much to see. There's an ice cream place on the back side of Kawaihae Center that has fairly good ice cream. **Café Pesto** is your best bet for food.

This is the driest part of the state, with annual rainfall averaging less than 10 inches. (Contrast that with 240 inches on the slopes northwest of Hilo.)

At the junction of Highways 19 and 270 is the impressive **Pu'ukohola Heiau.** (Entry is free and the visitor center is open 7:30 a.m. to 4 p.m.) This massive struc-

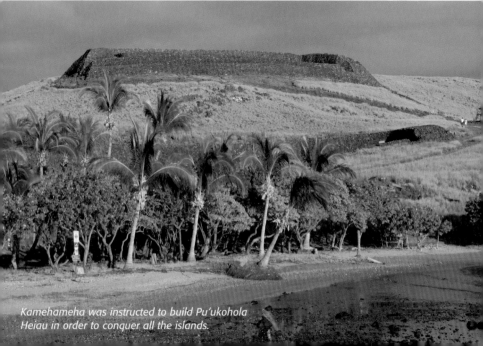

Kamehameha was instructed to build Pu'ukohola Heiau in order to conquer all the islands.

Kohala Resort Area
Waikoloa & Mauna Lani

Puako Road

Malama / Petroglyph Trail

19 73

74

Fairmont Orchid

Parking

Pauoa Bay

Mauna Lani North Golf Course

Mauna Lani Dr.

Mauna Lani Bay Hotel & Bungalows

Public Parking

Mauna Lani Terrace

Islands at Mauna Lani

Makaiwa Bay

Secret Pond

N E S W

0   1/2 MILE

Mauna Lani Point

⌒ Indicates Foot Trails

67 Roadside mile markers

⋯ Unpaved Roads

Kanikū Dr.

Ala Kahakai Trail

Mauna Lani South Golf Course

Honoka'ope Beach

49 Black Sand Beach —Lava freshwater pool

Ala Loa / King's Trail

Waikoloa Road

75

Colony Villas

Hilton Waikoloa

Waikoloa Kings' Golf Course

Queen Ka'ahumanu Hwy

Waikoloa Beach Golf Course

Shores at Waikoloa

Vista Waikoloa

Fairway Villas

Gas

76

Waikoloa Beach Dr

Parking

Kolea

Waikoloa Beach Marriott

Kings' Shops

'Anaeho'omalu Beach

Parking

19

Note: From this area (clouds permitting) you can see four of the Big Island's five volcano mountains. Looking away from the ocean, from left to right, they are Kohala, Mauna Kea, Mauna Loa and Hualalai. The most massive, Mauna Loa, seems the least impressive from this perspective. Offshore, Haleakala on Maui is often seen.

ture was built by King Kamehameha in 1790–91. He had sent his wife's grandmother to visit a kahuna on Kaua'i to ask how he could conquer Hawai'i. The kahuna said that if he built a fabulous heiau (temple) at Kawaihae and dedicated it to his war god, he would prevail. Thousands of "volunteers" worked on the project, carrying boulders from miles away. Workers were routinely sacrificed at different portions of the structure during construction to ensure that the gods would be pleased. When completed, Kamehameha dedicated the temple by inviting and then sacrificing his enemy Keoua (see page 91). During construction Kamehameha himself participated to inspire his workers. When his brother picked up a boulder to help, Kamehameha slapped the rock out of his hand saying, "No, brother, one of us should keep the kapu (meaning staying pure)." Kamehameha then instructed that the rock his brother had touched be taken far out to sea and dumped into deep water. Pu'ukohola Heiau is best viewed from Kawaihae Harbor Road (the one that leads out to the breakwater) in the late afternoon with Mauna Kea in the background. Just offshore are said to be the remains of a shark heiau, called Hale-o-Kapuni, where human remains were offered to sharks. Its precise location is unknown, and it has been buried for decades.

KOHALA RESORT AREA

Continuing *south* onto Highway 19 (called *Queen K* by most locals, short for Ka'ahumanu) toward Kailua-Kona, you will pass the Kohala mega-resort area. Ensconced in this desolate sea of lava and scrub, multi-zillion dollar resorts dot the coastline offering the luxury and amenities that have made this region famous. Golfing is top notch (and *expensive*) here; see

ACTIVITIES. Ocean activities, such as snorkeling and SCUBA, are very good. Though you wouldn't suspect it from the road, some of the best beaches in the state lie between here and Kailua-Kona. Some, such as Hapuna and Mauna Kea, are well known. Others, such as Manini'owali and Makalawena, are less known or deliciously secluded. The section on BEACHES describes them all in detail and tells you *exactly* how to get to each one of them.

See that barren lava field on the mauka (mountain) side of the highway? A Japanese company purchased the 3,000 acres in 1990 for a *mere* $45 million. They had big plans for it, including six golf courses and 2,600 homes. After paying taxes on it for nine years, the shrewd investors unloaded it in 1998 for $5 million.

Most of the lava you see here flowed thousands of years ago. In other parts of the island it'd be covered with forest. But the very thing that brings visitors here—the utter lack of rain—keeps the lava looking so uninviting.

Hold on to your hat along this stretch. The wind can be fierce in the afternoon. As the lava fields heat up during the day, it causes the air to heat and rise. Air from the ocean rushes in to fill the void, creating strong afternoon breezes.

Hapuna Beach is off the road near the 69 mile marker. This beach is often featured in travel shows and is a *superb* place to frolic. We like to snorkel from there to 69 Beach on calm days, or boogie board till we're raw. Otherwise, just gallivant on the fine sand.

The road to the Mauna Lani between the 73 and 74 mile markers is worth consideration. See map on previous page. To the north is the Malama Petroglyph Trail. This simple 25-minute walk through kiawe forest leads to a very large field of petroglyphs—or carvings—in the lava. Though not as extensive as the Pu'u Loa field at Kilauea Volcano, it's one of the largest in the state and worth a stroll if you want to see how ancient Hawaiians expressed themselves through their tenacious carvings.

The Mauna Lani Bay Hotel sits adjacent to some of the most fascinating grounds of any Big Island resort. Huge fishponds surrounded by palm trees to the south make for wonder-filled strolling. We like to wander back to Secret Pond (see map) for a cool, refreshing dip in the crystal clear water. (I know: the other ponds aren't clear—*this* one is.) Park at the public parking area and wander along the trail toward the fishponds. Allow an hour for this pleasant diversion.

Continuing south, the road at the 76 mile marker leads to 'Anaeho'omalu Beach. If you're low on gasoline, there is relief on this road. 'Anaeho'omalu

has a gorgeous palm-fronted fishpond behind the beach. If you're looking for the perfect location to take a sunset photo, the backside of the fishpond is as good as it gets. When clouds cooperate, even the most photographically challenged (present reader excluded) can take postcard-quality shots.

KOHALA LAVA DESERT AREA

Back on Highway 19 heading south, the large cluster of palms toward the ocean at the 79 mile marker surround a large freshwater pond and a pretty but secluded beach called Ke-awa-iki. The pond itself is not available to visitors (the barbed wire, half-starved Dobermans, and snipers with night vision glasses see to that), but the beach is accessible via a 15-minute walk, and there is a special freshwater golden pool available to hikers. (See Ke-awa-iki hike under ACTIVITIES.)

Take a look at the "graffiti" strewn about the lava field. It's sort of an island tradition to compose messages from

Even the harsh lava deserts hide jewels, such as the golden pools of Ke-awa-iki.

pieces of coral on the black lava canvas, and families often come out here to do it together. They're almost always friendly messages, like *Al* ™ *Sandy, I Love You Mom,* or *In Memory of Dan,* and rarely contain the nasties often seen in real mainland graffiti.

The scenic turnout at the 82 mile marker overlooks **Kiholo Bay.** Down there you will find a saltwater bay with freshwater calmly floating on top, lots of turtles and a lava tube with fresh spring water just 80 feet from the ocean. Intrigued? I hope so. You can drive part of the way during daylight hours and hike around. (See HIKING on page 198.)

Throughout this part of the island you'll occasionally see palm trees along the barren coastline. These are almost always an indication of freshwater spring-fed pools. Since there's no permanent stream on the entire west side of the island, water percolates into the lava and often bubbles to the surface near the shore, forming pools. We look for them when we're hiking along the coast. When you're hot and tired, you can't beat splashing like a fool in a cold, clean freshwater or brackish pool.

If you're looking for a stunning secluded beach, and don't mind walking for 15–20 minutes, **Makalawena Beach** (described in BEACHES) is west of the 89 mile marker.

You may still see some DONKEY CROSSING signs along here. Until recently there was a small herd of wild donkeys that crossed the highway at night and early mornings on the older lava north of the 85 mile marker. They came down out of the mountains to lick the salt off rocks by the shore, drink from springs and occasionally putt on the Hualalai Golf Course. (Now *there's* a hazard.) Known locally as **Kona Nightingales,**

they were the descendants of coffee-hauling pack animals that escaped a century ago. Every so often one got whacked by a passing car, leaving both pretty bent out of shape, and they were finally rounded up and hauled away to spend the rest of their days in a corral. Wild goats still work the area and are fairly easy to spot.

Just north of the 91 mile marker is a **large lava tube** from the Hualalai lava flow of 1801 that bisects the highway. On the ocean side of the road it has collapsed, leaving a large chasm in the lava. On the mauka side it forms a cave, which is collapsing in several spots. This cave looks rickety and unstable.

Located just south of the Kona airport is the **Natural Energy Laboratory.** Started by the government in the 1970s to respond to the energy crisis, they monkeyed with making electricity using temperature differences between 80° surface water and 37° deep sea water. The technology wasn't particularly scalable and has since been abandoned at this location. But their giant 55-inch pipe sucking water from 3,000 feet down is now being used by dozens of private companies taking advantage of easy access to cold seawater and year-round sunshine. Industries, such as raising clams, coral, sea horses, blue green algae, oysters and mushrooms, are thriving out here.

An example is **Kona Cold Lobster.** When the lobsters arrive from the mainland they have a nasty case of jet lag. (If you flew here from the East coast, you can probably relate.) The beasties are put in the cold water to rejuvenate so that they are bright and alert when you boil them for dinner.

Surprisingly, once you pump seawater out of the ocean, federal environmental laws make it *illegal* to return it, even if it's perfectly clean. So they're forced to pump it into a deep hole (more like a *loop*hole) where it naturally seeps back into the ocean. The energy lab gives a 2-hour-long lecture/presentations Tue., Wed. and Thur. at 10 a.m. for $8. Reserve at 329–8073.

An excellent tide-pool is nearby at **Wawaloli Beach**. (See page 163.)

Near the 97 mile marker is the parking lot for **Kaloko-Honokohau National Historical Park**. Despite its appearance, this area was once a thriving community, and Hawaiian artifacts are still scattered about the lava field. There's even a holua (stone slide) that was used by chiefs. They would cover it with grasses and leaves and go zooming down on a sled. Commoners weren't allowed to do it, but they could cheer. (Yippee!) See BEACHES for more.

If you are into deep sea fishing, you'll want to check out **Honokohau Harbor** listed under BEACHES. Fishing boats leave from here, and weigh-ins take place daily at 10 a.m. and 6 p.m. (You can tell what they caught by the fish flags they hoist.) If you want to buy some, **Marina Seafoods** (326–2117) gets the fish right off the boats as they come in.

KOHALA SHOPPING

In Hawi, **The Gallery at Bamboo**, inside the Bamboo Restaurant, is excellent. Be sure to go upstairs for additional art works and furniture. There are other shops in Hawi worth a look. They offer antiques, crystals, local artists' studios, etched glass and clothing. Grab an ice cream at **Tropical Dreams** or a chocolate covered banana at **Shady's** while you shop.

Heading north in Kapa'au, the newly remodeled Nanbu Building has the **Kohala Book Shop**, offering a large selection of used books on Hawaiiana. Grab a coffee drink or sandwich next door at the **Nanbu Courtyard** or browse the gallery there. And across from the Kamehameha Statue the **Ackerman Galleries** has a nice assortment of art, glass and woodwork.

All of the mega-resorts have shopping areas, but especially noteworthy are the shops at the **Hilton Waikoloa** and the **Mauna Lani**. An additional shopping area at the Mauna Lani Resort called the **Shops at Mauna Lani** was in the works at press time.

The main shopping area in South Kohala is the **Kings' Shops** located at the Waikoloa Beach Resort. Just about anything can be found here from the **Louis Vuitton** shop to the **Ukulele House**. There's also a Food Pavilion and a **Starbucks**, if you're hungry. Expect higher prices here as this is a resort shopping area.

KOHALA'S BEST BETS

Best Sunsets—Behind the fishponds at 'Anaeho'omalu Beach
Best Place to Get the Willies—Mo'okini Heiau, Hawi
Best Treat—Tropical Dreams, Hawi
Best Pizza—Café Pesto, Kawaihae
Best Koa Carvings—Gallery at Bamboo
Best Secluded Beach—Makalawena
Best Resort Grounds to Stroll Around— Mauna Lani Bay Hotel & Bungalows
Best Lu'au—Kona Village
Best Golf—Mauna Kea Golf Course
Best View of Maui—Coming down Highway 250 into Hawi
Best Overlook—Pololu Valley
Best Boogie-Boarding—Hapuna or Mauna Kea Beach
Best Remnant of Ancient Hawaiian Art—Puako Petroglyph Field

Kamehameha the Great, the first king to rule all the islands, could live anywhere he wanted. He chose Kailua-Kona. This is his 'Ahu'ena Heiau.

Kailua was a tiny fishing village in days gone by. Fishermen would haul in giants from the deep, bountiful waters, while farmers tended their fields up the slopes of Hualalai. Many of the great chiefs of old chose this part of the island as their home. Kona weather and Kona waters were known throughout the islands as the very best, and that hasn't changed. Though no longer the sleepy little village of yesteryear, this is a charming seaside town where the strolling is pleasant, the sunsets are mesmerizing, the food is diverse, and the activities are plentiful. Some guidebooks badmouth Kona because it's not the same as it was 20 years ago—what is? Kona is still great; there are simply more people who know it.

The town is alternately referred to as Kailua-Kona, Kona, Kailua, or sometimes Kailua Town. See page 30 for an explanation of this confusing situation.

Kailua-Kona is nestled in the lee of Hualalai Volcano, meaning that it is sheltered from the trade winds coming from the other side of the island. The winds we do get are usually from wraparound sea breezes. The rains from them have already been wrung out.

The heart of Kailua-Kona is the mile-long oceanfront stretch of Alii Drive starting at the Kailua Pier. As with any town, traffic can be heavy. (And it's gotten consideraby worse in the past few years.) Alii Drive is a particularly good area to take a walk after a meal, although *on occasion* at night there might be unsavory-looking characters hanging around. Public parking is somewhat limited and is shown on the Kailua-Kona Map. This part of town has lots of shops and restaurants overlooking the water. If you start strolling from the Kailua Pier, keep an eye out for some of these sights.

AROUND DOWNTOWN KAILUA-KONA

To the right (north) of the pier is the 'Ahu'ena Heiau. Now wonderfully maintained and very picturesque, this was King Kamehameha the Great's personal heiau (temple) that he had restored in 1812, and it was here that he spent his later years until his death in 1819. Note the bird on top of the tallest ki'i akua (statue of a god). It is a golden plover, the bird that may have guided the first Polynesians here. (See page 15.) Kamehameha dedicated this heiau to the god Lono and filled it with European and Chinese furniture. Nearby is Nane Mahina 'Ai, where the King went

Kona Airport ✈
90
(190)
95
19
Hualalai 8,271
(180)
Kailua-Kona
100
Kailua Bay
120 **Holualoa**
Keauhou Bay
115 **Honalo**
Kainaliu (1,400 ft)
0   5 MILES
Kealakekua
110 **Captain Cook**
Kealakekua Bay
Pu'uhonua o Honaunau (Place of Refuge)
105
Honaunau
11 **(1,000 ft)**

to get away from it all. There was a famous portrait painted here of Kamehameha wearing a red vest, white shirt and a yellow silk necktie. The artist pleaded with him not to wear the fancy sailor's outfit, but Kamehameha insisted.

The tiny beach in front of the heiau is Kamakahonu Beach, one of the calmest beaches on the island. There you can rent kayaks, paddle boats, snorkel gear, etc. (though at confiscatory prices).

To the left of the pier is a starting gate to end all starting gates. Every year in October an athletic event occurs on the Big Island that draws national attention. The Ironman Triathlon is a profound testimony to the power to challenge, to the ability to reach down to the very core of our spirit and summon the impossible. Three events, any one of which would seem *insurmountable* to most of us mere mortals, are stitched together in a triathlon that seems almost ludicrous. Swim 2.4 miles in the open ocean, then get out and ride a bike 112 miles on a hot road cut through a lava field. Finally, dismount and run a 26.2 mile marathon. All this is done consecutively under the tropical sun. This is the best opportunity you'll ever have to look into the faces of mass excellence, and not just the young. We have a friend in his late-60s who usually breezes by most of the 25-year-olds, completing the race in under 12 hours.

The seawall near the pier is usually a great place to fish. During abnormally high seas, water crashes over the wall and is quite a sight to see. Even better fishing is at the wall in front of the Hulihe'e Palace (329–1877) farther down. This palace, built in 1838 by Governor Kuakini, quickly became the house of choice for vacationing Hawaiian royalty until 1914. Now a

A REAL GEM

museum lovingly run by the Daughters of Hawai'i, inside you'll find a nice collection of koa furniture, including some stunning armoires, and a 6-foot diameter table cut from a single piece of koa. Most of the furniture was auctioned off in the 1920s but fortunately was cataloged. Later, the buyers were contacted, and many have graciously lent the items to the museum for display. There are many photos of Hawaiian royalty, including Princess Ruth. (History books *never* mention her without mentioning her size, but we're above that...no, we're not. Estimates range from 6-foot-2 to 6-foot-10, 400–450 lbs. She slept in a hut outside.) Spears, fishhooks and other artifacts make this museum a worthwhile stop. Most who give the tours (under an hour) are very knowledgeable and friendly, but occasionally you'll get some bad historical information. Admission is $6. The Palace Gift Shop next door has some interesting items and hard-to-find books and is worth a peek.

Outside, on the south side of the Palace to the right of the drinking fountain, is a rock with a hole in it. It is the top of a Pohaku Likanaka. It was used for executions out at Kahalu'u Beach Park. People would be forced to stand in front of it while a rope was passed through the hole, around the neck, and back out. The executioner would then pull back for a few minutes...and that was that.

Across the street from Hulihe'e Palace is the Mokuaikaua Church. This was the first Christian church built in the islands, in 1820. The initial building was a thatched hut, with the current structure erected in 1837. You're welcome inside; admission is free. Built of lava rock and crushed coral with koa hardwood gracing the tall interior, this is a magnificent remnant of the era. Look at the joints inside the building, which were painstakingly attached with pins made from gnarly 'ohi'a trees. There are exhibits relating to early Hawai'i and the work of the missionaries, along with a model of

With moonlight on one side and sunlight on the other, altars (called lele ho'okau), such as this one at the Ku'emanu Heiau, are still used by some for a morning prayer.

the *Thaddeus*, which brought the first missionaries here. Sometimes referred to as the Mayflower of Hawai'i, the *Thaddeus* left Boston in October 1819 for a five-month trip to the islands. These men and women left comfortable lives in the United States to come to an alien and mysterious land. Unbeknownst to them, their chances for success were greatly enhanced en route when Kamehameha II and his step-mother Ka'ahumanu orchestrated the overthrow of the Hawaiian religion less than a month into their ocean journey.

There's a large shopping area at Kona Inn. If you're looking for a place to watch the sunset or have a picnic, the grass on the ocean side of this center is ideal.

If you want to watch the sunset from a restaurant along here, the best views (from south to north) are: Huggo's, Bubba Gump, Kona Inn, Hard Rock Café and Hang Loose. Lulu's sunset views are not quite as good. See individual reviews under DINING. During months around the summer solstice (June 21), the sun may set behind the point from the northernmost restaurants.

ELSEWHERE ALONG ALII DRIVE

As you drive further south along Alii Drive, keep an eye out for joggers. They trot up and down Alii Drive in large enough numbers to constitute a flock. (Or is it a gaggle?) There are mile markers every half mile here, which we put on the Alii Drive map. Between Kona By The Sea and Kona Isle is a 100-yard access trail that leads to something that even most longtime Alii Drive residents don't know about. It's a public saltwater swimming pool fed by the splashing of waves. It was privately built decades ago and reverted to the state when the owner died without heirs. The pool directly abuts the ocean and even has some fish in it most of the time. There's a smaller tide-pool to the left. If you want to swim in seawater but are hesitant to go into the ocean, here's your chance. Unmaintained, the pool occasionally isn't refreshed enough if the surf has been flat for too long, meaning it sometimes gets green and yucky.

Keep an eye out on the mauka side of Alii Drive for a farmers' market. Near the 3½ mile marker is Pahoehoe Beach Park. No sand here, but it's a nice place to have a picnic, or to just sit on a bench and watch the surf. White Sands Beach (it has several other names) is a little farther down with good boogie boarding when the sand is in town. (See BEACHES.)

There are scads of oceanfront condos and apartments along this road. Traffic noise is going to be your penalty for staying on Alii Drive, but it's a penalty most are quite willing to endure.

Soon you'll come to the quaintest little church you've ever seen. St. Peter's Catholic Church is known locally as the "Little Blue Church." This tiny building, with its picturesque location, ever-open doors and less than a dozen simple *small* pews, is the most photographed in the islands. Weddings of all denominations take place there almost every weekend. Sunsets through the etched glass can offer dramatic photo opportunities.

To the right of the church is the Ku'emanu Heiau. This is the only heiau (temple) in the state known to be associated solely with surfing. This surf spot was available only to chiefs (commoners caught surfing here were put to death) and they came here to pray for gnarly conditions. (They usually got them, too.

Even today this is one of the most dependable breaks in Kona.) To this day, Hawaiians still come here to pay homage to the spirits. The small notch in front was a luapa'u, where discarded bones were tossed—perhaps bones of commoners caught surfing. Incidentally, surfing in the old days was usually done naked (giving new meaning to the term *hang loose*).

Next to the church is Kahalu'u Beach Park where you'll find some of the easiest access to good snorkeling on the island. It gets crowded on weekends. See BEACHES for more on this gem. Kahalu'u had a large population in the old days, and there are very extensive lava tube caves tucked away in the jungle up mauka (toward the mountain).

After you pass Keauhou Beach Resort, you'll see a parcel of land to its left. Fronting this parcel on some of the lava at low tide, you can see petroglyphs carved in the rock. They are at the northern end of the salt-and-pepper sand and gravel beach. In the 16th century, Kamalalawalu, the King of Maui, was impaled alive by Lonoikamakahiki at Ke'eku Heiau for 10 or 11 days. Kamalalawalu was then taken to a flat rock nearby and slain. His body was towed out to sea and fed to the sharks. The petroglyphs on the rock date back to that incident and detail the event. (Lonoikamakahiki had a good reason to be miffed at Kamalalawalu. His general had been captured by invading Maui forces, had his eyes gouged out and his eye sockets pierced with darts *before* being killed. That was considered uncool even by the standards of the time.)

The land contains several heiaus, including one where thousands of Hawaiians were sacrificed to their gods. Local lore says that any business that operates there is cursed. If you don't believe it, ask the Japanese company that paid millions

Alii Drive

❶ King Kamehameha Hotel
❷ Kona Seaside Hotel
❸ Uncle Billy's Kona Bay Hotel
❹ Kona Islander Inn
❺ Kona Alii
❻ Royal Kona Resort
❼ Hale Kona Kai
❽ Kona Reef
❾ Kona Tiki
❿ Sea Village
⓫ Alii Villas
⓬ Kona Makai
⓭ Royal Sea Cliff Resort
⓮ Casa de Emdeko
⓯ Kona Isle
⓰ Kona By The Sea
⓱ Hale Pohaku
⓲ Kona Nalu
⓳ Kona Bali Kai
⓴ Banyan Tree
㉑ Royal Kahili
㉒ Kona Magic Sands
㉓ White Sands Village
㉔ Kona Seaspray
㉕ Kahalu'u Bay Villas
㉖ Makolea
㉗ Outrigger Keauhou Beach
㉘ Keauhou Kona Surf/Rac.
㉙ Kona Coast Resort
㉚ Kanaloa at Kona
㉛ Keauhou Palena
㉜ Keauhou Resort
㉝ Country Club Villas
㉞ Sheraton Keauhou Bay
㉟ Keauhou Akahi
㊱ Keauhou Punahele

Downtown Kailua-Kona shown in the darker shade.

Kailua Bay

Henry

Farmer's Market

Royal Poinciana Drive

Pahoehoe Beach Park

White Sands Beach

Kahalu'u Beach

Ke'eku Heiau

Petroglyphs

Keauhou Shopping Center

Keauhou Bay

Kona Country Club Golf Course

End of the World

Burial Grounds, Kuamo'o Battle

Holua (Hawaiian Slide)

© 2006 Wizard Publications, Inc.

for the lease to a 454-room hotel here in 1988. They closed the hotel, called the Kona Lagoons, planning extensive renovations. Then they ran out of money. It sat vacant and dilapidated, until they finally gave it up in 1994 to the landowner, Bishop Estate, who bulldozed a decade later.

As you ascend Alii Drive toward the Keauhou Shopping Center (the bakery at KTA there *on occasion* has wicked taro bread pudding), keep an eye on your right, in the golf course, for the strangest corkscrew-shaped palm tree we've ever seen. No interesting story here—just weird. There's a flock of imported **wild parrots** that cruises around these parts. Keep an eye (and ear) out for them.

If you stay on Alii for a mile, it'll go back toward the ocean. There is a lava road near the dead end. If you walk on the road for a minute (actually you can see it from your car), you'll be able to see, on your left, terraces in the side of the mountain. You are at an extraordinary place. It might not look like much, but this is where the battle between Hawaiians to kill their religion took place one day in 1820. (See page 17 for the extraordinary story.) The terraces are the graves from that battle.

With a name befitting the area, a cliff-jumping spot past the battlefield called *End of the World* is listed under ADVENTURES on page 233.

UP MAUKA OF KAILUA-KONA

Hualalai Volcano erupts sporadically every few hundred years. The last time was in 1801 when it covered part of

The Hawaiians planted coconut trees wherever they could. In ancient times Kahalu'u Beach was heavily populated. Today, it is heavily snorkeled.

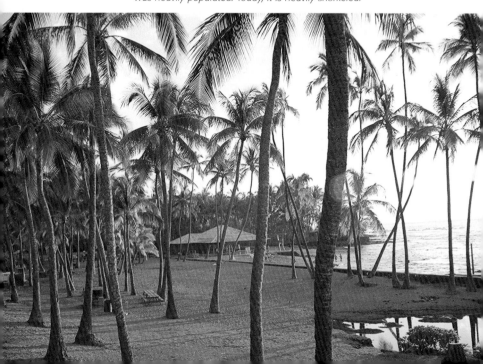

A Fish Story

Keauhou was dominated by the legacy of a king in the 1600s named Lonoika-makahiki (called Lono by his friends). Lono (not to be confused with the Hawaiian god of the same name) got into a series of bets with the king of O'ahu. Each time Lono won. On one occasion, Lono and the O'ahu king were out fishing. Lono's advisor told Lono not to go because he (Lono) didn't know how to fish. They went anyway, and while fishing, Lono got all worked up while the O'ahu king was hauling in a beauty and asked to borrow fishing gear. As Lono's advisor feared, the O'ahu king mocked Lono for not bringing his own gear. Lono's advisor, in order to save his master's honor, volunteered the solution to Lono. He whispered it into his ear and Lono agreed. Lono then shouted, "Hey, I don't need your gear. I'll bet you I can catch a fish on my own." The O'ahu king accepted, knowing that Lono had not brought any fishing gear with him. Then Lono, at his advisor's suggestion, clubbed his advisor to death, ripped open his belly and used his intestines for fishing line. Lono splintered the man's thigh bone for a fishhook. His flesh was used for bait and his head for a sinker. He lowered the gear into the water and immediately caught an ahi. Lono won the bet (a large piece of O'ahu) and later went on to win all of O'ahu in another bet.

The moral: If you think you sacrifice a lot for your boss, try working for Lono.

(Incidentally, Lono's bones were in the Bishop Museum in Honolulu until 1994 when they were stolen by Hawaiian activists and buried in Waipi'o Valley.)

what is now Kona Airport. The top of Hualalai is mostly covered with 'ohi'a and eucalyptus forest with occasional koa and pine. The clouds usually roll in around mid-morning, blanketing the 8,271-foot summit in a rich fog that can reduce visibility to zero. Wild goats and pigs scramble about the uninhabited top portion of the mountain. The views of Mauna Kea and Mauna Loa, as well as its own caldera, make Hualalai a hiker's haven. Unfortunately, it's all owned by Bishop Estate, which routinely denies access to the public. (Bishop Estate is a trust set up in the 1800s to help Hawai'i's kids. It has grown to where it now owns 11% of the state and has astonishing power. Many of the houses you see on the island are actually on Bishop land leased for several decades by individuals.)

Hovering above the town of Kailua-Kona is the "artist community" of Holualoa on Highway 180. There are several galleries worth stopping for if you are in the neighborhood. Hours can be sporadic. Otherwise, there is not as much to offer the visitor in this quiet, peaceful bedroom community as visitor literature might imply.

Although Kona itself doesn't convey the lushness many associate with Hawai'i, it *does* exist on this side of the island. Kaloko Road meanders up into a luxuriant cloud forest. See page 43 for more.

Kealakekua Bay to Honaunau

Greenwell Coffee
Farm 1 Mile

1300'

11

110

Mamalahoa Hwy

11

109

11

This 4WD road is very nasty and should
only be used as a hiking trail.

**Cook's
Monument**

Exceptional
Snorkeling here

10

108

Kealakekua Bay

*Kealakekua Bay is a great
place to spot dolphins.*

☐ **Hikiau Heiau**

Napo'opo'o Beach Park
(Sand now mostly gone)

Old Coffee Mill

160

Kayakers usually
launch here

Napoopoo Rd

8

Manini Beach

Keawi

11

107

Ke'ei Beach

↓

Moku-a-Kae Bay

Middle Keei Rd

Painted Church Rd

106

160

Bayview Coffee Farm ↗

N

W   E

S

✝ **Painted
Church**
■

1

105

2

Ke Ala o Keawe Rd

0   1 MILE

3

104

160

Honaunau Bay

Keoneele Cove

**Pu'uhonua o Honaunau
National Historical Park**
(Formerly City of Refuge)

11

Picnic Area

1871 Trail

Legend

∿	Indicates Foot Trails
67	Roadside mile markers
⋯	Unpaved Roads

SOUTH OF KAILUA-KONA

If you head south out of Kona, you'll come to a series of small towns, all above 1,000 feet. It's usually cool up here, sometimes even foggy. The theme to these towns is often coffee. Free samples are offered at many establishments. Some are mediocre. Others, such as Greenwell and Bayview, sell very good quality coffee to take with you. There are places to eat along here, such as Aloha Angel Café and The Coffee Shack, both good for breakfast. Look for Antiques—Art—Ice Cream on the ocean side of the highway in Kealakekua. They serve Tropical Dreams ice cream, as sinful here as in Hawi on the north shore. Near the antique shop is a massage school (323–3800) in the Pualani Terrace. Several times a week they offer hour-long massages by their students for $30. Between the 113 and 114 mile marker in Kainaliu, stop at Surfin' Ass for some of their donkey balls. (Wonderful chocolate covered mac nuts with thick chocolate.) Available in any quantity. (Not just pairs.)

In Kealakekua (you'll be forgiven if you don't readily see the transition between towns up here) between the 112 and 111 mile markers on the ocean side of the road is the Kona Historical Society Museum (323–3222). Located in an old general store built during the 1800s, there are lots of old coffee-related photos and other items of historical interest. Worth a stop if you have an interest in the past. Closed Sundays, $3 admission.

There are good views down the coast from some spots along here. After you pass the 111 mile marker on Highway 11, you'll see Napoopoo Road on the ocean side of the road—take it. There are lots of coffee farms down here. (See gray box on next page.) A coffee tour might be worth the effort. You may get to try delicious coffee or meet offbeat characters you'll remember for years to come.

Napoopoo comes to an intersection of itself and Middle Ke'ei Road. Turn right here and head toward the ocean. The old Mauna Loa Coffee Mill near the 8 mile marker is now a tourist shop run by another company and is of marginal interest. Stop only if you need to stretch.

KEALAKEKUA BAY & PLACE OF REFUGE

When you get to the sea, hang a right to Napo'opo'o Beach Park. The stone

A REAL GEM

structure you see in front of you at this southern end of Kealakekua Bay (at the end of the road) is Hiki-au Heiau. This was a luakini (a temple where human sacrifices were made). Here Captain Cook was first worshipped as the returning god Lono. During the ceremony, an elder priest named Koa, in the honored tradition of the Hawaiians, chewed the food first before spitting it out and offering it to Cook. (He politely declined.) It was also here that the first Christian ceremony was held in Hawai'i. Ironically it may have contributed to the death of Captain Cook. When one of his men died, Cook ordered him buried near this heiau and personally read the service. This event was proof to some Hawaiians that the strangers were mere mortals, not the gods others felt them to be.

Napo'opo'o Beach used to be a fabulous beach fronting the heiau. Most "current" guidebooks still rave about it. Too bad it doesn't really exist anymore. It had been eroding for years, being gradually replaced by boulders. When Hurricane 'Iniki sideswiped the island way

Kona Coffee

Of all the products produced on the Big Island, none is more well known or has received more accolades than Kona coffee. Though now out-produced in quantity by Kaua'i,

Kona coffee is unmatched in terms of quality. With the possible exception of Jamaican Blue Mountain coffee, Kona coffee is widely considered to be the best in the world. Good Kona coffee lacks the bitterness of coffees from other parts of the world. By the way, contrary to nearly everyone's belief, lighter roasts have more caffeine than darker roasts. (Caffeine cooks away during the roasting process.)

A quality cup of coffee has little resemblance to mass-produced coffee you see on most supermarket shelves. (Of course, you pay more for the good stuff.) Good Kona coffee will set you back $20 or more per pound. Surprisingly little profit is made by the farmer at that price. Most small farmers grow coffee as a labor of love. If you see 100% Kona coffee (not a blend) selling for $12 per pound, it might be poorly chosen, broken, or poorly roasted beans. You usually get what you pay for. And if you're told in a restaurant that they serve Kona blend because pure Kona is too strong, it's like saying that champagne needs to be blended with gasoline because pure champagne is too strong. Kona blends (which are blended with cheap beans from elsewhere) are less mellow than pure Kona. Blends are usually served because it's cheaper, not better.

Being wretched coffee addicts, we've tried them all. For what it's worth, we like **Fike Farms** (808–328–2265), **Holualoa** (800–334–0348), **Greenwell** (808–323–2862) and **Bayview** (800–662–5880). Some aren't available in stores, only by phone or mail order. **Kona Joe** (866–566–2563) grows their trees on a trellis, like grapes, and the Trellis Reserve medium roast is very good. But at $50 per pound you'll be forgiven if you want to pursue a less expensive vice.

Coffees that we've tried and didn't like are Bad Ass Coffee, Ferrari Mountain Gold, Royal Aloha, and Starbuck's Kona coffee. (The last one is surprising.) We are not saying that these companies are bad, just that we didn't like their coffee and didn't think it was worth the money.

Coffee tours are available from many growers, but coffee farms that claim to offer tours are often poorly marked and owners and employees sometimes seem shocked when you show up to buy coffee. Greenwell and Bayview have nice tours. They are on the map on page 66.

back in 1992, its surf removed most of what sand was left. Over the years very little has returned.

One mile across the bay you can see a white obelisk, the Captain Cook Monument, which was erected in 1874 by British sailors. It was near this spot (a rarely visited plaque to the left of the monument marks the *actual* spot) in 1779 that Cook was killed by the Hawaiians. (See INTRODUCTION for more on this event.) You won't need your passport to go there, even though it is British soil that the monument rests on. The small plot was deeded to the United Kingdom by Princess Likelike.

Kealakekua Bay is also popular with dolphins. A large number of spinners reside in the bay, so keep an eye out for them. We see them almost every time we kayak to the monument. Toward the monument side on the bay, up the steep cliff, there is a grayish impression. Local lore says this was made by a cannonball fired from Cook's ship.

These cliffs hold even more secrets. In the past, important chiefs were buried in small caves in the cliff face. After the bones had been separated, volunteers were lowered down the face of the cliffs by rope to place the bones in crevices. No one had a long résumé for doing this. That's because the person doing the burying, once finished with his task, would signal to those above that he was done. The officials on top would promptly cut the rope, sending the burial person, and all knowledge of the location of the bones, crashing to the rocks below. (It was actually considered an honor to be the volunteer at the end of the rope.) All this was to prevent the bones from being desecrated. Bones were often turned into fishhooks and other implements. Skulls were turned into refuse pots or toilets.

(*Really* good joke edited out here upon further reflection.)

Today, if you hear something fall from the cliff, it won't be a person. Brainless cows from above occasionally wander off the ledge, pleasing the fish below with a refreshing change from their seafood diet.

The waters near the monument are crystal clear and teeming with coral and fish. This is some of the best snorkeling in the state. The local community wants to keep it somewhat difficult to access to prevent it from being overrun with "casual" visitors. If you are wondering how to get there, you have several choices:

You can swim it. This takes us about an hour each way with fins and is guaranteed to tucker you out.

You can walk along the edge of the bay for about 98% of the distance. You'll have to scramble on boulders the whole way and will have to swim for a couple of short patches. You expose yourself to the ocean's whims with this method.

You can rent a kayak and paddle over. (See KAYAKING on page 208.) This is our favorite method. It's a relatively easy 30-minute paddle across the usually peaceful bay, and you stand a good chance of cruising among dolphins along the way. Make sure you bring water, lunch and snorkel gear. This is an excellent way to spend the morning.

Another way to get to the monument is to take the trail near the intersection of Highway 11 and Napoopoo Road. (The trailhead is a little over 1/10 mile from the highway across from 3 large palm trees. See map. You may have to park a short distance up the road.) It used to be a road but is now suitable only for hiking. It's two miles each way with a 1,300-foot constant descent to the water. It's a pretty good puffer coming back up with little shade and some obnoxious footing. It takes most people more than an hour each way. Drink *plenty* of water before and during the ascent, and be careful not to pull your calves during the steady, grueling climb. Along the way you'll pass (but won't see due to brush) the Puhina

Is there anything more tranquil than coconut trees, like those here at Honaunau?

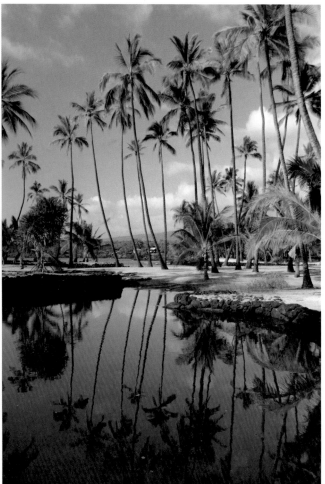

o Lono Heiau. It was here that Cook's bones were...well, cooked. (See below.) For $135–$150 per person, Kings' Trail Rides (323-2388) brings small groups down this trail on horseback for a 4-hour ride and snorkel tour. (See HORSEBACK RIDING in ACTIVITIES.)

Lastly, you can take one of the boat trips on page 210. They stop for snorkeling near the monument. They also offer SCUBA, SNUBA, and all-around fun.

What Finally Happened to Cook?

The Hawaiians traditionally scraped the flesh off the bones of great men. The bones were then bundled together and burned or buried in secret so they wouldn't be desecrated. If the dead person was really loved, the bones were kept in a private home for a while. Because Cook was so respected by the Hawaiians, his body parts were distributed among the chiefs. His head went to the king, his scalp went to a high-ranking chief, his hair went to Kamehameha, etc. Some of his organs, including his heart and liver, were stolen and eaten by some local children who mistook them for dog innards. *(Yuck!)* Eventually, when two Hawaiians brought a bundle to the ship, the

British solemnly unwrapped the bundle and discovered a pile of bloody flesh that had been cut from Cook's body. Even though the Hawaiians were bestowing an honor upon Cook, the British sailors didn't see it that way and were naturally shocked and horrified. The anguished sailors begged Captain Clerke to allow them to go into the village and extract revenge, but he refused, fearing a bloodbath. Some went anyway, killing several villagers. Most of the bones were eventually returned to the British, and Cook was buried at sea in Kealakekua Bay. The ship's surgeon wrote, "In every situation he stood unrivaled and alone. On him all eyes were turned. He was our leading star which, at its setting, left us in darkness and despair."

The steep cliffs around Kealakekua Bay seem strangely out of place on this otherwise gently sloping mountain. There's a good reason, and it happened in one day. See page 77 for the explanation.

As you leave Napo'opo'o Beach, stay on the oceanmost road heading south. There is a side road leading to Ke'ei Beach. Pretty but not real usable, its historical legacy is a Hawaiian legend, bolstered by Spanish records, which states that white men straggled ashore in the 1520s, 250 years before Cook arrived.

Lots of blood has been spilt on this part of the island. One particularly important battle took place just south of Ke'ei Beach at Moku-a-Kae Bay. You can't access it, but it was near here in 1782 that Kamehameha the Great finally became king of this half of the island after defeating Kiwala'o. During a bloody battle, one of Kamehameha's generals, named Ke'eaumoku (call him Ke for short), got tangled in his own spear and tripped, savagely impaling himself. Presuming Ke to be mortally wounded, Kiwala'o ran over to the enemy general to finish him off and seize his prized neck ornament. (Taking it off your enemy's body was symbolic of defeating him.) As he was leaning over Ke's body, Kiwala'o was beaned on the head by a sling stone hurled by one of Kamehameha's warriors, and fell backward. Ke, who wasn't dead from his spear wound, painfully crawled to the unconscious Kiwala'o and slit his throat with a leiomanu (a Hawaiian version of brass knuckles, but with razor sharp shark's teeth embedded on the outside). Thus Kamehameha was able to defeat his nemesis and rule western Hawai'i.

Battles such as these are a constant throughout Hawaiian history after the 12th century. Rival chiefs or kings were quick to take each other on. Warriors would often congregate on opposite sides of the battlefield and shout insults at each other in an attempt to intimidate. (Insults about lineage were always a real hit.) During battles, spears, sling stones and clubs were used with remarkable efficiency. Shark tooth-studded leiomanus were often given to old men who would go out onto battlefields after the fighting was over to slit the throats of those still alive. Though it may sound harsh (OK, OK—it *is* harsh), this was their way and not considered abhorrent to them.

Soon you come to Pu'uhonua o Honaunau (pronounced HOE-NOW-NOW). Also called Place of Refuge, this is an *awesome* spot to visit. It is a site of great importance and a fun place to explore. In ancient times, commoners' lives were governed by the

NOT TO BE MISSED!

Lawbreakers had one chance to escape the inevitable death penalty: Reach the area's place of refuge before your enemies reached you, and all was forgiven.

kapu system. There was a dizzying number of laws to observe. Those of lower classes weren't allowed to look at or even walk on the same trails as the upper classes. Men and women were forbidden to eat together, citizens were not allowed to get close to a chief or allow their shadows to fall across them, etc. All manner of laws kept the order. The penalty for breaking any of the laws was usually the same—death by club, strangulation, fire or spear. (Well, it's nice to have choices, at least.) If the offense was severe enough, the offender's *entire family* might be executed. It was believed that the gods retaliated against lawbreakers by sending tidal waves, lava flows, droughts and earthquakes, so communities had a great incentive to dispatch lawbreakers with haste. If a lawbreaker could elude his club or spear-wielding pursuers, however, he had one way out of his mess—the area's Pu'uhonua (Place of Refuge). This predes-

ignated area offered asylum. If a lawbreaker could make it here, he could perform certain rituals mandated by the kahuna pule (priest). After that, all was forgiven and he could return home as if nothing had happened, regardless of the violation. Defeated warriors could also come here to await the victor of a battle. They could then pledge their allegiance to whoever won and live out their lives in peace.

Pu'uhonua o Honaunau is such a place. Designated as a national park by Congress in 1961, it is the finest example of a Place of Refuge in all the islands. Here you will find neatly kept grounds featuring a remarkable stone wall, called the Great Wall. Built in the 1500s, this massive wall is 1,000 feet long, 10 feet high and 17 feet thick in most places. It separated the Pu'uhonua from the Ali'i's palace grounds. Though the wall has a chiseled appearance, it was made without dressed (cut) stones and without mortar. Also on the grounds you will find reconstructed Hawaiian houses, temples, and a few petroglyphs (rock drawings). There are wood carvings of gods (including one that is anatomically correct, assuming that's how the gods were endowed). The reconstructed thatched structure called Hale-o-Keawe was originally a mausoleum, containing the bones of 23 chiefs. Bones were thought to contain supernatural power, or *mana*, and therefore ensured that the Place of Refuge would remain sacred.

There are many other sights here, as well. Overall, this place is easy to recommend. The walk around the grounds is gentle, and there are facilities such as drinking water and restrooms. Coconut trees (which have an almost magical, calming effect) are scattered all over. There is a $5 per car entrance fee, but sometimes no one is there to collect it because they "can't afford the manpower to collect the money." (Only the government could come up with that kind of logic.)

Honaunau is particularly enchanting an hour before sunset, the best time to visit. Swaying coconut trees have a golden glow as large turtles munch near the canoe landing. You won't find a

The Green Flash

Ever heard of the green flash? No, it's not a super hero. We'd heard of the Green Flash for years and assumed that it was an urban myth, or perhaps something seen through the bottom of a beer bottle. But now we know it to be a real phenomenon, complete with a scientific explanation. You may hear other ways to experience the Green Flash—but this is the only true way.

On days when the horizon is crisp and clear with no clouds in the way of the sun as it sets, you stand a reasonable chance of seeing it. Avoid looking directly at the sun until the very last part of the disk is about to slip below the horizon. Looking at it beforehand will burn a greenish image into your retina, creating a "fool's flash" (and possibly wrecking your eyes). The instant before the last part of the sun's disk disappears, a vivid flash of chartreuse is often seen. This is because the sun's rays are passing through the thickest part of the atmosphere, and the light is bent and split into its different components the way it is in a rainbow. The light that is bent the most is the green and blue light, but the blue is less vivid and is overwhelmed by the flash of green, which lingers for the briefest of moments as the very last of the sun sets.

For a variety of reasons, including our latitude, Hawai'i is one of the best places in the world to observe the Green Flash. North Kohala is usually better than Kona due to the clarity of the horizon, but we've seen excellent Green Flash from all along the west coast.

If you aren't successful in seeing the real Green Flash, try the beer bottle method—at least it's better than nothing.

And so ends another day in paradise...

more relaxing or soothing place to finish off the day. Then head over to the middle/southern end of the park where picnic tables and BBQS await. Local families often bring their keikis (kids) to play in the nearby tide-pools. Drive to that area using the dirt road to the left of the visitor center after you enter the park.

For the less cerebral, you'll find unbeatable snorkeling and SCUBA diving in Honaunau Bay to the right of the boat launch. There are also hiking trails including the 1871 Trail, so named because area residents paid their taxes in 1871 by fixing up this formerly dilapidated trail. (We have a call in to the IRS to see if the offer's still good.)

Leaving Honaunau, you'll continue up Ke Ala o Keawe Road to Painted Church Road. Hang a left onto it to get to St. Benedict's Catholic Church, known simply as the Painted Church. It's a charming little build-

A REAL GEM

ing dating back to the 1800s. Between 1899 and 1904, Father John Velge dedicated himself to creating frescos on the inside walls and ceiling. Everything from hell to the Temptation of Christ is represented in loving detail. There is a sign on the door explaining in detail Father Velge's efforts. Termites and age are starting to take their toll, but this is always worth a stop.

Either continue on Painted Church Road to Middle Keei Road, or backtrack to get back up to the highway. (See map.)

When deciding where to eat in Kailua-Kona, see ISLAND DINING on page 244.

KONA SHOPPING

If you've ever wanted to own a lamp that does the hula (and after all, who hasn't?), you can purchase one at Hula Lamps of Hawaii located off Luhia Street in the Old Industrial Area. These are not cheap but are individually cast sculptures from table-top size to life-size floor lamps. Also in the same area, off Kaiwi Street, is the French Bakery at the east end, a good place for that sweet tooth.

Continuing south on Kuakini is the Kona Wine Market at the King Kamehameha Mall, which offers an outstanding selection of wine, spirits and gourmet food.

Along Alii Drive, starting at the north end is the Made on the Big Island Outlet located at the King Kamehameha Beach Hotel, which, as the name implies, carries a good selection of items grown or made on the Big Island. Across the street at the Seaside Shopping Mall is the Sandal Stop, a good place to pick up hiking and walking sandals. At the Kona Square is Country Samurai Coffee Company where you can get a buzz off their Buzz Beans, a coffee and chocolate jolt that will wake the dead.

Those interested in antiques should stop at Paradise Antiques & Gifts at the Kona Banyan Court.

Other shops to visit are Crazy Shirts for their unique T-shirts and Blue Moon for women's clothing. Across the street at the Kona Inn Shopping Village you'll find Hula Heaven, Honolua Surf Co., Sgt. Leisure and Island Salsa for casual island-style clothing and T-shirts. Kane Malia for men's and women's clothing, and for the kids there's Giggles.

There are three Farmers' Markets in Kona. One at the corner of Hualalai and Alii Drive (Wed.-Sun.), one at Kaiwi Square (Sat. & Sun.), and the Alii Garden Marketplace (Wed.-Sun.) near the 2.5 mile mark on Alii Drive.

Other stops in Kona are Hilo Hattie near Kopiko Plaza behind Burger King for reasonable prices and a great selection of aloha wear and souvenirs. Our Wal-Mart offers good prices on coffee, T-shirts, souvenirs, reef shoes and suntan lotion. Near the Wal-Mart is Borders Books for Hawaiian music or videos of island sights. Don't forget about Costco for beach towels, books, aloha wear and bathing suits, plus the best gasoline prices in Kona.

Keauhou Shopping Center south of Kailua-Kona has the Showcase Gallery and ForDuns for fine gift items. For women's clothing try Paradise Found or Borderlines.

The Bong Brothers in Honaunau is a good stop for a smoothie, fresh fruit, coffee or some Bong Brothers logo items. Gotta love the name.

KONA'S BEST BETS

Best Place to Meet Fish for the First Time—Kahalu'u Beach Park
Best Kona Coffee—Fike Farms
Best Pizza—Kona Brewing Company
Best Shave Ice—Tropical Island Flavor
Best Fish Sandwich—Quinn's
Best Treat (Despite the Name)—Donkey Balls at Surfin' Ass
Best Sunset Cocktail Location—Veranda at Keauhou Beach Resort
Best Place for a Coffee and Cinnamon Roll in the Morning—Island Lava Java
Best Snorkeling—Captain Cook Monument or Honaunau
Best Place to Spot Dolphins—Kealakekua Bay
Best Dessert to Go—Mac Nut Pie, Hwy 19 between 97 and 98 Mile Markers
Best Sunset Picnic—The BBQS at Honaunau or the tide-pools of Wawaloli Beach, if the surf's crashing
Best SCUBA Adventure—Manta Ray Night Dive
Best Place For a Man to End Up Wearing a Coconut Bra—Captain Beans' Cruise

At Broken Road near South Point, crystal clear waters are the norm.

The southern end of the island from Honaunau (near the 104 mile marker on Highway 11) to Hawai'i Volcanoes National Park is the least developed part of the Big Island. Long stretches of lava fields on the western side of Mauna Loa's flank give way to green as you round the southern part of the island, where rain is allowed to fall with less interference from Mauna Loa volcano. Along the way you'll pass roads leading to, among other things, a (usually) deserted black sand beach, a sparsely inhabited 11,000+ acre housing subdivision and the southernmost place in the United States. Since most people drive this stretch on their way to the volcano from Kailua-Kona or Kohala, we'll describe it from that direction.

These districts, called South Kona and Ka'u, are littered with the financial corpses of big businessmen with big plans and big wallets who took a big bath. Most didn't have a clue how business in Hawai'i works and lost their 'okoles as a result.

Three examples, all mentioned in detail later, are:

HOVE—*If you build it, they won't come.*

Hawaiian Riviera—*He who underestimates his opponents will ultimately be crushed by them.*

SeaMountain—*How to turn $30 million in cash into $3 million in real estate.*

From Highway 11 heading south from Honaunau, you'll have several opportunities to visit beaches below the road. Ho'o-kena (a decent gray sand beach) and Pebble Beach (a violent 'okole kicker) are described under BEACHES. Distances between gas stations are large, so gas up when you can. Just after Honaunau between the 104 and 103 mile marker is the best fruit stand we know of on the west side. South Kona Fruit Stand usually has excellent quality fruits all organically grown on the adjacent farm.

While driving along the flanks of Mauna Loa along here, consider this: Mauna Loa was built from countless thin layers of lava flows, usually less than 15 feet thick. (Flows since 1800 are shown on the map.) About 120,000 years ago, there was a plain below you where there are now steep hills. At that time, a humongous piece (that's a technical term) of the island, from roughly around the 109 mile marker to an area north of Miloli'i (20 miles to the south), broke off and slid into the ocean, creating what is now Kealakekua Bay and the steep hills south of Honaunau. The resulting tsunami (tidal wave) was so huge that it washed completely over the 1,427-foot-high island of Kaho'olawe, continued on and washed almost completely over the 3,370-foot-high island of Lana'i, where it deposited chunks of coral over a thousand feet up the mountain. This area is, geologically speaking, still unstable. Just didn't want you to run out of things to worry about.

Usually referred to as the last remaining fishing village on the island, Miloli'i is just past the 89 mile marker. As a beach destination, it won't offer you much (especially on the weekends—see BEACHES for more information). From the highway, 2²/₁₀ miles into the beach access road, look off to your left, and you will see a narrow a'a lava flow. The nearby village of Ho'opuloa was wiped

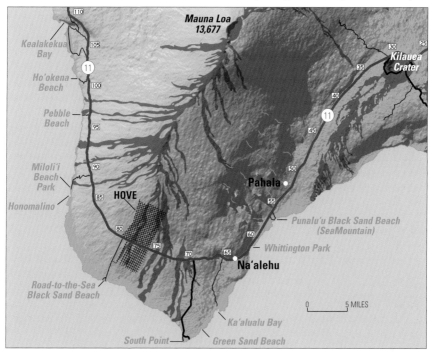

Mauna Loa
13,677

Kealakekua
Bay
Ho'okena
Beach
Pebble
Beach
Miloli'i
Beach
Park
Honomalino
HOVE
Road-to-the-Sea
Black Sand Beach
South Point

Kilauea
Crater

Pahala
Punalu'u Black Sand Beach
(SeaMountain)
Whittington Park
Na'alehu

Ka'alualu Bay
Green Sand Beach

0   5 MILES

out entirely when the lava marched down the slopes of Mauna Loa in 1926. Miloli'i's residents gained notoriety when they and their lawyer managed to kill the Hawaiian Riviera Resort, 17 miles to the south. (See below.) A 20-minute walk from Miloli'i leads to an exceptionally picturesque coconut-lined bay called Honomalino. It's usually deserted and worth the walk. See page 170 for more.

The main highway, called the Hawai'i Belt Road, follows an old Hawaiian road called the Mamalahoa Highway. If you want to see what driving this area *used* to be like (and why it took so bloody long to circle the island), take the 2-mile stretch of the old road. The intersections are at the 88 and 86 mile markers on the mauka (mountain) side of the road.

You'll see lots of macadamia nut trees along this stretch of the island. (By the way, keep the mac nuts away from dogs; they cause paralysis in certain species.) The Big Island is a major player in the macadamia nut world. The inner shell of the macadamia nut is impossibly hard. We've been told by nearly every macadamia farmer we know that if you roll over them with your car, they won't break. So we did it. The result? They all broke. Another urban legend shot to...

Back on the highway, Manuka State Park is near the 81 mile marker. There's a 2-mile loop trail that wanders through lava flows of several ages, giving you perspective on how things grow over different times. See HIKING for more info. There are restrooms and phones.

The arrow-straight dirt road ⅔ mile past (south of) the 80 mile marker off Highway 11 is a perfect example of why 4WD vehicles are so useful here. It's called Road to the Sea. (Gee, I wonder where it goes...) Two stark, deserted black sand beaches, unknown even to the vast majority of island residents, are at the end. (See BEACHES on page 172 for an explanation.) It's hard to conceive of a lifeless, arid area being inviting, yet these beaches somehow are. We've even seen plankton-eating whale sharks more than once near the beach. The road is a *public access*, misleading sign notwithstanding.

Another beautiful bay south of here is called Pohue, but access to it from the dirt road has been scuttled for decades by a revolving series of petty lawsuits. Separately, there was a several *thousand* acre resort called Hawaiian Riviera slated to be built from Road to the Sea to Pohue Bay. Even though the developer had big bucks, he was thwarted by a handful of residents from Miloli'i, 17 miles to the north, who protested that a planned marina here (and the resort in general) would interfere with their rich fishing grounds and their way of life. They got a lawyer to take up their cause, and together they successfully killed the project.

Continuing along, Hawaiian Ocean View Estate (known locally as HOVE) lies up mauka of the highway along here. Look at the map on the previous page. Notice all those roads? Until a couple years ago, if you had driven on them you would have noticed countless empty lots. About 11,000 one-acre parcels on harsh lava are spread amongst those roads. An oil company built it in the '60s, with the dream of creating a new community. Acre lots originally sold for $995 each and until just a few years ago, you could still pick up lots for $1,500. Buyers were lured by photos of palm tree-backed Pohue Bay (which is distant, private and not reachable) and talk of the HOVE Yacht Club (which never existed). It's changed owners many times since then. They used party line phones until 1998 and only recently got electricity. Rain catchment is their lifeline. There's not even a school. Streets have lovely sounding names like *Paradise Parkway* and *Tree Fern Avenue.* But after driving around, you'd expect names like *Lava Lane* and *Rocky Road.* Most of the lots were sold or given away free with a full tank of gas *(just teasing).* It took the current land boom to finally shake up HOVE land values. Oh, by the way, part of it lies in an area that was overrun by lava from Mauna Loa in 1907. Just thought you'd like to know. Not to be outdone, another company built a subdivision below the highway (also shown on the map) with 1,200 three-acre lots. They, too, were long-forgotten until recently.

To be fair, everyone we've met who lives in HOVE loves it there. They have formed a tight-knit community and seem happy as can be with their location.

Whenever we drive around here, however, we're reminded that the Big Island is often rumored to be one of the largest repositories of people from the FEDERAL WITNESS PROTECTION PROGRAM. What a perfect place to lose one's self.

A few places to eat here are reviewed under DINING on page 273.

SOUTH POINT

Between the 69 and 70 mile markers is the road to South Point (called

Ka Lae meaning "the point"). This is the southernmost part of the island, making it the southernmost spot in the entire nation. (Not the Florida Keys, as most trivia books claim.) At one time the road was nasty and very hard on rental cars. It has since been repaved and is in fine condition the whole way. The only hazard is that the road is

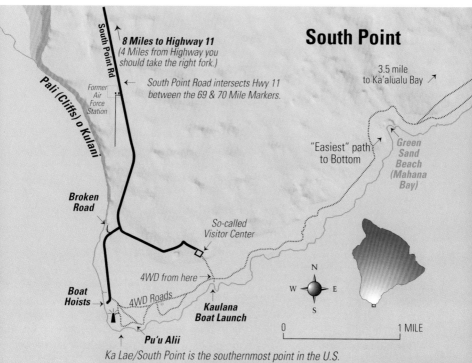

South Point

South Point Rd

8 Miles to Highway 11
(4 Miles from Highway you should take the right fork.)

3.5 mile to Ka'alualu Bay ↗

← South Point Road intersects Hwy 11 between the 69 & 70 Mile Markers.

Pali (Cliffs) o Kulani

Former Air Force Station

"Easiest" path to Bottom

Green Sand Beach (Mahana Bay)

Broken Road

So-called Visitor Center

4WD from here →

Boat Hoists

4WD Roads

Kaulana Boat Launch

Pu'u Alii

N
W E
S

0   1 MILE

Ka Lae/South Point is the southernmost point in the U.S.

Wind farming has long been a landmark of the South Point area.

one lane for much of its length. It is mostly straight, and there is space to pull over for on-coming cars. Try to resist the temptation to speed on the seemingly wide open parts of this road; there are some surprise blind hills and turns.

The wind is always blowing out on this grassy plain, hence this location for the old Kamoa Wind Farm you cross on South Point Road which at press time was being replaced by the Pakini Nui Wind Project. The trees here are all wind-blown in the same direction (west), vividly showing what happens to deflected trade winds coming from the northeast. (The foldout back cover map puts it in perspective.)

As you get near South Point, turn right at the fork. (Don't go left to the "Visitor Center.") South Point is the site of some of the oldest artifacts yet discovered in Hawai'i (as early as 300 AD) and was probably the first place the Polynesians came ashore and settled when they discovered these islands. Dry and desolate with no permanent streams, this might seem a surprising place for people to set-

tle. The reason for its settlements, however, lies offshore. The waters off South Point are incredibly rich fishing grounds. Large pelagic game fish, such as tuna, mahimahi and marlin are plentiful. The ancient Hawaiians quickly discovered this but had a problem harvesting the fish. The wind and current together form such a strong offshore force that it would require all their attention just to stay put in a canoe. Those who went out too far were considered lost due to these forces since fishing canoes were not as maneuverable as voyaging canoes, and since the currents are uninterrupted all the way to Antarctica. The bottom drops to great depths quickly, so anchors aren't the answer. Their clever solution was to carve holes into the rock ledge and feed ropes through them so their canoes could be tied to shore while fishing. Some of those holes are still visible near the boat hoists at the cliffs.

Freshwater is very scarce here, even from wells, and what is available is barely potable. In the 1700s a chief named Kalani'opu'u, tired of having to bathe several miles away, asked his kahunas if there was water under the ground. One know-it-all assured him there was water at a certain spot if he dug *really* deep. After much digging, they found nothing. The big-mouth kahuna was promptly executed for his bad advice.

Today, you're likely to see long lines strung from the sea cliffs just to the northwest of the actual South Point. These lines are usually held afloat by empty bleach bottles and are sometimes pulled so taut by the wind and current that you'd swear you could walk on them. Fishermen use toy sailboats to drag the rope out to sea and dangle 10 foot leaders from the main line at every bleach bottle. When they get a strike, they haul the whole line in.

At the cliffs near South Point are old hoists, used to lower small boats from the low cliffs. Metal cliffside ladders are present, as well. Larger boats use the Kaulana boat launch less than a mile to the east. People lived at Kaulana until the beginning of the 20th century. Most visitors make the mistake of assuming that the cliffs with the boat hoists *are* South Point. The real South Point is past the light beacon at a place where a rock wall trails down into the sea. There is no cliff there. The beacon will be behind you. Next to the beacon is the small Kalaea Heiau.

Since ancient times this entire area has had a reputation for having exceptionally strong currents, and during all but calm seas this is no doubt true. Even so, we know people who love nothing better than to leap into the water from the boat hoist area and come back up via the metal ladder adjacent to a boat hoist. There are also a few spots along the cliffs where you can scramble down to the water. Some people even like to snorkel here at night when fish and clouds of small, beautiful shrimp greet the eye. The water is unbelievably clear and seems quite inviting when calm, especially when you can see lots of fish swimming below. With this in mind, I've repeatedly snorkeled here below the boat hoists to assess the currents. I was so wary the first time out that I tied myself to the cliff ladder with a long rope—just to be safe. It turned out to be unnecessary. *When calm,* I have yet to detect much current *below the boat hoist area,* probably because it's protected by the point. The water is teeming with life and visibility is usually over 100 feet. But (and I can't stress this enough) I've *never* gone into the water when it's not calm, I don't swim too far, and I don't endorse swimming there. The surge there

Bring your extra-strength hairspray when you visit South Point.

demonstrates the extreme power of the ocean and I'm excited and nervous every time I swim at that spot. South of the cliffs at the actual South Point, the water is always violent and unswimmable. I mention all this so you will know what I've experienced here in case you are crazy enough to do it on your own. Check to see that your life insurance policy is in order before you go, and buy a good guidebook to Antarctica—just in case.

South Point was used during WWII for army barracks. Later, the Navy installed a missile tracking station on 33 acres. Not to be left out, the Air Force later took over the facilities and renamed it South Point Air Force Station. The station was closed in 1979, and little remains except the shabby buildings on your right as you are approaching South Point.

Just north of the boat hoists (see map) is a road that leads you off a cliff. There is nothing to stop you except your own good judgment, so don't take it all the way. The road was built in 1955 along with a concrete landing below to service fishing boats. Representing the finest county quality, it lasted less than a year. The surf erased the landing and part of the road. What remains is called (you see this one coming, don't you?) Broken Road. The view from the end of Broken Road is spectacular, but the snorkeling isn't as good here as it is below the boat hoists. Off in the distance you see Pali o Kulani, which rises 350 feet from the ocean. At the place where the cliff appears to end, it actually turns inland and runs north to an area just south of Highway 11. The inland cliff was caused by another catastrophic landslide, similar to (but pre-dating) the one described earlier. It slid to the west and caused a similar splash.

If you had gone left at the aforementioned fork you'd have come to the "Visitor Center." There is no such thing. This is a former military base now occupied by whoever wants to stay there. The area is part of the Department of Hawaiian Homelands and parking is free. Many times in the past, official-sounding squatters have tried to extract $5 for parking here. You *don't* have to pay, according to DHHL officials. You can keep driving to the boat launch ¼-mile away and park.

Off to the east of South Point is a strange phenomenon called Green Sand Beach. (See BEACHES.) It features a beautiful mixture of green and black sand and is a fascinating place to visit. If you have 4WD you should be able to drive it, unless squatters close the gate, which they've done on occasion. It's 2¼ miles each way on the flat, grassy plain. Many readers have written us to say we're *way* off on that distance. We promise, we're not. We've checked it by car odometer and on foot with GPS. It just *seems* longer since the wind is in your face going out.

A REAL GEM

Back on Highway 11, as you continue, you'll wrap around the island and enter the wetter, windward side. Almost instantly, our old friend green has returned to the scene. This was the edge of sugar country. Big Island sugar died here in 1996 (as a business—some of the cane still lives on), and most of the fields here are supposed to be replaced with the more profitable macadamia nut trees. Waiohinu and Na'alehu are the first towns you come to. Waiohinu's claim to fame was the Mark Twain Monkeypod Tree, planted by the author himself. It blew down in the '50s, but its shoots have grown into a respectable new tree. There are restrooms here.

While in Na'alehu, stop by the best restaurant along this part of the island is Hana Hou Bakery.

As you come down the hill near the 62 mile marker, you'll see **Whittington Park** and the remains of its wharf in the distance. Picturesque from a distance but less so close up. Best to drive past or see BEACHES. From the vantage point up the hill you truly appreciate the vastness of this Big Island.

Just after the 56 mile marker is the road to **Punalu'u Black Sand Beach**. This is the easiest volcanic black sand beach to access on the island now that the more famous one in Puna is gone. (That one was buried by lava in 1990—see page 119.) The water here is cold due to the large amounts of freshwater percolating from the floor just offshore. At one time the ancient Hawaiians at Punalu'u (which means *spring dived for*) obtained their freshwater here by diving down with an upside-down, dried, hollow gourd to where the freshwater was streaming out. There they would flip the gourd, fill it with fresh water, put their thumbs over it, and come to the surface.

Don't adjust your book. The sand really is green here.

There are scads of turtles in the bay, and it's one of the few areas where we've seen them beach themselves. There is also a picturesque fishpond backed by lots of coconut trees. (Incidentally, there were no coconuts in Hawai'i before the Polynesians came. Though ubiquitous in the South Pacific, Hawai'i is fed by the North Pacific Current, precluding the possibility that a live coconut could have floated here from any place warm. Just thought you needed to know that for your next appearance on *Jeopardy*.) The only eyesore at this exotic black sand beach is the closed and ramshackle restaurant behind the fishpond. Fortunately, it's mostly covered over from the beach side, which tells you how long it's been closed—long enough to choke off their lovely view with vegetation. It's been condemned and might be bulldozed by the time you arrive.

When the Japanese attacked Pearl Harbor in 1941, Army troops dynamited the concrete wall over near the boat launch to keep it from being used by the enemy in case of an invasion.

Tour buses sometimes bring groups to Punalu'u, but it *usually* isn't crowded since it is 60 miles from both Hilo and Kona. Forgive us for nagging, but please resist the temptation to take black sand home as a souvenir. Since it is finite, it would eventually deplete the beach for everyone. (Or you can see CURSES under BASICS.) The sharp edges of the sand grains ensures that swimmers will inadvertently take some home anyway. You will find plenty of stowaways in the lining of your bathing suit, which will stay there for years. The concessionaire at Punalu'u sells black sand and, though they *claim* it's from another beach consumed by the volcano, that certainly can't be said of their green sand, so we hope you won't buy any. OK, end of nag.

This area is sometimes called Sea-Mountain, named by a developer for the Lo'ihi Seamount. That undersea volcano, 20 miles offshore from here, will be the Big Island's next volcano attraction. It's still 3,200 feet underwater and won't surface for another 100,000 years, but be sure to look for it when we release our 99,000th edition of this book. (Call now to reserve your copy early.) The whole property was purchased by a Japanese investment company for more than $30 million at the height of a real estate boom in 1989. After five years and countless challenges to their plans by local residents, they sold it for less than $3 million, not even a *tenth* of what they paid for it. *(Ouch!)* At press time, it was being sold yet again for $20 million. There are places to stay here and a golf course. See BEACHES for more on Punalu'u.

From Punalu'u you'll start your gradual 4,000-foot ascent to Kilauea Volcano. Along the way you pass Pahala, a former sugar town. (This is also a speed trap, so watch it. Another bad speed trap is when the limit changes after the 38 mile marker.) Though friendly, the town is quiet and a little depressing, and the economic harm is, to a certain degree, self-inflicted. Pahala residents were crucial in killing the expansion plan at Punalu'u in the mid '90s, confident that their sugar plantation jobs were sufficient and fearful of altering their way of life. After that, the coastal land below Pahala was slated to be a spaceport where private satellites would be launched. Again Pahala residents were able to successfully fight the plan, even though it was backed by the state, the governor and the mayor.

Then in the late '90s the last Big Island sugar plantation opened the books and told the workers they either needed to accept a 15% pay cut or the company would have to close down due to ongoing losses. (Every other sugar plantation on the island had failed in the previous years due to a changing marketplace.) The sugar workers voted to reject the pay cut, and the sugar company promptly shut down, putting nearly every resident of this one-industry town out of work. Their way of life changed anyway, but they had nothing to fall back on. For a decade they paid the price in the form of a downward economic spiral. Only now is the land boom that hit the Big Island finally starting to trickle down to this part of the island.

A couple miles past the edge of Hawai'i Volcanoes National Park, take note of the rugged looking a'a lava. It's hard to believe that barefoot armies marched through this stuff, but they did—sometimes under extraordinary circumstances like those described on page 91.

Lava sometimes forms surreal images as it's flowing.

If you had to name the one thing the Big Island is most famous for, it would undoubtedly be **Kilauea Volcano**. In all the world there isn't a more active volcano, and none is as user-friendly as Kilauea. People often refer to it as the drive-in volcano.

Kilauea is an enigma—you can't really see the mountain from anywhere on the island, or even recognize it when you are standing on it. It seems more like a wound on Mauna Loa, whose flanks it resides upon. In the past, everyone thought that it was *part* of Mauna Loa, but today we know that it is separate and distinct, with its own separate (though possibly interrelated) magma chamber. One part of Kilauea, the actual Pu'u 'O'o vent itself, is teasingly inaccessible. You can't get very

close to it without a long hike. The "quickest" way is described in ADVENTURES on page 229.

We feel strongly that most people allow far too little time for visiting **Hawai'i Volcanoes National Park**. Many simply blow through on an around-the-island driving frenzy, stopping long enough to snap a shot of Kilauea Caldera. There is much more here than meets the eye, and this might be the highlight of your Hawaiian trip. Whether Kilauea is erupting or not, this park is the most fascinating place you may ever visit, and you *surely* don't have anything like this back home. The finest hiking on the island is here. The lushest rain forest you've ever seen is here to stroll through. Vents spewing steam, brand new land, birds-a-plenty, giant chasms, ancient Hawaiian petroglyphs, lava craters, walk-through lava tubes, unrivaled vistas—it's all here. Once you know what to look for, you will want to spend at least a whole day, preferably two. Since driving to the volcano can take four hours round trip from Kona and five hours from Kohala, consider reserving a place to stay at Volcano House or in the town of Volcano (see WHERE TO STAY). This allows you to experience it at a more leisurely pace and is a nice way to go, if you can swing it. You'll probably want to stay until after dark if there are accessible surface lava flows, and the drive back to Kona or Kohala is a drag (with no place to eat at night until Kealakekua). If you are staying in Hilo, it's an easy drive back.

WILL I GET TO SEE LAVA FLOWING?

Historically (meaning since 1778), most eruptions have lasted days or weeks, rarely months. Until this eruption, only once, from 1969–1974 at Mauna Ulu, has an eruption outside the crater lasted more than a year. The current eruption, originating from a newly created vent called Pu'u 'O'o, is redefining our understanding of an eruption. It started on January 3, 1983, shifted to a vent called Kupaianaha from 1986 to 1992, then shifted back toward Pu'u 'O'o and was still going strong as we went to press with an occasional hiccup in its flowing activity.

When you visit Kilauea, you either *will* or *won't* get to see a surface lava flow. (Now *there's* a gutsy prediction!) Hawai'i Volcanoes National Park has a recording at 985–6000, but it's not always updated when it should be. They also have weather updates. As we went to press, there were no signs of an impending work stoppage by Madame Pele, the fire goddess of Hawai'i, but that doesn't mean you can come here and be assured of being able to stick your toe into liquid lava. Madame Pele can be kind of a tease. The lava has stopped and started many times, shifted from vent to vent, gone straight into the ocean from underground lava tubes, and flowed in inaccessible places. It has also flowed just feet from the end of Chain of Craters Road, in Kilauea Caldera and other very accessible places. It's a gamble as to whether you will get to see it. Kilauea might go months without *accessible* lava flows, then put on a flawless show for months after that. If you have Internet access, we have an eruption update on our Web site at www.wizardpub.com. We also have links to other eruption Web sites.

When you hear that the volcano is erupting, you might think of a cone-shaped mountain, of going up to the top and peering into a boiling lake of molten rock. Maybe some will be pouring rapid-

Mauna Loa Trail

Glenwood 15 11

Mauna Loa Caldera 13,677

Bird Park

Volcano Village 20

0   5 MILES

Glenwood Road

Pu'u 'O'o Eruption Origin

Mauna Loa Road 35

30

25

Kilauea Caldera

130

40

Napau Trail

Kalapana (Destroyed)

45

Road destroyed by lava flows

11

Chain of Craters Road

50

Light brown indicates major trails

Beaches of jet black sand can form almost overnight when lava shatters as it's quenched by the sea.

ly down the mountain, consuming everything in its path as people flee in panic. In Hawai'i, things are *far* different. Here, even the volcano is laid-back. Though it has erupted from the main crater in the past, most of the time (including the current eruption) the lava breaks out from a vent along what's called the rift zone, a linear belt of fractured rock on the flank of the volcano. From this vent the lava travels downhill, usually to the sea. After it starts flowing, pahoehoe lava rivers crust over, forming tubes. These tubes act as excellent insulators (the lava usually loses a mere 20°F over miles of travel in these tubes) and carry the lava to the ocean. Sometimes these tubes break the surface downhill of the source, forming surface flows. When this happens, you can often walk right up to it. Otherwise, there might be an enormous steam plume at the sea (which glows at night).

Many activity companies and nearly every guidebook shows photos of a helicopter or viewer directly in front of gigantic fountains of lava. You won't see any pictures like that in our book for two reasons. One, you're more likely to see *Elvis* than to see that. It might happen a few times each decade for a few hours. What are *your* chances? The other reason is that a few of those photos are fake. (A stock government photo of a Kilauea lava fountain taken by scientists, a shot of a helicopter or person, a computer, and *voilà*—the unreal looks real.) The close-up photographs of surface lava flows you see in this book were all taken by us at accessible sites. We didn't get special permission to go to special spots or go through any unusual procedures. We didn't use a camera lens longer than a rental car to make it *seem* like it was close (and I had the singed leg hairs to prove it). We also didn't charter helicopters and use zillion dollar cameras on loan from NASA. Granted, we didn't get to see this kind of lava our first time out there, but these are the kinds of things that mere mortals like us might get to see *if* Madame Pele is cooperating.

THE SCENE

We've been to the volcano countless times, with and without surface lava. It's always a fantastic experience, though not what people expect.

During a relatively calm flow, pahoehoe lava is silvery coated, red or yellow as it oozes its way toward the sea. It is a humbling experience to stand there and observe Earthly creation, like seeing the planet during its fiery adolescence. In most parts of the world, people dread active volcanoes, fearing death and destruction. A huge explosion will send clouds of ash and pumice into air, killing everything in its path. In Hawai'i, people drop whatever they are doing and drive out to see it. Rather than apocalyptic explosions, Kilauea mostly drools and dribbles. (In historic times, it has exploded only twice, and one had astonishing consequences—see page 91.) Though the total volume of lava erupting ranges from 300,000 to more than a million cubic yards *per day*, it is so spread out that it rarely rushes down the mountain in a hellish river of liquid stone. Usually, it's small rivulets of molten lava separated by large distances from other rivulets. When it hardens (which occurs very quickly), it crunches beneath your feet like shards of glass.

There are not many places on this planet where you can walk on ground younger than you are, where you can be assured that there is absolutely nothing alive beneath your feet except for the earth itself. We've been there when people from all over the world stand in awe, tears streaming down their cheeks as they tell their children, "You may never see anything like this again in your lifetime."

As freshly hardened pahoehoe lava cools, it stresses the silica coating on the outside. This natural glass then crackles and pops off the rock, creating subtle sounds that bewitch viewers. Heat from the flows can be intense. Many times we've been less than a yard from the molten lava and felt like we would suddenly burst into flames. Other times, the

A father and daughter standing around watching the world get made. Not a bad way to spend the afternoon.

Lava comes in many flavors and textures.

wind has blown from the other direction so we could enjoy the liquid earth in comfort. Sometimes there is unpleasant black smoke and fumes (especially when the volcano is gobbling up more road or forest). Other times it seems to have absolutely no fumes or smoke and no offensive smell. (What smell it does have is hard to describe but never forgotten.)

At night, the lava may glow in numerous spots like a prehistoric scene from yesteryear. Sometimes, as the lava flows into the ocean, brilliant red and orange steam clouds light up the immediate area, creating dazzling light shows as the flow drips or gushes into the ocean. Sometimes, when it burns scrub vegetation at night, the methane emits a blue flame. A scene at night might go like this: A crowd of about 50 people on a bluff overlooking a field of fresh pahoehoe. It pops, crackles and glows as the night consumes all. What amazes us is how reverent everybody is. Couples hold each other tight. People speak in soft whispers. They try not to move much for fear of disturbing others as they watch Earth's most primordial show. Nobody wants to leave. Watching the lava enter the sea at night never fails to impress, and we've been told more times than we can count by visitors that it is an unsurpassed highlight.

A FEW BASICS

Despite the fact that it is operated by the federal government, the park seems very well run. Much of the staff are friendly and professional. (We've seen other parks where the staff can be real curmudgeons.) The rangers are pretty good at letting you see the action close up. We've been there when they lead people across smoldering lava, the heat coming up through their shoes. They will only keep you away if they *truly* perceive danger, unlike some other parks where they sometimes keep you away from imaginary dangers on orders from the lawyers. Because of this, you should heed their cautions seriously. If they say you can't go to a certain area because they expect a lava bench might collapse, don't go there. At least one person has died because he didn't heed this warning. (The ocean drops quickly off the coast of the park, and new lava land is usually destined to break off when it reaches a critical mass.) If rangers say an area is off limits because of the dangers of methane explosions, believe it. Methane from plant matter in older flows can heat up when a new flow covers it. This usually escapes by hissing or by small pops, but sometimes it can be more dramatic. We were there once with many other visitors when a large

A river of stone plunges into the sea.

methane explosion occurred 25 feet from us. It was powerful enough to rip through 12-inch thick lava, pieces of which jumped into the air. Under certain circumstances, these explosions occur 100 yards in advance of a lava flow.

In the park we like to arrive at surface flows about an hour or two before sunset. That way we get to see it during the day and at night. As the sun sets, the light-emitting lava doesn't have to compete with the sun, resulting in brighter and seemingly more abundant lava. Bring plenty of film and a polarizing filter if you have a camera that will accept it. (Wipe your camera off when you are finished; the air can be acidic and is hard on electronics.) The best shots will be late in

The Explosion That Changed History

Mild-mannered Kilauea has exploded only twice in recorded history, once in 1790 and once in 1924. (There is evidence that it may have exploded more often in the distant past.) These eruptions are phreatomagmatic, meaning steam-induced (but you knew that). In 1790, Kamehameha ruled much of the island. While he was distracted with plans to invade Maui, a rival chief named Keoua seized control of this part of the island. Kamehameha sent troops to do battle. Eventually both armies pulled back to their strongholds. As Keoua's troops and their families camped at Kilauea that night, fire and rock spewed from Kilauea Caldera. Keoua thought he had offended Pele, the volcano goddess, by rolling stones into the crater the day before and spent two days trying to appease her. It didn't work. On the third day they tried to leave, organized in three divisions. Right after the first division left, the mountain exploded. Darkness enveloped the area, punctured by volcano-induced thunder and lightning, and streams of red and blue light from the crater. Huge amounts of hot ash rained down, then a suffocating gas belched up from the volcano.

The first division to depart escaped mostly intact. The second division disappeared. When the third division came to the scene, they found their comrades of the second division huddled in circles, some hugging each other with their noses pressed together. Relieved, the third division rushed forward to greet them, only to discover that every last member of the second division—around 400 men and their wives and children—were dead. (Not 85 as the park sign says.) Most had been asphyxiated by the noxious gas. The only survivor was a solitary hog. If you take the Ka'u Desert Trail (page 102) you can see the faint outline of steps preserved in the ash—steps created by other soldiers at the time of the disaster.

As for Keoua, everyone now knew that Pele was against him and his army. He kept fighting more battles but never turned the tide. Not yet defeated, he was invited by Kamehameha to peacefully dedicate the new Pu'ukohola Heiau in Kawaihae. When Keoua's boat approached the shore of Kawaihae, he was immediately murdered by one of Kamehameha's officers and had the dubious honor of being the temple's first official human sacrifice. Thus was Kamehameha's rule over the island forever solidified.

Kilauea Crater

This map is rendered at an angle in order to convey the lay of the land at Kilauea. Visualize it as a solid cast of the land sitting on a table. Each "terraced" contour line represents an elevation change of 20 feet.

Volcano Village

Gas

Old Volcano Rd

11 / 27

26 miles to Hilo

Park Entrance

28

Park Visitor Center

Kilauea Military Camp

Sulphur Banks

Volcano House

Old Crater Rim Road now collapsed and part of Crater Rim Trail

Steam Vents

Sandalwood Trail

Crater Rim Trail

Kilauea Caldera

Bird Park

Volcano Golf & Country Club

Tree Molds

Mauna Loa Scenic Road / 31

Kilauea Overlook

Crater Rim Drive

Hawaiian Volcano Observatory

Jaggar Museum

88 miles to Kailua-Kona

Namakani Paio Cabins & Campgrounds

11 / 32

Ka'u Desert Trail

Halema'uma'u Crater

Halema'uma'u Trail

Thurston Lava Tube

Kilauea Iki Overlook

Park Boundary

Escape Rd

Crater Rim Drive

Kilauea Iki Trail

Kilauea Iki Crater

Kilauea Iki Trail

Crater Rim Trail

Devastation Trail

Chain of Craters Rd

Pu'u Pua'i

Byron Ledge Trail

Byron Ledge Trail

Keanakako'i Crater

Lua Manu Crater

Crater Rim Drive

Puhimau Crater

1

Pu'u 'O'o Vent is 8 miles this way. It is not easily accessible. The hike to Pu'u 'O'o, from outside the Park is described on page 229.

Crater Rim Trail

0 | 1 MILE

Indicates Foot Trails

67 Roadside mile markers

Unpaved Roads

N E S W

© 2006 Wizard Publications, Inc.

the afternoon. If you get close to the lava, the heat might consume your camera battery faster than you think. (Trust me on that one.) Bring water—you'll get hot and thirsty. If it rains, you'll be grateful for something waterproof, and so will your camera. Depending on the flow, a flashlight might be invaluable. At times, they let you walk to places at night that can be spectacular. Contact lens wearers will want to bring drops—maybe even your glasses if it gets uncomfortable. Bring sunscreen if you are there for the day. Add more film and water. During really good flows the question you hear most is, "Does anybody have any film I can buy?" What you don't want to bring are your preconceptions. No matter what you expect, the flow will be different. Come with a blank slate, and you will leave full of wonder.

And remember, if there are no accessible surface flows (which is quite possible), don't despair. The volcano area is eminently fascinating and exciting, with or without surface flows, and is always worth at least a day of exploration. Below are some of the other delights waiting for you at Hawai'i Volcanoes National Park.

AROUND KILAUEA CRATER

A quick note: We decided not to use our **Real Gem** and **Not To Be Missed** icons in this section because they would fill the pages. The entire park is *a real gem* and is *not to be missed.*

A REAL GEM

As you arrive at the park, which is open 24 hours a day, there is a recording playing on 530 AM radio. It has information that is promptly updated every leap year or so, so don't expect up-to-the-minute reports.

Remember that Kilauea Caldera is located at an altitude of 4,000 feet, so make sure you bring your warmies for those days when it's misty and chilly at the summit.

After paying your $10 car entrance fee (what a deal!) at the gate, stop by the Visitor Center on your right. They have up-to-date information, a nice display of books, videos, artifacts, a movie showing and—most important if you've driven a long way—restrooms. Check out the 3-D miniature of the island near the restrooms to get a perspective of the island. Some guided hike notices are sometimes posted at the Visitor Center if you're interested. From the Center, you might want to walk across the street to **Volcano House** for your first peek of Kilauea Caldera from their enviable view. You can also eat at the restaurant or snack bar there. (See ISLAND DINING for review.) This is the only place to eat *in* the park.

We should probably take the opportunity to confess here that the park used to sell this book at the Visitor Center. After undergoing a lengthy reviewing process, they called it the most accurate book they'd ever seen on the Big Island, and it became the only guidebook sold there. Quite a coup. The book's not there anymore. Why? Because some park bureaucrats became upset when they realized that we revealed things, such as a trail to Pu'u 'O'o that doesn't go through their park, the hike to Mauna Ulu, and several other things. Well, we're not going to stop telling you about these attractions even if it means they won't carry our book at the Visitor Center. The trail is described in ADVENTURES on page 229; Mauna Ulu is on page 225. (A few other things we revealed also got under their skin.)

You'll want to do a counter-clockwise tour of the caldera to start. The first thing you come to is **Sulphur Banks** on your right. There is a road to this stinky

A'a lava on the left (named by the first Hawaiian to walk on it bare-footed?) is rough and clinkery. Pahoehoe on the right is smooth and ropy, like thick cake batter.

phenomenon, where hydrogen sulphide gas and steam form deposits of sulphur, gypsum and hematite on the ground. This should be avoided by those with a heart condition, respiratory problems, children or anyone eating lunch in the car.

Going farther on Crater Rim Road, you see the **Steam Vents** on your left. Here, rain that has seeped into the ground is heated by Kilauea and issues forth as steam. The amount varies daily depending on the level of rain in the past few days, and it is rarely smelly like Sulphur Banks—in fact, there is usually no smell at all. Make sure you take the trail for 2–3 minutes toward the crater rim for a smashing view of the crater, and where additional, more powerful and unobstructed steam vents are present.

Rounding the crater, you come to **Kilauea Overlook**. This is a different perspective on Kilauea Crater and its progeny, **Halema'uma'u Crater**, and is definitely worth a stop. Look for white-tailed tropic birds soaring on the thermals down in the crater.

Just past the overlook is **Jagger Museum** and the **Hawaiian Volcano Observatory**. The museum has some very interesting exhibits and is worth a stop. (The view is *da kine,* as well.)

Continuing on, you start to round the bottom of the crater. Note that there are no walls here. The crater summit is tilted, and lava has spilled over the sides at the southern end many times in the past.

Soon you come to **Halema'uma'u Crater**. This crater-within-a-crater is said to be the home to Madame Pele, the Hawaiian volcano goddess. Though crusted over now, for most of the 19th century this was a boiling lava lake. Mark Twain and other celebrities of his time visited here, and described it as viewing the fiery pits of hell. When Isabella Bird saw it in 1873, she wrote:

Suddenly, just above, and in front of us, gory drops were tossed in air, and springing forwards we stood on the brink of Hale-mau-mau, which was about 35 feet below us. I think we all screamed, I know we all wept, but we were speechless, for a new glory and terror had been added to the Earth. It is the most unutterable of wonderful things. The words of common speech are quite useless. It is unimaginable, indescribable, a sight to remember forever, a sight which at once took possession of every faculty of sense and soul, removing one altogether out of the range of ordinary life. Here was the real "bottomless pit"–the "fire which is not quenched"–"the place of hell"–"the lake which burneth with fire and brimstone"–the "everlasting burnings"–the fiery sea whose waves are never weary. There were groanings, rumblings, and detonations, rushings, hissings, and splashings, and the crashing sound of breakers on the coast, but it was the surging of fiery waves upon a fiery shore.

Halemaʻumaʻu is quieter now with the lava action occurring elsewhere. It takes a few minutes to walk to the crater overlook and is well worth the walk. Though usually not as strong, fumes *can* call for similar warnings as at Sulphur Banks. The crater has risen and fallen over time—going from 1,335 feet deep to overflowing its top. Right now, it's less than 300 feet deep and 3,000 feet across.

Some Hawaiians today still make offerings to Pele. You might see these gifts near the edge of the crater, though most of the time these come from visitors and are considered an irritant by park personnel. It is said that Pele will appear as a beautiful young woman in the mountains and as a very old and very ugly woman at the shoreline. (Hence the Hawaiian saying, "Always be nice to an old woman; it might be Pele.") Though Halemaʻumaʻu is said to be her home, she seems to be spending more time these days at her summer house at Puʻu ʻOʻo.

Continuing, you come to another crater called **Keanakakoʻi**. The Hawai-

ians used to fetch abnormally hard rock from here until it was covered by subsequent lava flows. Across the road from Keanakakoʻi is a lava fissure. These fissures are usually long cracks where lava erupts in a curtain of fire, as this one did in 1974.

Past Keanakakoʻi you will notice a gravel-like substance on the ground. That's **tephra**, airborne gas-frothed lava from fountains, which cools as pumice cinders.

Soon you pass **Chain of Craters Road**, which leads 20 miles down to the shore and ends abruptly where the current lava flow has cut it off. Just pass it by *for now*.

The road will pass through an incredibly lush area. Ferns and ʻohiʻa trees rule this forest—it's hard to believe that a few minutes ago you were in a lava desert.

On your left will be a road to the **Puʻu Puaʻi Overlook**. The overlook just past the parking lot is great. It overlooks **Kilauea Iki Crater** and **Puʻu Puaʻi**. This crater (meaning little Kilauea) had been asleep for almost a century when it became active in 1959. Then it erupted into gargantuan fountains of lava, some reaching a staggering 1,900 feet—that's more than four times the height of the crater walls and is the highest on record. Scientists had warnings that an eruption was going to occur. Earthquake swarms and a swelling of Kilauea told them it was coming. So they set up their instruments and waited for the inevitable—*at Halemaʻumaʻu.* They were stunned when the lava instead shot from the southwest wall of Kilauea Iki (right below you) 2 miles away. Ground zero was near the Puʻu Puaʻi (meaning gushing hill) cinder cone. It was created as fountains of lava, blown southwest by the trade winds piled high into a cone. The vent spewed enough lava at one point to bury a football field 15 feet deep in lava—*every* *minute!* Each time the showers ended, the lava would drain back into the vent opening, only to be shot out again. When it ended, 36 days after it began, the crater floor was a dead zone with a lava bathtub ring above the floor to tell how high the lava had reached. The lava lake cooled and cracked as sheets of lava buckled and warped, giving the crater the look of dried, crusted-over gravy. Today, steam usually issues from cracks in the crater floor, and the rock is still molten a couple of hundred feet down. There are still vents on the crater, though the main vent was covered by falling cinders. Kilauea Iki offers one of the best hikes on the island. See HIKING on page 193.

From here you can stroll for 10–15 minutes along the **Devastation Trail**. This is where the fallout from the 1959 Kilauea Iki eruption killed the fern and 'ohi'a forest. The line of demarcation is abrupt, going from healthy forest to a field of tephra littered with bleached tree trunks. The forest is working to come back, and you will see the results along the way. You can either walk back the way you came, loop around on Crater Rim Road, or have someone pick you up at the other end.

Back on Crater Rim Road, you come to a parking lot (probably full of buses). This is **Thurston Lava Tube**. If you are looking for an easy way to see what the inside of natural lava plumbing looks like, Thurston Lava Tube is worth a stop. It is considered one of the "must sees" at the volcano. If you get there between tour buses, it can be an interesting experience. The entrance is a few minutes walk from Crater Rim Drive (see map). You exit about halfway through the tube. This part of the tube is lighted and is the most widely visited. Most of the lava stalactites have been removed over the decades, but you can still see enough tube detail to get the idea of how the lava travels. Undisturbed tubes often have floors littered with rocks that fall from the ceiling (either from when the tube cooled or from rainwater seeping through the cracks over the years). Thurston has been cleaned up and lighted to make it easy to visit. The more adventurous might want to see Thurston's *darker* half. At the stairs at the end of the tube tour and past the gate, Thurston continues for another 1,000 feet (it seems like more) before it ends abruptly. You are welcome to go. (The rangers used to keep a book for visitors to sign at the end of the tube, protected by a PVC pipe, but say they had to pull it out because visitors kept mistaking the PVC for a pipe bomb.) Make sure you bring a good flashlight (or two) for the journey, as you will be in total darkness most of the way. At the end turn off the light. You've never seen *real* blackness until you've seen *this* blackness.

If you want to get a feel for what Thurston Lava Tube looked like before it was tamed, see ACTIVITIES.

That dirt road that leads south of Thurston Lava Tube is an **escape road**. It is well maintained in case Chain of Craters Road is ever obliterated by a lava flow (again). That dirt road is the only place in the park where **mountain bikes** are allowed. It goes through very lush forest and is a delight. Just make sure you close all gates behind you. Some areas are fenced off to prevent pig damage. Wild pigs are amazingly destructive, and rangers fight an unending war to minimize their impact.

Just past Thurston Lava Tube is the **Kilauea Iki Overlook**. This, too, is worth stopping for. You look at Kilauea Iki from the other side. The Ki-

The 1959 eruption of Kilauea Iki punished this part of the forest when it showered the land with falling bits of gas-frothed lava from the 1,900-foot-high fountains. But it's the forest that will prevail. Take the short Devastation Trail and see for yourself.

lauea Iki hike mentioned a moment ago starts from here. Kilauea Iki is separated from Kilauea by a narrow shelf of land called **Byron Ledge**. It was on this ledge in 1824 that Princess Kapiolani publicly stood and, to the horror and fear of many, denied the volcano goddess Pele and embraced Christianity. She initiated this by eating 'ohelo berries without offering any to Pele first. (It was thought that Pele would strike you dead if you didn't offer her some first by tossing a fruiting branch into the crater.) When the Princess didn't die after snubbing and denying Pele, Christianity was more widely embraced by her people.

If you continue on Crater Rim Drive, you will end up back at the Visitor Center. If you need a break, walk over to the building on your left, the **Volcano Art Center Gallery**. Built in 1877, this was the original Volcano House before it was moved here to make way for another building. Now an art gallery, they have an exquisite selection from some of the island's top artists, including higher-end wood carvings, glassworks, paintings, and the like. This is also a good place to check out what's going on in the area in terms of events and demonstrations. Open 9–5.

There is another nice hike that starts near Volcano House. (See HIKING on page 194.) Part of it is on the *old* Crater Rim Drive—before it fell into the crater in 1983—and the results are dramatic.

DOWN CHAIN OF CRATERS ROAD

From the Visitor Center, you could head back the way you came on Crater Rim Drive, past Kilauea Iki and onto **Chain of Craters Road**. This is a 19-mile descent to the sea. (At least it was 19 miles when we went to press, and getting shorter all the time.) The road was so named because it passed numerous craters along the rift zone before veering off to the shore. It was rerouted after Madame Pele repaved 12 miles of the road with lava during the 1969–74 Mauna Ulu flow and now visits fewer craters than in used to. Mile markers are on alternating sides of the road, and we will refer to some of them. There are still some craters along the way you might want to check out (but don't bother with Ko'oko'olau). Remember to check your gas gauge; we've seen people run out of gas coming back up.

A little more than 2 miles into Chain of Craters Road is **Hilina Pali Road**, 8³⁄₁₀ miles long. It may be closed during nene nesting or if there is a perceived

Lava sometimes bursts from fissures such as this one from the 1970s Mauna Ulu eruption. But life always reclaims the land.

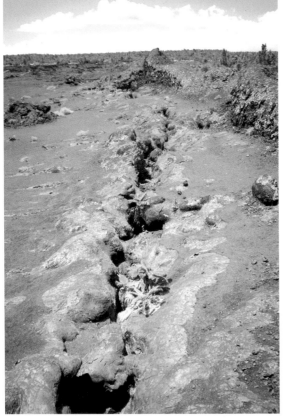

fire danger. The drive isn't impressive, but at the end is **Hilina Pali Lookout**. Walk down the path for 100 feet or so, and you are treated to an amazingly expansive view. You're perched above the vast shoreline below, and on a clear day you can see the entire shoreline for over 30 miles south. It's very quiet, desolate and peaceful, with the sound of the distant ocean sometimes present. If you take it, please drive very slowly as the endangered nenes are usually in the road and aren't very impressed by cars. The Kulanaokuaiki campgrounds are also on Hilina Pali Road.

Less than ¹⁄₁₀ mile past Hilina Pali Road, on the left (east) side is a 60-second walk to **Devil's Throat**. (It's unmarked.) This small collapsed crater is impressively sheer and a genuine heart-stopper. It's *straight* down. Be careful at the edge; it looks pretty fragile.

Along this stretch of Chain of Craters Road, keep an eye to your left. You *might* see steam coming from a hill. This is **Mauna Ulu**, the source of the second longest flank eruption of Kilauea. From 1969–1974 it poured lava and harassed park road builders, forcing Chain of Craters Road to be rerouted. There is a trail off the spur road past Pauahi Crater that goes near Mauna Ulu. (See ADVENTURES on page 225.) In 1997 a couple camping way out at Napau Crater (3½ miles east of Mauna Ulu) were awakened when lava suddenly began gushing from the ground half a mile away.

Just south of the 4 mile marker is a field of tephra. We've

walked to the east along here and discovered incredible lava fissures from 30 years ago (such as the one shown on the facing page), with ferns and trees already growing in them. But there is no trail, so you are on virgin, and untested, ground.

Proceeding down the road, you will get an appreciation in several spots of how lava actually flowed down the mountain during the 1969–74 Mauna Ulu eruption. At the **Alanui Kahakai turnout** (near the 14 mile marker) you will see a segment of the old, partially covered Chain of Craters Road. At the **Holei Pali Lookout**, just before the 15 mile marker, there is a great view of the mountain lava flows, where you get a feel for the volume of a'a and pahoehoe that drooled down the mountain. The newer highway cutting through the lava flow is dramatic.

About ⅓ mile past the 15 mile marker, you will pass by a lava tube on your left. Road crews bisect them every time they cut a new road in this area.

Past the 16 mile marker you will see the **Pu'u Loa Petroglyph Trail**. This fairly easy 15–20 minute walk is over an old pahoehoe lava flow with cairns (mounds of rock) marking the way. It leads to an area studded with thousands of petroglyphs (rock carvings) representing everything from birth to death. This is the largest petroglyph field in the state. A circular boardwalk has been built near some of them to allow you to view them without walking on them. *Many* more carvings are located past the boardwalk, but they request that you avoid walking around to protect the perishable petroglyphs

The Hawaiians, like people since the dawn of time, were compelled to leave a lasting legacy of themselves to the ages. These ancient petroglyphs are on the short Pu'u Loa trail.

from wear. The small holes bored in the rock were usually cut by parents who placed the umbilical cords from their newborns there for good luck. The area is very peaceful and worth your time if you wish to see a direct expression of ancient Hawaiian life. It's 1½ miles round trip.

Just before the 19 mile mark is the **Holei Sea Arch**, where the ocean has undercut the rock, leaving an arch. You walk less than a minute to it.

Past here should be the **end of Chain of Craters Road** (unless the lava advances to the sea arch). This is where the lava was pouring as we went to press, sometimes on the surface, sometimes into the sea, sometimes too far inland to walk to. Old maps showing Kamoamoa Campgrounds, a visitor center, Waha'ula Heiau, Lae 'Apuki, Waiaka Pond, Queen's Bath, Royal Garden, Kalapana Gardens and more are all tragically out of date. These were victims of the current eruption. Before you is a newly paved lava wasteland,

← *Trail described on page 229*

1983–1986 Flow

**Jan. 1997
Hiccup**

10 miles to Kilauea Caldera

● **Kupaianaha**

Pu'u 'O'o Crater
(Heart of current eruption)

2500'

1986–1992 Flow

N
W   E
S

2003—Present

1983–1986 Flow

1992—2003 Flow

Park Boundary

1992—2003 Flow

2000'

1500'

1000'

500'

**Visitor
Center/
Closest
Parking**

**Royal Gardens
Subdivision**

**End of
Chain of
Craters
Road**

19

*Former
Campground*

Kohola

Wilipe'e

W. Highcastle

Laeapuki

Kamoamoa
Pre-eruption Coastline

Brand new land

Kamokuna

Waha'ula He
(now destroye

0   1 MILE

© 2006 Wizard Publications, Inc.

Since the eruption began at Pu'u 'O'o (which conveniently materialized just within the park boundary) on January 3, 1983 the lava flows have been quite prolific. Each day 300,000 to 1,000,000 cubic yards of lava erupts, which has dramatically changed the landscape. Note how the lava concentrates in one area until another area opens up. The town of Kalapana was erased from the map in 1990. The famous Black Sand Beach at Kaimu is gone, now under 50–75 feet of lava. But a new, unnamed black sand beach now exists a third of a mile in front of where the old one was.

One of the most important heiau on the island was Waha'ula Heiau. Oral tradition states that it was constructed by Pa'ao, a priest from Tahiti who arrived during the second wave of colonization in the 12th century. It was he who was said to have introduced the concept of human sacrifice. Mu, whose role was to gather people to be sacrificed, would go out at night in parties of three and eavesdrop on houses, listening for any breach of kapu (rules of conduct). When one occurred, they would rush in and seize the victims and lead them off to this heiau. Sacrifices here were deemed so important that priests were sometimes sacrificed if others could not be found by the required time. Even smoke from its altars was sacred, and it was death to anyone who passed under the shadow of the smoke. Abraham Fornander states in his epic work of the late 19th century that this was the last heiau to be destroyed after the kapu system was abolished by King Kamehameha II in 1819. The heiau's foundations were finally buried by lava in 1997.

The doomed village of Kalapana is said to be named after an old man from Kaua'i trying to make a pilgrimage to Pele. He landed at what was Kaimu Beach and tried to make it to Kilauea but was unsuccessful due to severe storms. That night Pele came to his hut and appeared to him. The next morning nearly all of the old man's long hair was burned off. When he died some time later, the people named their village after him. It is said that because Kalapana could not make it to Pele's house, she sometimes visits his.

Interesting facts at a glance…

Total amount of lava erupted since 1983—3,100,000,000 cubic yards
Number of dump trucks that would fill—Over 200 million
Temperature lost while traveling in lava tubes—20°
Average temperature of flowing lava—2,000°
Length of public highway covered—8 miles
Amount of new land created—600 acres
Owner of all new land—State of Hawaii
Total area covered—40 square miles
Number of homes destroyed—182

1500'

1000'

500'

Kalapana Gardens and most of Royal Gardens were destroyed by lava flows in 1990.

End of lava road (at press time)
19°20.324'
155°00.542'

2WD Lava Road

Kalapana

Kalapana Gardens Subdivision

Former Kaimu Black Sand Beach

Pre-eruption Coastline

New Unnamed Black Sand Beach

Brand new land

Cave of Refuge

Punahaha

Brand new land

Kupapau Point

where liquid rock has poured above and below ground, reaching the ocean and building more land. The park "Visitor Center" at the bottom is now a motor home, which has had to be moved many times to avoid the fate of the last visitor center down here. Check with the rangers to see what's shakin'. Ask if nighttime offers good viewing conditions. Often at night the skylights, holes in the ceiling of a lava tube, are visible in the distance. Usually the only way to see a skylight during the day is on a helicopter flight. When the lava is flowing inland, you are usually allowed to hike to it. (They may *imply* that you can't but will usually admit that it is permitted if pressed.) See ADVENTURES on page 238.

HIKING IN THE PARK

Much of the best hiking on the island is in Hawai'i Volcanoes National Park. The ACTIVITIES chapter has a HIKING section on page 192, which lists scads of great hikes in the park. There's also a couple of spookier park hikes listed in ADVENTURES. Note that strolls of less than 30 minutes were described above in the tour of the volcano.

OUTSIDE THE PARK ENTRANCE

Just outside the park entrance there are a few sights that are worth checking out, either before or after your park visit.

Mauna Loa Scenic Road leads past the **Tree Molds**. These holes are created when a lava flow encounters a sopping wet tree trunk, which resists bursting into flames just long enough to harden the lava around it, giving the holes the texture of the tree bark. Better tree molds are found on the easy beginning of the **Napau Crater Trail** hike listed on page 194. Farther up the road

is **Kipuka Puaulu (Bird Park)**. This 30-minute hike goes through a kipuka, an old growth of forest surrounded by newer lava flows. This kipuka features many native trees and plants. Birds abound in this park—hence its nickname, Bird Park. The entire 1-mile stroll takes only 30 minutes plus stopping time. There are several benches scattered along the trail, which ascends gently for the first half.

Mauna Loa Scenic Road becomes very winding past here and switches to one lane (with several blind turns), as it passes through forest. At the end of the 13-mile road (at 6,650 feet) is the trailhead to **Mauna Loa Trail**. This is where you start your multi-day trek through the cold and altitude to ascend the summit of Mauna Loa. (Maybe another day.) There are picnic tables and a nice view of the park at the road's end. Though pleasant, this road is dispensable if you are budgeting your time.

Off the main highway south of the park entrance near the 38 mile marker is the **Ka'u Desert Trail**, which leads less than a mile to **Footprints**. Most of these were created during the explosion of 1790 (plus a few from an earlier explosion in the 1500s). You may read or be told that the footprints are worn away because they were vandalized. The truth is apparently a little more embarrassing. Park sources have told us that park personnel tried to protect the footprints many years ago by placing a glass case over them. Their intentions were pure, but when it rained, water condensed on the underside of the cracked glass and dripped onto the prints, wearing them away. That's why the display case is gone, but the vandalism rumor persists. Most personnel believe the vandalism explanation to be

Creation meets destruction. The ocean begins dismantling the land even before it cools.

Why you Shouldn't Pick a Lehua Blossom off an 'Ohi'a Tree

According to legend, 'Ohi'a was a young, handsome Big Island chief. The volcano goddess Pele knew that 'Ohi'a was courting a beautiful young girl named

Lehua. Pele became enamored with 'Ohi'a and desired him for a husband. One day as 'Ohi'a went up into the mountains to cut kukui bark to stain his surfboard, Pele appeared to him. She was dressed in her finest clothes and was quite striking. After a time, she announced to 'Ohi'a who she was and asked him to be her husband. Nervously but very diplomatically, he turned her down, professing his eternal love for Lehua. In her anger, Pele told him he was as gutless as a piece of wood, and changed him into a gnarled tree with grey-green leaves. When the other gods saw what Pele had done, they felt bad and tried to reverse it, but failed. The best they could do to reunite the broken-hearted Lehua with her beloved 'Ohi'a was to turn Lehua into a beautiful blossom on the same tree. To this day, it is said that picking a lehua blossom off an 'ohi'a tree will produce rain. These are the tears from heaven for separated lovers everywhere.

true to this day. Regardless, if you look around, you can still find better footprints elsewhere when shifting ash dunes permit.

Just outside the park is **Volcano Golf and Country Club** (see GOLFING in ACTIVITIES). Their restaurant (see ISLAND DINING) has pretty good food. A mile down Pi'i Mauna Road, you'll find **Volcano Winery** (967–7479). This is a good place to stop for a sip of some locally made wines. They have several unusual wines, including a local favorite,

Mac Nut Honey Wine. They also have wines made from fruits—*even grapes.* Hard-core oenophiles might turn up their noses, but less finicky palates might enjoy a snort or two of the exotic. A sign there says NO LARGE TOUR BUSES. Wow, *that's* a switch.

THE TOWN OF VOLCANO

When you first see the town of **Volcano** on a map, you figure they must spend all their time biting their nails over the active volcano crater less than

2 miles away. In fact, since they're upslope of the crater, they're safer from lava flows than Hilo or even the Kohala Resort area 50 miles away, as far as the geologists are concerned. Though extensive lava flows did cover this area about 500 years ago, the summit has since been reshaped so that today nearly all the lava flows happen on Kilauea's southern flank (away from the village). Their main threat is from falling tephra or ash from the occasional crater explosion like the one in 1790—annoying, but not as bad as a lava flow. And as for volcano smoke, normal trade winds send the smoke around the bottom of the island and up the coast where it harasses Kailua-Kona. It's ironic that this dreamy little community, set in a misty, lush fern-filled forest, can be so snug living on an active volcano.

Volcano is also a convenient place to pick up some supplies and gas (which is *breathtakingly* expensive here). If you enter the loop road from near the 27 mile marker, you pass by the **Volcano Store** and **Kilauea General Store and Gas Station** farther down. If you're driving back to the west side of the island, you can grab some gas or a snack before the long drive back. We often pick up some tasty pumpkin bread, 'ohelo berry turnovers, or sandwiches on Hawaiian sweetbread at Kilauea General before heading back.

In addition to the hotels and inns, there are cabins and free tent camping at **Namakani Paio Campgrounds** (967–7321) and **Kulanaokuaiki**, both in CAMP-ING on page 179. Current and retired military can rent clean cabins at **Kilauea Military Camp** (967–8333) right in the park. Higher rank, higher rent.

Looking more like the gates of hell, a rare vertical skylight allowed us to peek into a lava falls. You never know what you'll discover on an ever-changing lava field.

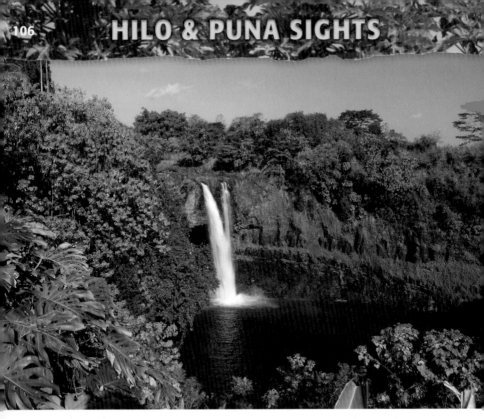

If you like waterfalls, Rainbow Falls is a perfect example of why you'll want to drive to the Hilo side.

Hilo is a charming mix of old and new Hawai'i. Once a thriving town bolstered by limitless sugar revenues, the demise of the sugar industry has kept Hilo in a time warp. And that's the charm. Though a full-fledged city, things move slower here, and the community is tight. They've been through a lot. Lashed by tsunamis, threatened by lava flows, racked by a changing economy, Hilo has withstood it all. Hilo is also a strikingly beautiful town. Abundant rains give the flora a healthy sheen that soothes the soul. Though the exodus of business has left many of its buildings looking worn and neglected, Hilo's charms lie deeper.

Hilo's Achilles' heel is weather. Only in Hilo would water officials quake in fear and declare a drought, even encouraging water conservation, when they receive *only* 70 inches of rain in a year. (All you Arizona residents can stop laughing now!)

This rain translates to an unacceptable gamble to many visitors. People are hesitant to spend precious Big Island days in a place that might get rained out. But they forget that even if it's rain-city here, elsewhere along the eastern side things might be sunnier. Hilo is the logical gateway for exploring Puna, the easternmost part of the island, where you'll find lush rain forests, a black sand beach, thermally heated pools and volcano-ravaged towns. Puna is also famous for its outlaws from the '60s, guerrilla gardeners and bizarre characters.

Hilo has a reputation for being less friendly to visitors than other parts of the island. Sort of a *let da buggahs go to Kona* mentality. Though this reputation is not entirely unearned, it is also not entirely accurate. Some of the friendliest, nicest and most helpful people we've run into have been in Hilo. But we've also gotten more blank expressions and outright nastiness here.

Hilo is a ghost town on Sundays. Don't expect much of anything to be open. We'll describe sights around Hilo in a scattershot manner before heading toward Puna.

AROUND HILO TOWN

Starting at the corner of Kamehameha (which fronts the bay) and Waianuenue (in northern Hilo), head southwest on Waianuenue. (See map on next page.) When you pass the Hilo Public Library on your

right, take a look at that oblong stone out front, six full strides long. Think you can move it? At age 14, Kamehameha risked death (if he failed) and agreed to try to move that Naha Stone (estimated at 7,000 pounds). He did it because legend said that whoever could overturn the stone would be the first king of all the islands. At that time the stone was slightly imbedded in the ground. The ox-like youth, whose strength was unprecedented, squatted and gave a huge push—nothing. He tried and tried but could barely nudge it. As people gathered round and the priest started to come over (to condemn him to death), he summoned a final burst of strength and overturned the boulder, shocking everyone and beginning the fulfillment of his destiny.

Just off Waianuenue St., on the corner of Haili and Kapiolani, the Lyman Museum (935–5021) is worth a stop. The Earth Heritage exhibit alone justifies the $10 admission. It has incredible displays

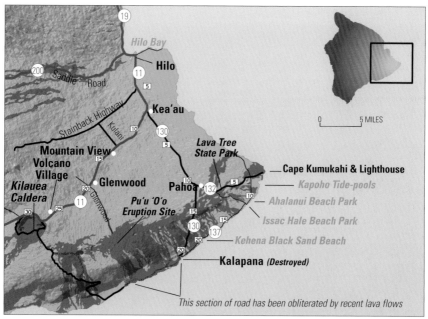

This section of road has been obliterated by recent lava flows

of Hawaiian geology, plant, animal and fish life (nicely done), plus an exceptionally beautiful rock and mineral collection from around the world. Elsewhere **A REAL GEM** they have Hawaiian history displays and a few other interesting items. Tours of the Lyman missionary house next door are given at various times throughout the day.

Take the right fork after the 1 mile marker and follow the signs to Rainbow Falls. These **NOT TO BE MISSED!** falls change dramatically depending on water flow. Moderate flow is best. (Too little and the wishbone shape is gone; too much and it's an undefined, roiling mess.) The falls are best seen in the morning when the sun is behind you. (Rainbows can only be seen when the sun is behind you, so if you ever see a photo with the sun and a rainbow in the same frame, it's fake.) The cave below the falls is where Kamehameha is said to have buried the bones of his father. Take the trail to the left for different views and the shady comfort of a large banyan tree. From the left a trail leads to the top of the falls, but you are on your own in assessing whether to go down there.

A mile farther up the road is Boiling Pots. This series of bowl-shaped depressions roil and boil when the water flow is heavy, creating dramatic photo opportunities. To the left is Pe'epe'e Falls. (No, it's *not* pronounced pee-pee, but rather PEH-EH PEH-EH, so wipe that smirk off your face.) One look and it's obvious you can't swim in Boiling Pots when it's boiling. (During calmer times we see daring dudes jumping from pot to pot to pot.) There's a trail to the right of the viewing area that leads down to the rocks below. From there you could scramble over the boulders to the other side (without getting your feet wet if the flow is low enough, as in our photo on the next page) and continue to Pe'epe'e Falls. This waterfall and deep pool are an idyllic place to sit in solitude and ponder. You'll usually have it to yourself. Be careful on the rocks; don't go if the river is raging and don't fall in. Also, don't go down to the falls without mosquito repellent unless you've checked with your life insurance company to see if excessive bloodletting is considered an accident rather than suicide. While we're nagging, this is probably a good time to tell you that Boiling Pots and Rainbow Falls are common places for car break-ins. We often see thieving scum casing the lots looking for unsuspecting tourist cars to rob while they are away lost in the beauty.

Less than a mile up Waianuenue the road veers right. From a bridge you can see Wai'ale Falls. The amount of water is considerably more than what you saw downstream at Rainbow Falls, an impressive demonstration of how much actually seeps into the porous lava bed along the way. (It's *not* tapped at the nearby dam.) You can hike there and enjoy some wonderful pools. See HIKING on page 204.

Over on Kaumana Drive (see map) is Kaumana Cave. This lava tube can make for fun exploring and is described in detail in SADDLE ROAD SIGHTS on page 146 since it's usually visited by those coming into Hilo from the Saddle.

Along the bay, the grassy park fronting the town is the Hilo Bayfront. It used to be the main Japanese district, Hilo's Japantown. On April Fool's day 1946 a tsunami (tidal wave) of unprecedented size was generated from a horrific earthquake off Alaska. The tsunami lashed the entire state, but punished this part of the Big

Offerings are common at Pe'epe'e Falls.

Townsfolk refurbished the clock but refused to rebuild it in honor of those who died.) Tsunamis have unimaginable power. The water first recedes, exposing the ocean's floor, and then bulldozers of water come crashing in. The event can last for hours.

The Pacific Tsunami Museum (935-0926) is on Kamehameha and Kalakaua. (Open 9 a.m. to 4 p.m.) It's in the old First Hawaiian Bank Building. (You sit in the old bank vault while they show a movie of the tsunami.) The quality of the tour is dependent on the quality of the docent showing you around, and the ones we've seen are excellent. (Most of them have lived through a tsunami.) Lots of photos, and you'll leave with a good understanding of what a tsunami is—and why it's not really a wave. It's $7, closed Sundays.

Banyan Drive, where most of Hilo's hotels are located, is named after the graceful and stately banyan trees that line the road. If a tree can look wise, then banyan trees definitely qualify. Each tree was named after the person who planted it. Familiar names such as Amelia Earhart, King George V, Babe Ruth, FDR and Richard Nixon. (In one of those ironies of life, the first one Nixon planted was washed away on election day when he became VP.) Also on Banyan Drive is Lili'uokalani Gardens. This is one of several graceful and serene parks in the area worth checking out. If you're a bit warm, look for the nearby ice pond. (See map.) Cold water intruding into this part

A REAL GEM

Island the most. In all, 159 people, including 21 school children in Laupahoehoe, were killed in the worst natural disaster in Hawai'i's history. After another tsunami killed another 38 people in 1960, town fathers decided to make this area a park rather than risk more lives during the next tsunami. (The clock on the side of the road on Kamehameha Street in front of Naniloa Golf Course stands with its hands frozen in time—1:04 a.m.—from the 1960 tsunami.

of the bay (you can sometimes see it percolating to the surface) creates water so cold it'll give you *chicken skin kine.*

If you were to continue east along the shoreline on Kalanianaole, you would pass by most of Hilo's beach parks. See BEACHES for more on these. You *might* not want to drive past the part where the road is paved. In the past it contained Hilo's underbelly, but the county was addressing it at press time. On your way out to the parks check out a beach access across from Lokoaka Street. It is very jungly and draped with vines. The beach is worthless, but the short walking road is kind of cool as is the trail on the left, which ends at James Kealoha Beach Park. You'll also pass Hilo Homemade Ice Cream (933–1520) on the ocean side. Although owned by our favorite, Tropical Dreams, this ice cream is not as sweet or rich as other gourmet ice creams, has more air and less butter fat. Lots of exotic flavors like ginger and 'ohelo.

HEADING SOUTH ON HIGHWAY 11

As you head out of town, you will pass by Hilo's biggest shopping area. Prince Kuhio Plaza, Waiakea Center, and Puainako Town Center are where you will find Safeway grocery store, Longs Drugs, Wal-Mart, Borders and a zillion fast food restaurants. On Hinano Street off Kekuanaoa is Big Island Candies (935–8890). Their locally made chocolates and cakes are excellent, though their prices are confiscatory. (This is a favorite stopping place for tour buses.) Good place for chocolate if you don't mind paying double-extra-super-retail. On the Highway before the 4 mile marker, Makalika Street heading east leads to Nani Mau Gardens (959–3500), 20 acres of flawlessly groomed tropical and sub-tropical plants. Most of their business comes from Japanese tour groups (who are fussy about their gardens). Whereas the mother of all gardens, Hawai'i Tropical Botanical Garden (on your way out of town heading north, described on page 124) is much more exotic, Nani Mau Gardens will appeal to those who want a more manicured, controlled and artistically arranged setting. Nani Mau is also a popular place to get married. Allow 30–60 minutes, cost is $10 (for the garden, not the wedding). They also have a lunch buffet for $11.

The road past the 4 mile marker heading west leads to Stainback Highway and the Pana'ewa Rain Forest Zoo (959–7224). The zoo is a mixed bag. In the past it was downright dismal, but their recent attempts to improve exhibits shows. One exhibit—with a wire mesh tunnel going through it and lots of animals roaming around a well-designed area—is contrasted by dreary, spartan cages with sole occupants. Kids should like the zoo, adults may not. Price is right—it's free.

Between the 5 and 6 mile marker is Macadamia Road and the Mauna Loa Visitor Center (966–8618). This is the mac nut giant's main processing plant. You can see the process through the glass or pick up some of their products; otherwise, it's expendable.

If you're going to explore Puna, your best route is to take Highway 11 to 130, then take 132 to 137, and 137 to Kalapana where you link back up to 130. See maps on pages 107 or 113 if you aren't too dizzy to flip the page. If you want a meaningless diversion, you could continue along Stainback Highway until it ends at the Big Island's least popular visitor attraction—our prison. This one-lane road goes for miles through an otherwise impenetrable forest. There are signs saying that it is illegal to drive the road, but they were put up by the prison to cover their 'okole—they told us that it's perfectly OK to drive it as long as you're not planning to spring anyone. Some 13¾ miles into the one-lane (and dead-on straight) road is the Pu'u Maka'ala Forest Reserve. The roads in there are 4WD only, and the trails (if you can find them) are lush and wet.

EXPLORING PUNA

Head south on Highway 130 and you come to the town of Pahoa. Known as the Big Island's outlaw town, this is where

Free energy. In Puna they don't drill for oil; they drill for steam.

guerrilla gardeners (pakalolo farmers), dreadlock enthusiasts, FBI fugitives and the never-bathe crowd coexist without stepping on each other's toes—usually. You'd be surprised to learn how many homes you see are built on vacant land— at least according to the County Tax Assessor's Office. Permit? What's that? To be honest, their reputation is a little exaggerated—probably. People-watching here can be a hoot sometimes. There are a couple places to eat here that you may like, reviewed in ISLAND DINING. By the way, Pahoa usually has *comparatively* **cheap gas**.

After Pahoa, turn onto Hwy 132 and you'll soon come to Lava Tree State Park. Lava trees form when fast flowing pahoehoe encounters wet 'ohi'a trees. As the flow drains away, it leaves a thick coating around the dying tree. Most of these free-standing tubes are moss-covered. You can saunter around the park in 30–60 minutes. Look for the huge chasms created during the explosive eruption of 1790. Even if you don't want to hike (there are better lava trees on the Napau Crater Trail), take a minute to drive into the park and gawk at the regal monkey-pod trees that dominate the area. A while back, the park semi-massacred some of the trees here to eradicate a pest. (Didn't work.)

Past Lava Trees, the canopy of trees is absolutely lovely. If you have a con-

5 miles to Hilo

11
Kea'au Town

Kea'au/Pahoa Rd

130

Hawaiian Paradise Park Subdivision

Kaloli

Paradise

Makuu

This stretch 4WD only

2WD OK

Lava Swimming Pool
19°32.747'
154°51.224'

Kazumura Lava Tube Cave

Kahakai

Hawaiian Beaches Subdivision

1840 Flow

1790

1960

Cape Kumukahi Lighthouse

Grey Lava 4WD Road

Champagne Pond
19°30.114'
154°49.000'

Pahoa Town

132

Lava Tree State Mon.

Frogs

1840

1790

Pahoa-Pohoiki Rd (very pretty)

1790

1955

Kapoho Tide-pools

137

Kapoho Kai Rd.

Ahalanui Warm Spring

Natural Lava Steam Rooms

Opihikao-Kamaili Rd

1955

1790

Pohoiki Warm Pool (small)

Issac Hale Beach Park

Black Sand Beach Community

130

1790

Mackenzie State Recreation Park

1955

1790

137

Kehena Black Sand Beach

Star of the Sea Church

1990

New Kaimu Black Sand Beach

Punahaha

Pre-1990 Shoreline

Cave of Refuge

N
W   E
S

0   5 MILES

© 2006 Wizard Publications, Inc.

vertible, look up; it's kind of hypnotizing. If it's after sunset, pull over and listen. Millions of tiny Caribbean tree frogs now fill the air with their whistle. Islanders consider these new arrivals a pest and are trying to eradicate them by spraying various chemicals, including caffeine. Though it gives you and me a morning lift, it'll make these little guys...croak. (Sorry, I just *had* to get that one in.)

Shortly after Lava Trees take the left fork (near a papaya grove) where Hwy 132 continues toward Kapoho. Ever wonder where people on an island get their electricity? Well, here on the Big Island 25% of our juice is volcano-powered. They drilled a basketball-sized hole a *mile* deep and when they did, steam shot up at pressures similar to what you'd find inside a SCUBA tank. They use the steam to turn turbines. The underground water source is naturally replaced by the ocean's pressure, so it'll last indefinitely—at least until the surrounding rock cools. Interestingly, though the land is private, *all* mineral rights in Hawai'i belong to the state government (as all first-time landowners here discover to their shock). This includes *steam*. So, even though the private company returns the

water vapor back to the ground, they have to pay the state almost $1 million a year for the steam they temporarily borrow because it's considered *state steam*. (Just thought we'd pass that along, in case you were thinking of opening a gold mine here.)

Across from the 5 mile marker on the left (north) side is the lava vent from the 1955 eruption. The vent is interesting to walk on. It's made up of loose and cemented blobs of airborne lava (called tephra) that fountained out of the vent. It's worth a few minutes if you want to poke around. There are opportunities for a good fall, so be careful.

The end of Hwy 132 is on lava flows from 1960. A dirt road leads out to the point. Fountains of lava $\frac{3}{10}$ mile high produced enormous amounts of lava that wiped out the town of Kapoho, leaving only two subdivisions. Having hiked through countless lava fields on the island, this wins the prize as the harshest and most difficult to walk through we've ever encountered. (You'd have an easier time walking through the minefields of the demilitarized zone between North and South Korea than hiking through this stuff.) At the end of the unpaved road leading to the sea is a **light tower**.

Take a deep breath. This is the easternmost part of the island, and since our winds come from that direction, scientists use it to test "virgin air" that has drifted over the landless Pacific for many weeks. Air from here is considered as pristine as any in the world, and it is analyzed by governments around the globe and used as a benchmark to compare to their air.

While you're out on this point, you'll see a 4WD gray lava road on the right. If you take it and a right then left onto the lightest gray road at the first confusing intersection, it heads for $1\frac{2}{10}$ miles

Champagne Pond

Light Beacon

To Hwy 137 & Hwy 132

Main Lava Road—Walk or 4WD

Private Gated Roads

N

0   1/4 MILE

19°30.114'
Champagne Pond 154°49.000'

An oceanside lava swimming pool—the original black bottom pool.

to Kapoho Bay. A gate may or may not prevent 4WD access halfway into it (there were posts but no gate at press time), possibly necessitating walking the rest of the way to Kapoho Bay. Why would you want to do that? Simple. A truly awesome experience called Champagne Pond awaits.

Imagine a calm, protected ocean inlet filled with *crystal* clear water. A scattering of fish and sometimes a turtle or two (or *nine,* our personal record here) await. Fine, you say. There **A REAL GEM** are lots of places with that. Maybe. But how many of them are *heated*? Sparkling clean freshwater heated by the volcano percolates from the ground. It's not Jacuzzi-hot, but rather relaxing-warm (around 90° on top) and changes with the tide. The more it's been raining lately, the deeper the floating warm water goes. Bring a mask and you can *see* the layers of temperature differences (warm is on top). This isn't Ahalanui Park (listed later). This is in a gated residential community,

and the cove is next to an A-frame house. But from the 4WD public *lava* road *anyone* can access it. Weekends and holidays are crowded with locals, and it's best to leave it to them during those days. But during the week it's lightly used. Make sure you take out anything you brought in, and wear reef shoes in the water or you are *guaranteed* to stub your toes. Don't worry if the water's cool when you first get in, just head to the back of the cove where its warmer. And remember: The best way to avoid scaring a turtle away is to act disinterested and keep your distance.

Back at the corner of Hwys 132 and 137, you'll want to head south on 137. But if you feel like a different kind of forest drive, head north first for 5 miles or so. It goes from stark lava to a luxuriant jungle filled with birds almost instantly. Along the way there's a delightful natural lava swimming pool if you don't mind walking ³⁄₁₀ mile (each way.)

The enormous pool (250 feet long) is naturally ensconced in a rugged lava shoreline. It's 5 feet deep in spots and backed by a thick grove of lovely hala trees. (Sometimes unusually ultra-low tides virtually erase it.) Meandering around the pool is fun while you scramble over the occasional lava obstacle. (If you don't have some cheap water/reef shoes, navigating the rounded-boulder floor will be unpleasant.) There is shade near the pool until noon. Water splashes into the pool from the ocean. Only during big surf or very high tide is it anything but gentle in the pool. Bring a mask (though the water is so incredibly clear, you almost won't need one). Fishermen sometimes use it on weekends, but it's usually vacant during the week.

To get there, drive about 1⁹⁄₁₀ miles from the end of the pavement (or 2⁸⁄₁₀ miles from the corner of Hwys 132 and 137—see map on page 113). The beautiful jungle-side road (which looks more like a tunnel drilled through hau bush) is easy to find: It's the first road on the right at the bottom of a short paved segment on the otherwise unpaved main road. It's 1,500 feet to the shoreline, and the pool is another 100 yards to the left.

Return to Hwys 132 and 137 when you're done.

Heading south on Hwy 137 leads past Kapoho-Kai Road. This road goes to one of the more unusual locations on the Big Island. Dozens and dozens of spring-fed, brackish pools and tide-pools, some volcanically heated, are strewn throughout the area known as the Kapoho Tide-pools. Many of the land-locked pools have been incorporated into people's front and back yards as swimming pools. The large pools adjacent to the ocean (called Wai'opae Ponds) are on public property and contain some of the most fascinating snorkeling around. If you wish to snorkel here, take Kapoho–Kai Road

A vast area of interconnected tide-pools await at Kapoho, providing endless snorkeling possibilities.

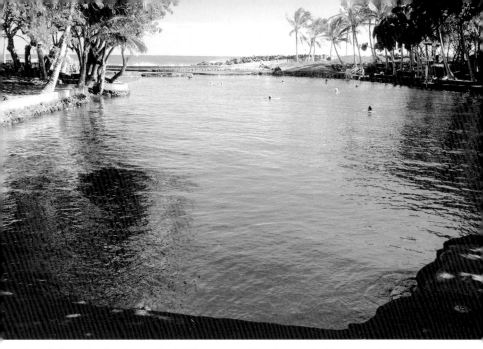

There's no such thing as a quick dip in the soothing volcanically heated pool of Ahalanui.

(just before the 9 mile marker). When it seems to dead end (on Waiopae), turn left, go ⅒ mile and park when the ocean is visible. Snorkel exploration is possible even for novice snorkelers. The largest pool snakes its way to the ocean and rises and falls each day with the tide. This creates slight currents that are fun to ride if the surf's not high. These pools are usually (but not always) very calm and protected. Closer to the reef edge brings more fish, but sometimes there's a current. We've spent many hours here and counted eight kinds of coral. Toward the back (west) a couple of pools are slightly heated by the volcano. The weather is sometimes snotty in the morning but usually clears up in the afternoon.

Note that the tide-pools are best visited during the week. Weekends are crowded since Puna residents have comparatively few beaches to choose from.

There are lots of vacation rentals available here (called Vacationland) and next door in the gated community of Kapoho Beach Lots. Make *sure* you see

what you're getting beforehand because there are a number of charming sounding dumps there alongside wonderful vacation rentals.

Farther down Hwy 137 past the 10 mile marker is Ahalanui. (Formerly called

A REAL GEM

Puʻalaʻa, the state discovered that they had accidentally misnamed it for decades— *oops*.) This delightful gem is definitely worth stopping for. It's a spring- and ocean-fed pool with a manmade wall and an inlet separating it from the ocean. Although the original builders created this spot when the water was *ice cold*, the Kapoho eruptions of 1955 and 1960 reworked the lava plumbing here so that now, instead of coming out cold, this pool is *volcanically heated* to a toasty 91–95 degrees. (It occasionally gets *much* cooler and we're not sure what the mechanism is.) With palm trees all around and the sound of

A lonely Puna road.

the surf over the seawall, you may have trouble hauling yourself out once you've experienced this genuine Pele bath, and it's easier to access than Champagne Pond, though it's more crowded, as well. *On occasion* we've noticed a slight sulphur smell on the skin when we've gotten out, but even then it's worth it.

As mapmakers we couldn't help but notice that this area called Puna, which receives *lots* of rain and is the size of Moloka'i, doesn't have a *single* river or stream—not even an intermittent one. The reason? The land's too new. Rain that falls simply seeps into the porous lava. If you get a chance to hike in a lava tube, you'll see it dripping from the ceiling on its way to recharging the vast water table below.

Isaac Hale Beach Park farther down the road is where local fishermen launch their boats, and they are not known for extending gobs of aloha to visitors. (There's also a lunch wagon here that serves the worst shave ice we've had on the island.) The swimming is poor and the surfing is for experts. So why bother? Because if you take the shoreline trail to the right of the boat launch for two minutes, where it veers inland, you'll come to a surprise. There, set in the vine-covered jungle but only 40–50 feet from the shore, is a small (8-feet by 14-feet) warm water pool similar to Ahalanui but completely natural. The setting is heaven sent. The only caveat is that some residents don't always appreciate the paradise that they live in and occasionally spoil the area with litter. But if you come during the week, there's a chance you may have it all to yourself.

As you drive along this stretch, realize that this is one of the least known parts of the Big Island. The vast majority of island residents and visitors never see this area, and that's a shame. It is mostly untouched and exceptionally beautiful. Take your time here.

Less than 2/10 mile past the 13 mile marker is a turnoff to the ocean. Check out the massive squared-off rock at the lava bluff's edge. Then try to imagine the kind of wave it takes to *toss* it up from the ocean, because that's how it (and others you see around you) got here. This area is a nice place to watch the humbling power of the ocean when the surf's up. Just be careful not to let a monster wave surprise you. Another good wave-watching place is 2/10 mile past the 14 mile marker. It's a 700-foot walk if you don't have 4WD and leads to a series of tide-pools that are created on this short bluff when waves explode against the lava, showering the pools.

If you look at the map, you'll see that this part of the shoreline was covered by a lava flow in 1790. The flow killed everything in its path, leaving nothing but barren, unforgiving rock for new life to work with. Yet look at what life has managed to accomplish in these two centuries. Remember this natural rejuvenating power when you come to the modern devastation that lies ahead on this road.

Near the 19 mile marker is Kehena Beach. This is a powerful testament to the changing nature of the Big Island. This beach wasn't even here until it was created by the 1955 lava flow you just drove through. Officials created stone steps leading down to the western part of the beach. Then an earthquake in 1975 sank the beach 3 feet all at once. The lower portion of the stone steps collapsed. If you take the path *to the right* of the turnout, it leads to the stone steps, which, upon descent, end abruptly 10 feet above the shoreline. Those wishing to use Kehena Beach will need to go back up and take the trail to the eastern section of the beach. The trailhead is *to the left* of the parking area. Swimming is dangerous during high surf, and the beach is often used by nudists. Be care-

ful not to leave anything in your car here, as we've noticed lots of thieving scum casing cars.

Shortly after the 22 mile marker, you're confronted with the consequences of the current Kilauea eruption. A rolling sea of hardened lava stretches in front of you. This particular flow occurred in 1990, annihilating the towns of Kalapana, Kaimu and the Royal Gardens subdivision beyond. (See map on page 100 to get an idea of the scale of the devastation.) Kalapana was a treasured Hawaiian fishing village, richly steeped in the traditions of the past. Its loss was a stunning blow to those wishing to keep the old ways alive.

Until the 1990 lava flow, this was also the site of the most famous black sand beach in the world. A long curving bay of jet black sand with numerous stately palm trees sprinkled about, the black sand beach at Kaimu was universally regarded as the finest. Today, it is gone, forever entombed under 50–75 feet of lava.

When the road stops, get out and walk to the top of the lava and look toward the shore. You'll notice young, sprouting coconut trees in the distance. The campaign to bring the plantings was begun by a local resident. She encouraged others in the community to take trees out to the new black sand beach 1/3 mile in front of you to begin the process of rebuilding their precious beach. Even as she was dying of cancer, residents and school children continued the tradition in her honor. Today, there are vast numbers of sprouting coconuts along the new black sand beach, a testament to the vision of one resident who refused to let her community die, even in the face of her own death.

Imagine what it must be like to have grown up in Kalapana. Sights that seemed so permanent to you like the

The sprouting coconut trees of the new Kaimu Beach are a tribute to one woman's dream and represent community hope for another beautiful family beach for tomorrow's generation.

freshwater queen's bath you played in as a child, the fishing shrine that your grandfather used every day before he went fishing, that beautiful coconut grove where you had your first kiss. All these things that seemed so timeless, that came before you and you *knew* would always be there, are now gone, erased without a trace, as if your whole world had been nuked. Kalapana residents didn't just lose their home; they lost all traces to their past and share the unique experience of having outlived their world.

A 5–10 minute walk straight out across the lava leads to the new black sand beach. Don't even consider swimming there for the surf is treacherous. Until recently the state (or more likely their lawyers) posted signs telling you to stay away. The public—rightfully—ignored the signs in droves and today the signs are gone. To the right of the trailhead are some perfect impressions of palm trees. Their dying act was to cool and harden the lava around their trunks, forever capturing the bark texture of a vanished Kalapana coconut tree. There are even some hala tree fruit moldings in the lava.

Once at the beach most people stop, say, "Wow, so *this* is a black sand beach," then dash back to their car. *Hey, what's the hurry?* Take your shoes off and wiggle your toes in sand that might have been born after you were. Watch the perfect white ocean foam as it slithers across the black sand, leaving a sheen that disappears into the sand. It's the contrasts that make this such a beautiful place, not the oddity that the sand happens to be black.

Also from this beach you can see the top of **Pu'u 'O'o** behind you (clouds permitting), the source of all this lava.

Back at your car, to reward yourself for your walk, you should know that Verna's across the street makes a deadly (and utterly massive) banana split.

If you look at the map on page 100 you'll see another road, Hwy 130, leading toward a demolished neighborhood. Most of the subdivision is now buried under lava. There's not much to see in the area itself: A handful of hardy souls still live in the ravaged subdivision without power or water. Birds have rediscovered this island of green in a sea of lava (called a kipuka). During the devastating lava flows, the media and the public focused their sympathy on the people who lost their homes. The *real* people to feel sorry for are the people who *didn't* lose their homes. You see, insurance covers loss of property, not loss of *access* to property. Imagine an insurance adjuster walking up to your now worthless house, surrounded but untouched by a sea of hardened lava and saying, "Nothing wrong with this house; claim denied."

Most of the end of Hwy 130 is a sifted lava road, cut in 2001 on top of the lava. Despite any misleading NO TRESSPASSING or RESIDENTS ONLY signs you may see, this is a *public* road and you *are* allowed to drive on it. (The land on *either side* is private, but not the road.) Depending on *where* the ever-changing lava is flowing during your stay, you might have to drive on it (with a regular car) to see lava flows. When lava viewing requires this road, the county sometimes charges $5 per car, which is very reasonable when you consider how much work it is to keep the road open. Less than two weeks after the state's grand opening of this road, lava crossed it again, requiring yet another trip for the bulldozers. See page 238 for more on lava viewing.

You may be wondering what happens if you own oceanfront property, and the volcano creates new land in front of you (called *accreted land* for the trivia deprived). Do you now own a larger parcel? No. You don't even own oceanfront anymore! Apparently Madame Pele signed a quit claim deed over to the state, because all newly created land goes to our hungry state government.

As you head north on Hwy 130 on your way back toward Hwy 11, look for the church on the right (east) side of the road near the 20 mile marker. Formerly the Star of the Sea Church built in 1928 by the same priest who did the Painted Church near Honaunau, the building was in the path of an advancing lava flow in 1990. Community members had to wrench it from its foundations to save it just in the nick of time. After sitting on the side of the road for years without a home, it was finally decommissioned and is being turned into a Hawaiian cultural center.

Subdivisions in East Hawai'i often have names at odds with reality. Places like HAWAIIAN BEACHES SUBDIVISION (there are *no* beaches there), PARADISE PARK (it's not a park and it sure ain't paradise) and our personal favorite that you pass, up the mountain of the 17 mile marker on Hwy 130. It's surrounded by jungle, miles from the ocean, and is called BLACK SAND BEACH COMMUNITY. (The lots were probably easier to sell than if they had named it SURROUNDED BY JUNGLE COMMUNITY.)

Here's something I'll bet you've never seen. Just before you get to the 15 mile marker (south of it) is a pullout area, a scenic overlook with seemingly no attraction. Take the very quick trail to the 'ohi'a trees (60 seconds or so), and from there a maze of short trails lead to natural lava steam rooms ranging in size from one person pukas (holes) to rooms big enough for large groups. Unusually pasty lava flowed here in 1955, and, depending on how much rain we've had lately, varying amounts of steam issue from the ground. The pukas have been enhanced by regular users with wooden benches and even a ladder for the deepest room. Occasionally, regular local users can be found basking in the steam in their altogethers.

When you take Hwy 130 back to Hwy 11, you can either head to Hilo or toward the volcano. If you head to the volcano, look for the Hirano Store before the 20 mile marker. From their parking lot you get the easiest view on the island of Pu'u 'O'o belching 7½ miles away. (A better, less obstructed view is from 100 feet down S. Glenwood Road, just past the Hirano Store.) This is the headline-grabbing vent that has been the lava source for most of the current eruption. Look across the road and slightly to your right. Unless you hike to it or fly over it, this is as close as you'll come. If you *are* up to a long hike, the trek through the virgin rain forest to Pu'u 'O'o is the trek of a lifetime. See ADVENTURES on page 229 for more on this beautiful hike.

Kilauea Volcano is just ahead.

HILO SHOPPING

Shoppers may want to visit Hilo on Wed. as this is Farmers' Market day. The Market is also held on Saturdays but will be more crowded with local residents. Park along the bayfront (Kamehameha Ave.) to visit the shops along this street. Start by heading north along Kamehameha and end at the Farmers' Market at the corner of Kamehameha and Mamo before returning to your car.

Some of the shops you may want to visit along Kamehameha are The Most Irresistible Shop in Hilo for souvenirs and gifts; Hana Hou for vintage Hawaiiana; Basically Books for maps and Hawai'i related titles; Sig Zane, next to the Tsunami Museum, for original island print clothing; Ets'ko (up Waianuenue) for their vast assortment of fine gifts; and the Rock Island Gallery on Furneaux for an excellent selection of rocks and minerals.

While window shopping, Tropical Dreams Ice Cream is available in the Kress Building and Hilo Homemade Ice Cream is available on Waianuenue. Shave ice and addictive, chocolate-covered sunflower seeds can be purchased at Wilson's By the Bay, (on Kamehameha). There's also shave ice at Hilo Snack and Seed (on Waianuenue).

On Highway 11 heading south you'll see Waiakea Center which has Borders Books and Wal-Mart. Across Maka'ala Street is Prince Kuhio Plaza and Hilo Hattie on the corner. Hilo Hattie is the popular stopping place for visitors, and for good reason—their aloha wear is excellent and priced right.

If you're interested in the beautiful bonsai plants you've seen on many countertops around the island, Fuku-Bonsai (982–9880) is 10 miles south of Hilo in Kurtistown. Call first to be sure they'll be open when you'll be driving through.

HILO & PUNA'S BEST BETS

Best Cerebral Stimulation—Lyman Museum

Best Dessert—Double Chocolate Truffle Cake at Pescatore

Best Snorkeling—Tide-pools at Kapoho

Best Place to Soak Your Bones—Champagne Pond or Ahalanui Park

Best Way to Pull Your Back—Duplicating Kamehameha's Feat of Lifting the Naha Stone

Best Waterfall—Rainbow Falls

Best *Secluded* Waterfall—Pe'epe'e Falls

Best Shakedown—State Charging for Use of Steam at Puna Geothermal

Best Healthy Food—Island Naturals Deli in Waiakea Center

Best Mexican Food—Luquin's in Pahoa

Best Chance of Finding Turtles—Champagne Pond

Best Place to Nuke Your Cholesterol Count—Café 100

Best Place to Catch an Easy Glimpse of Erupting Pu'u 'O'o—Glenwood Road near the Hirano Store

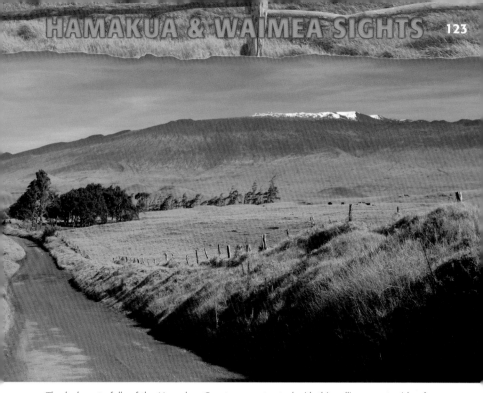

The lush waterfalls of the Hamakua Coast are contrasted with this rolling countryside of Waimea creating one of the best drives on the Big Island.

When local residents speak of driving between Hilo and Kona, they either "drive the saddle" or they "take the upper road." The upper road is the stretch of Highway 19 between Hilo and Waimea. It passes through magnificent country reminiscent of old Hawai'i. Along the way you can check out numerous waterfalls, drive along stunning gorges, gaze over (or go into) an Eden-like valley, or check out Hawai'i's premiere ranch town, home of largest private ranch in the U.S., Parker Ranch. Part of this drive is actually in the districts of North and South Hilo, but that distinction is lost on the driver.

We'll start our description from the Hilo side. (If you're coming the other way, just turn the book upside down.) It's best to start this drive in the morning since the waterfalls and much of the best scenery face east.

Highway 19 was constructed to make it easier and faster to travel this part of the island. Consequently, most people are totally unaware of the almost forgotten stretches of road that make up the old highway. We have a particular fondness for these diversions off the highway and point them out as DIVERSION ALERTS.

LEAVING HILO BEHIND

Heading north (see map on page 125) you will see a sign on the ocean side past the 4 mile marker that says ALAE. Take Nahala Road, then turn left at the T. You pass by **Honoli'i Beach Park**. This is the primo surfing and boogie

DIVERSION ALERT!

boarding spot on this side of the island. There are stairs leading down to the black sand beach. The road continues around the back of the stream. When it ends, hang a right to go back to the highway, then left. This is probably a good time to mention that, while stopping at scenic spots along here, during certain times of the year, it's a good idea to have mosquito repellent. Sometimes they are absent; other times they are ferocious. Feeling lucky?

Past the 7 mile marker is the only part of the old highway that is marked. This 4-mile **scenic route** is breathtaking—do *not* miss it—and leads past the **Hawai'i Tropical Botanical Garden** (964–5233). (Consider the 4-mile drive a NOT TO BE MISSED.) You don't have to be a "garden person" to appreciate this *stunningly* beautiful area that fronts Onomea Bay. For $15 (kids 16 and under are $5), you wander on a self-guided tour for about an hour through over 2,000 exotic types of marked flora.

A REAL GEM

(Umbrellas are thoughtfully provided but mosquito repellent is extra.) Birds abound in this Eden-like setting. The smell of flowers and fruit (especially mangos) fills the air. Onomea Falls is located on the grounds, which makes a nice place to stop and take in the surroundings. Views of the bay are unbeatable. $15 is pretty steep for a garden, but this is the Big Island's best. A mile past the garden is a food stand called **What's Shakin'** (964–3080) that serves exceptionally good smoothies. (They make 'em the way you're *supposed* to make 'em—starting with frozen bananas, not ice—*oh, yeah...*) They also have a small lunch menu with dependably great food.

Back on the highway between the 13 and 14 mile markers is a 3¾-mile road through former sugar land to **'Akaka Falls**. This free-fall plunge of 420 feet is best seen in the late morning. (This is a popular place with tour buses.) If you're in a hurry, walk left 3–5 *beautiful* minutes through lush

NOT TO BE MISSED!

Pololu Valley
Waimanu Valley
Waipi'o Valley
Kukuihaele
240
Honoka'a
0   5 MILES
19
19
Waimea
190
Kalopa State Park
Laupahoehoe
Mana Road (4WD)
Douglas Pit
200
Umauma Falls
Mauna Kea 13,796
Akaka Falls
19
Saddle
Road
Onomea Bay
Hawai'i Tropical Botanical Garden
Hilo

vegetation and over streams to the falls. There you'll find silver/white strands forming as the water hits the rocks on the way down. Otherwise, there is a 15–20 minute amble (and a few hills) through the lush bamboo-filled woods along with another waterfall. The latter is recommended if you have the time. Everything's paved. After visiting Akaka Falls, you'll want to stop at the Woodshop Gallery and Cafe for some homemade ice cream and the best collection of Hawaiian wood products we've seen on the island. Woodworkers can even purchase a plank of Hawaiian hardwood to take home. For food here see ISLAND DINING.

As you continue on Hwy 19, there is another piece of old road to take. It's shortly after the 14 mile marker on the mauka (mountain) side. It leads past Kolekole Park. The massive highway bridge in **DIVERSION ALERT!** front of you was part of an old railway. The great tsunami of 1946 carried away many of the girders, rendering the bridge useless. This was the deathblow for the railway, sparking the construction for the entire highway. During the week this is a great place to bring your Briquettes and cookables to make good use of the stone BBQs, full facilities and tranquil setting. (Though quiet during the week, it gets too rowdy on weekends to recommend.) The small waterfall and swimming hole is where most swim when the river isn't raging, since the black sand beach itself is too hazardous to swim. This is where the water from 'Akaka Falls ends up, so if you lost something up there, maybe you'll see it again here.

If you stay on this road, it crosses the highway, curves left and empties into Hakalau Bay. A rich, vine-filled forest dripping with life ushers you into the bay. A gate at the hairpin turn means you'll have to walk the last part. The ruins at the mouth on the east bank were from a mill destroyed during the tsunami. The swimming here is poor, but you can't say that about the view. Backtrack to the highway.

The bridge past the 16 mile marker boasts nice views of two waterfalls. As impressive as they are, they don't even come close to the multi-tiered beauty of Umauma Falls upstream. This may be the most stunning waterfall setting in the state. You can only

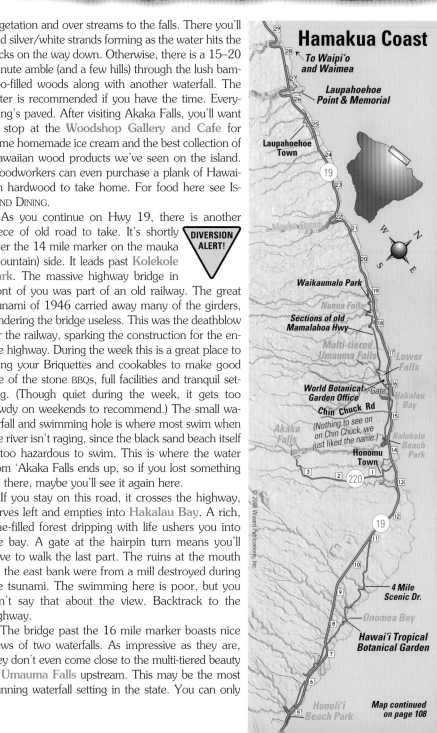

Hamakua Coast

To Waipi'o and Waimea

Laupahoehoe Point & Memorial

Laupahoehoe Town

Maulua Stream

Waikaumalo Park

Nanua Falls

Sections of old Mamalahoa Hwy

Multi-tiered Umauma Falls   Lower Falls

World Botanical Garden Office   Gate   Hakalau Bay

Chin Chuck Rd

(Nothing to see on on Chin Chuck, we just liked the name.)   Kolekole Beach Park

Akaka Falls   Honomu Town

4 Mile Scenic Dr.

Onomea Bay

Hawai'i Tropical Botanical Garden

Honoli'i Beach Park

© 2006 Wizard Publications, Inc.

Map continued on page 108

see it by visiting the World Botanical Gardens (963–5427). This is a relatively new garden, so don't expect much. Although they're obviously putting in a lot of effort, it'll be a long time before it's ready for prime time. A short stroll called the Rain Forest Walk has a few things to see and the garden adjacent to the visitor center has numerous plants neatly marked. Visitors are given free fruit. But their exclusive view of Umauma Falls from their road (⁶⁄₁₀ mile from the old highway—see map) is really the only reason to stop by and pay the $11 per person entry fee. (See the photo on page 128 to see if it's worth it to you.) Whether you plan to pay for the gardens or not (closed Sunday), *be sure* to backtrack ²⁄₁₀ mile from the highway bridge turnout, then take the road on the mauka side across from the 16 mile marker and turn right at the T. This 4-mile-long, one-lane country road passes through sugar land before it takes you to a small tree tunnel and several striking gulches. This is the Hawai'i of yesteryear, when life moved a bit slower. You might want to do the same. Stop at one of the old bridges and enjoy the peace. Vine-covered trees and ever-chirping birds give this area an unforgettable feel. One of the small Depression-era bridges crosses Nanue Stream (it's stamped into the bridge). The guard-rail 75 feet beyond the bridge has a crude and steep trail that leads down to the stream. From there a person could walk over to the top of the falls (don't fall off), or go upstream where taller waterfalls await. (The up-stream falls, though only 900 feet away, require *very* awkward stream hiking.) If you don't have mosquito repellent, be prepared for the bloodletting of a lifetime.

DIVERSION ALERT!

Bypass any opportunities to reconnect with the highway until you pass rarely used Waikaumalo Park near a pretty stream.

When you reacquire the highway just north of the 19 mile marker, you may want to backtrack less than a mile to see the densely jungled gulch and waterfall visible from the highway that you missed before continuing north.

What a drop! Akaka Falls tumbles 420 feet.

From a picnic table at Kolekole Beach Park you can either watch the ocean or watch kids swinging off a rope swing next to a waterfall. Talk about an embarrassment of riches!

As you effortlessly cruise these gulches on our modern bridges of today, try to visualize what a nightmare it must have been to cross them in days gone by. It took many days to get from Hilo to Waipi'o Valley. When Isabella Bird toured this area by horse in 1873, she wrote of the utter dread she felt as she plunged down and then trudged up gulch after harrowing gulch on her way to Waipi'o, fording raging streams on a snorting, terrified horse. Today, the hardest thing about traversing these gulches is resetting the cruise control after a sharp bend.

Just past the 25 mile marker is the road leading mauka to the town of **Laupahoehoe**. (The short road on the ocean side sports a nice view of the point mentioned below.) The town itself doesn't offer much other than a '50s-style restaurant (see ISLAND DINING), plus a store down a road on the *ocean* side of the Hwy ³⁄₁₀ past the 24 mile marker. It's just a store and they usually only have one hot meal to eat, so just ask what's for lunch today. (Their curry stew's not bad.)

Also on the highway is the **Laupahoehoe Train Museum** (962-6300). This assortment of artifacts and photos of Hamakua's history with trains is somewhat interesting. They have over a dozen volunteers. Some are extremely knowledgeable…and some aren't. It's $4.

Just past the 27 mile marker is a road on the ocean side that leads 1 mile down the cliffs to **Laupahoehoe Point**. To many on the Big Island, Laupahoehoe is associated with tragedy. During the April Fool's Day tsunami of 1946, twenty-one schoolchildren and three adults were swept to their deaths. Following this, the village was moved topside. The views from the road down to the rugged point sport dramatic views of the sea cliffs beyond and is well worth the stop. There is a memorial at the bottom to those who lost their lives. From out on the jetty, the ocean's energy feels raw and menacing. Waves come in with powerful anger. You feel (and are) exposed to the ocean's fury on the jetty and here it's not

DIVERSION ALERT!

Umauma Falls is the only waterfall on the island you have to pay to see. Is it worth it? You decide...

the calm, soothing ocean of Kona, but rather the unpredictable, hot-tempered ocean of Laupahoehoe. Away from the jetty the surf pounds against the twisted and jagged lava and is spectacular to watch, especially when surf's up, but don't even *think* of swimming here at any time. In 1985 a barge full of brand new Toyotas broke loose from its tug and washed ashore near here, spilling the entire cargo. When an insurance adjuster from Lloyd's of London came to check it out, he insisted on landing on the deck of the wrecked ship in a helicopter. Then a wave knocked the chopper over, drowning the adjuster. Surf is almost always violent here.

This whole area was once dominated by sugar. Over 70,000 acres of the Big Island were under cultivation. Even with generous government subsidies, the last mill shut down in 1996, ending 150 years of sugar production. Today this area has a new look and a new crop. More than 24,000 acres of fast-growing eucalyptus trees have been planted, and now Hamakua is known as tree-farming country.

Between the 39 and 40 mile markers is the road to **Kalopa Native Forest State Park**, which offers nice hiking and camping. See ACTIVITIES.

HONOKA'A

Near the 42 mile marker is a road through the town of **Honoka'a**. Most merely use it to get to **Waipi'o Valley**, described below, but while on the main road in Honoka'a, stop by **Mamane Bakery** for limited but extremely delicious baked goods. You have a few other eating options described in DINING.

WAIPI'O VALLEY

Waipi'o Valley is as beautiful a place as you will ever visit. With unimaginably steep walls on all sides, waterfalls etching

A REAL GEM

the perimeter, fields of taro and a luscious mile-long black sand beach, Waipi'o never fails to impress. The instant you arrive at the lookout above this awesome spectacle, you realize why this place was so special to the ancient Hawaiians. Because of its inspiring and tranquilizing effects, Waipi'o was often chosen as the meeting place for chiefs when important decisions, such as the succession of the king, were made. Even the kings who resided in sunny Kona had residences in Waipi'o Valley. According to Hawaiian legend, Waipi'o Valley was gouged out by a powerful warrior with his club to demonstrate his power. (Unfortunately, the warrior was himself clubbed to death by the one he was trying to impress.)

At one time thousands of people lived here, meticulously cultivating the lush valley floor with everything from bananas to taro to coconuts. Even Waipi'o pigs were considered tastier here in the Big Island's breadbasket. During times of famine, you could always count on Waipi'o Valley for much-needed sustenance. Fifty generations of Hawaiians have lived and died here, and they believe that the spiritual *mana*, or supernatural power left by those departed, is preserved and felt to this day.

As an infant, Kamehameha was hidden away here soon after he was born to avoid a death sentence by the king of the Big Island, who feared the prophecy that the child would one day rule the island.

The peace of Waipi'o Valley was shattered by the great tsunami of 1946 that washed away nearly everything. Most people moved away and the valley was left mostly wild for two decades. Then in the '60s and early '70s people started trickling back in. Most were hippies and recently discharged veterans who wanted to "get away from it all." Others soon joined. These days Waipi'o is populated by a colorful assortment of 50 or so characters (including an inordinate number of people named Dave). Many have turned their backs on traditional society; others simply live there to experience the grace of nature at its grandest. Lots of feuds take place down here, and it's not uncommon for one to result in a building getting torched. Police hesitate to get involved in Waipi'o disputes, so residents usually settle things on their own.

Those who live in the valley have no power, water, sewage, phones, cell or TV coverage. Solar power and generators provide the electricity they need. (A few nearside residents have phones and power courtesy of small lines stretching down into the valley.) They share their valley with two herds of wild horses (the swamp horses and the bush horses) that were left by the departing residents after the tsunami of '46. There are some who live "topside" and come down daily or on weekends to tend their taro patches.

Land ownership is a big issue. Even the biggest landowner in Hawai'i, Bishop Estate, has trouble proving how much of the valley they own. Dueling surveyors keep boundaries in flux. When Bishop tried to block access to a beach parcel in 1997, all of their signs were torn down and Bishop gave up.

Today the allure of Waipi'o Valley is beckoning outsiders. Visitors and residents alike enjoy the splendor of Waipi'o. Experienced surfers and boogie boarders ride the waves off the black sand beach. Hikers are enthralled by the scenery. Horseback rides are popular. And Waipi'o Valley Shuttle takes groups down the steep road. Does all this mean that Waipi'o is ablaze with activity? Not really. To you and me, Waipi'o is a quiet, peaceful place. But if you've had the

place all to yourself for years, even a few people a week would seem like a crowd. The residents here range from the friendly to the grouchy to the *very* weird. We've found that we are less likely to get a smile or a wave in this valley than anywhere else on the island, in sharp contrast to the friendly folks in Kukuihaele and Honoka'a above. Stink eye (dirty looks) and overall unfriendliness from some residents is common. Perhaps it's because they see visitors as antithetical to the reason they chose to live in Waipi'o in the first place. Whatever. At any rate, you should feel free to explore and enjoy the valley; just don't expect a big hug from some of the people who live there.

Getting Into the Valley

Don't even think about driving a regular car down Waipi'o Valley Road. The paved one-lane road down into the valley has a ridiculously steep *25%* grade. Vehicles with 4WD and low gears (so you don't burn up your brakes) can make it down the 900-foot descent (in less than a mile). Regular cars simply can't. (There is a wad of metal that was once a two-wheel drive truck below one of the turns left by someone who thought otherwise. He miraculously survived by jumping from the vehicle just as it started tumbling down the almost vertical plunge.) You would probably be violating your rental car agreement if you brought your SUV down here, meaning that they won't come save your bacon if it breaks down. Downhill traffic yields to uphill traffic, so use the turnouts. While driving down the road, the extreme angle makes it feel like the back of your vehicle is about to flip right over the top of you.

While the overlook sports an unforgettable view of the valley and along the coast, it gives you only a taste of what the valley has to offer. The view from the valley floor with its numerous waterfalls is even better. If you don't have an SUV (or nerve) you can take Waipi'o Valley Shuttle (775–7121). For $45 they'll take you into the valley on a 1½-hour *limited* tour. You can get off and try to catch the next shuttle back up, but don't count on an open space. (Or any cooperation—they can be downright rude to deal with.) They are nearby in the town of Kukuihaele (shown on map on next page). A better way is Waipi'o Valley Wagon Tours (775–9518). For $45 they take you on the same 1½-hour tour in a mule-driven wagon. (A half hour of it gets you into and out of the valley by 4WD.) Wagons hold 10 passengers and the driver narrates the sights in a similar way, but with the added charm of being in an open-air wagon. Neither of the above operate on Sunday.

If you want a better tour, Waipi'o Na'alapa Trail Rides (775–0419) has outstanding horseback rides in the valley. They'll shuttle you down into the valley and take you back a ways. See HORSEBACK RIDING for more.

If you want to hike down into Waipi'o Valley just walk the road to the bottom. (Oh, is *that* all?) Though less than a mile going down, you'd swear it was 5 miles coming up. Just take your time. Waipi'o is a great place to spend the afternoon. At the bottom, the beach is to your right. Past the right (eastern) side of the beach at the shore is Kaluahine Falls. (The falls are sometimes dry.) If you kept walking along the beach boulders below the cliff for 20–120 minutes (depending on your surefootedness),

you'd come to the larger Waiulili Falls ⅔ mile from the beach. It drops almost directly into the ocean and is nearly always deserted. Bear in mind that even on calm days, the ocean could always toss a rogue wave at you while you are walking on the dry boulders, and that could ruin your day. Waipi'o Beach is often treacherous to swim unless the surf is real calm. Rip currents are a problem, and the power of the waves is impressive. Legend states that the door to the underworld is near Waipi'o Beach, so Hawaiians were always careful where they camped, lest they should take the one-way trip there themselves.

The back part of Waipi'o Valley is awesome. In the first nook you'll find

Waipi'o Valley is a lush wonderland where taro farming is still the main occupation.

Waipiʻo Valley & Old Mamalahoa Hwy

© 2006 Wizard Publications, Inc.

N
W E
S

2 MILES

Nearly all of the coast in this area is composed of sea cliffs.

40 Miles to Hilo

42

Old Mamalahoa Hwy

19

Golf

1

Maile

Lehua

240

Honokaʻa

43

44

Kalehua Rd

Ahualoa

2

3

45

Kahana Rd

46

Old Mamalahoa Hwy

4

5

Hamakua Coast Hwy / Mamane St

6

(New) Mamalahoa Hwy (Hawaii Belt Rd)

47

(Hamakua Ditch)

7

Indicates Foot Trails
67 **Roadside mile markers**
Unpaved Roads
Cave

48

Cave #3
20°02.834'
155°32.563'

8

49

Waiulili Falls

Kaluahine Falls off the coast

Dahana Ranch

240

9

Kukuihaele

50

Hamakua Ditch

Exceptional view from this switchback

Waipiʻo Bay

Hiʻilawe Falls

Waimea Golf Course

51

52

To Waimanu Valley

Perfect pool for a dip

Waipiʻo Valley

Falls
Gate

Falls

Mud Lane

Note: Dirt roads shown as dashed lines in Waipiʻo Valley are county roads.

53

19

1 Mile To Waimea

Map continued on page 135

twin falls of staggering heights. The upper part of the one on the left was shut off by a now-defunct sugar company when they diverted the water. *(Grumble, grumble.)* At press time it was supposed to be turned back on at any time. The other, Hi'ilawe Falls, is 1,450 feet high with a free fall of 1,200 feet, the highest on the island. You'll see it when you head inland after you've reach the bottom of the road. Hikers can get there with some difficulty; see ADVENTURES.

Mosquito repellent should be required by law for hikers here. The bugs are not always around, but when they are in a foul mood—watch out! Remember while walking around that the roads are county roads and are public access. At one place there is a sign saying END OF COUNTY ROAD. According to the county official we spoke to, that's a crock. The sign was stolen from a construction site to dissuade you. Part of the road near the sign *looks* like a stream. Two hundred feet or so are flooded with taro runoff, but it is usually driveable. See map. Other illegal signs farther back also falsely indicate road closures. Just before the apparent end of the road a waterfall via a short trail on the left side provides a grand respite. The falls are intermittent.

The trail you see zig-zagging up the wall on the far side of Waipi'o Valley goes up then down into the next valley, Waimanu. The third switchback (400 feet up the trail cut pretty deeply into the mountain) offers a far grander view of the valley than from the automobile lookout. You can see the back of the valley, the twin falls and lots more. Waimanu is much farther along the trail. It is utterly gorgeous, devoid of residents, and camping is allowed for those who are willing to make the trek.

Call Forestry & Wildlife (974–4221) for permits one month ahead of time. Don't try to go and come back as a day hike. It's too long, and you can't see Waimanu Valley from the trail until you have mostly descended.

OLD MAMALAHOA HIGHWAY

Leaving Waipi'o and Honoka'a behind, get back on Hwy 19. Along this stretch of the highway, between the 43 and 52 mile markers, there **DIVERSION ALERT!** is another forgotten piece of The Old Mamalahoa Highway. Again the scenery on Old Mamalahoa is much nicer than Hwy 19 and worth the diversion. Lush, green hillsides bracket this old, country road. Mist and rain mean that lovers of green will be very happy. If you like caves, there are several along Old Mamalahoa Highway. The best, by far, is labeled on the map as cave #3. You should bring two flashlights. (There are lots of long chambers snaking pitch black into the mountain and, though tall enough to walk upright in, you'd be groping till the cows come home if you lost your only flashlight toward the back of some of these chambers.) The entrances are often dripping with ferns. Cave #3 has lots of structures inside (such as walls and platforms), presumably built by early Hawaiians, and a few empty drinking bottles, presumably left a bit later. The other caves labeled are much less impressive. These caves are in old Mauna Kea flows, and it's unusual for lava tube caves to last so long.

WAIMEA

This town is often labeled Kamuela on maps. That's because there are two other Waimeas in the state, so the Post Office named the local branch Kamuela— Hawaiian for Samuel (as in Samuel Parker; see below). Many locals object to the use of Kamuela, so we will use the original name in deference.

On the surface, Waimea seems like the least Hawaiian town in Hawai'i. In fact, if Scotty had beamed you here and asked you where you were, Hawai'i would probably be the last state you'd guess. At 2,600 feet, the air has a cool crispness to it. Clouds slither over the saddle between Kohala and Mauna Loa volcanoes, often bathing Waimea in a cool fog. Evergreen trees and cactus sit side by side, and the trees all seem blown in one direction. (Kind of like your hair if you've rented a convertible.) Rather than seeing surfers in shorts and aloha shirts, you're more apt to see Hawaiian cowboys (called paniolos) wearing blue jeans and driving pick-up trucks. (A brief visit to a magazine rack, and you'll think, "I never knew there were so many *truck* magazines.")

Life runs a little slower here, and families are a bit closer knit. Many people compare its appearance to a Northern California rural town, but prettier. As you drive through town from the east side of the island, note how quickly the terrain changes from lush upland forests and green pastures to dry lava scrubland. If it's raining in Waimea (a common occurrence) and you're heading to Kohala via Hwy 19, it'll stop raining less than 5 minutes after you leave Waimea—*guaranteed, brah*.

Don't be lulled into thinking that Waimea is a hick town. It is remarkably over-represented when it comes to fine shopping and has several restaurants that are utterly superb. Some of the homes up in the Waimea Homesteads where the descendants of cattle magnates live are absolutely beautiful.

PARKER RANCH

The town is dominated by the legacy of John Palmer Parker. When Captain George Vancouver brought long-horned cattle to Kamehameha as a gift in 1793, the king made them kapu (off limits) for 10 years to build up the numbers. By 1815 the wild herds that roamed Kohala were so ferocious that locals steered clear of them. Marauding cattle were known to drive Hawaiians from their homes by munching and goring everything in sight, even the homes themselves. Kamehameha the Great hired Massachusetts-born John Palmer Parker to shoot them, salt the meat and bring it to the harbor to sell to passing ships. This was no easy task. Long-horned cattle of that time were not like the tame, mindless morons we know today. They were wily, lean and stealthy. They would charge men on horseback, goring them. They lived in the valleys and canyons as well, making them very difficult to detect. Good horses became the equivalent of hunting dogs—they would smell the wild cattle before they saw them, and their ears would perk up, warning their rider to the danger. Because Parker possessed a musket and good shooting skills, Kamehameha made him the first person ever allowed to kill the cattle. Parker took great pains to select cattle with favorable traits and kept them for himself as payment. These he domesticated, starting the Parker herd.

As a totally irrelevant aside, one of the casualties of these cattle was the Scottish botanist David Douglas. He's the guy for whom Douglas fir trees were named. He was walking near Mana Road on the slopes of Mauna Kea one day when he fell into one of the covered pits used as a cattle trap. (Some said he was thrown in.) Although he was lucky enough to survive the fall, so was the bull already occupying the pit. The unhappy bovine made his displeasure known by goring Douglas to death. Douglas Pit is 28 miles into Mana Road from Waimea.

Back of Waipi'o Valley

Map continued on page 132

20 Miles to Hawi

Waimea Park

Waimea Center

250

19

59 Kawaihae Rd

9 Miles to Kawaihae

53 Miles → to Hilo

White (Lindsey) Rd

Mana Road

Mana Road

Mamalahoa Hwy

Kahilu Rd

Kamamalu

Mamalahoa

Kapiolani

Opelo

Indicates Foot Trails

67 Roadside mile markers

Unpaved Roads

N W E S

0 — 1 MILE

Upper Hamakua Ditch

Restaurant Row

Parker Ranch Historic Homes

Parker Ranch Center / Visitor Center

Paniolo Park

36 Miles to Kailua-Kona ↓ 190

Waimea-Kohala Airport

To Parker Ranch Land
Dirt road leads 44 miles around base of Mauna Kea to Mauna Kea Road (near Saddle Road). After 18 miles, there is a 5 mile stretch that is 4WD or mountain bike only.

❶ Jacaranda Inn
❷ Kamuela Inn
❸ Waimea Country Lodge

John Parker himself was a colorful character. A lover of adventure, he was a natural born risk-taker who, though a long-range planner, felt strongly that part of wisdom is to know the value of today. He was well loved and respected by his contemporaries. (But he sure wasn't very photogenic—in his dour photo he makes Ebenezer Scrooge look like Mr. Rogers.)

In 1816 John Parker married Kamehameha the Great's granddaughter, forever cementing the bond between him and the royal family. He was eventually allowed to purchase two acres of land. His wife, because of her royal blood, was later granted 640 acres, and he bought another 1,000 acres. Thus was born what would become the largest privately owned cattle ranch in the entire United States, peaking at over 225,000 acres, 9% of the Big Island. Parker and his descendants would go on to become very powerful on the island.

Later, when Kamehameha III realized that Hawai'i was lacking in people knowledgeable in the ways of cattle ranching, he arranged for three Mexican cowboys to come to the Big Island and teach the locals about ranching. Nearly all Big Island paniolo traditions descend from these three cowboys.

Parker Ranch was severely neglected by subsequent Parkers. John Parker's grandson, Samuel Parker, was a flamboyant playboy who spent money like water and had a genius for making profoundly stupid investments. Unlike King Midas, everything *he* touched turned to manure. As the aging Parker II saw money pouring down Samuel's many ratholes, he began to squirrel away funds as fast as he could. But when the time came to retrieve the money, the old man could not remember where he had hidden most of it. To this day, much of the fortune Parker II hid away has never been found. In 1900 the family hired a Honolulu attorney to manage and rejuvenate the ranch. This he did with a vengeance, turning a dying relic into a powerful and very lucrative operation.

The serenity of Waimea was broken in the 1990s when Richard Smart, the descendent of John Palmer Parker, died, leaving some of his $450 *million* estate to his family, but the bulk of the land (139,000 acres) to a non-profit trust. Lawsuits started flying from disgruntled family members angry about their share, and it was beginning to look as if the ranch might be broken up and fed to the lawyers and tax collectors. Fortunately, the dispute was finally settled and peace once again returned to sleepy little Waimea.

Most of Parker Ranch is mile after mile of rolling, grassy hills and wide open plains interrupted by rows of trees for windbreaks. Owls, pheasant and wild turkeys crisscross the ranch, while ever-chewing cows wander about. The ranch consists of several non-contiguous segments of land, and its 35,000 cattle are controlled by a mere 12 paniolo (Hawaiian cowboys). The road across from the 55 mile mark (see Waimea map, on previous page, or graphic below) slices through Parker Ranch. Called **Mana Road**, it goes 44 miles around Mauna Kea mountain to Mauna Kea Road (off Saddle Road). 2WD vehicles can drive it for the first part to see what the ranch looks like. After 18 miles there's a 5-mile segment that requires 4WD (it'll seem like more than 5), plus there's an area with confusing but *presumably* parallel roads. Otherwise, you can go as far as your desire takes you. Close any gates that you open (all 4 of them). According to the county, it is a *public* right of way, despite any signs you may see that *imply* the contrary. Avoid if it's been too rainy; some of the puddles can be big enough to waterski in.

DIVERSION ALERT!

Parker Ranch gives 45-minute **wagon tours** of a *small* section of their ranch for $15. Not a thrill-a-minute tour, it's... *marginally* interesting. Call them at 885–7655. They also have ATV and horseback tours available.

A successful cattle ranch is first and foremost a grass farm. After being raised on sweet Hawaiian range grass for 5–6 months, most of the cattle are shipped by boat or 747 to the mainland or Canada, then fattened in various areas before slaughter. (Ironically, cattle class on a 747 has more leg room than what you had in coach.) In the old days, just getting the cows to the ship was a traumatic process. They were driven to Kawaihae, forced into the ocean, then lashed to the outside of small boats, which ferried them to the main ship

Parker Ranch Shown in Dark Areas

19

190 200

Mana Rd→

where they were belly-hoisted aboard. Now they simply walk onto an old cruise ship, into stalls, and off they go. If you want to get an idea of what Big Island beef tastes like, the best (and most consistent) source is Foodland (885–2022) located in Parker Ranch Center. The range-fed beef is darker and stronger than grain-fed beef and is particularly good marinated. Fresh deliveries are usually Tuesdays and Thursdays. Grocery stores around the island usually have beef flown in from the mainland.

Visitors to Waimea often stop by the Parker Ranch Historic Homes (885–5433). One of these homes was purchased in 1879 by John Palmer Parker II. It was used as a ranch home until it was converted to a French provincial home in the 1960s by his descendent, Richard Smart. Full of fine European art and furniture, the home's entrance fee is $8.50. This fee also allows admittance to the house next door. It contains the original koa interior of the Parker home located 12 miles away at Mana, which was built in the mid-1800s. With Hawaiian koa wood everywhere (floors, ceiling, stairs, etc.), you'll see the kind of house the rich lived in a century and a half ago. (Floors of that era make a surprising amount of noise when you walk on them.)

The Parker Ranch Visitors Center (885–7655) in the Parker Ranch Center shows a video of the Parker Ranch history and has a small museum. It's $6.50 to get in.

One of the prettiest hikes on the island is above Waimea. It overlooks the back side of Waipi'o Valley and is off White Road and described under HIKING.

Past Waimea heading into Kohala, sights are described in the Kohala section.

HAMAKUA & WAIMEA SHOPPING

The Parker Ranch Center has lots of shops including Journeys and Reyn's, which both offer men's and women's aloha wear. Parker Ranch Store has all kinds of paniolo and Parker Ranch logo items.

Heading down Kawaihae Rd., The Quilted Horse in the High Country Traders Building is a good place to pick up island-made foods, clothing and gifts.

Next door is Parker Square with many outstanding shops such as Bentley's and Gallery of Great Things. Pick up something for your kids at Imagination Toys. Mauna Kea Galleries across from the Edelweiss Restaurant is a good stop for vintage Hawaiiana.

After leaving Waipio Valley lookout, drive by Kukuihaele for Waipio Valley Artworks, which features an outstanding selection of Hawaiian wood pieces and other gifts. Ice cream is next door. Up the road in Honoka'a on Mamane St., there are some stores worth stopping for. Taro Patch, Maya's Clothing & Gifts, and Mary Guava Designs have some unique clothing, home and gift items. The Honoka'a Marketplace has the Mary Guava Boutique with a large selection of Hawaiian design quilts.

HAMAKUA & WAIMEA'S BEST BETS

Best Garden—Hawai'i Tropical Botanical Garden
Best Waterfall—Umauma Falls
Best Place to Ride a Horse—Waipi'o
Best View (Easy)—Waipi'o Overlook
Best View (Hard)—From the zigzag trail on *other* side of Waipi'o Valley
Best Treats—Mamane Bakery in Honoka'a
Best Place to Get Stink Eye—Waipi'o
Best Hole to Avoid—Douglas Pit
Best Picnic Table—Kolekole Beach Park

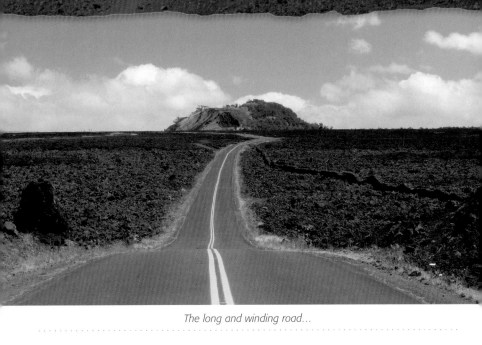

The long and winding road...

Saddle Road runs between our largest volcanoes, Mauna Loa and Mauna Kea. The entire area is called the Saddle because of the saddle-shaped valley between the two mountains. It travels through some unpopulated and very surreal-looking country and is worth considering if you are driving from one side to the other.

The saddle crests at an impressive 6,578 feet. That's some saddle. The 53-mile-long road has a bad and outdated reputation. It was hastily built by the military in 1942 for strategic purposes. This was wartime and they wanted a road connecting the two sides of the island, and they wanted it fast. They didn't design it with general traffic in mind; it was meant for military vehicles. Even today, driving on Saddle Road is prohibited in many rental car agreements, meaning your Collision Damage Waiver with them won't cover you. A few years ago their fears were quite well founded. The road had been paved by *Sadists-R-Us* and was a body shop's dream. But now it's in decent shape. It's still a winding, hilly road with blind turns that aren't banked. Think of it as a roller coaster for your car. Traffic is almost always sparse. It's two (narrow) lanes wide, but most drive the road's center (on the Kona side of the saddle) when nobody's coming their way. There are no lights and only a fool drives it at night. (We came out here in the middle of the night to watch a comet a few years back and *got chicken skin fo days*—i.e., it was spooky. The only sound was a lone birthing cow screaming in the blackness.) The road is often licked by fog toward the center crest. But all in all, it's not as bad as when the rental car companies first made the decision to keep you off it.

Some companies, like Harper and Alamo (See BASICS), have no qualms about letting you drive on it. The government is in the process of straightening portions of Saddle Road. It'll take place over several years and should provide some relief when it's finished.

So why drive Saddle Road? Three reasons. First, it's the only way to drive to Mauna Kea. Second, it cuts between Mauna Kea and Mauna Loa and has some nice sights. The landscape is otherworldly in places and decidedly different. Third, it's kind of fun (if you like winding roads). If your question is, "Yeah, but do *you* bring your personal car on it?"—the answer is yes. (As we all know, *drive it like a rental* is like saying, *drive it like it's stolen*.) It's not necessarily a shortcut, though. It's a shorter distance, but you can't drive it as fast as Hwy 19, known locally as *the upper road.* Some people love taking Saddle Road; others feel intimidated. I guess it depends on your personality. We like to take it from the Kona side and return from Hilo on the upper road. In 50 miles the terrain

goes from dry lava scrub land to rolling green hills and plains to young lava fields to dripping fern-covered forests. With this in mind, we'll describe it from west to east. There's no **gas** on this road; get it in Waikoloa Village or Waimea in the west, Hilo in the east.

Look at the foldout back cover map to familiarize yourself with the route and to put it in context. From the intersection of Saddle Road (200) and Hwy 190, you leave lava land behind and enter rolling plains of grasses. Keep an eye out for wild turkey (the bird, not the booze) and pheasant, which are plentiful here.

As you ascend to the crest of this saddle, you'll get an idea of the scale of Mauna Kea on your left and Mauna Loa on your right. The military often drive this road in their HUMVEES and other camouflaged vehicles. If you stop and listen, you'll often hear the booms of artillery from the Pohakuloa Military Training Area. Sometimes you'll see their choppers swooping low like a scene out of

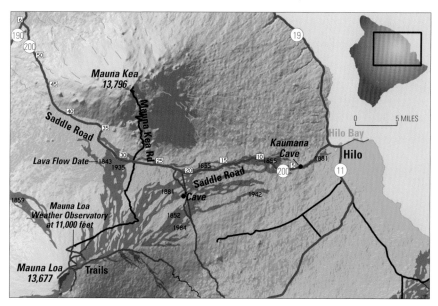

Apocalypse Now. Tanks and Armored Personnel Carriers also use this road on occasion. (We respectfully suggest that you *always* give armored tanks the right of way.)

Near the 44 mile marker is a dirt road on the left side. If you have a 4WD, check out the adventure described on page 236.

Mauna Kea State Park is at the 35 mile marker. After you turn into the park, there are restrooms and a phone to your right. Cabins are available (See CAMPING on page 180.)

Back on the highway, note the rock wall just before the 29 mile marker on the right (southern) side. Follow it and you'll see where it was covered by the Mauna Loa flow of 1935.

You'll find the road up Mauna Kea (on your left) is marked by a large mound, called **Pu'u Huluhulu** (hairy hill) shown on page 138. This pu'u is a good place to stretch if you want to walk to the top. (If you have kids, this is a good place to let 'em burn off some of that extra energy.)

It's an old cinder cone created by Mauna Kea long ago and has been surrounded by more recent lava flows from Mauna Loa. (You can tell by scars on the side that it was once mined for its cinders.) The main trail is on the far (east) side of Pu'u Huluhulu, just off the road to Mauna Loa, on your right. There are several trails on top of this forested mound. Just generally stay to the right at major intersections, and it'll take you around and to the bottom on the other side. The splendid view, as well as the birds, make it a short but worthwhile diversion.

MAUNA KEA

If someone asked you to climb from the base of Mauna Kea to the summit (which is more than 13,000 feet above sea level), you'd have to climb over 30,000 feet. (The base of Mauna Kea just happens to be 17,000 feet *below* sea level.) Those wimps who climb from the base of Mt. Everest to the summit only have to climb a mere 12,000 feet. (Its base just happens to start at 17,000 feet

Mauna Kea

Summit

Ancient Adz Quarry
19°48.068'
155°28.097'

Unpaved Rd.

Mauna Kea Trail

Visitor Center
9,200 feet

Mauna Kea Rd.

Mana Road

Summit Close-up

Keck

Summit
●13,796'

U of H Scope

Mauna Kea State Park
35

Restrooms & Telephones

Saddle Road

31

28

22

25 200

14.7 Miles to Mauna Kea Summit

17.4 Miles to Mauna Loa Weather Observatory

Pu'u Huluhulu
Crest of Saddle at 6,578 feet

Lake Wai-au
19°49.020'

19°48.662'
155°26.629'

© 2006 Wizard Publications, Inc.

With clouds below you and clouds above you, the summit of Mauna Kea feels like you're half way to heaven.

above sea level.) Everest, too, is located in a warm latitude, 28°, as far south as sweltering Orlando, Florida. But people still freeze to death in the summer on Everest because the summit's high altitude (29,035 feet) offsets the warm latitude.

The second of the five surviving volcanoes to create the island, Mauna Kea (meaning White Mountain) pokes its head 13,796 feet above the ocean. In its prime, half a million years ago, Mauna Kea was 3,500 feet higher. But it gets shorter with age. It shrinks every day, settling under its own weight, and bending the ocean floor beneath it. The ancient Hawaiians considered it the home of Poli'ahu, the snow goddess. She and Madame Pele, next door on Mauna Loa, didn't always get along very well, and the saddle between Mauna Loa and Mauna Kea was said to be their battleground. The ancient Hawaiians were uncomfortable in this region, not wishing to get in the middle of this domestic disturbance.

Atop the mountain, the air is thin and incredibly clear. Scientists recognized this spot as possibly the best place in the world to observe stars and have been placing the world's finest telescopes up here for years. (The *twinkle, twinkle* of the little star is caused by air turbulence, and the air above Mauna Kea is some of the least turbulent in the world—windy, but not turbulent.) With little precipitation (except for the occasional blizzard), little in the way of city lights below, and relatively easy access, Mauna Kea is the pride of the astronomical community. Two dozen of the finest telescopes in the world are sprinkled about the summit or are in the works. One area up there is called Millimeter Valley since its peepers are designed to look not in the optical wavelength, but rather at the high end of the radio band, in the much longer millimeter and sub-millimeter wavelength. This allows scientists to look through cosmic clouds and watch stars being born. Some of these telescopes can look at objects over 12 billion light years away, meaning that the light they are seeing left those objects long before the earth and sun were even born. The mighty Keck telescope has a 33-foot wide viewing surface. The moveable part weighs 300 tons but is so perfectly balanced that it can be moved *with one hand.*

Here's a thought for you: Look around at all the infrastructure necessary to look at the stars—the roads, the buildings, the computers, the people, the research, the scopes themselves. All of these things and the hundreds of millions of dollars they cost are here for a single purpose: to hold *one tenth of an ounce* of metal in a specific shape. That's how much aluminum coats the giant mirrors that gather all the starlight and where all the information comes from.

Tours of the **University of Hawai'i Telescope** are given Saturdays and Sundays. Call 961–2180 beforehand for more information. Call 935–6268 for a recorded weather update of Mauna Kea. (It's not usually updated in the summer.) Except during summit tours, visitors won't be able to visit the inside of any of the telescopes except U of H and Keck (labeled on map), which has a visitors' gallery open weekdays, as well as restrooms. You'll get a glimpse through the window of the telescope itself there. (As cold as it gets outdoors, it feels even colder in the temperature-controlled rooms housing the telescopes.)

The view from atop Mauna Kea can only be described as majestic moonscape. The Apollo astronauts did considerable training up here because it was deemed uniquely moon-like. Looking down on the clouds *below* is mesmerizing. It's a cliché but true—you feel like you're on top of the world! Off in the distance, the still-active volcano of Mauna Loa seems bigger than life, especially from a place about 2 miles down the road from the summit. Ironically, Mauna Loa's massive size makes it appear smaller than Mauna Kea. *(Huh?!)* Because Mauna Loa rises so gently to its 13,677-foot height, you don't get the sense of size that you would if it were steeper, like Mauna Kea. But that very gentle slope hides a volume of rock far greater than Mauna Kea—10,000 *cubic miles* of stone. From atop Mauna Kea, the islands of Maui, Moloka'i and Kaho'olawe can

The only one of its kind—a tropical lake fed by permafrost.

be seen on clear days. From this area people ski down the mountain to link up with the road below. The actual summit is a quick (5–10 short-of-breath minutes) hike from the University of Hawaii Observatory. (You'll see a faint trail before the pavement ends.) Sunsets from up here when clouds cooperate are an unrivaled splendor of unequaled expansiveness. The summit appears utterly lifeless except for a few unlucky bugs blown up from below and a few flightless native insects that feed on them. No trees, no plants. Just a lifeless void. The mountain last erupted 4,500 years ago and is considered dormant. (If it erupts when you are up there, please disregard this last statement.)

Also located near the top are two oddities. **Lake Wai-au**, at 13,020 feet, is one of the highest lakes in the United States and at first its existence defies explanation. What could be feeding it? There are no rivers at the top of a mountain, and natural springs need a higher source to gravitationally feed them (like water in a siphon tube). Rain and snow are insufficient, and the lake is here year round. The answer is *permafrost*. During the last Ice Age (and until 13,000 years ago), Mauna Kea was covered by a 20-square-mile glacier that was up to 350 feet thick and extended 3,200 feet below the summit. It carved and scoured the mountain and left permafrost several feet below the surface. Each day, as the sun heats up the mountain, it melts a fraction of the permafrost, which then works its way into Lake Wai-au. Though shallow, the ancient Hawaiians thought the lake was bottomless—probably because they couldn't find anyone crazy enough to venture into it at this frigid altitude. Lake Wai-au can be accessed by a 15–30 minute walk from the road. (See map and turn right when the trail intersects another trail. The upper trail, near the hairpin turn on Mauna Kea Road, is the easier trail.) Many of the gulches you see on the side of Mauna Kea were created when the glacier melted, sending the snowmelt to scour the sides of the mountain.

The other oddity up here is **Keana-kako'i**, an ancient Hawaiian adz quarry. (Adz is a stone cutter used for shaping wood.) When Mauna Kea erupted during the last ice age, the glacier cap cooled the lava very quickly. The result is the densest and hardest rock in all the islands (tougher than spring steel) and was the hardest substance in the state (except for the bread at a Kona restaurant we reviewed recently). What's impressive is that the ancient Hawaiians discovered this site (at 12,400 feet) and were able to successfully mine it for generations, trading it to other islanders for assorted goodies. The only trail to the adz quarry is down from Lake Wai-au. Coming back up involves a grueling 800-foot ascent, a genuine 'okole kicker at this altitude.

DRIVING UP TO MAUNA KEA

From Saddle Road it's 14⁷⁄₁₀ miles to the summit. About 2 miles into Mauna Kea Road is a dirt road on your right called **Mana Road**. It leads 44 miles *around* Mauna Kea Mountain all the way to Waimea and passes through tranquil forest. There's rarely anyone on Mana Road, and you need 4WD (or a mountain bike) to take it. The **Onizuka Center for International Astronomy** is 6 miles up Mauna Kea Road at 9,200 feet. Ellison Onizuka was a native of Kona and part of the crew of the Space Shuttle Challenger in 1986 that *"slipped the surly bonds of Earth to touch the face of God."*

The Visitor Center has a few displays and small telescopes that they break out at night for visitors. They also sell warmies (for those who came in shorts) and brake fluid (for brake-riders coming down the mountain), as well as water and some snacks like freeze-dried ice cream (really weird). They have some "interpreters," but they must spend a lot of time alone, because every time we try to get information out of them it's like interrogating a Klingon POW. There are restrooms available. About 50 people live up here (tending the 'scopes) and they have to bring their water in several times a week by truck.

While driving up this part of Mauna Kea Road, watch out for mindless, wayward cows occasionally wandering onto the road.

After the Visitor Center the road is unpaved for 5 miles before it becomes paved again for the last 3⁷⁄₁₀ miles. You are allowed access to the top of the mountain in any vehicle. 4WD is what astronomers are *hoping* you're driving because it causes less road wear, but countless regular cars drive it anyway. 4WD is also nice because the unpaved portion of the somewhat steep road

coming down can get a bit slippery at times, especially when wet. 4WD vehicles usually have a gear low enough to obviate this situation. We've found, however, that 4WD vehicles seem to fishtail *going up* more than 2WD cars do. The road is a bit washboardy and they'll often close it for a short time after a snow until they can plow it. (Finding a good snowplow repairman in Hawai'i must be about as easy as finding a good surfboard shaper in Kodiak, Alaska.)

If you don't want to drive it, several companies will pick you up on the west side and take you to the summit for sunset, then come down a bit for some stargazing and hot chocolate sipping for around $150 per person. They'll provide warm coats for you, and the total time is 7½ hours. See STARGAZING on page 222 for more.

Those who *really* want a challenge can opt to hike the trail from the Visitor Center to the top. (See map.) It's 15 miles round trip and a *very* tough day hike, even for the fittest. You need a very early start and should take precautions mentioned in the hiking section. Expect blinding headaches, extreme nausea and bewildered looks from anyone who ever finds out that you did it.

If you drive up, drink *plenty* of water before, during, and after, as dehydration is a severe problem at that altitude. Children, pregnant women and those with respiratory problems should avoid the summit. Try to avoid soft drinks and (how do I put this delicately?) foods that produce gas. (You figure it out.) Bring a can of unopened Pringles with you and watch how they explode when you open them up top. And consider chewing gum on the way down to help with your ears. Don't come up here within 24 hours of a SCUBA dive. As far as your nitrogen is concerned, you're flying. Altitude sickness can strike anyone, causing weakness, dizziness and nausea. Some claim that ibuprofen *before* the trip will help this, similar to the way aspirin is said to forestall hangovers, but we won't swear by it. Go slow and don't exert yourself too much. Acclimating for a half hour or so at the 9,200-foot visitor center can help.

Then there's the cold. Between November and April, snow is not uncommon. Even summertime brings the occasional freak snowstorm. During the rest of the year, it's often bone-chilling up there. Dress warm. *(Like you packed your parka for your Hawaiian vacation!)* The wind can be exceptionally fierce. It's often warm and calm up there, but you shouldn't *count* on it being this way. During the winter, you can snow ski short distances. See Snow Skiing under ACTIVITIES. When it snows, local residents often rush up the mountain to frolic. We've seen people dashing down the hill below the summit on every conceivable mode of transportation: skis, snowboards, sleds, boogie boards, surfboards, tarps—we've even seen people sliding down in *ocean kayaks,* complete with paddles!

According to King Kalakaua, the Hawaiians had their own version of the Ironman Triathlon. Here, the objective was to climb Mauna Kea during the winter, grab all the snow you could carry, bolt back down the mountain, and run all the way to the ocean. If you had enough snow for a snowball, you won. (If you didn't, you probably grabbed the winner's snowball and stuck it in his pants.) Ironically, this is still done. Only today people bring the snow back in pickup beds and throw a party when they get home. This may be the only place in the world where you can experience snow less than 30 miles from an 85° tropical resort area.

On your way down, a couple of miles below the Visitor Center, you *may* (clouds permitting) see the smoldering Pu'u 'O'o cone at Kilauea Volcano 30 miles to the southeast. Without question, the best views from Mauna Kea are while coming down, not going up.

MAUNA LOA

Across the saddle from Mauna Kea is the more active Mauna Loa (long mountain). This is the most difficult volcano summit on the island to access. You've got two choices, and both are a *buggah.* (See HIKING.) However, off Saddle Road a quarter mile east of the road up Mauna Kea, there is a narrow, paved road leading 17⁴⁄₁₀ miles up to the **Mauna Loa Weather Observatory,** just above the 11,000-foot level. From there the view across the saddle to Mauna Kea is stunning, especially if there is snow on top. Otherwise, Mauna Loa Observatory Road offers little for you. Created in 1958, the observatory is now used to measure gases to determine if global warming is occurring. Built near the top of a semi-active volcano, it is protected by a first-of-its-kind lava barrier on the upslope side designed to redirect any lava flows long enough to get the scientists out during an eruption. Someone (with *way* too much time on his hands) has painted a squiggly center line on this entire road, creating the illusion that this is a two-lane road. (Actually it was to help when driving in fog.) You might want to check out the pit crater across the street from telephone pole #200. It's about 50 feet from the road and 50 feet deep where lava drained after overflowing.

APPROACHING HILO

As you continue on Saddle Road, you'll descend toward Hilo. There's a pristine mile-long cave that you can hike to. See ADVENTURES on page 227. Look at the foldout back cover map to get an idea of where the lava has flowed during historic times. You'll be periodically passing through fields of it. The pavement is much nicer on the Hilo side of Saddle Road. Cynics would say that's because the politicians, who make the road maintenance decisions, always visit the summit from where they live (Hilo is the county seat), but we would *never* be so cynical.

You're on the windward side now, and things will start to get greener. One mile after the 7 mile marker (the 6th was missing at press time) you'll have to turn left to stay on Kaumana Dr. and Hwy 200. (Otherwise, the bypass—Hwy 2000—will take you to Hwy 11 if you remember to dog-leg to the right at the end of Hwy 200 onto Puainako—see Hilo map on page 108.) As you approach Hilo, before Hwy 200's 4 mile marker, you'll see **Kaumana Cave** on your left. Created by the Mauna Loa

lava flow of 1881 that traveled 25 miles and threatened Hilo, this lava tube skylight is saturated with green. Full-grown trees and ferns have taken over the cave and its entrance. It stands in stark contrast to other caves throughout the island. Elsewhere, a century-old lava tube would be little changed from when it was created. But here, in lush, wet Hilo, geologic time marches at a rapid pace. The cave looks old, worn and rickety. You can take the stairs to the bottom and peer in. Once down there, most people are immediately attracted to the large opening to the right, never even noticing the cave entrance to the left. Remember, this is simply an interruption in a 2-mile long lava tube. If you have a flashlight (make that two—it's so dark you can't tell whether your eyes are open or closed) and sufficient nerve, you can go cave exploring. (Called spelunking—in case that's the only word you forgot in your last crossword puzzle.) The cave to your right has more low overhangs between long stretches of tall ceilings, but the formations are more fascinating. To your left, after an initial low overhang, the cave is more cathedral-like. Tree roots occasionally poke through the ceiling. You could spend hours exploring this lava tube if you wanted.

This flow came within 1½ miles of Hilo Bay. Princess Ruth was sent from Honolulu to save Hilo. She stood in front of the lava flow beseeching Pele to stop the lava. That night she slept next to the advancing flow and by morning it had stopped. Today several hundred homes are built on the 1881 flow and can easily be recognized by their rock gardens.

Rainbow Falls and Boiling Pots are off Waianuenue Road in this area. See HILO SIGHTS for more on these.

In addition to the popular beaches, lesser known gems such as Kikaua Beach are scattered along the west side of the island.

The Big Island has the reputation of being the island without beaches. That's because in the past, lack of roads and lack of knowledge caused most of its more glorious beaches to go unnoticed. Granted, the island has fewer sand beaches per mile of shoreline than any of the other islands. It's newer, and plentiful beaches are the blessings of older, more mature islands. However, what beaches we *do* have, especially on the west side, are among the very best in the state. The water off the west side of the Big Island is the clearest, cleanest and often calmest water in all the islands. There is not one permanent stream on the entire west side, so cloudy river runoff is not a problem. And the shape of the island, along with the prevailing current, often gives the west side relatively gentle water. Rough water usually comes from the northeast. Kona and Kohala's calmer waters can be dramatically seen from the air.

During normal conditions, the inbound flier will notice that the transition from coarse, choppy channel waters to fine textured leeward waters is almost instantaneous, just south of the northernmost tip of the island.

On the Big Island we have white sand, black sand, salt-and-pepper sand and even green sand beaches. As for beach quality, Hapuna Beach is consistently named the best beach *in the entire country* by travel magazines. Mauna Kea Beach is not far behind. Kahalu'u and Honaunau offer outrageous snorkeling. And secluded gems like Makalawena and

Road to the Sea, along with unusual delights such as Kiholo Bay, Kapoho Tidepools, and Green Sand Beach probably makes beach-going on the Big Island the best in the state.

BEACH SAFETY

The biggest danger you will face at the beach is the surf. Though it is calmer on the west side of the Big Island, that's a relative term. Most mainlanders are unprepared for the strength of Hawai'i's surf. We're out in the middle of the biggest ocean in the world, and the surf has lots of room to build up. We have our calm days where the water is like glass. We often have days where the surf is moderate, calling for respect and diligence on the part of the swimmer. And we have the high surf days, perfect for sitting on the beach with a picnic or a mai-tai, watching the experienced and the audacious tempt the ocean's patience. Don't make the mistake of underestimating the ocean's power here. Hawai'i is the undisputed drowning capital of the United States, and we don't want you to join the statistics.

Other hazards include rip currents, which can form, cease and form again with no warning. Large "rogue waves" can come ashore with no warning. These usually occur when two or more waves fuse at sea, becoming a larger wave. Even calm seas are no guarantee of safety. Many people have been caught unaware by large waves during ostensibly "calm seas." We swam and snorkeled most of the beaches described in this book on at least two occasions (usually more than two). But beaches change. The underwater topography changes throughout the year. (White Sands Beach is a dramatic example.) Storms can take a very safe beach and rearrange the sand, turning it into a dangerous beach. Napo'opo'o

Beach vanished after a storm in 1992 and has yet to come back. Just because we describe a beach as being in a certain condition does not mean it will be in that same condition when you visit it.

Consequently, you should take the beach descriptions as a snapshot in calm times. If seas aren't calm, you probably shouldn't go in the water. If you observe a rip current, you probably shouldn't go in the water. If you aren't a comfortable swimmer, you should probably never go in the water, except at those beaches that have lifeguards. There is no way we can tell you that a certain beach will be swimmable on a certain day, and we claim no such prescience. There is no substitution for your own observations and judgment.

A few standard safety tips: Never turn your back on the ocean. Never swim alone. Never swim in the mouth of a river. Never swim in murky water. Never swim when the seas are not calm. Don't walk too close to the shorebreak; a large wave can come and knock you over and pull you in. Observe ocean conditions carefully. Don't let small children play in the water unsupervised. Fins give you far more power and speed and are a good safety device in addition to being more fun. If you're comfortable in a mask and snorkel, they provide considerable peace of mind, as well as opening up the underwater world. Lastly, don't let Hawai'i's idyllic environment cloud your judgment. Recognize the ocean for what it is—a powerful force that needs to be respected.

If you're going to spend any time at the shoreline or beach, reef shoes are the best investment you'll ever make. These water-friendly wonders accompany us whenever we go to any beach. Wal-Mart or Kmart in Kona sell cheap ones, perfect for your short-duration usage. Even on sandy beaches, rocks or sea life seem magnetically attracted to the bottom of feet. With reef shoes, you can frolic without the worry. (Though don't expect them to protect you from everything. Some beaches are backed by kiawe trees, and their thorns could probably penetrate an armored car.)

The ocean here rarely smells fishy since the difference between high and low tide is so small. (In other words, it doesn't strand large amounts of smelly sea plants at low tide like other locations.)

Theft can be a problem when visiting beaches. Visitors like to lock their cars at all beaches, but piles of glass on the ground usually dissuade island residents from doing that at secluded beaches. We usually remove anything we can't bear to have stolen and leave the car with the windows rolled up but unlocked. That way, we're less likely to get our windows broken by a curious thief. Regardless, don't leave anything of value in your car. (Well...maybe the seats can stay.) While in the water, we use a waterproof fanny pack (available at many outdoor stores) for our wallet, checkbook and keys, and leave everything else on the beach. Sometimes we only bring car keys and tie them to bathing suit drawstrings. We don't take a camera to the beach unless we are willing to stay there on the sand and baby-sit it. This way, when we swim, snorkel or just walk, we don't have to constantly watch our things.

Consider one of those disposable underwater cameras. Even if you don't go in the water, they will withstand the elements. Their quality is better than most people think. Between the Kodak and the Fuji, we give a slight quality edge to the Fuji, as it seems to have a sharper lens.

Use sunblock early and often. Don't pay any attention to the claims from sunblock makers that their product is waterproof, rubproof, sand blast proof, powerwash proof, etc. Reapply it every couple of hours and after you get out of the ocean. The ocean water will hide sunburn symptoms until after you're toast. Then you can look forward to agony for the rest of your trip. (And yes, you *can* get burned while in the water.) Gel-based sunblocks work best in the water. Lotions work best on land.

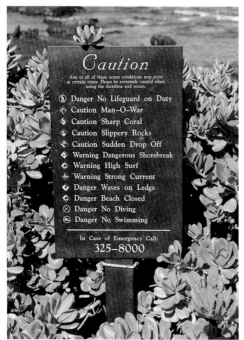

Tell me a lawyer didn't write this beach sign!

People tend to get fatigued while walking in sand. The trick to making it easier is to walk with a very gentle, relaxed stride while lightly striking the sand almost flat footed.

Always remember that in Hawai'i, all beaches are public beaches. This means that you can park yourself on any stretch of sand you like. The trick, sometimes, can be access. You might have to cross private land to get to a public beach. We'll try to point out a way to nearly all beaches

In general, surf is higher and stronger during the winter, calmer in the summer, but there are exceptions during all seasons. When we mention that a beach has facilities, it usually includes restrooms, showers, picnic tables and drinking water.

Lastly, remember that just because *you* may be on vacation doesn't mean that residents are. Consequently, beaches are more crowded on weekends.

To get ocean safety information, call 974–6200 for state beaches or 961–8694 for county. The beaches that had year-round lifeguards at press time were:

West—Hapuna, Kahalu'u, White Sands
Puna—Ahalanui (north of Isaac Hale)
Hilo—Honoli'i, Richardson's

Those with lifeguards on weekends and whenever school's out were:

West—Spencer
Hilo—Leleiwi, Onekahakaha, James Kealoha

We'll start our descriptions at the end of the road at the top of the island and work our way counter-clockwise. The first few beaches have marginal swimming.

❖ Pololu Beach

Located at the end of Highway 270 on the northern end of the island, this beach is very pretty. High surf and currents usually make this a poor swimming or snorkeling beach. Access is via a 15–20 minute trail from the Pololu Valley Overlook 400 feet up. No facilities.

❖ Keokea Beach Park

Although the swimming is usually poor, the exception is a small cove created by a manmade boulder breakwater. It was constructed as a community project by locals with the help from some heavy equipment donated by a long-gone sugar company. Not worth driving to unless you're in the neighborhood. Access road near the 27 mile marker on Highway 270 in North Kohala. Full facilities.

❖ Kapanaiʻa Bay

Tell anyone outside North Kohala that there is a beach below Kapaʻau, and they'll look at you like you're crazy. Kapanaiʻa Bay is one of the best kept secrets in North Kohala. This small pebble-and-sand beach is backed by trees and was carved out of the cliffs by a small brook. Even during moderate surf, you may see keikis boogie boarding in the back part of the bay. Surfers venture farther out where the waves are completely unobstructed. While there's not much sand and the water is a bit murky, the bay is very picturesque and a wonderful place for a picnic. The catch is that the access road requires a 4WD vehicle and the nerve to punish it. See map on page 46.

❖ Kapaʻa Beach Park

No sand at this beach, just rocks and a little coral rubble. The attractive assets here are the exceptionally clear water for snorkeling and SCUBA, usually abundant fish (sometimes large pelagic fish), coupled with somewhat protected waters except during periods of high surf (which can bring rips and surges). Be careful of surge here. Clear water makes it a good place to take underwater fish pictures. Not much coral but plenty of life. Rarely visited during the week, but easy to access just north of the 16 mile marker on Highway 270. Facilities include restrooms, as well as a BBQ and picnic tables. Excellent view of Maui and a nice place to watch the sunset. Bees are sometimes a problem here.

❖ Mahukona

When the seas are calm, it's *really* calm here. Not a beach, but an old abandoned sugar company harbor, Mahukona boasts crystal clear water and ridiculously easy access for snorkeling or swimming. You can practically drive up, open your door

Normally placid, Spencer Beach Park is a popular place for families with keikis (kids).

Kawaihae to Puako

and fall in. (But use the ladder at the entrance to the right, OK?) Though there's not much coral, the underwater relief is interesting. There's usually a large variety of fish, as well as abandoned sugar equipment (giant chains, wheels, etc.) and sparse remains of an old shipwreck. If the surf's up, don't go. When it's calm, check for surginess. During the week you'll most likely have it all to yourself. Facilities, except drinking water. (Don't drink the shower water!) The dirt road from the other side of the harbor heading north leads to the navigational heiau shown on page 14. See map on page 46.

❖ Lapakahi

We feel kind of funny putting this in the beaches section. Located in Lapakahi State Historical Park near the 14 mile marker on Highway 270, this is a reserve and there is no real beach here. (See page 52.) In fact, swimming is not even allowed. But *snorkeling* is and it's exceptional. (Yes, they *do* differentiate.) The water is clean and clear in Koai'e Cove between site 11 and site 7 near the coconut grove (see brochure at entrance). Not much coral but usually *lots* of fish. Stay inside the cove; the waters get unfriendly outside of its protection. Speaking of unfriendly, don't expect to be overwhelmed with aloha from park personnel. They seem to resent snorkelers here.

❖ Spencer Beach Park

A great family beach. Located just south of Kawaihae Harbor, the beach is protected by a long offshore reef and the extensive landfill of the harbor to the north. The beach slope is very gentle and the swimming is usually quite good. Keikis (kids) enjoy the usually calm waters of Spencer. Though the water is a bit cloudy due to its proximity to the harbor, this shouldn't deter you from enjoying the ocean here. If you snorkel, you will probably see miniature underwater volcanoes from small amounts of cold freshwater seeping from the floor. The amenities include several showers, restrooms, a pavilion, lifeguard, picnic tables, barbeques, a lawn area, lots of shade and basketball/volleyball courts. Camping is permitted by county permit (see CAMPING). As you approach the park from the access road between the 2 and 3 mile marker on Hwy 270, you can go to the right or left side of the park. Whether by design or not, the right (northern) side seems to be used mostly by locals and the left side by visitors. Since it's so popular with locals, expect it to be a little messier than other, more pristine beaches.

Just north of here is a small beach in front of the Pu'ukohola Heiau called **Pelekane Beach**. No swimming or sunbathing is allowed there out of deference to the sacred heiau complex.

The **Ala Kahakai Trail** between **Spencer** and **Hapuna Beach** hugs the shoreline. It crosses hole #3 on the golf course but otherwise is easy to follow and passes some pretty shoreline.

❖ Mau'umae Beach

Pretty, secluded, uncrowded during the week and decent swimming when calm. Nice place for a picnic, and you may have it to yourself during the week. Snorkeling is only fair due to slightly cloudy water. Access is through the Mauna Kea Resort entrance, right on Kamahoi, park at pole #22. 10-car maximum is rarely a problem (see map). Less than 5-minute trail walk from your car. No facilities. Usually pronounced MOW-MY. This is one of the most underrated and unknown beaches in this part of the island. Winter usually thins the sand out a bit. Sometimes frequented by nudists.

❖ Mauna Kea Beach (AKA Kauna'oa Beach)

This is a great beach! Probably the most classically perfect beach in the state. This gorgeous crescent of sand over ¼-mile long offers *very fine swimming*

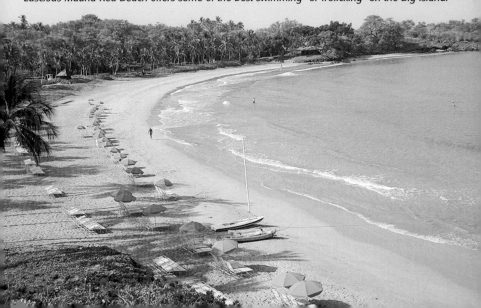
Luscious Mauna Kea Beach offers some of the best swimming—or frolicking—on the Big Island.

and boogie boarding during calm seas. On the left side of the beach are a bunch of rocks composing a linear reef that offers outstanding snorkeling.

A REAL GEM

Don't venture too far out unless calm (the outer portion of this reef is more surgy and unpredictable). The northern (right) side of the beach also offers interesting snorkeling but is more exposed and should only be snorkeled by strong swimmers. There is a big light there that attracts plankton at night, which in turn sometimes attracts large manta rays. This beach and Hapuna are the two best frolicking beaches on the island, if not the state. This beach is usually less windy than Hapuna. Full facilities. Only 30 cars allowed in the Mauna Kea Resort parking lot at a time, which is sometimes a problem, so try to arrive before 10 a.m. or take the 1-mile shoreline trail from the north end of Hapuna Beach. Located 32 miles north of Kona in the Kohala resort area off the 68 mile marker. See map on page 152.

❖ **Hapuna Beach**

A REAL GEM

If you close your eyes and picture a perfect beach, there's a good chance you'll see Hapuna in your mind's eye. Half a mile long and 200 feet wide during the summer, beautiful Hapuna is the ultimate frolicking beach. Fine golden sand slopes gradually into the ocean. Clean, clear water and excellent swimming conditions during calm seas, full facilities, easy access and gorgeous scenery. The boogie boarding here, when the surf's not too high, is exceptional. These are some of the elements that account for the fact that *Condé Nast Traveler* magazine has often voted this beach the best in the entire nation. During the week it usually isn't too crowded, but weekends and holidays bring lots of locals who know a great beach when they see one. Most people who live here bring their guests to Hapuna at least once to gloat. The lifeguard is usually stationed near the sign saying that there's no lifeguard on duty. Swimming is not safe during periods of high surf, which will kick the living daylights out of you. Also note that the wind sometimes kicks up in the afternoon. We've noticed that the southernmost (left) part of the beach is usually more protected during strong winds. All in all, this is a beach to savor. The only shade *on* the beach is a tree at the southern end. (Though there are shaded pavilions behind the beach.) You know how frenzied dogs can get when they go to the beach? That's how most people act when they come to Hapuna or Mauna Kea Beach.

For the more advanced snorkelers on calm days, the area directly south of the sand beach offers superb snorkeling, and it's usually empty during the week because no one knows about it. The waters are usually teeming with fish, and coral is abundant. The sea is unprotected here, so don't do it if it isn't calm or you'll get beaten up. Check for currents. If it starts to get rough, get out. We often start at the southern end of the beach and snorkel along the rocky coastline all the way to a little black gravel cove half a mile down the coast near a sea arch. Then we walk back along the shore in our reef shoes via a poor trail or use the dirt road (don't do it bare-footed). Be careful of the wicked kiawe thorns—they can penetrate nearly any shoe and probably most bulletproof vests. If you have some energy left, keep snorkeling past the little gravel cove to Waialea (69) Beach. The area just past the cove is absolutely heavenly.

Hapuna is located 30 miles north of Kailua-Kona in the northern part of the Kohala mega-resort area near the 69 mile marker off Highway 19. The only ding is that the state has historically done a terrible job of maintaining the facilities. Sometimes the restrooms look like they're from the third world.

❖ Waialea (Beach 69)

A REAL GEM

Sigh! Just another kickin' Kohala beach. This beach slopes gently into the water, giving it nice swimming conditions most of the year when the sea is calm. Not as long or as well known as Hapuna or Mauna Kea, this beach is popular with *akamai* (savvy) residents who sometimes bring their families for a day at the beach on weekends. To the north (right) of the main beach is a secluded little cove, which people sometimes claim for the day. The snorkeling around the northern part of the beach can be excellent. There's a sea arch at the northern tip, but refrain from walking on it; it looks like it's getting ready to go. Located 30 miles north of Kona near the Kohala resort area off Puako Road. (See bottom of map on page 152.) The short road is near telephone pole #71 (it used to be pole #69—hence the name). The pole had been stripped of its number at press time, so you'll have to count poles from one that's marked. Park next to the toilets (no showers). High surf occasionally strip mines the beach of its sand, which can take months to naturally replenish itself.

❖ Puako

Great snorkeling and SCUBA (see page 217 for directions to best spots, and photo of the reef), but the swimming is marginal. The reef at Puako is *very* extensive. The somewhat cloudy water on entry usually gives way to very clear water at the reef's edge. You stand an excellent chance of sharing the water with multiple turtles. (Oh, yeah, what's a multiple turtle?) The tops of the reefs are not the most interesting part (and can subject you to the prospect of being raked over them). The best fish and scenic action are at the outer edges of the reef. Check for currents and give the ocean respect. People occasionally bring their dogs to this beach (which end up chasing the catfish, no doubt). Wind often creates chop on the water here, but that doesn't usually affect the underwater experience much. There are six legal public accesses along the bay from the boat launch. Some are *conveniently* unmarked. A check of the county tax map and a site check shows us that they are by telephone poles #106, 110/111, 115, 120, 127/128 & 137, plus the dirt road at 143.

❖ Mauna Lani

The Mauna Lani Bay Hotel and the Orchid at Mauna Lani both have small, manmade (or enhanced) beaches. The Mauna Lani Bay Hotel beach to the south is usually *very* protected. Access is via the public parking lot shown on the map on page 53. You'll have to walk for about 15 minutes, but the trip through the fishpond area is worth it.

❖ Honoka'ope Beach

This small salt-and-pepper beach is located between the Hilton Waikoloa and the Mauna Lani. Until recently it was unknown and isolated. A recent development of 49 houses now surrounds it, and the road from the Mauna Lani resort area is open to you from 6 a.m. to 6 p.m. It's a 2-minute walk from your car. Like other beaches in this area, it can get windy in the afternoon. If you're seeking a hike, the ancient Ala Kahakai shoreline lava trail takes 30–60 minutes to reach the beach. (See map on page 53.) This trail segment, which starts near the Mauna Lani fishponds and ends here, goes through some fabulous lava cliff scenery. When surf's up, waves explode onto the twisted, gnarled lava fragments in the ocean. Facilities.

At the beach the swimming and snorkeling are fair if it's calm, ugly if it's rough. (Visibility is often poor here.) If the surf's right (not too big, not too small), you can float face down with a mask and snorkel at the surf's edge. As the waves rake you back and forth, listen as the black pebbles mixed with the sand make a great sound as they, too, are raked back and forth.

❖ 'Anaeho'omalu Bay

A REAL GEM

Another nice Kohala beach. (Even those born and raised here usually call this 6-syllable tongue-twister **A Bay**.) This long, curving salt-and-pepper sand beach is popular with both locals and visitors. The swimming is best in the sandy center, whereas the snorkeling (though not great) is best on the right side past the sandy area. The water is not as clear as what you'll find at other nearby beaches, but it's so tranquil here, you won't care. Protected by an offshore reef, this bay is usually safe except during very high surf. Windsurfing is popular here. Say *meow* to the wild cats that live near the restrooms.

'Anaeho'omalu is well known throughout the islands for its two large fishponds. These exceptionally picturesque and placid pools were used by ancient Hawaiians for raising mullet. Hawaiian royalty were the beneficiaries of these ponds—commoners weren't allowed to partake. The ponds are ringed by palm trees, making sunset photos from behind the trees a sure-fire winner.

There's a pleasant paved path on the mauka side of the fishpond that's worth a stroll. Numerous signs along the way give information about the fishponds and the area in general. Toward the center of the path are the remains of an ancient dwelling, probably a combination of sleeping and eating quarters as well as a

While not as flashy as some of the other beaches in the area, Honoka'ope Beach is a good place to listen to what's going on under the water.

shrine. The pond itself contains brackish water; fresh water flows from a natural spring and mixes with ocean tide water. The ancient Hawaiians covered the opening to the fishpond with a grate, which allowed small fry to enter from the ocean. Once inside, they gorged themselves on algae and small shrimp and became too fat to get back through the grate, at which time they were sitting ducks (so to speak) for the ancient Hawaiian pond keepers.

On the right (northern) side of the beach is a hut that rents snorkel gear, kayaks, boogie boards, windsurfers, etc. (at confiscatory rates). They also have guided snorkel and SCUBA tours. If you're hungry, Nalu's Bar & Grill at the Waikoloa Beach Marriott behind the beach has pricey but available burgers and hot dogs.

There's a marvelous shoreline trail north between the two Waikoloa hotels that leads through sand, lava and large amounts of brilliant white coral rubble. All along the trail you'll find various tidepools tucked against the shoreline. Turtles tend to hang out at one particular tidepool just a few feet from shore. At the north end of this trail is the Hilton Waikoloa. What a way to see this place for the first time! A sunset stroll along this path is unforgettable. Footwear is a must. There is an alternative place to park along this stretch—see map on page 53.

A few minutes walk south of A Bay on a narrow ribbon of sand leads to Kapalaoa Beach, a series of sand pockets. There is shade and a pleasant cove for snorkeling at the last pocket. If the surf's not high, the cove is amazingly protected. The short walk to this beach goes by numerous Hawaiian petroglyphs, some ancient and some modern. The more ambitious will want to take the lava trail farther south for about half an hour until you reach a lone palm tree in the lava, a

Ke-awa-iki Beach
House
Weliweli Point
Watch for Intersection
Lava Road used as trail
Freshwater Pools
19°53.688'
155°54.180'
Pueo Bay
Large rock & ground cover
A'a flow of 1859 from Mauna Loa (30 miles away)
Kiholo–Puako Trail (King's Hwy)
78
Ke-awa-iki Bay
Lava Trail
Brown Estate
Lava Road used as trail
Queen Ka'ahumanu Hwy
0   19   1/2 Mile
© 2006 Wizard Publications, Inc.

hundred feet or so from the shore. Here, you are rewarded with an outstanding spring-fed brackish pool with lots of charm. It is very deep in spots and is great for dipping after a hike. You will rarely see anybody else here as it is only accessible by foot, and it's a favorite stopping place of ours. The lava trails in this area offer good hiking, but they can get a bit hot in the middle of the day. The trail leads mostly along the shoreline for miles, all the way to Ke-awa-iki below.

❖ Ke-awa-iki Beach

This black sand- and gravel-lined bay is never crowded due to the access—to get there you have to walk on a lava road half the time, and a rougher a'a trail to the right of the fence the other half. Few on the island even know it's there. (It takes about 15 minutes to walk to.) The water off the left (south) is clear and offers good snorkeling when calm, but be wary of currents. There's also some shade there (and sometimes a swing from one of the trees). The best snorkeling is usually in the center of the bay. If you keep walking past the southern edge of the bay, there are lots of tide-pools to explore on an older, smooth pahoehoe lava shelf at low tide. (This is a good place to be wearing reef shoes.) Past that are numerous salt deposits from evaporated seawater. These deposits attract goats from the dry scrub inland who warily come and lick the salt off the rocks. Past the right (northern) side of Ke-awa-iki Bay is Pueo Bay, lined with black pebbles and semi-protected with nice swimming on calm days. There are off-shore freshwater springs here, causing areas of perturbations in the water, visible as waves of underwater distortion. You will almost certainly have this bay to yourself. No shade here because it's backed by an a'a field. If you feel like an extended stroll, you can walk past Weliweli Point and take a lava road inland to circle back to the highway. Mauka of Pueo Bay are some beautiful golden pools, described under HIKING on page 200 and shown on page 55.

Both of these beaches were created in 1859 when a'a from Mauna Loa drooled down the mountain and exploded when it hit the ocean, creating black sand. The eruption only covered half the bay and some white sand is still sprinkled at the southern end because there hasn't been enough time to evenly distribute the newer black sand. The entire area has a desolate but pretty character to it and is one of the least known beaches on the west side of the island. The only pockmark is the Brown Estate lining the center part of the beach with its barbed wire fence and its unwelcome feeling. Francis I'i Brown was an influential and beloved Hawaiian businessman in the early 1900s, and in turning his estate into a historical landmark, they seem to have taken away all its charm. They have tours of it for a few hours on the third Tuesday of every month. (Gee, *that's* convenient!) Located 20 miles north of Kailua-Kona just after the 79 mile marker.

❖ **Kiholo Bay**

A REAL GEM More of a region than a beach and there are a few surprises. Access to much of it requires a little hiking. See HIKING on page 198. It's certainly worth it.

❖ **Ka'upulehu Beach (Kona Village)**
Most of this long sand beach is fronted by a lava bench, making the swimming poor, but there is a pocket of sand in front of the Kona Village that allows easier access to the water. You can access this beach either from the Four Seasons, which is closer to the water from your car, or the Kona Village. (Kona Village guards at the guard shack imply that you can't go through. Just say these magic words—*public access.* They *have* to admit you, but expect dirty looks.) Public access is in yellow on the map on the next page.

❖ **Kuki'o Beach**
Near the Four Seasons Resort between Kona and the Kohala Resort area, this is yet another pretty Kohala beach. This long, fringing crescent of white sand is backed in parts by palm, ironwood, and kiawe trees offering inviting shade. At the southern end of the bay is a small, but very protected sandy cove. The swimming in the bay itself is only fair during calm seas, and the snorkeling offers somewhat murky water. There is public access from the resort area (see map on next page). While Kuki'o Bay might sound like a pretty name, in Hawaiian it means to *stand and defecate* (traditional definition) or *settled dregs* (modern definition). You probably won't be seeing

that on the back of a postcard. The reason behind the *lovely* name has been lost to the generations, but it's probably safe to say that whoever named it was having a bad hair day.

❖ Kikaua Beach

A REAL GEM

One of the things that makes the Big Island so different is its ever-changing nature. Active volcanos sometimes create new beaches overnight. But in this case, we have modern man—developers, no less—to thank for this one. Kikaua Point was once an isolated area with a pretty, but rocky cove defining it. Since our last edition, a private golf and beach club has been built behind this point and it seems obvious that a lot of sand has been transported to this cove, whether by man or by nature we can't say. But the result is a dreamy, softly padded sandy bottom and a protected cove that offers easy swimming and wading most of the time. The 27 parking spaces fill up on weekends, but weekdays are usually not bad. To get there, take the Kuki'o Nui Road just south of the 87 mile marker. The guards at the entrance can get snotty, so just smugly tell them you're exercising your beach access rights. It's a 5-minute walk from your car. Full facilities.

❖ Manini'owali/Kua Bay

A REAL GEM

This is one of our favorite beaches. (Most on the island know it as **Kua Bay** but the state recently starting pushing Manini'owali Beach as its name.) Off the beaten path, beautiful fine white sand, clear, clean water, gentle slope and a picturesque setting. When the ocean is calm, the swimming is fabulous. The snorkeling off to the right (north) is interesting not for its coral, but for the underwater relief. **Boogie**

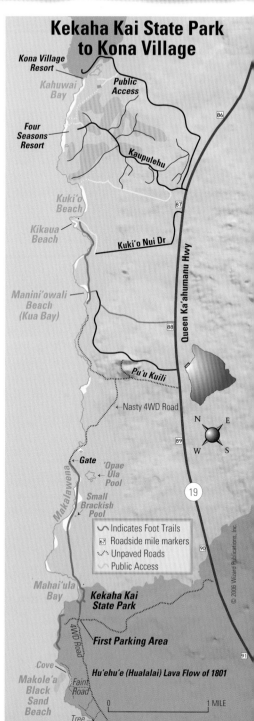

Kekaha Kai State Park to Kona Village

Kona Village Resort

Kahuwai Bay

Public Access

86

Four Seasons Resort

Kaupulehu

Kuki'o Beach

87

Kikaua Beach

Kuki'o Nui Dr

Manini'owali Beach (Kua Bay)

88

Queen Ka'ahumanu Hwy

Pu'u Kuili

← Nasty 4WD Road

N E
W S

89

← **Gate** 'Opae 'Ula Pool

Makalawena

Small Brackish Pool

19

⌒ Indicates Foot Trails
67 Roadside mile markers
∴ Unpaved Roads
⌒ Public Access

90

Mahai'ula Bay

Kekaha Kai State Park

4WD Road

First Parking Area

91

Cove

Makole'a Black Sand Beach

Faint Road

Hu'ehu'e (Hualalai) Lava Flow of 1801

0   1 MILE

Tree →

© 2006 Wizard Publications, Inc

Isolated and unknown, Makalawena is one of the finest beaches on the island. Access requires a 15–20 minute walk or a 4WD.

boarding is excellent during moderate surf, but the waves can be strong and deserve respect. There is sand here most of the time, but it is most abundant during the summer months. During the winter, high surf sometimes shifts the sand offshore for a time, leaving the area rocky and undesirable. Many residents consider this one of the best swimming beaches near Kona when calm, and on weekends they sometimes make their presence known. Crowds are less common during the week. From Highway 19 take the paved access road between the 88 and 89 mile markers. Note that the waves here have a lot of power, so if the surf's up, don't go in. No shade here, but restrooms are available. One caveat: Behind the northern end of the beach are a couple of palm trees adjacent to a freshwater spring. The water looks like a nice place to splash the saltwater off. *Don't!* What looks like inviting sand on the bottom is actually quicksand created from the rotting palm fronds of countless generations of palm trees. If you jump in, you

will find yourself up to your chest in the most putrid, disgusting rot you ever saw or smelled and will require help getting out while you recoil from the stench and pull snails off you. If this warning sounds particularly detailed...let's just say we're still picking scum out of our gear.

❖ **Makalawena**

A REAL GEM

To many, this is the choicest beach on the island...if you don't mind walking to it. In fact, Makalawena is as idyllic a beach as you will find anywhere in the islands. Gobs of superfine, clean white sand, plentiful shade and no crowds. The setting is utterly beautiful. Consisting of a number of coves and rocky points united by a long, curving stretch of beach, the best swimming is in the largest inlet backed by high sand dunes. Boogie boarding can be great here. There's a freshwater pond (see map on previous page) where we like to rinse off the saltwater before walking back. A herd of wild goats visits this area often, so keep an eye out for them.

Backed by private (Bishop Estate) land, you get there over the trail from Kekaha Kai State Park (about a 20-minute walk). It's a lava trail through an a'a field, and the footing is a little annoying. As you walk this trail, try to imagine how ridiculously difficult it would be to walk through the field itself without the trail. Then imagine doing it *barefoot*, as the ancient Hawaiians did. As you approach Makalawena from the Kekaha Kai side, the a'a trail suddenly gives way to sand dunes. But if you climb the dunes, rather than finding ocean, you find more a'a, indicating that this had been shoreline until a lava flow of a'a came along and added more real estate, cutting off the dunes from the sea.

If you have a 4WD (and your fillings are tight), you can take the nasty road from the highway between the 88 and 89 mile marker. It'll take you just north of the beach before a gate forces you to walk like the rest of us dogs. By the way, because it's so isolated, people some-

times travel light to this beach, omitting such extraneous things as their bathing suits. (Yeah, *that* must be the reason.)

❖ Kekaha Kai (formerly Kona Coast) State Park; Also Mahai'ula/ Ka'elehuluhulu

A REAL GEM

This beach is outside of Kona town and pretty. It's usually fairly uncrowded. **Mahai'ula Beach** (which you access after a 5-minute walk to the north from the first parking area) offers good swimming and interesting strolling. Just around the southern corner is a pocket of sand called **Ka'elehuluhulu Beach** (park at the second parking area at end of the lava road), not as good as the northern beach. The entire area was once owned by a prominent part-Hawaiian family called the Magoons. They sold the land to a Japanese investor who had visions of a resort. When the state refused permission, the investor sold it to the state which turned it into a park. The abandoned

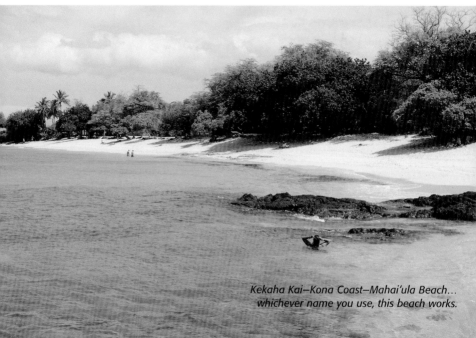

Kekaha Kai–Kona Coast–Mahai'ula Beach… whichever name you use, this beach works.

Magoon house is still located at the northern end of Mahai'ula Beach. This area abounds with freshwater springs that bubble to the surface, occasionally forming ponds. At the farthest northern part of the beach near some palm trees and a rock wall, you may see strange indentations in the sand at low tide. Here, freshwater gurgles right out of the sand and into the ocean. The snorkeling is only fair because the water can be a bit cloudy, especially during spring. This is a good beach to get away from it all, yet still have fairly easy access. There's plenty of shade at the backshore. Access is via a bumpy, but *usually* driveable, semi–paved 1½-mile road halfway between the 90 and 91 mile markers on Queen Ka'ahumanu Highway north of Kailua-Kona. (They were contemplating paving it at press time.) The only negative is the occasional plane overhead as it lands at Kona Airport. Facilities include picnic tables and toilets. Bring your own water. The gate to the beach is open 9 a.m. to 8 p.m., *closed Wednesdays*.

Legend states that before 1801 there was a 3-mile-long fishpond here. That year an old lady came to the village and asked for fish. The village overseer refused, saying that it *all* belonged to the chief. On her way out she was stopped by one villager who gave her food. After eating, she told the kind stranger to place kapu (forbidden) sticks outside his house. That night lava from Hualalai roared down the mountain to the village, destroying the great fishpond but sparing the man who fed her. The villagers realized that the old woman was the volcano goddess Pele, avenging the selfishness of the chief.

Check out some of the lava on the road leading to this beach (you'll certainly be driving slowly enough). There are lots of interesting formations where different flows meet. It has patches of gold/rust colored lava, streaks of blue,

Did you spring for 4WD? If so, Makole'a Black Sand Beach near Kona is all yours today.

red and other colors indicating the presence of numerous elements and gases present during cooling.

❖ Makole'a Beach

A REAL GEM Ask a hundred residents of Kona about a black sand beach just north of town named Makole'a Beach, and you'll get a hundred blank stares. Aside from a handful of shoreline fishermen, few seemed to have known about this beach—until we stumbled upon it for a previous edition. Created during the 1801 lava flow of Hualalai, this small pocket of jet black sand is the only black sand beach on this part of the island.

To get there you have two options. After driving to Kekaha Kai State Park (see page 161), those with 4WD can take a left at the first parking lot and drive the lava road heading south. Just under $\frac{7}{10}$ mile is a faint car path marked by some coral that leads 800 feet over lava to the sea. (Though driveable, you can walk this last part if the lava there dissuades you.) The other way is to park at the beach at Kekaha Kai State Park and walk along the shoreline for 15–20 minutes. At one point the sandy trail is interrupted. Best to walk on the smooth pahoehoe lava behind the beach boulders for this part. Just before the black sand beach is a small cove protected at low- to mid-tide during calm seas. It's a perfect place to take a quick dip. The snorkeling and SCUBA diving are great at the black sand beach. Though the visibility is only fair (it's better when you get away from the beach), there is a beautiful field of coral to the north (right) of the beach and to the south farther out. Enter at the sandy part in the center, and beware of unchecked waves. If you walked here, consider cutting across the lava field on your return for different scenery.

This beach, while certainly not on par with Mauna Kea or Kua Bay, deserves the GEM rating because it's the *only real black sand beach* anywhere near Kona, it's not overly difficult to access, and you are likely to have it all to yourself on weekdays. (Some fishermen use it on weekends and sometimes leave their beer bottles.) It's that rare treat—an undiscovered black sand beach.

❖ Wawaloli Beach

A REAL GEM This is our favorite tide-pool area on the west side of the island (shown on next page). The instantly accessible sand beach is cut off from the ocean by a large tide-pool that offers warm swimming when the surf is too high elsewhere. There are restrooms and showers here, making it popular with local families who bring their keikis (kids) to play in the mostly protected area. The largest pool (mostly sand-lined) is best near high tide most of the year, only best at low tide if the surf's cranking. The other, less protected tide-pool is better at low tide. A water channel in the lava closer to the restrooms can be fun to wander in. In late afternoon you might want to pick up a pizza on your way out, bring the kids, if you have 'em, and watch the sunset. Take the road to the Natural Energy Lab (near the 94 mile marker on the main highway north of Kailua-Kona), and park just as it veers to the right along the shoreline. Some equipment to the south is an eyesore, but try to ignore it, and airplanes sometimes shatter the quiet. Near here is a 4WD road that leads a mile south to Pine Trees, one of the island's premier surf spots. (So named because of the mangrove in a brackish pool. Surfer dudes thought they were pine trees.) The road is fairly poor.

The quiet tide-pools of Wawaloli Beach at the Natural Energy Lab are an excellent place to go when the surf's pounding.

❖ Honokohau/Kaloko Fishpond

Honokohau is an area rich in archaeological treasures. This part of the coast was inhabited for centuries and is filled with relics. Consequently, it was made a national park in 1978 in an effort to preserve what remains (entrance is free). At first it might seem surprising that people thrived here. Barren and rocky with particularly harsh 'a'a fields in many areas, the draw here was the freshwater springs. The Hawaiians took advantage of the water to create large fishponds to raise mullet and other fish.

Located just south of the airport (see map on following page), you can access the park between 8:30 a.m. and 4 p.m. from a parking lot near the 97 mile marker on Hwy 19 just north of Kailua-Kona or a gravel road between the 96 and 97 mile markers that leads to Kaloko Fishpond. You can also access the park from **Honokohau Harbor**, off the paved road between the 97 and 98 mile markers. From the harbor, a brief walk north will take you to **'Ai'opio Beach**. This lovely beach, located *so* close to town, has been largely forgotten by most Kona residents due to a nasty dispute in the past, now settled, that intimidated residents from even *walking* there. There are scads of turtles munching on grasses in the cloudy cove water. This was an ocean fish trap in ancient days, where fish entered at high tide and were easily captured. A protected area here is perfect for keikis (kids). An impressive heiau called Hale o Mono rests at the south end. Park at the north end of the harbor (past the restaurant) and take the trail for a minute or two. Turn toward the ocean before you reach the restrooms. This is a nice beach for relaxing. Farther north is **Honokohau Beach**. You may read elsewhere that this is a nude beach, but it is no longer permitted and they cite violators. This long stretch of salt-and-pepper sand offers reasonable swimming at the center. One nearby highlight is known as **Queen's Bath**. (Even locals get confused by Queen's Bath. There are several of these scattered throughout the islands. Essentially, any place that was considered an outstanding place to bathe was called Queen's

Bath.) This 15-by-20 foot natural lava pool of brackish water was lovingly enhanced by the Hawaiians to make it a fine place to congregate and splash in relatively fresh (and very cool) water. They lined the pool, located in the middle of a harsh a'a field, with smoother stones, built areas to sit, and generally made it a pleasant place to visit. These days, it is only sporadically visited by hikers and beach-goers from the nearby beach. To get there from Honokohau Beach, walk north along the beach. At 200 yards past the *end* of the beach you'll come to a rock wall. Look mauka (toward the mountain), and you will see numerous large piles of rocks. These are also ancient in origin—the largest is 10 feet high and 15 feet thick—and are part of 12 rock piles placed in a rectangle around the Queen's Bath, possibly used for lookouts. The trail to them from the south end of the wall is along the dividing line between the lava and yellow clumps of grass. Go toward, then between, the two largest mounds. The pool is about 100 feet north of the largest mound near the only large green shrub in the area. Enjoy!

At the south end of the Honokohau Harbor is **'Alula Beach**, a small, pleasant crescent of sand which is fairly protected during calm seas; a good sunning beach.

❖ Old Kona Airport Beach Park

A REAL GEM This beach park is located at (do we *really* need to say it?) the Old Kona Airport, closed in 1970 because it was unable to accommodate larger aircraft. You park anywhere on the runway (you may taxi as long as you like) and enjoy the patchy beach and full facilities. On the south end are ball fields where Little League parents battle for supremacy. The long beach is an easy one to access, and the sunsets from here are nice. Though you won't be overwhelmed by an abundance of thick sand, it's rarely crowded *during the week*. Located ½ mile (15–20 minute walk along the lava coastline) north is the finer **Pawai Bay**. The **snorkeling** in Pawai Bay is very exciting, especially for the experienced snorkeler. There's a little of everything with crystal clear water, lots of life, caverns, arches, drop-offs, small caves and some pinnacles along the shoreline. Here you may see the elusive and extraordinary frog fish (an angler fish) on the coral and Spanish dancers (a contorting nudibranch). During tricky surge, novices should stay away from the more interesting shore. Some snorkel boats bring groups. If you walk here, you will find the cove in the center of the bay is the best way to enter. Be careful of the channel that leads out to the bay; it can be surgy. The shady backshore of Pawai Bay has plush camping facilities that are private and belong to the Queen Lili'uokalani Trust, used for Hawaiian children. The walk to Pawai Bay from the Old Airport

Kaloko/Honokohau

Map:

Kaloko Industrial Park
96
Hina-Lani St
Olowalu
Kaloko Fishpond
Old Mamalahoa Trail
Queen Ka'ahumanu Hwy
2WD OK
Kaloko Honokohau Nat'l Hist. Park
Entire area rich in Hawaiian ruins
Kauhola
Maiau
Costco
Cheapest gas in town if you're a Costco member.
Queen's Bath
Rock Mounds
97
'Aimakapa Fishpond
Holua
(Ancient Hawaiian Slide)
Parking & Visitor Center
19
Honokohau Bay
'Ai'opio Beach
Parking
Small Boat Harbor where most fishing boats leave
Kealakehe
'Alula Beach
Parking
Two Miles to Kailua-Kona

© 2006 Wizard Publications, Inc.

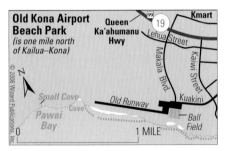

Old Kona Airport Beach Park (is one mile north of Kailua–Kona)

Queen Ka'ahumanu Hwy

99 19 Kmart

Lehua Street

Makala Blvd.

Kaiwi Street

© 2006 Wizard Publications, Inc.

N

Small Cove
Pawai Bay
Cove

Old Runway

0 1 MILE

Kuakini

Ball Field

is best experienced at low tide. Lots of pukas (holes) in the lava are exposed, creating fissures where water often surges and air escapes in loud gasps. This lava fractures easily, which is why the underwater relief along here is so good.

❖ Kailua Bay

Located in the heart of downtown Kailua-Kona. (See map on page 60.) Usually areas around piers have nasty water. This one is surprisingly clean due to the daily flushing action of the sea. There's a surprising number of fish in Kailua Bay. We've seen super-schools numbering in the many thousands off Hulihe'e Palace. On calm days we like to snorkel from the pier to the sand pocket across from Kona Islander Inn or the boulder beach across from Lulu's. If you are looking for *exceptionally* calm water and a sandy beach, the very small **Kamakahonu Beach** to the right of the Kailua Pier (in front of the King Kamehameha Hotel) is perhaps the gentlest and safest water on the island (with the *possible* exception of your hotel bathtub). Children love frolicking in the water here, though freshwater springs sometimes make it cold. This is where King Kamehameha chose to spend the last years of his extraordinary life, so you gotta figure it has something going for it. His personal 'Ahu'ena Heiau is right in front of you. The sand at the beach does-

n't extend very far into the water, but it is shallow the whole way. If you swim out from the beach, you'll notice a private ocean entrance to the right. It leads to a house owned by billionaire Paul Allen, the less famous co-founder of Microsoft. He bought this gloriously located house several years ago for $11 million. (Don't worry, it was probably a mere rounding error in his checkbook.) That was before the current land boom. It would probably be triple that amount today. A recently discovered map hints that this might be the location of Kamehameha's tomb, but if so, it was probably destroyed when the shoreline was rearranged in the 1950s.

There is a concessionaire at Kamakahonu renting various beach accouterments at the usual confiscatory prices—but it's convenient. Large schools of fish sometimes congregate on the other side of the heiau. It's about 300 yards from the public parking to the beach, so you may want to drop off your stuff (and a person) at the pier first.

To the left (south) of the pier is another pocket of sand. (They sometimes do SCUBA intros there.) It's a bit less protected but still relatively calm. Boogie boarders like to ride the normally small but long lasting swells. The grueling Ironman Triathlon (see page 59) starts here. They swim 2⁴⁄₁₀ miles before starting their 112-mile bike ride and 26-mile marathon run—*all in the same day!* (Makes you sore just thinking about it, huh?) If it's rained recently, snorkelers should look for little calderas of what looks like boiling sand, like a mini volcano. It's caused by small amounts of cold freshwater bubbling to the surface.

❖ Pahoehoe Beach Park

Though there's little sand here to speak of, this is a nice place to have a picnic and enjoy the surf and sunset from the benches. We've never seen it crowded. Backed by pretty trees and a lawn, there is a small gravel entrance to the water, but swimmers are discouraged from entering unless equipped with snorkeling gear. Even then, advanced snorkelers only need apply. That's because there are numerous holes, arches and pockets on the lava shelf offshore, making exploration very exciting. But surf can sometimes rake you over and even under the reef, making it *too* exciting. Lots of fish here, as well. Located north of the 4 mile mark on Alii Drive in Kailua (just north of White Sands Beach).

❖ White Sands Beach Park

Also known as Magic Sands, Disappearing Sands, and La'aloa Bay Beach. Located just north of the 4 mile mark on Alii Drive in Kailua, this small beach has particularly nomadic sand that retreats at the first sign of a surf assault, settling in a repository just offshore. Once the surf subsides, the sand slowly drifts back onto the shoreline until the next high surf. This occasional flushing of the sand tends to keep it clean and white. Those who live here can tell you of countless instances where the entire beach washes away in less than a day. Much of the time there is a shallow sandbar just offshore making the swimming and boogie boarding quite good. (The best wave break is on the left [south] side of the beach.) Watch for undertow and some rocks at the end of the ride. When the sand's thick, the frolicking is good. (But reef shoes are recommended in case you step on a rock.) When there's no sand or it's in the process of disappearing (i.e., when the surf's high), there is a strong rip current, making water activities hazardous. This small beach tends to be pretty crowded. Lifeguard and facilities are

here along with some shade trees. On calm days, the snorkeler will want to check out the area to the right (north), in front of Jameson's Restaurant. Especially large schools of fish sometimes hang out there. (Guess they don't know that Jameson's serves seafood.) We've also seen more moray eels here in front of the restaurant than at any other place on the island. *(If an eel bites your hand, and you bleed in the sand… that's a'moray.)*

Just south of here right at the 4 mile mark is a small cove where the SCUBA diving is excellent, offering short, easy access and good underwater relief and caves. The snorkeling is not bad either. Just offshore from this location we often see a pod of dolphins patrolling the waters. Why they hang out there, we don't know, but whatever the reason, keep an eye out for them.

❖ Kahalu'u Beach Park

A REAL GEM

This is one of the nicer snorkeling spots on the Big Island. It is teeming with fish and offers more variety of sea life than any other easily accessible spot in Kona. Among the many fish present are wrasses, parrotfish, convict tang, porcupinefish, needlefish and puffers, as well as the occasional lobster, eel, and octopus. Outside the reef you may occasionally see deep sea life, such as tuna, marlin and dolphin jumping about. When you first enter the water you might think, "What's all the hubbub about?" Well… it's about 100 feet offshore. The perimeter of this small, sheltered bay has numerous freshwater springs, making the near-shore water cold and cloudy. But once you swim out toward the middle, it gets warmer and clearer, and life is abundant. One reason is the Menehune breakwater offshore. Built in ancient times, it has been partially disassembled by countless waves, creating an excellent fish environment. There's usually a truck at the beach where you can rent snorkel gear (though it's more expensive—consider Kahalu'u Bay Surf & Sea almost across the street marked by a restored Woody) and boogie boards (but the boogie boarding here is not good—just surfing), and you can usually take surfing lessons at the beach. There is a full range of facilities. There's also a lunch truck with hot dogs, ice cream and bad shave ice. A family of turtles calls Kahalu'u home, and they usually won't dart away from you if you don't harass them. (We've noticed that near high tide, they often work the grasses that are otherwise exposed on the left/southern side of the bay.) Your odds of swimming with turtles are probably greater here than anywhere else on the island, with the possible exception of remote Punalu'u Beach. The best way to keep a turtle from fleeing is to act disinterested—like you don't give a

flying fish. (*Ooo*, sorry.) If you scope him out, he'll run off. If you pretend to eat the same grasses he eats, you aren't a threat. The more intrepid might venture around the breakwater on very calm days where life is also abundant. Exceptionally large mixed schools of fish sometimes congregate just outside the reef, but you expose yourself to the possibility of being strained through the reef—better stay inside unless it is real calm or you are real confident.

Crowds accumulate at Kahalu'u, but it's *usually* less crowded than White Sands Beach. During periods of high surf, large waves can wash over the reef and form a rip current flowing out the reef opening at the north end of the bay, making it unsafe.

Though we usually recommend against feeding fish since it upsets the balance, the fish here are already junkies. Read the snorkel section for tips.

To the left is a **tide-pool** in front of the Outrigger Keauhou Beach Resort. The water there is sometimes as warm as bathwater as it gets heated by the sun, a natural black-bottom pool. Cruise around in the shallows and look for eels, which like to be fed by people at the railings of the hotel.

Eight hundred feet to the left (south) of Kahalu'u is **Makole'a Beach**. (Not to be confused with the beach described on page 163 with the same name.) There are several heiaus along this beach, mostly in disrepair. The salt-and-pepper sand and gravel beach is usually empty and has a lonely, forgotten feel. The swimming is poor since you are facing large tide-pools. Look for the gory petroglyphs mentioned on page 63.

❖ Napo'opo'o Beach

We only mention this here because lazy travel writers *still* rave about the splendid

Kahalu'u Beach Park
Excellent surf break →

Ali'i Drive

Menehune Breakwater

N
W · E
S

Strong rip current when surf's high

Best snorkeling is in this area

Kahalu'u 5 Makolea
Parking

Tide-pool area between low & high tide on calm days is excellent for the timid snorkeler. Take care not to walk on the fragile coral.

Outrigger Keauhou Beach Resort

0   1000 Feet

Petroglyphs at low tide → ⊙ ⊙ Ke'eku Heiau

© 2006 Wizard Publications, Inc.

Good reef protected by a boulder breakwater have made Kahalu'u the most popular snorkel site in Kona.

beach at the south end of Kealakekua. *It's gone!* It disappeared when Hurricane 'Iniki sideswiped the island in 1992 and the surf wiped the beach clean, depositing boulders there. You'll find little more than a small patch of sand. This beach will probably never return to its former glory—part of the ever changing nature of the Big Island. Across the bay is the Captain Cook Monument, described on page 69. Slightly south is **Manini Beach** (shown on map on page 66). Coral rubble sprinkled with a'a lava, and poor swimming make this another must-miss beach.

❖ Ke'ei Beach

Between Kealakekua and Honaunau (see map on page 66), this pretty but small stretch of sand is backed by numerous coconut trees. Though picturesque, poor swimming and difficult parking mean that it is used almost solely by the small, adjacent community and by visiting SCUBA divers. This area seems to

have been a magnet for historical events. Local legend (bolstered by old Spanish records) states that foreigners washed ashore here during the 1520s. Several big battles took place nearby, including the one where Kamehameha became king. (See page 71.)

❖ Pu'uhonua o Honaunau

A REAL GEM This is a popular place to visit for reasons other than its water. It was the Place of Refuge in ancient times. See detailed description on page 71. For ocean lovers, the snorkeling and SCUBA just north of the boat launch are incredible, perhaps as good as the more difficult-to-reach Captain Cook Monument at Kealakekua Bay, making it some of the best in the state when conditions are good, though it's deeper. There are also picnic tables near the shoreline at the southern half of the park that make for absolutely splendid sunset picnics. We've made good use of

Honaunau

N

Less experienced snorkelers→

Most snorkelers enter here→

Excellent SCUBA↗

More Experienced Snorkelers Here→ Boat Ramp

Surgy→

Hale o Keawe Heiau→☐

Back Entrance

Main Entrance

To Picnic Tables

160

© 2006 Wizard Publications, Inc.

the BBQs there and can recommend them highly.

❖ Ho'okena Beach Park

South of Kona between the 101 and 102 mile markers is a paved road leading 2³/₁₀ miles to Ho'okena Beach Park. This pocket of fine salt-and-pepper sand is popular with local families on weekends, but mostly empty on weekdays. Tourists are not common because the beach is not well known and is off the beaten path, though access by car is a snap. Keikis (kids) ride the waves on calm days and splash about in a few of the tide-pools adjacent to the sand beach. (Decent snorkeling is to the left of the beach.) Once used as a boat landing in the days when steamships were king, the beach offers shade and facilities.

❖ Pebble Beach

Located down a *very* steep road. (You lose 1,050 feet of elevation in 6,000 feet of driving—that's almost as steep as the notorious road into Waipi'o Valley.) It's at the bottom of Kona Paradise (off Highway 11 between the 96 and 97 mile markers 20 miles south of Kona) and is one of the most violent beaches we know of. Even when calm it will kick your 'okole. We've seen fish tossed out of the

water on calm days. *(Seriously!)* The "beach" is actually countless large waterworn pebbles, which make a great sound when the surf's up. If you've got the nerve, it's fun to let the surge pull you up and down the steep beach (but stay away from the shore break).

❖ Miloli'i Beach Park

Located 30 miles south of Kailua-Kona, this is considered a very local beach, meaning that *on weekends* it's best to leave it to them. There is a very tight local community here, and, though Hawai'i is as friendly a place as you will find, you may get a little stink eye if you visit during "their time"—like crashing someone's family barbeque. This community beach sports a pavilion used by local bands playing outstanding Hawaiian music on weekends and holidays. There's not much sand, but the surfing is good, and the facilities are well-developed. (The sand was removed by a storm in the 1970s. The same storm also removed many houses. Some homeowners made the mistake of bulldozing their crumpled houses and were not allowed to rebuild. Shrewd owners knew that to stay that close to the water, they were required to keep and repair the *original* structure.)

Take the winding, one-lane paved road just south of the 89 mile marker. Drive slowly at the end of the road, and watch for local kids.

❖ Honomalino Bay

A REAL GEM

Ask most people who live here where Honomalino is, and they'll probably tell you it's on Maui. This lovely black-and-white sand beach is not well known. It's 100 yards or so long, backed by scads of coconut trees, decent swimming when calm (which is often), usually deserted, and is a 20-minute walk from your car. Though one of the larger *south* Kona beaches, it eroded considerably during the 20th century (as black sand beaches naturally tend to do—see explanation on page 174), and will probably be mostly a memory a hundred years or so from now. To get there, start at Miloli'i Beach Park (see previous page). Go to the end of the road, and you'll see bathrooms and a yellow church. The public access is between them. (A left fork is private property; the right fork is yours.) Don't be intimidated by the dizzying array of KEEP OUT and NO TRESPASSING signs at the trailhead. You are not necessarily the target audience for those signs. (It's a *looong* story and relates to four *decades* of litigation.) About 3–4 minutes into the trail after some tide-pools and a palm-backed spit of sand, follow the fenceline on your left up and over the black rock at the back of the beach and continue south for 15 minutes. There may be a few fallen trees to hop over. The snorkeling on the right side of the bay is interesting when calm in the cluster of rocks. There is a small cave there where a 6-foot white-tipped reef shark often rests. Don't worry, he's not a man eater—yet. If you plunge your hand into the sand at the water's edge at the south end of the beach, the sand's cold. That's freshwater (called a basil spring) percolating into the sand from below.

One of Honomalino's little-known joys is the pod of dolphins that sometimes cruise the sand-lined bay in the morning. Scientists think that, while resting, dolphins are able to turn off half their brain (including the half that runs their eco-location abilities). They do a sort of snooze and cruise, counting on the fact that the shallow water and light bottom will alert them to predators in the absence of their sonars. This means that, in the morning, dolphins are literally operating on half a brain. (Come to think of it, so am I before my coffee.)

Honomalino Beach on a crowded day.

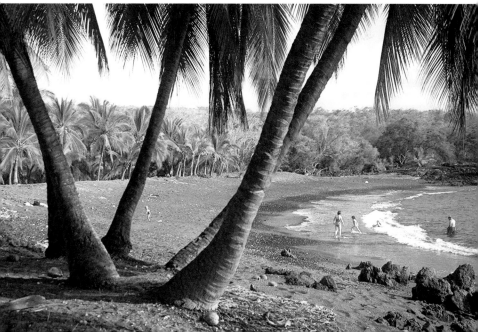

❖ Road to the Sea

A REAL GEM

This is one of Ka'u district's best kept secrets. In BASICS we mentioned that having a 4WD can come in handy. Here's a perfect example why. First, if you don't have a 4WD, you *probably* won't make it. It depends on the level of cruelty you normally inflict on rental cars. The access road is ⅔ mile past (south of) the 80 mile marker on Hwy 11. The first of two beaches is at the end of this 6-mile long dirt road with only a 20-foot stretch in the middle which will probably cause a problem for a *regular* car. Remember, you're far from Kona. If you get stuck, the first thing the tow truck driver will ask is, "Do you own your own home?" A 4WD will do nicely and is necessary to get to the second, better beach. Incidentally, misleading signs notwithstanding, you *are* permitted on the road down here.

Anyway, these two beautiful black-and-green sand beaches are nearly always deserted, especially during the week. The first beach is at the end of the road. Swimming *during calm seas* is fair and the beach is inviting; enter it from the left (south) side. Harmless plankton-eating whale sharks are sometimes seen in the area. To the right of the end of the road is a *deep* tide-pool—7 to 9 feet in spots. It makes a *great* wading pool, and there's even some coral in it—unusual for a tide-pool.

The second beach is reached via a 1-mile long *rough* but driveable 4WD road ³⁄₁₀ mile back up from the *very* end of the road. It dog-legs right, so don't take the first Fool's Road. The road leads to a much longer and finer black-and-green sand beach. (See Green Sand Beach next page for an explanation of green sand.) To the right are some palm trees, which means a freshwater pool. In this case it's saltier than most, but is great for dipping. There is some shade at the back part of the beach. Stay close to shore; the water can get tricky further out. (See aerial photo.)

This is a great beach to get away from it all and you will almost *certainly* have it all to yourself.

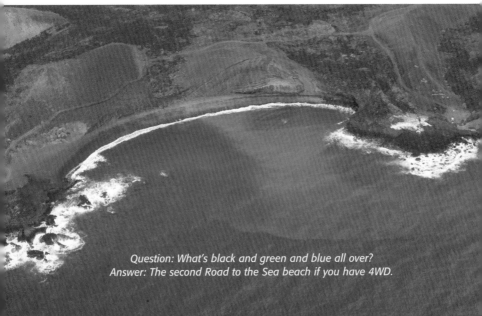

Question: What's black and green and blue all over?
Answer: The second Road to the Sea beach if you have 4WD.

The entire area out here is lifeless, arid and desolate. It was utterly assaulted by savage lava flows 250 years ago and on paper isn't worth a hill of beans. Yet despite this (or perhaps because of it), it is alluring. The lava field looks young and raw, and the beaches are desirable. If you have 4WD, it is a recommended trip. Located 40 miles south of Kona; see map.

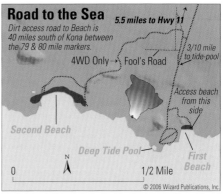

Road to the Sea 5.5 miles to Hwy 11
Dirt access road to Beach is 40 miles south of Kona between the 79 & 80 mile markers.
4WD Only → Fool's Road
3/10 mile to tide-pool
Access beach from this side
Second Beach
Deep Tide Pool
First Beach
0 — 1/2 Mile
N
© 2006 Wizard Publications, Inc.

❖ **Green Sand (Papalokea) Beach**

A REAL GEM
(Literally!)

So you say you've seen white sand beaches. You've seen plenty of golden sand beaches. Maybe you've even seen a black sand beach. But when is the last time you frolicked on a *green* sand beach? This unique beach owes its name and color to a large deposit of a semi-precious gem called olivine liberally mixed with black sand. After ancient volcanic eruptions created Pu'u o Mahana, a small littoral cone containing thick veins of the stuff, the ocean went to work dismantling it. It has already broken through one side, and when the surf is up, each wave rakes at the back side, revealing more and more olivine. Though most of the gemstones are in the form of sand particles, people occasionally find large nuggets. (Actually, your best chance of finding a nugget is at the rarely visited adjacent cove on the far side of Green Sand Beach. Access is from the far [northeast] side). See map of South Point on page 79.

Located near South Point, which (this will stun you) is at the southernmost point on the island, access to the beach requires a 2¼-mile (each way) walk or 4WD from Kaulana Boat Launch. There are more dirt roads than we showed on the map because people are constantly creating new ones. They all go to the beach and beyond. You'd have to try real hard to get lost since you always stay within sight of the shore. Keep an eye out for the remains of several Hawaiian structures dotting the area.

A parking lot ¼ mile from the boat launch has a so-called "Visitor Center." Don't believe *anything* you hear there. Statements like, "You have to pay $5 to park here" are nonsense. The Department of Hawaiian Homelands (which runs the area) says anyone can park there *for free*. If someone official-looking tries to charge you $5, it's a scam.

Once at the cone, most people take a "path" on the closest (southwest) side (see map), which requires a short hop off a rock at one point. Unfortunately, the path is more evident from the beach than from the top and might be tough to spot. Others walk down a path from about the middle of the cone, which can be slippery due to sand particles on the hard surface. Don't try to walk from the highest part of the cone; it's treacherous. Use your best judgment. Everyone from small keikis to the elderly go to the beach, but you are on your own in evaluating it. Check to see that the waves are not inundating the entire beach before you go down. The ocean is unprotected, so the waves are at full strength. Many books tell you that you will drown if you even *think* about swimming there. We swam there plenty of times, and if the surf's not up, it's not bad. The sand bottom is thick and there are few exposed rocks. We have yet to encounter nasty currents *in the bay,* but we're not stupid enough to venture out of the bay where the prevailing current will give you a splendid tour of Antarctica. Again, use your best judgment. There is a shorebreak, and the undertow can be harsh. You might see plenty of local kids (or us) playing in the surf, but this is not Waikiki. And if the surf is high, definitely stay out. Those same large waves that expose the olivine could pull you in. There's no shade here and the wind, which has beautifully sculpted the eastern side of the bay, is also the same wind that might get on your nerves if it is blowing hard, particularly in the late afternoon. Go earlier if you can. No facilities. Please resist the urge to take any of the sand with you. We've seen people taking large amounts, and the supply is finite.

The spooky snorkeling at South Point itself is described on page 81.

❖ Whittington Park

Located off the road between the 61 and 62 mile marker on the southern part of the island. Very pretty from a distance. Formerly run down but they've spiffied it up recently. Think of it as a nice pit stop with restrooms and picnic tables.

❖ Punalu'u **Black** Sand Beach

A REAL GEM

This is the most easily accessible black sand beach on the island (now that Kaimu Beach is under 75 feet of lava). Backed by palm trees and a freshwater pond, the sand is *genuine* black sand—the kind created when a chunky a'a lava flow meets the ocean and shatters into small pieces on contact with the water. These small chunks are quickly pulverized by the ocean, forming a delicious

black sand. This differs from older black sand beaches where the sand is made up of lava chipped from a river bed by coursing water. Genuine black sand beaches are relatively fleeting since the source of the sand ends as soon as the lava flow stops. This contrasts with white and golden sand beaches, which have organic sources (coral or shells) that continue to build up sand over time. (In fact, one large, coral-munching parrotfish can produce three *tons* of white sand per year by himself!) That's why you don't see genuine black sand on old islands—the black sand erodes into the ocean over time and cannot be recovered.

The swimming is a bit different here than at many other island beaches. Cold freshwater springs bubble up from just offshore. Consequently, the top 8–12 inches of the water is guaranteed to freeze your 'okole off. You can usually see the floating freshwater while swimming and will be tempted to swim below to get a semblance of warmth. The visibility here is only fair, and you need to be conscious of rip currents. Generally, you want to stay fairly close to shore and be aware of currents during all but the calmest seas. Past the boat launch on the left (north) side of the beach, the rips can be a problem.

So why swim here at all? Well, one of this beach's lesser known treats are its turtles. The waters can get almost crowded with them. We've been here when you could see small groups of turtles every couple of minutes. They munch on limu that clings to rocks on the sea floor. Please remember not to disturb or play with them. In addition to the possible harm, it might cause them to find a less accessible beach to frolic.

Near the southern tip of the island between the 56 and 55 mile markers on Hwy 11.

EAST SIDE BEACHES

Past Punalu'u your choices for beaches diminish along with their calibre. Put simply, the east shore, which is exposed to more hazardous surf and lots of river runoff, has fewer and mostly poorer beaches. Therefore, we are breaking them up into regions and deviating from our previous rules by describing many in the tours of the various regions.

❖ Puna Beaches

Located near the extreme eastern part of the island, **Kehena Black Sand Beach, Issac Hale Beach Park, Ahalanui Warm Springs,** and **Kapoho Tidepools** are described in HILO AND PUNA SIGHTS because you won't encounter them unless you are touring that area anyway.

❖ Hilo Beach Parks

To the east on Kalanianaole (where Highways 11 and 19 meet) are Hilo's most popular beach parks. **Onekahakaha Beach Park** has a boulder-enclosed pool that is popular with local keikis (kids). The sand-lined pool is utterly protected except during very high seas. The pool to the left is rockier and has lots of urchins on the floor. Past Onekahakaha

is **James Kealoha Beach Park.** Though picturesque, the swimming is poor, and you're likely to share it with young toughs drinking too much and giving you stink eye. Best to move on to **Leleiwi Beach Park.** This last park contains **Richardson's Ocean Center** at the far end and is particularly attractive with freshwater pools sprinkled about. The county Aquatics Division is located here, and they are friendly and full of helpful information. This is an excellent place for a picnic, though sometimes the James Kealoha crowd spills over to here. There's a small black sand cove where you can enter the water. It'll be cold from freshwater intruding into the area. Some of Hilo's better snorkeling is here. Dolphins often frequent the area, and turtles usually congregate a little further down the coast toward Hilo. Check with lifeguards because this area is subject to strong surf.

Other beach parks north of Hilo are **Honoli'i, Kolekole Beach, Hakalau Bay, Waikaumalo Park,** and **Laupahoehoe Point.** Farther north is the difficult to access but beautiful black sand beach of **Waipi'o Bay.** All are described in the HAMAKUA AND WAIMEA SIGHTS section.

| Kua Bay | Green Sand | New Black | White Powder |
| White Sand | Beach | Sand Beach | Sand from Florida |

The Big Island is a snorkeler's paradise. This is at the Captain Cook Monument in Kealakekua Bay.

Take a deep breath and do some stretching before you read this chapter, because the Big Island has so much to see and do that you're likely to pull something just reading about it all. Among the more popular are fishing, golfing, snorkeling, SCUBA, hiking, horseback riding, kayaking, helicopter tours, boat trips, submarine rides and whale watching. Whatever you're into—even snow skiing!—you're likely to find it here on the Big Island.

Activities can be booked directly with the individual activity providers or through activity companies. *Sometimes* you can get better deals through activity companies. Many resorts have activity directors and booths, sometimes run by the activity providers themselves, so be aware that their "recommendations" are sometimes biased. Many of the booths spread around the island are actually forums for selling timeshares. That's not a dig at timeshares; it's just that you need to know the real purpose of some of these booths. They can be very aggressive. (Don't get skewered by one of the long metal hooks.) Free breakfasts and "island orientations" are often similar to activity booths. So if you are steered to XYZ helicopter company and assured that they are the best, that's fine, but consider the source. We walk up to these booths frequently. Some are reputable and honest, and some are outrageous. We have no stake in *any* company we recommend;

we just want to steer you in the best direction we can.

These are those 4-wheeled things that look like Tonka Toys on steroids with knobby tires. They are often used by ranchers these days to chase cows. And they're quite a bit of fun to ride. **ATV Outfitters** (889–6000) is our favorite. They'll take you around private land near the northern tip of the island on ATVs. For $109 you cruise along for 1½ hours, taking in the coastal scenery. They'll provide beverages and long pants (if you left them at home). The ATVs are easy to operate with automatic transmissions. (Riding wimps will do fine on these.) You need to weigh between 90–300 pounds. They also have a 22-mile, 3-hour deluxe tour for $249. All in all, these trips are lots of fun, and the coastal scenery they show you is great.

Also available but less interesting is **Kahua Ranch** (882–7954) that has 1½-hour tours for $85 and $100 respectively.

With a moniker like The Big Island, you would expect an endless variety of biking choices. Unfortunately, most roads have bad or no shoulders, and most unpaved roads have lava that is murder on street bikes. With this in mind, your best opportunities are on a **mountain bike**.

If you are willing to transport a mountain bike somewhere, these three rides can be fun:

South Point—See map on page 79 and the description of the area. You can ride from South Point past Green Sand Beach on the 4WD roads—lots of fun. The wind is usually with you coming back. This is wide open country with good mountain bike roads.

Volcano—There's a dirt "escape" road that leads through beautiful rain forest from Thurston Lava Tube to Chain of Craters Road and the Mauna Ulu Trailhead. (See maps on pages 92 and 195.) The 4-mile road is well maintained and very scenic, with green assaulting your eyes from both directions. Return on the escape road, or take Chain of Craters road back up (right) 1½ miles, then take Hilina Pali Road as far down as you want to go before returning.

Mana Road—This road leads through Parker Ranch in Waimea and winds around Mauna Kea to near Saddle Road. It starts near the 55 mile marker on the main highway in Waimea. See maps on pages 124 and 135, and back foldout map to get an idea of the route. It's a 44-mile dirt road to Mauna Kea Road near Saddle Road. Unless you are motivated and arrange for transportation from Saddle Road, you'll probably just want to take it as far as you like, then turn around and come back. The first 18 miles are relatively easy and pass through *fairly* flat, sometimes foggy, quiet plains of grass and cows. Past 18 miles, it gets hillier and bumpier and enters a beautiful forest reserve. Be sure to close any gates you pass (all 4 of them) that are already closed. Cleverly worded or placed signs sometimes *imply* that you may not traverse the road. Actually, it's a public right of way. At 10⁴⁄₁₀ miles is a fork—take the right one.

If you are staying in Kona and want to ride on the street, cruise down Alii

Drive along the coast. If you're staying in Hilo, Stainback Hwy (described on page 111) is a great road to sail down on a mountain bike. You could then take North Kulani to Hwy 11 where the shoulders coming back to Hilo are usually wide.

Guided Tours

Several companies offer a variety of guided tours. Expect to pay $75–$145. Consider calling **Mauna Kea Mountain Bikes** (883–0130). **Red Sail Sports** (886–2876) also has a tour for $80.

Bike Shops

In Kona, the best bike shop we know is **HP Bikeworks** (326–2453), visible from the highway, off Kaiwi Street. Excellent selection of bikes and bike accessories. Full suspension mountain bikes (the best you'll find on the island) rent for $50 per day, half suspensions are $35. (Prices drop if you rent for longer.) **Hawaiian Pedals** (329–2294) rents cheap mountain bikes for reasonable prices. **Dave's Bikes** (329–4522) is a good repair shop. Their rentals are fair at $15 per day, and Dave's a friendly guy. In Kohala, **Red Sail Sports** (886–2876) rents bikes for $7 per hour, $20 for 8 hours. Restricted to the resort area, feel free to pass. **C&S Outfitters** (885–5005) is in Waimea on Hwy 19 near Kamamalu. $35 per day. If you're a serious biker and want to bring your own from home, **Hilo Bike Hub** (961–4452) will receive and assemble it and then pack it back up for you for $60. Adjustments and cartons are an extra charge.

BOAT TOURS

See OCEAN TOURS on page 210.

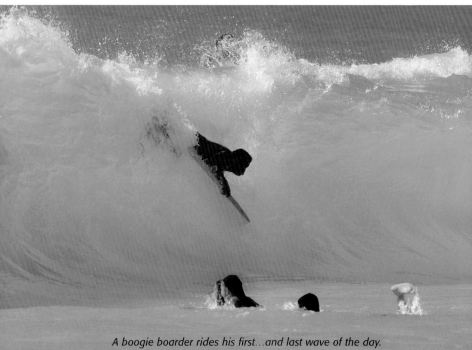

A boogie boarder rides his first…and last wave of the day.

Camp Sites–County Sites in Black, State Sites in Red, National Park Sites in

Kapa'a Beach Park & Mahukona Beach Park

Spencer Beach Park

Hapuna Beach Park

Waimanu Valley

Kalopa State Park

Laupahoehoe Beach Park

Kolekole Beach Park

Mauna Kea State Park

Mauna Loa Cabin

Ho'okena Beach Park

Miloli'i Beach Park

Namakani Paio

Kulanaokuaiki

Mackenzie State Rec. Park

Issac Hale Beach Park

Halepe and Keauhou Shelters

Punalu'u Beach Park

Whittington Beach Park

Boogie boarding (riders are derisively referred to as *spongers* by surfers) is where you ride a wave on what is essentially a sawed-off surfboard. It can be a real blast. You need short, stubby fins to catch bigger waves (which break in deeper water), but small waves can be snared by simply standing in shallow water and lurching forward as the wave is breaking. If you've never done it before, stay away from big waves; they can drill you. Surf is usually highest in winter months. Smooth-bottom boards work best. Men who don't do this often should—*this is important*—wear shirts, otherwise you can rub your *da kines* raw. (Women already have this situation covered.)

The section on BEACHES describes whether a beach is good for boogie boarding. Our favorite is **Hapuna** in Kohala. Conditions are usually excellent. We also like Mauna Kea, Manini'owali/ Kua

Bay and White Sands Beach. You won't have any trouble finding places to rent boards, so we won't bother mentioning them individually. Just keep an eye out for signs. Expect to pay $5–$8 per day, $15–$20 per week. You can buy them at Costco, Wal-Mart, etc. for $40+.

CAMPING

There's a drive-up campground at the **Kilauea Volcano** called Namakani Paio, just outside the park entrance at 4,000 feet. (See map on page 92.) They have 10 simple cabins for $50 each. Each has a couple of beds, community showers (good thing it's not the other way around) and a BBQ. 967–7321 for reservations. Tents are also permitted for free, and there's almost always plenty of space. No reservations. There's a campsite (pit toilet only) in the park called **Kulanaokuaiki** on Hilina Pali Road.

Also in the park are several campsites that require long hikes. Contact the park directly at 985–6017 to see which ones are open. You can pick up your permits when you get there, and there's usually not a problem in getting them.

Off Saddle Road at a chilly 6,500 feet, cabins are available at **Mauna Kea State Park**. They're $55 per night for up to four people, and have two bedrooms, range, refrigerators, toilet and cookware. Some are heated. Call 974–6200 for reservations. No water, and they close them for long periods during droughts.

Kalopa Native Forest State Park has decent cabins for $55 and covered campsites for tents. The limited hiking is good, and the park is in beautiful shape.

Many of the beach parks around the island are available for camping with a county permit. They are shown on the map on the previous page. Hapuna has A-frame cabins available from the state. There were other sites at press time that were too disgusting to recommend, so we left them off the map. Camping at state parks is $5 per family per night.

Waimanu Valley is utterly remote and stunningly beautiful. No facilities are available. It'll take most of a day to go down into Waipiʻo Valley up the trail on the cliff, then down into Waimanu. For this and other **state campsites**, call Division of Forestry and Wildlife at (808) 974–4221 or State Parks (974–6200). For **county campsites**, call Parks and Recreation at (808) 961–8311.

OK, so technically we should have put this under *spelunking*, but we had a sneaking suspicion that it might get overlooked there.

The Big Island is the land of lava tubes. The other islands had them, too, but most collapsed over time. Lava tubes are a characteristic of young, growing islands. And they don't get any younger than the Big Island.

In the ADVENTURE and HIKING sections we've identified some lava tubes that you can hike through *on your own*. If that prospect seems too much trouble or too risky for you, there are guided lava tube hikes that you may want to consider. Both are in the southern or eastern part of the island since it's the most geologically active. These companies seem very flexible and relaxed in their approach. About 2 hours seems the normal tour where you'll go 1–2 miles.

Lava Tube Tours (967–7208) takes you along part of Kazumura Cave near Glenwood, the longest lava tube known in the world. The guide's knowledge of geology is the best of the two. They'll supply the lights (though poor ones—if you have a dive light, we suggest you bring your own). The walking is pretty easy and you'll learn a lot. $10 or $15 per person.

Volcano Cave Adventures (960–5664) has an unusual cave from a Mauna Loa flow in Glenwood. Though their geology knowledge is poor, the tube is a bit more interesting. It's unusual in that there's lots of mud and some water flowing through it. The footing is much more awkward here (and the lights are weak, too), but it's fun and they're friendly if a bit unorganized. $35 per person (2-person min.). *Probably* only available on weekends.

If you had to pick the one sport Kona is most famous for, it would probably be its big game fishing. The waters off the Kona coast drop to great depths quickly and are teeming with big game fish. When there's a strike, the adrenaline level of everyone on board shoots through the roof. Most talked about are the marlin *(very hard fighters known for multiple runs)*, including blue, stripers and the occasional black. These goliaths can tip the scales at over 1,000 pounds. (Virtually all marlin above 300 pounds are female.) Also in abundance are ono, also called wahoo *(one of the fastest fish in the ocean and indescribably delicious—they strike very hard but tire quicker)*, mahimahi *(vigorous fighters—excellent on light tackle)*, ahi *(delicious yellowfin tuna)* and spearfish. With calm sunny conditions 300 days per year, quick access to the fishing areas, and strong competition among over 100 fishing companies, Kona has become a magnet for first-timers wishing to try their hand at catching the big one.

A Few Things You Should Know

Fish are plentiful year-round but more numerous in the summer, a bit less so in the winter.

The largest blue marlin ever caught in the state was a hull-popping 1,805 lbs.

Most boats leave out of Honokohau Harbor, just north of Kona. A surprising number of the thousand pounders (granders) have been caught just outside the harbor. This is probably because the harbor is flushed every day by freshwater springs, making the water clean and clear. This natural flushing expels the contents of the harbor on a daily basis. Perhaps passing fish like to hang around the harbor entrance to scoop up the results of that day's fish cleaning.

Most boats troll nonstop. Licenses aren't required. You will probably have to bring your own food and beverages.

Most boats here don't target a particular fish—they just troll for whatever they can get.

Most passengers on Kona fishing boats are novices, so don't feel self-conscious if you have no idea what you are doing. Deck hands will handle all of the arrangements; just sit back and relax.

You will either go on a shared charter (with other folks) or do a private charter. Nearly all charter boats are licensed for six people. Since boats range from 26–60 feet, how big a boat you charter will determine how roomy you feel. The fewer people on your boat, the greater the chance that *you* will be the one reeling in the fish since you share the lines with fewer people.

There are half-day (morning or afternoon) charters available, full-day, and overnighters. If this is your first time, do a half day to see if boat travel agrees with you. Mornings offer best conditions. Shared charters are getting harder to find. Sea Wife II has them for $80. You can do a private half-day charter for $400–$600. Full-day private charters go for $600–$900 or more for the big boats. *Usually,* the bigger the boat, the higher the price. Individual boat rates can change often depending on the season, fishing conditions and whims of the owners. Consequently, we'll forgo listing individual boat rates since this information is so perishable and instead list a few companies that we recommend. Call them directly to get current rates.

If you're easy-queasy, take an anti-seasickness medication. There are people who never get sick regardless of conditions, and those who turn green just watching *A Perfect Storm* on DVD. Nothing can ruin an ocean outing quicker than being hunched over the stern feeding the fish. Scopolamine patches prescribed by doctors can have side effects including (occasionally) blurred vision that can last a week. Dramamine II or Bonine taken the night before and the morning of a trip also seems to work well for many, though some drowsiness may occur. Ginger is a mild preventative. Try powdered ginger, ginger pills or even *real* ginger ale—can't hurt, right?

Tipping: 10–15% split between the captain and deck hand is customary if you are pleased with their performance. If the captain is a jerk and the deck hand throws up on you, you're not obligated to give 'em diddly.

You should know in advance that in Hawai'i, the fish belongs to the boat. What happens to the fish is entirely up to the captain and they usually keep it. You may catch a 1,000-pound marlin and be told that you can't have as much as a steak from it. If this bothers you, you're out of luck. If the ono or another small fish are striking a lot and there is a glut of them, you might be allowed to keep it—or half of it. You *may* be able to make arrangements in advance to the contrary, but I doubt it.

If you want to catch and release, or tag and release, make sure in advance that your boat will accommodate you. Most will, but some don't. If you do, use lures—live bait usually results in the fish coughing up its stomach, which kills it.

You might want to go down to the fuel dock at Honokohau Harbor around 11 a.m. or 3:30 p.m. for fish weigh-ins to see what's being caught and by whom. The boats hoist flags on their way back, each one representing a different species of fish caught on that trip.

If you fish from Kawaihae, expect ono and mahimahi rather than bigger stuff.

Whether you catch fish or not, it's great being out on the Kona Coast.

Popular boats can get booked up in advance. Making arrangements before you arrive can maximize your chances of getting a good boat.

Captains and deckhands come and go. Below are some boats that we've had good experiences with or that have good reputations as of press time. If you have a contrary experience with any one of them or have an experience with any company that you'd like to share with us, please contact us at the address listed on page 4 so we can stay on top of these boats. The number after each name is the boat length.

For the big stuff try:

Foxy Lady (46').................960–3009
Sea Genie II (39').............325–5355
Ihu Nui (35').....................325–1513
Camelot (34')....................936–9515
Sea Strike (31')................325–2108
Reel Pleasure (36')...........882–1413
Sea Wife II (38')...............329–1806

For light tackle try:

Reel Action (30')...............325–6811

To cut through the maze of companies, a reputable charter service company can be invaluable. Unfortunately, these come and go with amazing rapidity. **Charter Services Hawai'i** at 334–1881 or (800) 567–2650 has helpful personnel who gave the facts without the nonsense.

As a rule, we are always leery of activity booths—some are helpful and knowledgeable but some are scoundrels. However, at Honokohau Harbor, you might want to call 329–5735. They are right at the harbor, they have *lots* of boats to choose from and usually have the skinny on what's going on there.

Kona's famous **International Billfish Tournament** is held each year in August. Fishermen from all over the world come to compete for top prize. As a result, boats tend to fill up faster during this time.

Shoreline Fishing

The entire shoreline is available to you. If you want, you can find a secluded spot off any ugly looking lava road on the island. Otherwise, on Hilo side, Hilo Bay, especially near the mouth of the Wailuku River, is good. South Point is excellent. In Kailua-Kona, the seawall in front of Hulihe'e Palace is a great place and easy to access. As snorkelers, we've seen schools numbering in the many thousands congregate off this area.

Kona Fishing Tackle (326–2934) is located in Kona. They are your best source for supplies.

And remember: Never say, "I'm going fishing." Say, "I am going to the woods." Hawaiian legend holds that the fish will hear and avoid you if you warn them.

The Big Island is rapidly becoming known as *the* island to visit if you want to golf till you drop. This actually presented a problem for us in evaluating the individual courses. It would have been easy to froth at the mouth over most of them because compared to courses elsewhere, most are outstanding. But that would have missed the point. So with elevated expectations in mind, we have reviewed the courses *relative to each other*. This is important because if we get less than excited about a particular course, it doesn't mean it's a dump. It

just means that you can do better elsewhere on the island.

Prices at the top courses are higher than many are used to. If you stay at a resort near the course, you'll probably be eligible for much cheaper rates.

A Few Tips

Wind is often a factor at Kohala courses and is usually stronger in the afternoon. Sunshine is *almost* guaranteed in Kohala. Conditions are usually best in the mornings at all courses around the island.

Greens tend to break to the ocean, even when they look uphill.

Kona's driving range near Old Kona Airport is **Swing Zone** (329–6909).

Some courses offer big discounts after noon or 3 p.m. Check with individual courses for these or other discounts.

We also list kama'aina rates here. These are fees that Hawai'i residents pay. Though less, bear in mind that there are often restrictions on playing times.

Mauna Kea Golf Course (882–5400)

According to local lore, in the early 1960s, Laurence Rockefeller flew Robert Trent Jones, Sr., to an isolated, barren, mostly unknown place on the Big Island called Kohala. He took him out to an a'a lava field, pointed to the rock and asked, "Can you build me a golf course out of that?" Jones supposedly knelt down, picked up two pieces of a'a and ground them together. They crumbled. He then said, "Mr. Rockefeller—you've got yourself a golf course."

Opened in 1964, Mauna Kea is still the course by which all others are compared. Fairly open and forgiving rolling terrain, this course epitomizes what a Big Island course can be. The layout is brilliant, the location is dazzling, and the course is just plain fun. Number 3 is a

Course	Par	Yards	Fees
Discovery Harbor	72	6,326	$30*
Hamakua Country Club (X2)	66	4,920	$20
Hapuna Golf Course	72	6,029	$145*
Hilo Municipal Golf Course	71	6,006	$29
Hualalai Golf Club	72	6,032	$195
Kona Country Club Mauka	72	5,976	$145*
Kona Country Club Ocean	72	6,281	$160*
Makalei Country Club	72	6,161	$99*
Mauna Kea	72	6,365	$210*
Mauna Lani North	72	6,086	$205*
Mauna Lani South	72	5,940	$205*
Naniloa Golf Course (X2)	70	5,615	$30
SeaMountain at Punalu'u	72	6,045	$50*
Volcano Golf & Country Club	72	6,190	$64*
Waikoloa Beach	70	5,958	$175*
Waikoloa Kings'	72	6,010	$175*
Waikoloa Village	72	6,146	$75*
Waimea Country Club	72	6,210	$90*

* Indicates power cart included in price. Yards are from the men's regular tees.

signature hole that hugs the shoreline—a very difficult hole. Number 9 shoots downhill toward the hotel. Hole 11, a par three, drops precipitously downhill—consider yourself lucky if you par. Hole 17 is 555 beautiful curving yards. If you were on island visiting us, this is the course we'd take you to. The rolling scenery and the time-tested play seem ageless.

Located at the Mauna Kea Resort just south of Kawaihae—the turnoff is near the 68 mile marker on Highway 19. Fees are $210 for standard, $150 for resort guests. Kama'aina rate is $105. Carts are included; walking is allowed only in the afternoon.

Hapuna Golf Course (880–3000)

This is the other course at the Mauna Kea/Hapuna Prince resort complex. Designed by Arnold Palmer and Ed Seay and opened in 1992, it features narrower fairways, so bring more balls than you would at Mauna Kea. The course is well

marked, well organized and well kept. Don't expect to be overwhelmed with hazards, however. The narrowness is your challenge. The course is ensconced in an older lava field filled with scrub, rather than the starker, yet more attractive newer lava fields, such as the Mauna Lani's South Course.

Hapuna is a very pleasant and well-run course, though not overly remarkable. (Services, however, are excellent.) Standard fees are $145, resort guests pay $120, and the kama'aina rate is $65. Carts are included. Walking is allowed but not recommended since the 9s are separated by a large distance.

Mauna Lani Resort (885–6655)

Called the Francis H. I'i Brown South Course and the North Course, these two courses are the result of the 1991 splitting of the 1980 course. North and South each got nine and added nine. Of the two, the **South Course** is by far the most popular. It is closer to the ocean and is nicely incorporated into the stark lava. Fingers of 'a'a seem to reach out and grab your ball, so the accuracy-challenged will want to bring more than usual. 'A'a is a notorious ball eater and shoe wrecker. The course is well maintained, and some of the holes are highly memorable. Number 13 is quintessential Hawai'i. Driving toward and along the ocean, make sure you drive *your cart* on the left side for incomparable ocean views. Look back toward hole 7 and the secluded Honoka'ope Beach—a stunning hole by anyone's definition. At 15 you can count yourself among the elite if you can make par. It shoots over a respectable ocean cove onto greens guarded by cleverly placed traps. Par 3...we'll see.

Whereas the South Course is more open and expansive, the less used **North Course** has more trees and a more "traditional" use of lava boundaries. There are several lava tubes sprinkled about, and the kiawe trees often define the fairway. (Remember to be careful of their penetrating thorns when looking for an errant ball.) Make sure you hit solid on number 4—the scrub-filled lava gorge is laden with muffed drives. Number 17 is a short 119 yards from the tournament tees, but the narrow channel and well-placed traps call for lots of concentration.

Mauna Lani courses are the best maintained courses on the island. If you can only play one, make it the South. Otherwise, you'll find that playing both will offer very different and enjoyable games. Our biggest gripe is that both courses are poorly marked, and the free map is not very accurate. Standard fees for South & North courses at $205. Resort guests pay $140. Kama'aina rate is $100. Discounted during certain times. Between the 73 & 74 mile markers on Highway in Kohala. See map on page 53.

Waikoloa Resort

You have your choice of the **Waikoloa Kings'** or the **Waikoloa Beach**.

Waikoloa Kings' (886–7888) is probably our second favorite Kohala course. This links-style course is the tougher of the two. Features include deep bunkers, clever use of lava terrain and confiscatory lava boundaries. You stand little chance of retrieving your ball in this 'a'a from hell. They made good use of lava balls (you'll know them when you see them). Golf balls seem magnetically attracted to them.

Hole 5 is deceiving. There are two enormous lava balls nestled in a sand trap larger than many Kohala beaches. The cup is 327 yards away, and if there is a wind at your back and you are in a hard-driving mood, you might make it over the lava—or you might want to chicken out and use two strokes to get over them... anything to avoid being *behind* them. From most of the course on a clear day, you can see five volcanoes—Kohala, Mauna Kea, Hualalai, Mauna Loa and Haleakala on Maui. Palms and plumeria are scattered about among the trees. Though challenging, this is a course to be savored.

Waikoloa Beach (886–6060) gets far more golfers than Kings'. That's probably because it is in a location that affords more visibility and because it is closer to the ocean. Kings' is not seen from as many hotel rooms. Waikoloa Beach is a par 70, and its resort style layout is a bit more forgiving. It has less personality than the Kings' but is a fine course nonetheless. Check out the petroglyphs on your left on your way to number 9. On number 9, the wind can play havoc since there is a water border on your left almost the entire 558 yards. Number 15 is a whopping 591-yard voyage from the champ tees.

Both courses are well groomed and surprisingly well watered, sometimes to the point of being soggy (as evidenced by the number of golden plovers during the winter months). These two courses can get more crowded than other Kohala courses because they actively seek local players. Standard fees are $195, resort guests pay $130, kama'aina rate is $75. Near 76 mile marker in Kohala. See map on page 53.

Hualalai Golf Club (325-8480)

Opened in 1996, this course is private, meaning that only those staying at the Four Seasons Resort or at the adjacent residential community can play. (Kona Village guests *may* be able to play.) This Jack Nicklaus course is more player-friendly than most of his designs. There's a constant 5% grade toward the ocean, so there's lots of ocean views from the lushly manicured fairways. Very fast greens and a bit less wind than most Kohala resorts. Rates are $195.

Waikoloa Village (883-9621)

Up mauka of the Kohala resort area, three words come to mind here—cheaper, windy and walking. At $75 for standard rates, it's cheaper than the big boys in Kohala. (And I'll tell you right now that you are better off at Waimea Country Club if the weather is cooperating.) This course is popular with locals who appreciate the $35 Big Island kama'aina fares (cheaper with specials). As for the wind, you may see a bird on this course lay the same egg three times. Play *early* if you want to avoid the wind. Lastly, you can walk the course if you so choose, unlike most Kohala courses.

There are more trees here than many other courses. Some like to compare it to a very good municipal course, which sounds fair. It is adequately maintained (though poorly marked—you may even get lost on occasion). Overall, you get what you pay for here. Look for lots of wild goats and turkeys here.

Waimea Country Club (885-8777)

One of the most underrated courses on the island. You may think you are in Scotland rather than Hawai'i. You are a long way from and above the ocean. *Wide* open fairways, plush, well-watered grass, fog and mist often, and a delicious rolling terrain. These, along with a visitor rate of $95, make it one of the better golf bargains you'll find. The caveat is the weather—it rains a lot here, so call and ask if it looks like it will be *pumping* that day. Or better yet, just play early. A windbreak of eucalyptus trees surrounds the course. Geese, pheasant and quail all grace the course's water hazards. Number nine is as picture-perfect as you will find. A graceful curving fairway rambles down, around and up to the green.

If you're scared off by the fees the big boys charge elsewhere, this is a nice alternative—weather permitting. The course is located between the 51 and 52 mile markers on Highway 19 in Waimea.

Makalei Country Club (325-6625)

This is one of the lesser known Big Island courses. Located 2,100-2,900 feet upslope, it's cooler and less windy up here than at the Kohala courses. There are beautiful views down the coast, and bougainvilleas dot the cart paths. The course is carved nicely into the forest. Wailing peacocks are scattered about, as well as pheasant and turkeys. Number 4 has a low rock wall to act as a speed bump for low shots. Hole 10 wanders 580 yards with impressive views of the

*Over the water and onto the green.
Mauna Kea's hole #3 is vintage Hawaiian golf.*

coastline below. Smile when you tee off on number 15—you're being watched. They videotape you, and if you get a hole in one, you get a prize. (It's an easy hole to overshoot.) Makalei is a fun course. You won't get pounding Pacific surf, but you will get a moderately challenging course that's well maintained and easy to recommend. Designed by Dick Nugent. (Any relation to Ted?) $99 for standard fees, kama'aina is $49. Seven miles north of Kona on Hwy 190. Carts are included and mandatory.

Kona Country Club (322-2595)

The four sets of nine here were built over a period of 25 years, and their personalities are all different. Courses are split into the **Ocean Course**, and the **Mauka Course**.

The **Ocean** has some fine ocean and upslope views. Number 12 is a signature hole that skirts the ocean, with enough palm trees to remind you of why you came to Hawai'i. At 13, look for the blowhole near the handicap tees. Note the fantastic corkscrew-shaped palm tree near the white tees at 14. The 124-yard

number 17 shoots over a lava gorge—one of the few lava hazards. There is a flock of wild parrots at this course, so keep an eye (or ear) out for them.

The **Mauka** is more modern, making use of, rather than denying, the natural lava in this area. Number 14 drops 62 feet, over a water hazard and onto the green, with smashing views down the coastline. In fact, holes 14–18 all sport nice coastline views.

Someone must have gotten scared by a lawyer once. There are more warning signs at these courses than any we've seen. Since this is the only course in Kailua-Kona, expect more people here. There are plenty of signs to prod you to keep it moving. *(If you are at this hole, you better have done it in 45 minutes.)* The fairways for both courses could use a little TLC. Greens seem fine. All in all, the course is only fair. If you pay the full standard price, you paid way too much. But check for specials—they often have one or two. Standard fees are $160 for the Ocean, $145 for the Mauka. Carts are included and mandatory.

Discovery Harbor Golf & Country Club

We're still trying to discover the harbor at this course 4 miles from the unreachable ocean. It is the southernmost course in the United States, but it's probably not quite far south enough. Rundown and dilapidated, this course is a must-miss. It's now used mostly by the adjacent community. On the positive side, at least you won't have someone prodding you from behind if you want to play slow. Standard fees are $28. It was temporarily closed at press time due to lack of use.

SeaMountain—Punalu'u (928–6222)

The layout and promise were excellent here, but the course has been a victim to the fortunes (or lack thereof) of the developer. As a result, it's getting pretty mangy in spots. SeaMountain was sold way back in 1994 (for less that a *tenth* of the purchase price), and we haven't seen much evidence that the current owners are keen to make it a grand course. It's hard to predict what you will encounter, but the price is cheap for a scenic seaside golf course in Hawai'i. If it's in good shape, you'll find the location a real winner. Even if it's not, the fees are still worth it if you are in the neighborhood. Located near Punalu'u Beach on the southeast side of the island, 56 miles from Hilo and 65 miles from Kona. Standard fees are $47–$50, kama'aina rate is $29–$32. Carts are included and mandatory.

Volcano Golf & Country Club (967–7331)

Who would ever think that you could have a lush course just 1 mile from the main crater of the most active volcano on earth? Bring your warmies—the 4,000-foot altitude brings a chill to the air. The play is straightforward with few hazards. Mother Nature and the groundskeepers keep the grass green and healthy. Unlike other courses, the afternoons here *may* be better in the summer. Mist and fog sometimes make it interesting, but wind is usually low. Remember to club down since the ball travels farther up here. This is a nice course offering a moderate challenge and a peaceful setting. Standard fees are $64.

Naniloa Golf Course (935–3000)

Much of the infrastructure is run down and dilapidated, but the course, aided by the fertile Hilo climate, is in fairly nice shape. The RACK rates seem high given that this is a nine-hole course. Overall, forgettable. Standard fees are $30. Carts are $5 per 9 holes.

Hilo Municipal (959–7711)

Fairly flat layout and no sand traps (too much rain) are the hallmarks of this course. The play is not overly hard and the setting is quite pretty. It gets soggy after a heavy rain, so consider this beforehand. This course is usually pretty crowded and about half walk, so weekends should be avoided for the delays. Standard fees are $29–$34. Carts extra.

Hamakua Country Club (775–7244)

Built as a community course in the formerly sugar-rich area of Hamakua, this *small* 9-hole course is popular with locals who come to play and talk story in the "clubhouse." Greens fees are $20. (You're on the honor system—just drop your money in the box in the clubhouse and grab a hand-drawn scorecard.) The holes are very close together and amazingly well tended. The community takes obvious pride in caring for it. You won't find a lot of challenges (and you won't find club rentals or power carts), but you will find a gentle course set in a gentle, friendly community.

From the main highway (19) east of Waimea, turn just before (west of) the Texaco station between the 42 and 43 mile markers and take the frontage road 100 yards to the "clubhouse."

Unlike most activities that I can review *anonymously*, powered hang gliders (know as trikes) are aircraft that I fly myself and I'm familiar with pilots of these aircraft since we're all members of the small ultralight community. So it's one of those rare cases when it's not possible for me to review the company without them knowing who I am.

Don't confuse this with hang gliding. This craft has an engine, it's bigger and more stable, and some even have a powered parachute attached to the craft...just in case (a safety feature they're just beginning to install on traditional airplanes). Trikes take off and land on regular runways, and the ease and grace of the craft are glorious. (Rent the movie *Fly Away Home* if you want to see what they're like.) It's as close to flying like a bird as any form of flight I know. Although I also fly traditional aircraft between the islands, trikes are what I have come to love for the pure joy of flying and, in my opinion, are the safest form of ultralight flight available. (I'm not a daredevil and wouldn't fly them myself if I felt unsafe in them,

though any time you're in the air you're potentially at risk, even on the airlines.)

Advanced Recreation (775–9393) gives lessons in a powered hang glider. Pilot Jeff Hoff has been flying for years, both ultralights and fixed wing airplanes. It's $85 for 30–40 minutes of instruction.

HELICOPTERS

If you've been on a helicopter or airplane flight on another island, especially Kaua'i, you've been treated to wall-to-wall, tongue-wagging sights. The Big Island, however, has lots of fantastic areas spread about with less interesting areas connecting them. The northeast side is a lush wonderland, the southeast side is where the active volcano is and the west side is dominated by lava. That's why limited tours are so different on each side of the island.

Here, more than most islands, your tour is affected by the passion (or lack thereof) of the pilot. A boring pilot will sound something like this: "On your left is such and such valley, and on your right is such and such hill, and in front is the such and such lava flow." *So what!?* What you really want is a knowledgeable pilot with a command of the island who also knows to speak only when it improves the silence. We're prejudiced toward companies that let you ask the pilot questions through a microphone, as opposed to those where the pilots tells you "everything you need to know."

In the past, air tour operators could fly at any altitude they wanted, often producing low-flying *Apocalypse Now!* type flights, but those days are gone. Air tour operators are now restricted to 500 feet over unpopulated areas. But that doesn't mean that you won't walk off the aircraft with drool running down your shirt from the mesmerizing experience. It can still happen; you just aren't *assured* of it anymore. When the music, helicopter, pilot, and sights all come together, it'll still blow you away. We've flown with pilots who have an undisguised passion for the island and those who may as well be driving a flying bus. Unfortunately, most companies don't use the same pilots all the time, so it's sometimes hard to steer you toward the good ones.

In general, we recommend that helicopter tours be taken from Hilo. Tours that leave from Kona bound for the volcano spend too much time over less interesting areas, and you'll pay through the nose. The exception is Blue Hawaiian's trip from Waikoloa to the Hamakua coast (described below).

A-Star helicopters are the most popular. They hold six passengers, with four in back and two beside the pilot up front. The middle seats in the back are so-so; the others are good. Think of the A-Star as a pleasant tour bus. One company is also using **Eco-Stars**, a much larger and quieter cousin to the A-Star. Windows are larger so you'll have better views and it's noticeably roomier inside. The downside is the price. Since these birds are so expensive, you may pay a hefty premium of around 20% more for the comfort. **Hughes 500Ds** have two passengers in the somewhat cramped back and two *outstanding* front seats next to the pilot. This copter feels like a sports car, and the side views from the back are excellent. Windows come off if you want. They are less popular because they are less profitable to the operators. Some companies, like Tropical, have them but use them more often for non-tour business. **Bell Jet Rangers** are less comfortable with three in back and one passenger up front. The back middle seat is a poor seat indeed. We like the Hughes, Eco-Stars and A-Stars. We're lukewarm on Bell Jets.

Air tours give you a perspective on the volcano that you can't get any other way.

Afternoon tours are sometimes bumpier. I can tell you that as a pilot myself, I do most of my flying on the Big Island in the morning when conditions are usually best. You may want to also.

If you want to get around the altitude restrictions, think about *chartering* the aircraft. It's worth considering if you have a group, or if you strike up a friendship with other travelers. It might not cost any more than a regular tour, and *you* get to call the shots. (Leave the doors off if you want on the Hughes.) Make sure you rent one that has two-way communication with the pilot.

The Companies

Blue Hawaiian (961–5600) uses nice A-Stars out of Waikoloa, near the Kohala resort area, and Hilo. They use the expensive Bose Acoustic Noise-Canceling headphones and have videos of your trip for an extra $20. (Pretty poor quality, though.) The two-hour volcano and Hamakua Coast tour, which lands in Hilo, is $450 and uses roomy **Eco-Stars**. (It's $50 cheaper on their A-Star.) They also have a Waikoloa to Hamakua Coast trip for $235. No volcano, just lots of beautiful valleys you won't see on a volcano flight. Overall, a good outfit. Their on-line discounts can be pretty decent.

Tropical Helicopters (961–6810) is our second choice. They use a Hughes from Hilo. They have a 35-minute quickie trip to the volcano from Hilo for

$142 as well as a more comprehensive (and really fun) volcano experience from Hilo *with no doors* for $190. Less recommended trips from Kona in their Bell are also available.

Sunshine (882–1223) uses A-Stars but it's hard to justify their prices— $198 for their 50-minute volcano trip from Hilo, $390 for the trip from Kohala. They charge Eco-Star prices for their A-Star.

Safari (969–1259) leaves from Hilo. Through the years we've had concerns about their product. We've found their narrations lacking at times. And their prices seem unjustifiably steep. Their 55-minute volcano tour is $227; the 40-minute is $167.

Mauna Loa Helicopters is a little different. *You* fly the beast. It's a 2-person chopper and they give lessons or you can charter it *relatively* cheap.

Airplanes

Because of its size and relative flatness, the Big Island makes airplane tours an acceptable alternative. Some, like Big Island Air, use large tour planes. The volcano experience is certainly diminished from a plane (since you rush by things), but if you insist on leaving from Kona, the price is tempting.

Island Hoppers (329–0018) uses small (four-person) airplanes out of Kona and Hilo for aerial sightseeing. Flights are cheaper and shorter from Hilo ($164 for

Company	Phone #	Departure	Helicopter Type	2-Way*
Blue Hawaiian	961–5600	Waikoloa, Hilo	A-Star, Eco-Star	No
Tropical Helicopters	961–6810	Hilo, Kona	Bell Jet, Hughes	Yes
Sunshine	882–1223	Hapuna, Hilo	A-Star	No
Safari Helicopters	969–1259	Hilo	A-Star	Yes
Mauna Loa Helicopters	334–0234	Kona	Robinson R22	Yes

Companies toward the top are recommended higher than the ones toward the bottom.
∗ Indicates whether craft has a microphone for you to talk to the pilot.

45–50 minutes) than Kona (2½ hours for $287). The more expensive Kona flight is round-the-island, so you'll get to see the awesome valleys of the Hamakua Coast. (Avoid the out-and-back $247 Kona–volcano flight.) Overall a good company.

Big Island Air (329–4868) flies large (nine-passenger) planes from Kona on round-the-island tours (well...*mostly* around) for $289. They do a pretty good job, the routes are interesting, and the pilot does his narrating well. It's bumpy at times, so consider motion sickness medicine. (Morning is definitely best.) We'd be remiss if we didn't let you know something about them, however. Two fatal crashes in less than a year leaves us uncomfortable. We know this throws cold water

Hamakua Coast by air is the only way you'll be able to see its waterfalls.

on the review and that's not our intent, but the truth's the truth and we've noticed that their prices have gone way up since the accidents.

Renting an Airplane

Island Hoppers rents 172s for $159. Check rides required.

The Big Island has plenty of hiking to keep you happy. You can wander through a lush rain forest, walk on a volcano crater floor, puff up a frigid, snow-covered mountain, hike along an empty tropical beach, teeter on the edge of steep canyons, or saunter along an old Hawaiian lava trail. The possibilities and diversity are incredible.

Footwear—We do much of our hiking here in hiking sandals or light trail shoes.

For really muddy conditions we occasionally use boots lined with Gore-Tex. And for stream hiking, nothing beats tabis. These look like green fuzzy mittens for your feet and stick to wet, mossy rocks better than any other kind of footwear. (Though without much stiffness, tabis may leave the bottoms of your feet feeling a bit sore.) You'll find tabis for about $25 at Wal-Mart in Kona, Wal-Mart or Longs in Hilo, KTA in Waimea.

If you're looking for the topographic maps of the island (it takes 74 to cover the island!), **Basically Books** (961–0144) in Hilo or **Hawai'i Forest & Trail** (331–8505) in Honokohau are your best bets.

We hike a lot and have become big fans of hiking sticks. We'll use two on some long hikes and find that they greatly ease the hikes and give us better balance. They have saved us several times from falling on nasty lava. Some have straps on the handles and are telescopic.

HIKING AT KILAUEA VOLCANO

Much of the best hiking on the island is found in and around Hawai'i Volcanoes National Park. In VOLCANO SIGHTS we've described lots of strolls of 30 minutes or less. They include **Bird Park** (a nice 30-minute walk through the forest), **Devastation Trail** (see how the volcano wiped out part of a forest with flying, frothed lava and how it is coming back), **Pu'u Loa Petroglyph Trail** (less than 2 miles round trip, it heads to a massive field of ancient rock carvings—this one takes a bit more than 30 minutes), **Thurston Lava Tube** (see what lava sees as it travels underground) and a few others. We've also described a trip to a pristine **Rain Forest Lava Tube** and a trek to the edge of the smoldering **Mauna Ulu Crater** in ADVENTURES.

ELSEWHERE IN THE PARK
Kilauea Iki

This is a great hike! If you are only able to do one hike while you are on the Big Island, this is one we'd recommend. It goes from ancient rain forest to a newly lava-paved crater and back through rain forest. At a little over 3 miles, it can take anywhere from two hours if you hoof it without distractions, to four hours if you stop and gawk as much as we do and enjoy lunch on the crater floor. It is a *reasonably* easy hike (well...maybe moderate) with only about 15 minutes of gentle but constant incline toward the end when you ascend about 450 feet. Before hiking, read some background on this crater and its attention-grabbing past in VOLCANO Sights.

We like to start this hike at the Kilauea Iki Overlook and go counterclockwise, through the forest first. The trip is gentler this way and is preferable to going into the crater first. (You could also start from the Visitor Center and get there via the Earthquake Trail and Byron Ledge Trail—see page 196.) You will go through a gorgeous and ancient fern and 'ohi'a forest as the trail skirts the edge of Kilauea Iki Crater. Take your time here, and enjoy the beauty and grace of the forest and birds. All along are short spur trails offering magnificent views of the crater. Judging size and distance is surprisingly difficult

Kilauea Iki

Kilauea Iki Overlook

Thurston Lava Tube

Kilauea Iki Crater

Pu'u Pua'i Spatter Cone

Devastation Trail

Pu'u Pua'i Overlook

Crater Rim Drive

0   1 MILE

© 2006 Wizard Publications, Inc.

First through lush rain forest, then across the eerie crater floor, the Kilauea Iki hike is smashing!

here until you see people walking on the crater floor. The abrupt contrast between the ancient fern forest and the newly created maw of the crater floor couldn't be greater. Though the forest is lush and cool, the 4,000-foot altitude seems to prevent mosquito problems here (though it's always a good idea to bring a repellent, just in case). Before the trail veers away from the crater for a bit, take a look across at Pu'u Pua'i and you will appreciate the scale of the eruptive event. Just keep to the left whenever you encounter a trail intersection. The descent into the crater is somewhat steep, but there are steps carved into the trail in spots and a few railings to help ease the way.

In a heartbeat you go from lush forest to barren lava. The trail bears to your left for a bit, then goes right. Cairns (piles of rock) mark the path across the floor. The lava here is more jagged since it contains remnants of lava spatters rather than the smooth lava farther ahead. Keep an eye out for a small sign pointing to the actual vent, where lava fragments are accumulating. Where you see steam escape from cracks, you will notice minerals leaching from the rock. The steam seems inoffensive compared to the nasty stuff that comes out of parts of Halema'uma'u. We like to have lunch near a steam vent about ⅓ of the way across the crater floor.

The crater floor is quiet and peaceful. You may be hot, cold, wet or dry here, depending on the weather. (Gee, *that's* a useful piece of insight.) Sounds bounce around the crater in an unpredictable way. You may hear the crunching of footsteps when no one is nearby. Plants and trees are already starting to make themselves at home in cracks on the lava floor. It's amazing to stand in this near-dead crater and to see and hear the profusion of life all around you just beyond this hostile field of Pele's destruction.

After you ascend the crater wall, keep to your left along the edge of the crater, and you are back at the overlook. Outstanding!

Napau Crater Trail

Another nice hike is the Napau Crater Trail to **Pu'u Huluhulu**. The trail (occasionally called the Mauna Ulu Trail) is the only place in the park where you can see Pu'u 'O'o, the heart of the current eruption. (There is an easier view of Pu'u 'O'o outside the park—see page 121.) This is a *long* day hike if you do the whole thing. Mauna Ulu (meaning growing mountain) erupted between 1969 and 1974, adding more than 200 acres of new land to Hawai'i's coastline, and its effects are dramatically seen on this trail. It was Kilauea's second longest flank eruption in recorded history. This trail starts on an old segment of Chain of Craters Road. (Twelve miles of this road were buried by the Mauna Ulu flow, and we've shown it on the map on the inside back cover as a stippled line.) This fairly easy trek wanders over the young Mauna Ulu flow, as well as through old forest. You'll notice stone sentries along the way, strangely shaped columns of rock. These are called **lava trees**. When lava from the Mauna Ulu flow coursed its way through here, it occasionally encountered exceptionally wet trees. These resisted the flow and the temperatures long enough for the lava to harden around the tree. When the lava level lowered, these piles remained. You will often see a circle in the middle of lava trees, the outline of the now-dead tree. Sometimes, there are half-circle outlines of the tree. These are on the upstream side of the lava, showing you which way the lava flowed.

At about 30 minutes, you come to Pu'u Huluhulu (shaggy hill), a heavily forested mound. There is a five-minute spur trail leading up to the top. From there you get an awesome view of Mauna Ulu, a third of a mile in front of you. You may see Pu'u 'O'o smoldering off in the distance (quite a bit to the left of Mauna Ulu, partially obscured by the Kane Nui o Hamo Lava Shield—see map). Be sure to look down into the pristine, fern-filled rain forest below you in the crater. It's utterly untouched, looking much like it did a thousand years ago. Looking off in the distance, you can see how the Mauna Ulu flow cut into the heart of the forest, going from green to black in a single footstep.

The view of Mauna Ulu is gorgeous. Looking over at it, you might be tempted to walk over to the top and peer into **Mauna Ulu Crater**. If so, check your insurance and see ADVENTURES.

Most people turn around from here. Past this point the trail footing gets more difficult and goes to the massive Makaopuhi Crater, then to Napau Crater, where camping is allowed. (Technically, you need a permit to go that far.) That's 6⅔ miles one way. Just before Napau, you will pass the remains of an old pulu factory. Pulu is the soft, down-like fuzz that covers the stems of some ferns. Someone thought it would make a great stuffing for pillows and mattresses, so they built a factory out

Napau Crater Trail

Escape Rd.

N
0   1 MILE

Pauahi Crater

3

Chain of Craters Road

4

Pu'u Huluhulu

Mauna Ulu Lava Flow 1969–1974

Mauna Ulu

To Makaopuhi Crater, the trail generally follows the old Chain of Craters Road, which was covered by this flow.

Kane Nui o Hamo Lava Shield

Best part of the trail starts here.

Campsite

Old Pulu Factory

Napau Crater

Makaopuhi Crater

Pu'u 'O'o Vent

Pu'u 'O'o Lava Flow

© 2006 Wizard Publications, Inc.

here. Unfortunately, pulu turns to dust after a few years. Consequently, so did their business.

Another 2 miles past Napau is **Puʻu ʻOʻo** and this is the best part of the trail. The menacing volcano looms ahead of you the whole way, reminding you why you've started this 17-mile round trip hike. The trail goes nearly to the base of the active volcano and if the trade winds are blowing in your face, you may have to contend with volcanic fumes for the last part of the trail.

Earthquake Trail/Byron Ledge

There is a cluster of trails around and below Volcano House. One of our favorite combinations is described below. It sounds more complicated than it is— use the map on page 92. All told, it takes 90–120 minutes and is moderately difficult (if that). You descend, then ascend about 400 feet. This is a good hike to take on a clear day because the views of the crater can be spectacular.

From the Visitor Center, you can walk around the right side of Volcano House, eventually heading to your left as you pass in front of Volcano House. Parts of the old trail and Crater Rim Road *fell into the crater* after an earthquake in 1983. This part of the road has become part of the Crater Rim Trail. It is eerie to see the road split in half, with guard-rails dangling into nothingness. Large, gaping chasms in the old road dispel any notions you may have that ground is inherently stable. Parts of the trail detour from the old road for safety reasons, but it is fascinating to try to safely glimpse as much of the crumbling road as you can, even if through the bushes at times. The best part shows the guard-rail and split road. Watch for this part as it's off the main trail. When the road forks, you'll usually take the right fork whenever you can. See map. The trail will eventually leave the road and descend through ʻohiʻa forest. You link up with the Byron Ledge Trail (where you turn right) and continue to the Kilauea Crater floor. (The map and trail intersection signs make it much clearer.) On the crater floor, you'll get an idea of the texture of a skimmed-over lava lake. You are only on the crater floor for a few minutes before you head back up. It's not overly steep. On the way back up, you will pass the remains of a recent landslide. Look up from the big rock. You are at *eye* level and can almost feel the slide coming at you.

At the intersection with the **Sandalwood (ʻIliahi) Trail**, you have the choice of continuing (which is a little steeper) or taking the Sandalwood Trail. We recommend the latter. It straddles the crater for awhile, featuring great views and several steam vents. Then take the Sulphur Banks Trail back to the Visitor Center.

You might want to add the **Kilauea Iki Trail** to this hike. You can access it early on from the Byron Ledge Trail. See map and description of Kilauea Iki earlier.

Rain Forest Lava Tube

In the summer of 1993 park personnel discovered a beautiful, pristine lava tube in the rain forest. Even the ancient Hawaiians apparently never discovered it. Similar to Thurston Lava Tube but with far grander details, it is accessible via a fairly easy one-hour (each way) hike through lush forest. This cave is long and loaded with lava stalactites and other treasures, making it an unparalleled hiking experience. The park wishes to control access, and they have asked us not give directions for fear that some thoughtless jerk might read it and damage some of the delicate features. Con-

Forests ruled by ferns and 'ohi'a trees make volcano hiking a time of wonder and magic.

sequently, they have started *guided* tours of 12 or so people. (Hikes were every Wednesday and some Saturdays at press time.) If you want to be on the list, call them at (808) 985–6017 in advance (it fills up) and make arrangements. Ask for the *Wild Lava Tube* (or Pu'u Po'o) guided hike; it'll knock your socks off.

They will provide helmet lights. (They don't charge for the tour, so bring batteries to help out.) Be prepared to scramble on or around large boulders on the floor that have fallen from the roof over the years. The ceiling is usually 20 feet tall, but severe claustrophobics need not apply. Take your time and expect to spend about an hour to go from one end of the cave to the other.

Also in the Park

Consider the **Crater Rim Trail**. It circles the entire Kilauea Caldera and makes for a long day. But segments such as the one between Volcano House and the Jagger Museum are dramatic. The part from the Escape Road to Chain of Craters Road passes through an exquisite fern canopy.

From the end of Chain of Craters Road, there may or may not be a trail to an **active lava flow**. See ADVENTURES for more on that.

There are long overnight trails (with camping) at **Halape**, **Keauhou** and **Ka'aha**. Hikes are down the mountain or along the coast and go for many miles. Contact the Park Service at 985–6000 for more information.

KOHALA AREA
Malama Trail to Puako Petroglyphs

Located near the Mauna Lani Resort in Kohala, this 10- 15-minute-long trail (each way) through a kiawe forest has a few petroglyphs sprinkled along the way. (Kiawe thorns are evil, wicked and hateful; be careful not to let them penetrate your shoe.) The real payoff is at the end (just past a dirt road intersection) with hundreds and hundreds of lava carvings adjacent to each other in this field in the middle of nowhere. The reasons for the Hawaiians' selection of this site has been lost to the ages. Perhaps the most obvious reason is that the slabs in this area make nice canvases. Regardless, some Hawaiians say that if you close your eyes and listen to the breeze, you can hear the sound of rock scraping against rock.

Kiholo Bay

This is a fabulous place. You can catch a nice glimpse of the bay from the scenic turnout near the 82 mile marker on Highway 19. (See map below.) Between the 82 and 83 mile markers a smooth gravel road leads almost to the shore. (The last short patch is rough, and some 2WD drivers may want to park the car and walk to the water.) From there you could walk 300 yards to the right along the shoreline to Queen's Bath. (See below.)

There's also a trail from the main highway just south of the 81 mile marker. If you take the latter trail, park at the north end of the guard-rail and take the trail toward the ocean. The trail from the highway to Kiholo Bay takes 15–20 minutes. When the trail becomes a gravel

road, it will eventually curve to the left. (At that intersection there's a gate to your right, but it's private. The public access is a bit farther along the road. The map makes this clearer.)

Kiholo Bay is a beautiful and uniquely shaped ocean inlet. It has several points of interest that make it great for exploring. First, the lagoon offers waters that are usually dead calm (but cold and fairly cloudy due to freshwater springs leaking into the bay, kicking up fine silt). Turtles *abound* here, grazing on limu in the bay. The fishponds inland, called Wainanali'i Pond, are on private property. Turtles swim through the manmade channel to the fishponds at night, perhaps to sleep unmolested. Walking around this part of the bay offers magnificent scenery. You can usually look right into the lagoon water and see the fish.

This whole area was once a gigantic freshwater/brackish fishpond, built by Kamehameha the Great in 1810 after another fishpond (where the airport is now) was destroyed by lava from the 1801 Hualalai flow. Enormous stone walls up to 6 feet tall and 20 feet wide were laboriously erected, creating a deep pool 2 miles in circumference where all manner of deep sea fish were stocked. It was said that half the population worked to complete it and it was considered one of the "artificial wonders of Hawai'i" at the time. The lagoon now composing the farthest reaches of Kiholo Bay was once part of that pond, and the water-worn stones were part of the wall. The Mauna Loa lava flow of 1859 traveled *30 miles* to fill in most of the pond and breach the southern wall, creating the lagoon. Freshwater, which initially fed the pond, still intrudes into the bay from springs. Since the water in the back part of the bay is usually as calm as a swim-

Kiholo Bay

Kiholo Bay is a fabulous place to wander around.

ming pool, the snorkeling there, though the visibility is poor, can be surreal. If nobody has been there to disturb the water (except for the ubiquitous turtles), the swimmer or snorkeler might encounter what appears to be a pane of glass suspended horizontally in the water about a foot down. That's the lighter freshwater floating on top of the heavier seawater. Left undisturbed, the dividing line between the two can be straight, razor thin and very visible. If you swim slowly with your hand extended vertically in the middle of the joining of these two layers, the top of your hand will be cold (from the freshwater) and the bottom will be warm (from the seawater).

Walking along the gravel shoreline from the bay heading southwest, you pass several houses. One is called the **Bali House**. It was built by the guy you see on TV who runs Paul Mitchell hair care products. He paid 200 Balinese workers $1.50 a day for two years to create the intricate carvings and assemble the house. All was then disassembled and shipped to Kiholo Bay, where American and Balinese workers reassembled it. To the

shock of many, they used large green logs from the *Borneo rain forest*, which shrank and split in less-humid Hawai'i, and much effort went into responding to the shrinking structure. While being built, the owner was amazingly gracious about letting people tour the house, so many on the island have gotten to see the inside. The Bali House is about midway between the row of houses on the beach, and you *will* know it when you see it.

Continuing south, you'll pass a big yellow house with security cameras, tennis courts and guards. (It was built by the guy who invented the pacemaker.) About 300 yards southwest of the house, only 80 feet from the ocean *and on state land* is a delight known as **Queen's Bath** (Keanalele Waterhole). It's just off the mauka (mountain) side of the gravel road and easy to miss. There you are, spitting distance from the ocean, in a fabulous crystal clear, spring-fed lava tube bath, open to the sky in two spots. (See photo on page 32.) It is attached to a dry lava tube cave, shown on the map. (By the way, the dry part of the lava tube has numerous petroglyphs carved into it and can be fascinating to visit, if you are careful and keep your eyes peeled.) Though filled with freshwater, its level rises and falls each day with the tides. (It goes back farther than it looks—a waterproof flashlight can make exploring it fun.) You can't help but think it doesn't get much better than this. Once you've refreshed yourself in the exquisitely cool water, you can make your way back to your car. (Our thermometer says it's 71°, but it sure *feels* colder.) By the way, if you have a lot of suntan lotion on, please consider rinsing in the ocean first, perhaps in the bay, to avoid leaving an oil slick in the bath.

There occasionally may be some yellowjackets flying around the area. Try not to make them mad.

Luahinewai

If you had a vast sea of blackened lava and found a beautiful, coconut tree-lined pond just 200 feet from a secluded black sand and gravel cove 1,000 feet long, what would you do? If you said build a mansion, you're out of luck. Somebody beat you to it. But hey, you can still hike to it. And although the owners of this enviously-located estate comically watch over what they imply is their private pond (using a high-powered camera lens, no less), you'll still get a peek at the pond and possibly have this long cove to yourself. (By the way, we seem to recall a former governor being quoted that the public has access to the pond, called Luahinewai, but we don't know if that's true.)

Anyway, the short hike of about 20–25 minutes each way is worth it. It's along the lava coastline and is pretty. Take the road toward Kiholo Bay mentioned on page 198 and toward the end take the left fork and park near the porta-potties. That round house you see is the old, unoccupied Loretta Lynn

home. Pick up the trail to the left and follow it toward your goal, marked by lots of coconut trees.

The Golden Pools of Ke-awa-Iki

How about a hike that leads to a deserted beach with white sand on one end and black sand on the other? A trail that leads over harsh a'a, along the beach, past a jewel-like freshwater pool and back to your car in 4 miles. We've taken friends on this hike, and they love it. It displays the raw nature of the Kohala coast, has a variety of sights you'll never forget and rewards you with a cool dip if you get warm. (See photo on page 55.)

Slightly north of the 79 mile marker on Queen K (Hwy 19) there are boulders blocking a road on the fresh (150-year-old) lava leading to the sea. (See close-up map on page 157.) Take the road-turned-trail toward the ocean and go around the right side of the fence.

The beach was created when lava from the 1859 Mauna Loa eruption flowed 30 miles, landing at the north end of the beach. The black sand created hasn't had a chance to mix with the previous white beach sand at the southern end, resulting in a nice blend from black to white along the stretch. Just past the south end there are tide-pools to explore if you have reef shoes.

Continuing north (right) you'll come to Pueo Bay. Large amounts of freshwater enter this tiny bay from underground, creating some strange snorkeling conditions. From Pueo Bay you can either take the trail toward the highway (to the right of a very large lava rock) to the pools, or take the other trail to Weliweli Point and link up with another trail. Look for the latter to Weliweli marked with pieces of coral. (The map makes these trails easier to visualize.) The pools (there are two of them) can be seen from far away because they are marked by hala trees. (The end of their branches look like palm tree-inspired pompoms.) Once at the pools, take a moment to savor the scene. Here in the middle of all this raw harshness is a magnificent oasis—freshwater (no hint of seawater at all) lined with golden-coated lava. (The gold comes from a growth on the rocks and makes the ponds too fragile to swim in.) If you want a quick, cool dip, walk just beyond the golden pools to the pool under the hala trees. It's sand- and gravel-lined and makes a good place to cool your legs off before taking the trail back to your car.

OTHER BEACH HIKES

For other beach hikes, often to secluded spots, check out **Honomalino**, **Makalawena**, **Honoka'ope**, **Green Sand**, **'Anaeho'omalu** (going south to the freshwater pool), and **Road to the Sea** (the second beach), all described under BEACHES. Also consider the trail between **Spencer Beach Park** and **Hapuna**. It's along the shoreline and is vague only where it crosses the golf course at hole #3.

WAIMEA TO BACK OF WAIPI'O VALLEY

This hike has some of the tastiest views of any hike on the island and is one of our favorites. Unfortunately, at press time, access was being restricted while the leaseholder contemplated issuing hiking permits. Check our web site for the latest updates. It leads from Waimea to the top of the back edge of Waipi'o Valley. It's moderately strenuous (if that; it depends on how far you go), has forest and valley views and is quiet. The trail was cut to facilitate the construction of the Hamakua Ditch system in the early 1900s. The first 1¾ miles (45 minutes) is through forest. After a mile you cross a cement ditch, and the road becomes a trail. Lots of pretty forest and the easy walking becomes a little more hilly. Then you come to the edge of the world—a

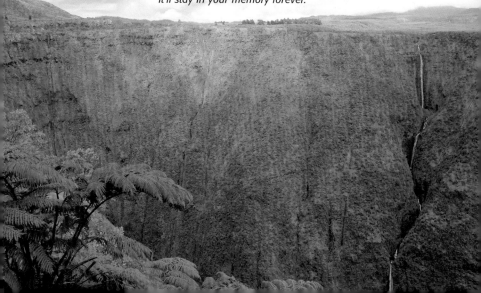

The grandness of the back of Waipi'o Valley is hard to capture on film. With a heart-pounding 2,000 foot drop to the river below and waterfalls etching the valley walls, it'll stay in your memory forever.

nearly sheer drop-off to Waipiʻo Valley. It's amazing how abruptly the back of the valley starts from the plains above. (Surprisingly, the large valleys in this part of the island were often created by unimaginably catastrophic landslides like the one described on page 77, *not* just erosion.) There *may* be a superb waterfall across the valley, if it's been raining. If you are vertiginous, picnic here before returning. Others will want to take the trail along the perimeter of the valley (since the view from the back is so incredible), then through a bamboo grove to a ginger grove (be careful of holes in parts of the ginger matting). Return when you want, 2–4 miles into it; don't try to loop it.

The trail is well cut, but be observant. A 2,000-foot tumble into the valley would be annoying. This is a truly great hike when the weather is good, a lackluster hike when the weather is bad. Winter months are *usually* best, but it's *real* hard to predict the weather here and it can change (either way) on a dime. Mornings *greatly* enhance your chance of good weather. The first part of the trail, at the end of White Road (one sign may incorrectly say Lindsey Road) in Waimea (right side of map on page 135) is through a pasture. (Cattle may be present at the beginning.) This is Hawaiian Homelands for the first few minutes, so please be respectful, leave nothing behind, and close the gates. There's debate as to whether the first part is public easement, so be nice. (County says it's a public easement, Hawaiian Homelands says it isn't and at press time the state said they wanted hikers to get permits, then said they wouldn't give any.) Locals and visitors alike hike this trail without problems. But at times we've heard from readers that someone has approached them saying they were the leaseholder and requesting $2 to traverse the land. We don't know if this person actually controls the land, but it's probably worth the two bucks to avoid the hassle.

MAUNA LOA SUMMIT

Getting to the top of Mauna Loa is tough, no matter which way you slice it. It's 13,677 feet high, and there are no roads to the summit. You can do it the hard way or the *very* hard way—it's your choice. The first is a 3- to 5-day hike from the Kilauea side up the Mauna Loa Trail. The trail starts at the end of the Mauna Loa Scenic Road. This hike has been known to humble even the most conditioned athlete. Though the gradient rarely exceeds 12°, it's 38 miles round trip through lava, and you gain 6,500 feet. Red Hill Cabin is 7½ miles into the hike at 10,035 feet, and Mauna Loa Summit Cabin is near the crater rim at 13,250 feet—another 11½ miles. Some prefer to break this second leg (*ooh*, bad phrase) by overnighting at Water Hole halfway to Mauna Loa Cabin. This trail is in Hawaiʻi Volcanoes National Park, and you need a permit from them to camp.

The other way up is a *tough* 8-mile round-trip day hike from the **Mauna Loa Weather Observatory** off Saddle Road. (See page 145 for directions.) You start at 11,000 feet, so you won't have a chance to get acclimated—count on altitude sickness from starting so high. (Savvy hikers often car-camp at the weather observatory the night before to acclimate.) This trail is steeper than the Mauna Loa Trail and over rougher terrain, but you can do it in a day if you're into punishment, and the views across the saddle will be superb. Make sure you get an early start.

It's always cold up there, and snow can come at any time of the year without warning. Altitude sickness is common, even among the fittest. For either of these hikes, thorough preparation is the key. Just because you are in the tropics doesn't mean you can take this mountain lightly. The *base* may be in the tropics, but the *summit* is in Alaska.

MANUKA STATE PARK

A pleasant nature loop walk through native dry and wet forest. Located in the southwest part of the island off Hwy 11 just north of the 81 mile marker, it takes 1–2 hours for the stroll, and sights are well marked by forestry personnel. There should be a decent map at the trailhead for you to follow, which includes lots of information. The latter half of the trail has some obnoxious footing on small chunks of 'a'a, so wear sturdy shoes. Otherwise, it's a pretty easy walk. Be sure to check out the lush pit crater. Kids seem to love climbing on some of the gnarled kukui and hau trees along the trail. There are tables and restrooms at the trailhead for you to follow, a nice place for a picnic. Not the best hiking on the island, but pleasant nonetheless.

KALOPA NATIVE FOREST STATE PARK

This is a nice forest hike, and the park is well maintained for a state park. You go through a beautiful and very lush forest of tall trees and glorious ferns. You'll be skirting along the edge of a large gulch part of the time, then heading down an abandoned 4WD trail back to your car, unless you choose to take the perimeter trail. It is less traveled than the old 4WD road, and the fence is always in sight. This hike is anywhere from 2–4 miles depending on your route, and the elevation gain from the bottom to the top is 400 feet.

This wet forest is heavenly. Take the time to notice the stunning forest around

you. If it has thorns (as the brambles do), it's not native. Native plants didn't need to develop harsh defenses since there weren't any large, foraging animals to ward off.

Now a few warnings. It rains about 80 inches per year here, so the weather *may* be a factor. It's often best to go early in the day. The park facilities are maintained by the state, *but the trails are not.* That duty falls to volunteers who come out every three to six months (or longer) to pretty up the trails, cut fallen trees, etc. That means that if you arrive at the tail end of a maintenance cycle, the trail will be in poorer shape or overgrown. Our map shows the trails as they are *supposed* to be. Intersections are usually marked, but you may need to keep an eye out for them if the signs have blown down. If you go along the gulch, it'll lead to the fence at the top of the park. (You'll need to cross a small and usually dry gulch about ¼ of the way along.) From the top it leads to the abandoned road (you'll see a gate). Either take the "road" (only a trail

Once the conduit of 2000° molten rock, this lava tube is now hikable.

now) to the bottom, or continue on the less-used horse perimeter trail. The compacted dirt on the "road" can get pretty slippery on the way down, so be careful. Hiking boots are preferred here.

All in all, this is a great hike for anyone who wants to see the splendor of a Hawai'i forest. If you just aren't up to it, take the ¾-mile nature loop near the parking area. It goes through a native 'ohi'a forest and is worth the stroll. Camping with tents or at the cabins is available here—see CAMPING. Located 40 miles north of Hilo off the main highway. Take the road between the 39 and 40 mile markers and follow the signs.

HILO'S WAI'ALE FALLS

Many people come to Hawai'i looking for an idyllic pool or waterfall to frolic in. Well, here it is, and it's only a 10-minute hike to get there.

Wai'ale Falls itself is a pretty and fairly high volume waterfall. Above the falls lie several beautiful pools and some small falls that can be a delight to play in (if the flow's not too high).

You start on Waianuenue Avenue past Boiling Pots. You'll see the falls from the bridge that crosses the river. (See map on page 108.) The trailhead is just past the bridge. The trail itself is plagued with mosquitoes, but once at the water we've haven't found them to be a big problem. Bring bug juice just in case. Follow the narrow trail up through the strawberry guava lining the north bank of the Wailuku River. There are several offshoots that allow you to visit the large pool below the falls (if you wish). The trail ends at the *top* of those falls. Remember that spot for your return.

At the top, pools and small falls await. The footing is much less slippery than many other stream banks around the islands, thanks to the consolidated lava here.

INSTRUCTIONS FOR WATERFALL USE: Prance, frolic and have fun. Repeat if necessary.

Stay out of pools that have a fast moving exit. Other pools are farther upstream. And, of course, always be aware that a flash flood can occur anywhere in nature. So if you see a large wall of water coming your way...well, you're already screwed, so what does it matter?

FIND THE CAVE IN THE FOREST

Across the street from the 23 mile marker on Hwy 11 near Volcano, exactly 80 yards from the road itself, is a lava tube cave. The main trail is about 20 feet to the left (east) of what's across the street from the mile marker. You *should* find a trail through the wiry Pacific false staghorn ferns and you *should* find the cave opening. Then it's two awkward drops to scramble before you stumble down the rubble of the collapsed roof (that's the cave opening) to the floor.

The first thing you notice is the lovely soda straw-like lava stalactites, some over a foot long. Here's where you must promise us—*c'mon, raise your hand and promise*—you won't break any of them off or take anything but memories from this cave. It's never been revealed before and is pristine. Please leave it that way.

The cave is about 1½ miles long and can take hours to explore. It's got an unusually fine assortment of different colored lavas, so take your time. In a few places you think it's choked off, but a little hands-and-knees action, and you're back to walking. (Knee pads or long pants help at those few low places.) The rest of the time it's 20 feet high. The temperature is a cool 64° and the humidity is high. Odds are you'll be pretty comfortable in there. You'll *know* when it ends; just retrace your steps.

See page 227 for info on flashlights and preperation.

PUNAHAHA

Although Kilauea Volcano ravaged this area in the 1990s, it spared one small sliver of its former glory. Punahaha is an idyllic oasis in a sea of lava destruction, and getting there can be tricky.

It's *way* out in Puna at the end of Hwy 130. (See map on page 101.) After the 21 mile marker the road ends. From here there is a lava road that the county *may* charge $5 to drive since it's used to view lava flows when the volcano is putting on a show in this area. (This is a *public* road despite any misleading NO TRASSPASSING signs.) If it's open (call 961–8093), the road alternates between lava and paved road. At 1⁷⁄₁₀ mile after the lava road starts (and in the third stretch of paved road) there's a road angling back on your left. A sign indicating private property seems incorrectly placed since this is still a *government* road. *If* there's a barricade, you'll have to walk 900 feet where you encounter a 100 yard lava interruption. Up and over the lava and another 1,250 foot stretch of paved road ends at some pine trees. Even here in the tropics the wind sounds cold as it whistles through the pine needles. Remember those trees for your return trip.

From here Punahaha is ¼ mile to the southeast. There's a trail, but the first part is vague and hard to find, and there's no practical way for us to tell you how to find it other than use your sense of direction and poke around. The trail is fairly straight.

Once at Punahaha we like to climb the short lava bluff on the right side of the beach and listen. Instead of sand, the beach is made up of countless marble-sized lava pebbles. The surf rolls them up and down, and the sound is hypnotizing. Behind you is a stunning grove of palm trees. The setting is utterly tranquil and uplifting, and it's easy to see why Madam Pele spared this area.

You won't want to expose yourself to the ocean here as the surf can be powerful. Just sit back and enjoy.

Return the way you came, which is easier said than done. You *did* keep track of how you got here, didn't you?

HIKES DESCRIBED ELSEWHERE

The hike to **Captain Cook Monument** is listed on page 69; the cold hike to **Lake Wai-au** on top of Mauna Kea is shown on map on page 140. Hiking in **Waipi'o Valley** is described on page 130, plus an ADVENTURE on 236. The awesome hikes through a *pristine* rain forest to the erupting **Pu'u 'O'o Volcano Vent**, **current lava flows** and a **lava tube** hike are all under ADVENTURES, as is the trip into **Pololu Valley** and over to **Honokane Nui**.

GUIDED HIKES

There are several companies that do these. The biggest is **Hawai'i Forest & Trail** (331–8505). Though the vast majority of people prefer to hike on their own, some might feel more comfortable with a live person along. This company has a tour that goes to an extremely unusual waterfall. **Kapoloa Falls** plunges 500 feet and is interrupted halfway down by an old ditch trail. So there *you* are, safely on the side of the cliff, able to walk *behind* the falls and look out at the valley. It's an incredible view and an easy 3-mile walk. Since it's on private land this is the only way you'll be able see it. Ten people max, $125. They have other hikes, as well.

HORSEBACK RIDING

If you want to let someone else do the walking, consider horseback riding. The Big Island has quite a tradition when it comes to horses. There are lots of companies offering wildly different kinds of rides. It just depends on the type of riding and terrain you want to see.

Waipi'o Na'alapa Trail Rides (775–0419) has excellent rides in Waipi'o Valley. (See page 129 for more on this spectacular valley.) Two hours on horseback, plus another half hour getting into and out of the valley via 4WD, this is an easy one to recommend. You cross several streams, see breathtaking waterfalls, walk along taro patches and generally get a taste of old Hawai'i. It's a nose-to-tail ride, but the scenery is great. $85 per person, 230-pound limit. **Waipi'o on Horseback** (775–7291) has a similar tour also with a 230-pound limit.

Waipi'o Ridge Stables (775–1007) has a different product. Instead of going *into* Waipi'o Valley, they walk part of the upper edge above Hwy 240. (See map on page 132.) Despite the name, most of the trip is through a tree farm, but the views from some of the overlooks are great. $85 for 2½ hours. Longer rides also available. Eight to ten people max. It's nose-to-tail, no running. Guides are good.

Paniolo Riding Adventures (889–5354) has nice quality horses and gear. Their 2½-hour trips are $96 and take you across a wide open working ranch featuring beautiful views. This is not one of those nose-to-tail rides. You go across open country, and you can canter if you like. (That means to go faster than a trot, for all you city slickers.) The guides aren't patronizing; they genuinely seem to want you to experience the peace of the Hawaiian countryside. Rides have between 2 and 14 people and aren't at all gimmicky. If it's calving season, you might get to see a calf being born. They also have 3-hour picnic rides for $124. Lunch is included in the price. Thick dusters and the like are available for free, but it's a good idea to bring a sweatshirt and long pants. Located ²⁄₁₀ mile north of the 13 mile mark on Highway 250 in Kohala. Easy to recommend.

Dahana Ranch (885-0057) has 1½-hour tours of their 2,500-acre ranch off the Old Mamalahoa Highway in southern Waimea for $60. You see lush, rolling pastures from open country, not from a trail. You *may* even get to ride their gentle but *enormous* Brahma bull (if he's in a good mood). Bring warm clothes; it's sometimes misty or rainy in this part of Waimea. (You might want to call them for a weather check.) They also have a round-up ride for $130. This is not the kind where you sit there while they do all the work. For at least 2½ hours, your group will do all the hard work from horseback while they bark out orders, and you'll probably have a great time doing it. Four people are necessary for this. (Call them to see if any others have signed up.) Dahana Ranch has a 300-pound weight limit, and kids over 3 are welcome (except on the round-up ride). Well run by good folks.

Kings' Trail Rides (323-2388) brings people down the 2-mile trail to Captain Cook Monument for some outrageous snorkeling, the best on the island. $135–$150. The 1,300-foot descent is constant, and novices might get spooked at riding downhill the whole way. Lunch and snorkel gear (minus fins) are provided. Bring reef shoes for scrambling on the rocks at the water's edge.

Horse-Drawn Wagons

Parker Ranch (885-7655) gives *(yaaawwn)* 45-minute rides behind a shopping center in Waimea for $15. Waipi'o Valley is toured for an hour by **Waipi'o Valley Wagon Tours** (775-9518) for $55. The Waipi'o carriage tour works, but the Parker Ranch ride seems a little goofy to us.

Call them Jet Skis, Wave Runners (which are brand names) or personal watercraft—whatever your name for them, these motorcycles of the sea can be rented in Kona. **Jet Ski Hawaii** (329-2754) has fairly powerful jet skis. They seem to get most of their business from the cruise ships and customer service isn't exactly a big priority. Early morning is usually very smooth, late afternoon choppy. Late morning seems a good balance to give the water some texture. It's $60 for a half hour on their small track, about the size of a Home Depot. Morning usually offers smoother waters. The half hour will tucker out most people, especially if you're like me and you drive it like it's stolen. Experiment with different ways to hold your feet while you sit. Extra riders are allowed for $15, but we recommend one person per craft. Doubling up seems to increase the risk of the passenger falling off, from what we observed. Some people seem to feel that these craft are hazardous to the ocean; others

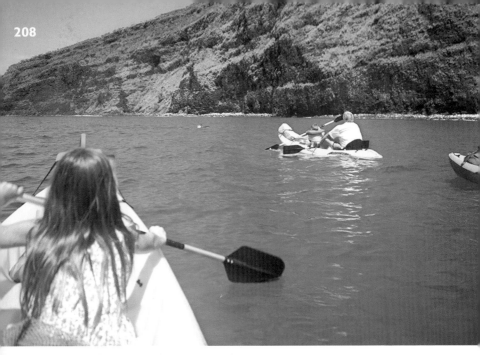

Watch for spinner dolphins during your kayak trip across Kealakekua Bay.

say modern jet skis are no different than regular boats. We honestly don't know which is the case; we're just saying what it's like to rent one. They leave from Kailua Pier.

KAYAKING

On the Big Island, kayaking is mostly an ocean affair. Although other islands, such as Kaua'i, have rivers to kayak, the Big Island lacks navigable rivers. But there are several areas on the normally calm Kona coast where ocean kayaking is excellent. Our favorite is across Kealakekua Bay to the Captain Cook Monument. (See page 67 for complete description of the bay.)

The 1-mile (each way) trip often features fairly calm waters, spinner dolphins and outrageous snorkeling at the monument. This is a *great* trip! Other kayak trips are from Kailua Pier to the north or south, or from Kohala beaches such as 'Anaeho'omalu. Old Kona Airport or Honokohau Harbor to Makalawena is a long, pleasant voyage. (See BEACHES for descriptions and locations of landings.) The area south of Keauhou Bay has numerous cavities (called "sea caves" by the more optimistic companies) that can be fun to paddle by.

Remember that the ocean, even in Kona, can be treacherous and unforgiving, especially during periods of high surf. We don't want to rain on anybody's parade, but if you don't give the ocean the respect it deserves, it can humble you quickly. Only paddle when it's calm, and always be wary near the shore where a rogue wave can beach (or rock) you.

Renting a Kayak

Aloha Kayak Co. (322–2868) up in Honalo just past the intersection of Hwys 19 and 180 has good gear. $35 for singles, $60 for doubles. **Kona Boys Kayaks** (328–1234) prices have crept *way* too high. It's $37 for a single, $67 for a double. Past the 113 mile marker on Hwy 11. **Ocean Safaris** (326–4699) also rents kayaks, in Kona at Keauhou Bay.

In Kona, consider picking up your kayak the afternoon of the day before, so you can be on the water early.

At Kealakekua Bay, put in on the left side of the cement landing before Napoʻopoʻo Beach Park. Parking can be a problem, and you can always launch at Manini Beach if necessary. (See map on page 66.) Be careful not to damage or walk on the coral when you land at the other side. Though people have been known to rent kayaks right at the bay, it's not legal and you can't count on it, so you'll have to let the kayak companies strap it to your car. At press time the state was contemplating requiring all kayak trips in Kealakekua Bay to be *guided*, meaning if they implement it, you won't be able to rent one on your own.

There's also a concession to the right of the pier in Kona that rents kayaks by the (expensive) hour for use in that area. Kohala companies rent them by the minute (OK, OK...by the hour). Among them are **Ocean Sports** (886–6666), which rents them at ʻAnaehoʻomalu Beach. You'll have to cash in your IRA for the Kohala rentals.

It's virtually impossible to rent a kayak with a **rudder** here. While rudders make it easier to stay on track in any ocean water, their absence is particularly felt in Kohala where winds will tend to annoyingly weathercock you sideways.

Guided Tours

If you want a guided trip, **Aloha Kayak Co.** (322–2868) has $129 guided tours of Kealakekua Bay which includes lunch. If snorkeling isn't a big deal, they also have $75 trips near Keauhou Bay that includes the "sea caves" and some cliff jumping if you're so inclined. Good company with a good attitude.

Also worth noting is **Kona Boys** (328–1234). They do group and private trips (where everybody knows each other) and will take as few as one. It's $159 for a half-day group tour, $225 for a private tour, and for that they'll meet you near Kealakekua, guide you across the bay and feed you before or after snorkeling. With advance notice they'll set up remote and camping trips to places like Waipiʻo, Miloliʻi and South Point. **Ocean Safaris** also has tours. **Hawaiʻi Pack & Paddle** (328–8911) has multi-day camping/kayaking trips, as well and will take children.

If ocean kayaking is not your thing, **Flumʻin Da Ditch** (889–6922) has a unique way to kayak—in the Kohala Ditch. This narrow ditch spends much of its time in mountain tunnels. Along the way you learn about how this engineering feat was accomplished. Five people per kayak. No whitewater here—remember the ditch designers wanted to lose altitude as *slowly* as possible. So if you're visualizing something like the logger ride at Disneyland where you rush down a steep grade and splash at the bottom, you'll be disappointed. You drift along slowly, but you may get wet when passing under intersecting streams. Views are marginal since you're sunken into the ditch. Do it for the novelty and a relaxing cruise, not for a thrill ride. $98 for 1½ hours.

LU'AUS

See ISLAND DINING on page 275.

Aspen has its ski slopes, Washington has its monuments, Orlando has Disney World, and the Big Island has the Kona Coast waters. Quite simply, if you visit the Big Island and don't ply the Kona waters, you haven't *really* been to the Big Island.

The waters off the Kona Coast are the finest in all the islands. Calmer, clearer, and teeming with fish, Big Island waters make residents of other islands turn *blue* with envy. A popular way to see it is on an ocean tour. If you take one of the many tours along the coast, you *may* see turtles. You are *likely* to see dolphins, flying fish off the bow and whales during whale season. You *will* see smiles from fellow passengers.

You're less likely to get **seasick** on Kona's calm waters than anywhere else we can think of. Nonetheless, if you take seasickness medication, do it *before* you leave. (The night before and morning of are best. It's useless to take it once you're on the boat.) Also, avoid any alcohol the night before. No greasy foods before or during the trip. And some think that citrus is a no-no. Ginger is a very good preventative/treatment. Below deck is a bad place to be if you're worried about getting seasick. Without a reference point, you're much more likely to let 'er rip down there. Scopolamine patches work but have side effects, including (occasion-

ally) blurred vision that can last a week. (Been there, done that, on a 10-day California–Hawai'i trip.)

Boats are usually less crowded on weekends since that's when visitors usually arrive and depart the island. And remember, most single-hull power boats are smoothest in the back.

Kealakekua Bay

The Captain Cook Monument in Kealakekua Bay is a favorite destination. Snorkeling near the monument is perhaps the best you will find anywhere in the state. If you've never snorkeled before, this is the place to start. Experienced snorkelers will be dazzled. A large number of spinner dolphins reside in the bay, and you're likely to see them—perhaps even swim with them, if you're *real* lucky. (They are called spinners because they are the only untrained dolphins that routinely leap clear of the water and spin on their longitudinal axis.) Companies sometimes offer morning or afternoon tours. Take the morning; it's calmer and the water is usually clearer.

Fair Wind II (322–2788) uses a 63-foot power catamaran to bring 100 or so people. They leave from Keauhou Bay, 7½ miles north and stay tied to their mooring for a couple hours of snorkeling, BBQ burgers and general frolicking. People seem to really enjoy this trip and make good use of the short waterslide into the water, the high dive platform and the cash bar. Restrooms, hose to rinse salt off, shade, ♿ accessible. Easy entry and exit from water, SNUBA also available for extra. Continental breakfast on board. It's not as crowded on board as it looks from a distance. Unfortunately, since they troll along the way, the boat travels too far from the coast to see much of the coastal features. The sail is for decoration—you will be motoring at 10 MPH the whole way—but the boat is pretty smooth. This is a good tour, especially for those who are wary about ocean travel. $105 for the 4½-hour morning tour, $69 for the 3½-hour afternoon tour. (An hour less at the bay and snacks instead of a meal—we much prefer the morning trip.) Note that sodas are free only during lunch; they charge the rest of the time. Also, no dessert after your burgers. Part of the year they also have a sunset cruise.

Sea Quest (329–7238) is totally different. They take six passengers on their 22-foot rigid-hull inflatables (which is a good design because it absorbs bumps better than a regular rubber raft) to the Captain Cook Monument and beyond to **Honaunau** (Place of Refuge) for snorkeling. It's bumpier than the Fair Wind II, and there's no shade. (But bumpier means more thrilling.) You won't have all that wandering room that you have on the Fair Wind II, and it's snacks instead of a meal. But these guys go near the coastline and do the best job of anyone narrating what you are seeing. Along the way they poke the boat into several "sea caves" (more like sea cavities), and show you how they are formed. We like them better than Captain Zodiac below because they snorkel in two spots, aren't nearly as crowded and take their time on the way back. (They can afford to because they depart from Keauhou Bay, 10 miles closer to the monument than Captain Zodiac.) $85 for the more recommended 4-hour morning trip, $64 for the 3-hour afternoon trip, which omits Honaunau. They also have 12-passenger crafts in case you have a big group.

Dolphin Discoveries (322–8000) has a very similar product for similar prices. They do a pretty good job, as well.

Sea Paradise (322–2500) has a 46-foot sailing catamaran that leaves from Keauhou Bay. They attempt to sail on every trip if there's wind. With juices and

With water this clear, it's easy to see why ocean tours are so popular.

muffins in the morning, sandwiches and an open bar at lunch a friendly staff and good boat, this is an easy trip to recommend. $95 for this less crowded alternative to the Fair Winds.

Captain Zodiac (329–3199) leaves from Honokohau Harbor 17 miles north of your destination at Kealakekua Bay. One and a half of the four hours is spent at the monument area with snacks provided. $87 per person. This is an adequate tour, but we recommend Sea Quest or the Fair Wind over Captain Zodiac.

Other Boat Destinations

Body Glove (326–7122) goes to a different location. Their two-deck, 50-foot trimaran cruises from Kailua Pier to Pawai Bay. (See page 165 for complete description of Pawai Bay.) They take almost a hour to cruise a mere 2 miles, so it's not like you'll be covered with sea spray. They can take 100 people maximum (but 100 is too crowded—we like it when there's 60 or less). Continental breakfast at boarding, deli lunch at site. In addition to snorkeling, they have SCUBA (for an extra fee), both certified and beginner. A good boat, crew and location make this a good deal, and we recommend it wholeheartedly. Lots of shade, water-slide, restrooms and a full bar on board. 4½-hour tour ($94), 2½ hours of which is at Pawai Bay. Inner tubes and see-thru boogie boards for the timid. Afternoon cruise to the same place is 3 hours ($61) and snacks instead of a meal. If we have one gripe, it's that they keep snorkelers on too tight a leash. The best snorkeling is nearer the shoreline, but they whistle at you if you get too close.

Kamanu Charters (329–2021) leaves Honokohau Harbor in their 36-foot *sailing* catamaran and heads 2¼ miles south to Pawai Bay. $75, 24 passengers at most, good snorkeling and snacks provided. Only a little shade for this 3-hour tour (like Gilligan's Island?). Though an acceptable trip, unless you *have* to sail, you're better off on the Body Glove—better boat, longer trip.

Kailua Bay Charter (324–1749) has quickie tours (under an hour) of Kailua Bay with a glass-bottom boat for $30. No food, just a quick jaunt through the water. Leaves from Kailua Pier. Not overly compelling.

In Kohala

Red Sail Sports (886–2876) uses their 50-foot sailing catamaran to take people out of 'Anaeho'omalu Beach to two of several locations for snorkeling. Motor one way and sail back. Four-hour trip includes continental breakfast and deli lunch for $79. Other tours offered as well as a dinner cruise. When we ask how many people they'll take on a charter, they answer, "As many as we can book."

For **Dinner Cruises**, see ISLAND DINING on page 277. **Submarine**, see page 222.

Parasailing is where you get pulled by a boat while attached to a parachute and a long line. We've done it, and to many people (including us), it *looks* more fun and thrilling than it really is and doesn't seem worth the money. If you have your heart set on it, **UFO Parasail** (325–5836) will drag you around for $60 or $70 using a 400 or 800-foot line, and a 1,200-foot line for $80. You're up for 7–10 minutes. Tandem rides available.

One tip (*especially* for guys): Don't wear any slippery shorts or you may cinch forward in your harness creating...the longest 7 minutes of your life.

Whether you're already a certified scuba diver or are interested in trying it out, you've found paradise on the west side of the Big Island. Whereas the east (windward) side of the island has poorer diving due to river runoff and rough waters, the Kona side offers some of the best in the state. There are no permanent streams on the *entire* west side (from the northern tip to the southern tip), so runoff is not a problem. Kona waters are mostly shielded from winds and the ocean's prevailing northeast swell, so calmness is the norm. Fish, coral and divers appreciate the warmer water of the Big Island, the southernmost of all Hawaiian Islands. It's 75° at its coldest in February, 82° at its warmest in October. 100+ foot visibility is common.

You have your choice of boat dives or shore dives. Boats mostly leave from Kailua Pier, Honokohau Harbor and Kawaihae Harbor. Typical dives here are two tanks at two different sites. When we list a price range in the table, it refers to those who have their own gear vs. those who need to rent it.

The island has no decompression chamber. Everyone knows not to fly after a dive, but don't forget that the heights of some of our mountains simulate flying as far as your tissues are concerned. Just the saddle *between* Mauna Loa and Mauna Kea reaches 6,600

feet. And if you decide to drive to Place of Refuge from Kona, you'll reach 1,400 feet—probably too high if you dove deep.

So you'll know our perspective when we review companies, we should tell you what we do and don't like when we go on a dive. On a bad dive, the dive master takes the group on a non-stop excursion that keeps you kicking the whole time. No time to stop and explore the nooks and crannies. Good outfits will give you a briefing, tell you about some of the endemic species here, what to look for and will point out various things on the dives, keeping it moving but not too fast. Bad outfits kick a lot. Good outfits explain the unique qualities of Hawai'i's environment. Bad dive masters may tell you what *they* saw (but *you* missed). Good companies work around your needs, wishes and desires. Bad companies keep everyone on a short leash. Good dive masters know their stuff and share it with you. Bad dive masters don't know squat but imply they know it all in order to impress you. As divers, we tend to like companies that wander toward the boat for the latter part of the dive and allow you to go up when you are near the end of your tank, as opposed to everyone going up when the heaviest breather has burned up his/her bottle. We define bad dive shop attitude as what you experience when you walk into a shop (or onto a boat) and the crew does nothing but convey the attitude, *I'm so cool, don't you wish you were as cool as me?*

During times when we feel the diving conditions are bad (poor vis or big swells), we like to call around and ask about conditions. We appreciate the companies who admit it's bad, and we hold it against those who tell us how wonderful conditions are.

Dive Operator	Services Available	Price of 2 Tank Boat	Rent Gear Shore Dive	Camera Rental	Dive Computer	Manta Ray Night Dive	Dive Certification	Rx Masks
Aloha Dive 325-5560	Boat Dives	$95 – $110	No	$20	Included	None	$600	No
Big Island Divers 329-6068	Dive Shop & Boat Dives	$100 – $135	$35	No	Included	$99 – $120 (1 or 2 tank)	$500	Yes
Dive Makai 329-2025	Boat Dives	$108 – $134	No	$20	Included	None	No	Yes
Jack's Diving Locker 329-7585	Dive Shop, Boat & Shore Dives	$125 – $155	$35	$45	$10 Extra	$145 – $180 (Includes 1 dusk dive)	$425 – $650	Yes
Kohala Divers 882-7774	Dive Shop & Boat Dives	$115 – $140	$30	No	$10 Extra	None	$575	Yes
Kona Coast 329-8802	Dive Shop & Boat Dives	$125 – $155	$35	$45	$10 Extra	$145 – $180 (2 tank)	$425 – $650	Yes
Kona Honu Divers 324-4668	Dive Shop & Boat Dives	$105 – $110	$35	$35	Included	$95 – $110 (Includes 1 dusk dive)	$450	Yes
Ocean Sports 886-6666	Boat Dives	$120 – $130	No	No	None	None	$1,000!	Yes
Pacific Rim Divers 334-1750	Boat Dives	$110 – $130	No	No	Included	None	No	Yes
Hawaiian Scuba Shack 331-8708	Dive Shop & Boat Dives	$119	$30	No	Included upon request	$119 (2 tank)	$250	Yes
Red Sail Sports 886-2876	Boat Dives	$109 – $138	No	No	None	None	$1,000!	Yes
Sandwich Isle 329-9188	Dive Shop & Boat Dives	$100 – $115	$35	No	$10 Extra	$110 – $125 (Includes 1 dusk dive)	$500	Yes

The Tops in Kona

There are lots of dive outfits on the island, some good, some bad. Three of them stand apart from the rest. Any of these three would make a good choice. If we had to pick one, it would probably be Pacific Rim Divers.

Pacific Rim Divers (334–1750) is a boat-only, husband/wife team. Their enthusiasm with diving is evident and contagious. Wife Patrice is one of the best we've seen at finding critters, and her knowledge of marine life is excellent.

With their warm attitude, comfortable 26-foot boat (though it needs shade) and reasonable price, we're as happy and relaxed as can be at the end of a dive. (Their killer homemade brownies don't hurt, either.)

Kona Honu Divers (324–4668) has a beautiful 46-foot boat with plenty of shade. It's comfortable and easy to get around on. Two dive steps into the water and two showers on board. They'll take up to 16 divers and their guides are professional. Good briefing, pineapple and cookies between dives and a relaxed pace. If you don't like small boats, these guys are worth considering.

Jack's Diving Locker (329–7585) is a good shop with three 38-foot boats for up to 12 divers each. Good ascent policy, hot shower, and dive masters carry slates. They do a lot of work with novices, but experienced divers will also be pleased. They are also careful with the ocean's critters. They're a big outfit and have had a few growing pains recently, but overall they're still a good company.

Others in Kona

Big Island Divers (329–6068) is a fairly good choice. We like how they pace the dives (not too fast, not too slow) and how they'll rinse your own gear if you like. We've noticed a certain fondness on their part for deep dives. There's shade on the boat. Our biggest complaint is that they tell you to be at the shop at 8 a.m. but you don't get on the boat for 1–1½ hours. They use a 24-foot 6-pack.

Aloha Dive Company (325–5560) has historically been among our top recommended companies. The boat is a fast, 28-foot custom-built craft that can exceed 40 knots. (It could use a little more shade area.) This means that they can do dives in areas too remote for other companies. Home-grown local boys Mike and Earl have had an enthusiasm about diving that is missing from many companies, and their knowledge of marine life is refreshing. We can't recommend them for one simple reason: They've been very bad in the past about returning phone calls from customers wanting to book. Sure enough, when we tried multiple times to review them for this edition, we were never able to get a call returned, even from the cell number they mention on their message.

(We knew they were in town, because we saw their boat at dive sites when we were reviewing *other* boats.) If you get lucky, let us know if they're still good at what they do.

Dive Makai (329–2025) has also been one of the best companies in Kona, but it had been sold at press time and with new owners it's difficult to predict the future of their quality. We'll keep an eye on them and listen to our reader input as well.

Kona Coast (329–8802) has a 42-footer. Their shop is technically good. We get intermittent dive shop attitude with them. At press time they were bought by Jack's Diving Locker.

Sandwich Isle Divers (329–9188) has an adequate shop and their boat is a 28-foot Force. Their attitude is good. Six divers max (which is tight). They're patient with introductory dives. Cheap snacks. Like **Big Island Divers**, Sandwich makes you wait more than an hour before they put you on the boat. (Yeah, we *know* they're not supposed to take money at the harbor, but they could tighten it up a bit.) **Manta Ray Dives** (325–1687) has a glass-bottom dive boat that also takes snorkelers and they only do manta dives. (I have to confess to having this overwhelming urge to swim under their boat where the glass is, take out my regulator and pound on the bottom as if I'm trapped.) **Hawaiian Scuba Shack** (331–8708) had the farthest to go before we'd recommend them, but they're cheap, and it's inexpensive to rent their gear if you're looking to rent and dive on your own.

In Kohala

The diving in Kohala is often richer in coral than Kona. Lush finger coral gardens are plentiful. It's a bit less protected than Kona and sometimes a little bumpy, especially Dec.–April. (Though less bumpy than most of the other Hawaiian Islands during those months.) There are only a few operators there. You best bet is **Kohala Divers** (882–7774) which has a 42-foot Radon that leaves out of Kawaihae Harbor. **Ocean Sports** (886–6666), doesn't have their own boat, but rather subcontracts from one of the Kohala resorts.

Red Sail Sports (886–2876) is a large Kohala Resort area concessionaire with a crummy 38-foot dive boat. Groups are rushed into the water and held on a tight leash. Get in, get out, let's go, next site. We received *no* briefing whatsoever. 18 divers max. Good cookies and cold shower on board. They charge a confiscatory *$1,000* for certification. Along with Ocean Sports, that's the highest price we've ever encountered any place *in the world.*

Mauna Kea Divers (882–1544) is what we think of when we think of bad dive shop attitude. The guy sitting on his stool, playing with some piece of equipment and not looking at you as he conveys, *Come with us and we'll drape an octopus on your arm or we'll catch a puffer fish and tap him on the head to puff up for you. And we'll troll when we're not diving.* Doesn't work for us.

In Hilo

Yes, they *do* dive Hilo side. Though the visibility and calmness are *much* better on the Kona side, life is abundant here and often overlooked. You may see more turtles in some spots here than Kona. There's only one dive shop, **Nautilus Dive Center** (935–6939), which sells and rents gear. They cater mostly to locals. In addition, **East Hawai'i Divers** (965–7840) gives guided shore dives for $70. Private groups—he promises that

you won't see any other divers where he takes you. He dives all over the east side. A good resource.

Manta Ray Night Dive

This dive is *so* good, we put it in the ADVENTURES chapter. If you are a diver or want to be, check out that section and make plans for the dive of a lifetime.

If You've Never Dived Before

Several companies will introduce you to SCUBA by giving instructions, then taking you down on a supervised dive. That's how we started, and we were smitten enough to get certified. **Jack's Diving Locker** does good intros. It's $55 for a one-tank shore dive plus $25 for a pre-dive in their nifty pool with its glass wall. $150 for a two-tank boat intro. If they're full, **Sandwich Isle** is also pretty good with intros; boat dives only.

Dive Sites

Mentioning specific boat dive spots isn't particularly helpful because different companies sometimes use different names for the same spots, and you will usually go where the boat goes. As far as *shore* dive spots are concerned, here are some beauties you may want to check out on the Kona side. For Hilo side, see Nautilus Dive Center.

Crystal Cove—Also used as a boat dive area, it is in Kohala, north of Kawaihae Harbor, off the main highway. About 140 yards south of the 5 mile marker there's a blocked road from the middle of the middle guardrail. It's a 4-minute walk on the lava road to your entry point on the right side of the cove if the surf's not up. (Entry is not too difficult, but not a breeze either.) Coral garden is thick and lush, fish are abundant. Depths are mostly less than 40. If there's no boat here, you'll have it all to yourself.

Puako—Virtually every dive shop and book tells you to go to the end of the road where the pavement becomes dirt. (You actually turn right *just before* the end.) They'll say go about 25 yards on the dirt, park and swim out about 50–75 yards. Turn right (north) and you should see several large vertical holes in the reef to drop through to the bottom. Exit the tunnel on the ocean side.

That's fine, but those sources don't know about the far better area. There are several public accesses along here, but the *best* is at telephone pole #120 (kitty corner from a church 2 miles from the highway). The PUBLIC ACCESS sign is *conveniently* missing, but a check of county records confirms it's public access. Park near the road and the water is a 175-foot walk away. Entry is easy. You can see the reef edge from the shore (polarized sunglasses really enhance it), so during the normally calm seas, kick almost straight out (slightly to the left) over the fairly shallow reef shelf so you'll end up seaward of a house with a corrugated roof. (Remember where you entered; other entry/exit points are harder on the diver.) Once at the reef wall (150 feet or so from shore) work your way northwest along the wall where countless chasms, arches and small caves, coupled with boundless coral, fish and the occasional turtle, create a delightful (though shallow 30–40 feet) dive. If you want to go deep (see photo where the boat is hovering),

simply leave the coral behind and continue a short ways farther off-shore where the sand slopes relentlessly toward the abyss, broken only by vast fields of garden eels. (Approach them slowly, or they'll disappear into their holes.) If you're not too narc'd, return to the heavenly reef edge and make your way back. This is one of the few dives where you can go to 135 feet yet still stay wet for an hour and be within your profile. Snorkelers, too, will enjoy the reef edge.

South Point—If you're a junkyard dog in search of a thrill, South Point has *lots* of fishing relics strewn about the ocean floor. Currents and surf can be unforgiving, so go only when calm.

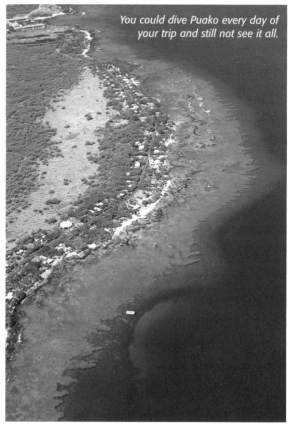
You could dive Puako every day of your trip and still not see it all.

(Winter is sometimes best.) Not-so-easy entry is from rocks to the left (southeast) of the the boat hoists. See page 79 for more information on this area. Stay away from the point.

Makole‘a Beach—One of our personal favorites. The variety, quality and quantity of coral is exceptional. This is a *very* healthy reef, and until now it's never been listed anywhere. We've dived it lots of times and have never seen any evidence that any other diver has been there. Unless you want to carry your gear for 15+ minutes, you'll need a 4WD vehicle to go over the lava road. This will allow you to drive right up to this black sand beach near Kona. The best diving is about 100 to 200 feet out from the right (north) side of the beach. From there, work your way south parallel to the beach. This is a fairly shallow dive (45 feet) and visibility is not the best in Kona (50–65 feet), but the quality of the dive site is hard to beat. Follow directions on page 163. Since we're sharing a hereto-fore unknown dive site (the one where we personally take visiting guests), please make us proud by being extra sensitive to the pristine reef.

The BEACHES section describes nearly all the beaches around the island. Divers should read the descriptions of Kohala beaches, such as **Kapa‘a Beach Park**, **Mahukona**, and **Hapuna** (the southern end). In Kona try the Alii Drive **Four Mile Marker** just south of **White Sands Beach** (from the cove head slightly south), **Kahalu‘u Beach Park** (outside the breakwater), **Ke‘ei**, and **Pu‘uhonua o Honaunau** (Place of Refuge).

If you've ever gazed into an aquarium and wondered what it was like to see colorful fish in their natural environment, complete with coral, lava tubes and strange ocean creatures, you've come to the right Hawaiian Island. Hawai‘i features a dazzling variety of fish. Over 600 species are found in our waters. Here's our dilemma: If we blather on and on again about how good the water can be on the west side of the island, you're probably going to get sick. But we *have* to! Because this is where Kona really pays off. Usually calm, clear and teeming with

We took this photo at the Captain Cook Monument with a disposable underwater camera to give you an idea of the quality you should expect. Remember to get close since the lenses are at a pretty wide angle.

fish, the Kona side offers some of the best snorkeling in the state.

We'll admit that we're snorkeling junkies and never tire of experiencing the water here. If you snorkel often, you can go right to our list below of recommended areas. But it you're completely or relatively inexperienced, you should read on.

For identifying ocean critters, the best books we've seen are *Shore Fishes of Hawai'i* by John Randall and *Hawaiian Reef Fish* by Casey Mahaney. They're what we use. You should see plenty of butterflyfish, wrasse, convict tang, achilles tang, parrotfish, angelfish, damselfish, Moorish idol, pufferfish, trumpetfish, moray eel, and humuhumunukunukua-pua'a, or Picasso triggerfish—a beautiful but very skittish fish. (It's as if they somehow *know* how good they look in aquariums.)

We know people who have a fear of putting on a mask and snorkel. Gives 'em the willies. For them, we recommend boogie boards with clear windows on them to observe the life below.

A Few Tips

• Feeding the fish is generally not recommended since it introduces unnatural behavior to the reef. That said, one place, Kahalu'u Beach Park, has experienced feeding for so long that humans are now part of the "natural" order there. Go ahead and feed them at Kahalu'u, but refrain from feeding them elsewhere. It's in your best interest anyway since fish in other locations won't be as receptive to your offerings because they haven't built up the habit. When feeding Kahalu'u fish, use fish food, rabbit food (cheaper) or a ball of bread rolled tightly in your hand. Contrary to popular belief, frozen peas and potato chips are harmful to fish since

they are unable to digest them properly. Dispense the food *sparingly*; too much and they will grab a bite and run. If they have to compete, they will increase in numbers.

• Fish are hungriest and most appreciative in the morning (before their coffee).

• Use *Sea Drops* or another brand of anti–fog goop. Spread it *thinly* on the inside of a dry mask, then do a quick rinse.

• Most damage to coral comes when people grab it or stand on it. Even touching the coral lightly can transfer your oils to the polyps, killing them. If your mask starts to leak or you get water in your snorkel, be careful not to stand on the coral to clear them. Find a spot where you won't damage coral or drift into it. Fish and future snorkelers (not to mention the coral) will thank you.

• Don't use your arms much, or you will spook the fish—just gentle fin motion. Any rapid motion can cause the little critters to scatter.

• If you have a mustache and have trouble with a leaking mask, try a little Vaseline. Don't get any on the glass—it can get *really* ugly.

• We prefer using divers' fins (the kind that slip over reef shoes) so that we can walk easily into and out of the water without tearing up our feet. (If you wear socks or nylons under the shoes, they'll keep you from rubbing the tops of your toes raw.)

• Try to snorkel in calm areas. If you're in rougher water and a large wave comes and churns up the water with bubbles, put your arms in front of you to protect your head. You won't sense motion, and may get slammed into a rock before you know it.

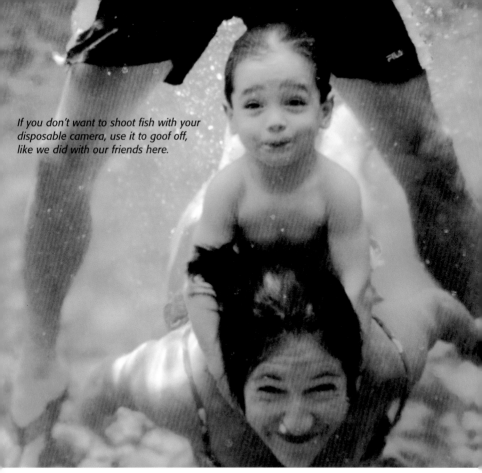

If you don't want to shoot fish with your disposable camera, use it to goof off, like we did with our friends here.

Prices

You'll find the least expensive gear in Kailua-Kona. The business can be cutthroat, so look for coupons in the free magazines scattered around the island. If you're going to snorkel more than once, it's nice to rent for a week, leave it in the trunk, and go whenever you have the desire. **Miller's Surf & Sport** (326–1771) has decent gear for $8 per day, $25 a week. The snorkel gear at **Jack's Diving Locker** (329–7585) is $8 per day, $42 per week. Divers' fins are available. **Snorkel Bob's** 329–0770 (near Huggo's restaurant on Alii Drive in Kona) has gear for $2.50–$15 per day, $9–$45 per week. Expect to get talked into the expensive stuff here. You can rent gear from a truck at Kahaluʻu Beach Park for use there or at the concessionaire to the right of Kailua Pier.

You won't find inexpensive gear in Kohala, but you can try **Ocean Sports** at 885–5555 who have a shack at ʻAnaehoʻomalu Beach. Convenient, but they rent snorkel gear for (hold onto your wallet) $6 *per hour* or $20 per day. They rent all kinds of other goodies there at rates that aren't *quite* as confiscatory.

Snorkel Boat Tours

These can be fun. They'll take you to a good spot, provide gear and show you how to use it, and sometimes provide lunch. OCEAN TOURS on page 210 reviews most of them and includes prices and where they take you. Our favorites are **Fair Wind II**, **Body Glove** and **SeaQuest**.

Snorkel Sites

The section on BEACHES has complete descriptions of all beaches. Our usual prejudice toward west Hawai'i for water activities applies here. Clarity and calmness just can't compare on the Hilo side, but sea life can be just as abundant there. On the west side, be sure to check out some of these beaches:

Kahalu'u—Easy access and lots of life.

Kealakekua Bay Near Captain Cook Monument—Some of the best snorkeling in the state.

Pu'uhonua o Honaunau—Easy access, excellent area, lots of turtles and coral make it almost as good as the Captain Cook Monument.

Pawai Bay—Very interesting underwater relief.

Hapuna to 69 Beach—Great stretch of reef.

Mahukona—Good underwater junk.

Puako—Very extensive reef.

Kiholo Bay—Strange conditions.

Kapa'a Beach Park—Interesting underwater sights.

Lapakahi State Park—Sometimes exceptional amounts of fish.

On the east side check out:

Punalu'u—Cold black sand conditions but *lots* of turtles.

Kapoho Tide-pools—Calm and unique.

Is this a misprint? Nope. Mauna Kea is 13,796 feet high, and in the winter it gets snow—sometimes a lot of it. **Ski Guides** **Hawai'i** (885–4188) takes small groups to the top of Mauna Kea. Their 4WD is your ski lift, and they act as guide. For $250 plus $50 if you need gear (and what are the odds that you *won't?)*, intermediate to advanced skiers get transportation from Waimea, lunch and lots of fairly short runs down from the summit to where the road loops around. Other runs are available if there's enough snow. Mauna Kea snow (called pineapple powder) is not reliable and neither is the company, so call them when you arrive to see if skiing is available. (It's sometimes tough to get them on the phone.) Granted, the conditions will be better at Aspen. But you can't go straight from the snow to the beach there, now can you? If you want to enjoy the snow yourself (or have trouble finding these guys), you can take a 4WD to the observatory area where everyone but the driver can slide down the mountain on boogie boards or anything you think will do, while the driver takes the vehicle to the bottom to act as a ski lift.

If you're a little hesitant about trying SCUBA, consider SNUBA. That's where you swim below a raft with tanks and a 25-foot hose, regulator in mouth and an instructor by your side. **SNUBA Big Island** at 326–7446 (part of a chain) takes you on a shore dive near King Kamehameha Hotel in Kona for $69, or off their boat for $135. Groups of 2–6 per trip; expect about 45 minutes of bottom time on the shore dives, a bit less on boat dives. Some of the boat trips listed under **OCEAN TOURS**, such as **Fair Wind II**, have SNUBA available for about $60 (plus boat trip).

SPAS

If you feel the need to lose yourself in the fog of a decadent overall body massage and treatment, you're in luck. The best is **Mauna Lani Spa** (881–7922). It's an open air spa that makes *wonderful* use of the lava surroundings. Also excellent is the **Fairmont Orchid** (885–2000) and their "Spa Without Walls." Couples can enjoy an outdoor sunset massage right at the shoreline. A curtain provides the privacy or at their waterfall tea houses. The **Kohala Spa** (885–1234) at the Hilton Waikoloa is a huge (25,000 square feet) full-service spa with all kinds of options. Enter a twitching ball of nerves, and you'll leave relaxed stupid.

STARGAZING

If you want to go stargazing on Mauna Kea, home to the world's finest and most coveted telescopes, **Hawai'i Forest & Trail** (331–8505) does the best job. They'll pick you up in Kohala or near Honokohau Harbor in Kona. Then they drive you to an old sheep-sheering station at the lower altitudes of Mauna Kea for a pretty good catered dinner, take you to the summit for sunset, then you come back down to the Visitor Center for stargazing from their own telescope. While you sip hot chocolate and eat cookies, their knowledgeable guides do a good job pointing out—with lasers—the night sky. It's 7½ hours altogether for $165. Another company, **Mauna Kea Summit Adventures** (322–2366), has a similar product but it's not executed nearly as well. It's

$20 more and you get a hot meal at the Visitor Center. **Star Gaze Hawai'i** (880–3155) will let you peek through their scopes at the Hapuna Beach Prince Hotel for $25. Kind of hard to get excited about that one.

submarine

You won't *Run Silent, Run Deep.* There won't be the sound of sonar pinging away in the background. And it's unlikely that anyone will shoot torpedoes at you. But if you want to see the undersea world and *refuse* to get wet, *dis is da buggah.* **Atlantis Submarine** (329–6626) has a 48-passenger sub that ambles about over a very healthy reef in Kailua Bay. This is the opposite of an aquarium—this is *their* world and *you* are the oddity. This 45-minute, $84 ride is a kick. Kids ($45) like it. Adults like it. Even certified divers like us like it. Claustrophobics will probably be too busy staring through the windows to be nervous. Photographers will want to use fast (at least 400 speed) film, and turn off the flash. Mornings are usually best. Wear a bright red shirt, and watch what happens to its color on the way down.

SURFING

Dudes, the most gnarly surfing on the west side is at **Pine Trees** just north of Kailua-Kona. (See Wawaloli on page 163 for directions.) It takes a 4WD vehicle to get there, but the breaks are outstanding. In Kona, the break off the "little blue church" near **Kahalu'u** is one of the most dependable. **Banyans** on Alii Drive just south of Kona Bali Kai has excellent waves. Other great surf spots are **Keʻei** and **Old Kona Airport**, described in BEACHES. You should know that Banyans and Lyman's (just around the bend) are notorious for surfers with bad attitudes. Outsiders will be as welcome as reef rash. (By the way, a collection of surfboards is known in surfing lingo here as a *quiver*. A little kid surfer who doesn't have a job or a car yet is called a *grommet*. If someone says your girlfriend is *filthy*, it's a compliment. And a *landshark* is someone who says he surfs... but doesn't.)

In Kona, **Pacific Vibrations** (329–4140) rents boards for $15–$20 per day. For lessons, **Hawaiʻi Lifeguard Surf Instructors** (324–0442) does an excellent job at Kahaluʻu Beach Park. It's $115 for 2 hours. Also consider **Ocean Eco Tours** (324–7873). They charge $95 per person for a group lesson.

TENNIS

If you feel like a lively game of tennis (or you simply like chasing the ball), the Big Island has plenty of courts. The WHERE TO STAY chapter mentions whether each resort has courts, lighted or not (and the phone numbers for each). The nicest courts on the island are at the **Fairmont Orchid** (887–7532). This fine tennis complex even has a stadium court. (Crowds are extra.) Rates are $15 per day per person. In Kailua-Kona, **Island Slice** (322–6112) at the Keauhou Beach Resort costs $10 per person. Lessons are $40 per hour. In Hilo, your best bet is the county **Hoolulu Park** (961–8720). Three indoor and

five outdoor courts. Indoor courts (preferred) are $4 per hour.

There are 43 *free* municipal courts scattered around the island. Rather than go into mind-numbing detail about all of them, just call the county at 961–8720 and ask for the courts nearest you.

Whale Watching

Humpback whales are common in Hawaiʻi between December and March or April. Humpbacks don't eat while they're here and may lose a third of their body weight during their Hawaiian vacation. (I doubt that many *human* visitors can make that same claim.) They're here to take advantage of Hawaiʻi's romantic atmosphere and mate in our waters (so don't stare), returning the following year to give birth. Though more numerous off Maui, the Big Island is still a splendid place to see whales blow and breach. From shore, you may see humpback whales causing a ruckus or just generally frolicking. But out on a boat, you can sometimes get up close and personal. Additionally, there are several other species—including giant sperm whales, pilot whales, false killer whales, beaked whales, pygmy killer whales and melon-headed whales—that reside here and require boats to see.

Captain Dan McSweeney's Whale Watch (322–0028) is our resident expert. He has spent approximately 1½ zillion hours studying whales off Kona. For $59.50 you and up to 41 other passengers take their 40-foot boat offshore for 3–4 hours of whale watching and education. Snacks provided, restroom on board.

They "guarantee" a sighting or you can come back for free and *claim* a 90% success rate in finding whales. **Living Ocean Adventures** (325–5556) offers year-round trips for up to 6 people in their 31-foot Bertram (a fishing boat). Like Captain Dan, the owner/operator is always present. Except during humpback season, they troll three lines while they whale watch—if they get a strike, you may get to reel it in. Only bottled water provided, restroom on board. $75 for 3½-hour trip. Several other boat companies listed in OCEAN TOURS in ACTIVITIES provide whale watching during humpback season, but these two companies do it year round and have more experience.

Lastly, during humpback season, we like to swim out beyond the sound of the breakers (say, 100 feet past the breakwater at Kahalu'u Beach) and listen to those soulful giants sing the blues. You certainly won't get to *see* them underwater, but their concert is often the best in town. (But I sometimes wonder if the fish all around me are thinking, "I *hate* it when the humpbacks come to town. They make such a racket when we're trying to sleep!") You can hear whales from much farther distances if your ears are a few feet underwater. (Hint: Hang upside-down.) Some years, the whale crowd is pretty raucous, constantly breaching, blowing and singing. Other years the behemoths may be strangely quiescent.

WinDsurfing

Windsurfing (also called sailboarding) is done in Kohala. Kona is a rotten place to windsurf—not enough wind. Kohala afternoons are best (since it's windier). At 'Anaeho'omalu Beach you will find rentals on the beach from **Ocean Sports** (886–6666) for $30 per hour, or take an hour lesson for $60.

It's unfair to say that windsurfing is a dying sport, but here in Hawai'i *many* long-time windsurfers are switching into kitesurfing.

Kitesurfing

Also called kiteboarding, you may not have heard of this. It's a fairly new sport, so we're putting it here. Imagine a modified surfboard, shorter and boxier than a normal board, with fins at both ends and straps for your feet. Then let a special, controllable two-line kite drag you along. Like windsurfing, you don't have to go the direction the wind takes you—you have control. Despite what some instructors tell you when they want to sign you up, it's harder to learn than windsurfing. But *oh*, what fun it is! More fun than windsurfing—if you can get over the steeper learning curve. One way you can prepare before you get here is to buy a two-string kite and master it so that you can instinctively maneuver the kite. It's not that hard, but it helps if you can steer the kite without thinking.

Geography and winds conspire to make kitesurfing somewhat difficult on the Big Island. In Kona there usually isn't enough wind to kitesurf. And in Kohala there's usually too much of an *offshore* component to recommend kitesurfing unless the weather's unusual. (Offshore winds can be unsafe because it'll drag you away from the land.) At press time we couldn't find anyone consistently doing kitesurfing lessons on the Big Island. Blaine at **Launch Our** (989–3900) might be able to help. Otherwise, consider saving your kitesurfing experience for Maui, which has the best conditions in Hawai'i.

Those willing to hike across the lava at night may be rewarded with visions of ethereal beauty.

The adventures described below (except for the dolphin encounter) are for the serious adventurer. They can be experiences of a lifetime. We are assuming that, if you consider any of them, you are a person of sound judgment, capable of assessing risks. All adventures carry risks of one kind or another. Our descriptions below do not attempt to convey all risks associated with an activity. These activities are not for everyone. Good preparation is essential. In the end, it comes down to your own good judgment.

MAUNA ULU CRATER

This short hike is not for the easily frightened or the faint at heart. Mauna Ulu erupted between 1969 and 1974.

When it was all over, it left a smoldering maw 400 feet deep and 600 feet across. (That's a guess—it gets bigger all the time.) This crater is accessible via a 45-minute hike from Chain of Craters Road in Hawai'i Volcanoes National Park. See map on page 196. From there, you just walk up to Mauna Ulu Crater.

We need to stress that this is new land. The part of the hill adjacent to Pu'u Huluhulu *seems* to be the most stable, but that is a relative term. There are several areas where thin, shelly lava breaks beneath your feet. You may only drop an inch or two, but your adrenaline tells you otherwise. There may be even less stable areas around the edge. The rim of the crater is nearly straight down and crumbling all the time. If you get too close, it may break off and you may fall in—and then you're *really* out of luck. If all this doesn't dissuade you, you'll get to see a view that is beyond belief. The crater seems raw, like an open wound on Kilauea. It usually steams heavily from several spots. There are empty river banks around it where huge quantities of lava coursed their way down the mountain. There are blobs where lava spattered where it fell, large cracks with heat still escaping. This is as close as you may ever get to experiencing an erupting vent—while it's not erupting. But remember, this hike is what we call an 'okole squeezer. Permits are only required if you hike beyond Pu'u Huluhulu to Napau, so you *are* allowed to hike to Mauna Ulu without

The Mauna Ulu hike is an 'okole squeezer, not an average stroll.

a permit or permission. That's official from the park, but some park personnel sometimes erroneously tell visitors otherwise. Morning is usually best for this hike.

MANTA RAY NIGHT DIVE

This one may stay with you for the rest of your life. Imagine the following scene: You take a boat to a dark piece of shoreline, leaving just before sunset. When you arrive, perhaps another dive boat is already there. *Damn,* you think. They'll ruin it. As you slip into the water and approach the action area, numerous lights already there beckon you toward them, like a porch light calling to the moths. Then you see gigantic shadows blotting out the lights. *Mantas!* As you approach, one zooms over your head, missing you by an inch. There you sit, with all the others, mesmerized by the performance before you. One, two, maybe three stinger-less manta rays, 6–10 feet across their wings, slowly swirling, looping and soaring all about you. Like a dance performed by extra-terrestrial beings, these filter-feeding leviathans are more graceful than you could possibly imagine. They seem to understand that they are on stage, and they rarely disappoint. When you think you have gotten used to their size, a goliath 14 feet across may swoop in, its enormous maw scooping up thousands of the tiny, darting shrimp that cloud the water along with the bubbles. You struggle to resist the urge to reach up and touch them—it's best to let them initiate any touching. Above the fray, a sea of needlefish gobble up what they can.

It all started 25 years ago when the Kona Surf Hotel (now a Sheraton) started flooding the shoreline with light, attracting tiny brine shrimp, a form of plankton. This plankton brought large manta rays, which gobble them by the millions. Then in 2000 the resort closed (and turned off their light), and the mantas vanished. By luck they were discovered to be congregating at a spot near the Kona Airport (perplexing dive operators since there are no lights there to attract their food source). Since the resort reopened in 2005, they've started coming back.

You will likely have plenty of air left since the dive takes place at about 35 feet, and you move very little. Diver etiquette dictates that you leave your snorkel on the boat; the protruding tube can scratch the mantas' belly. This is one of those rare dives where a crowd, as long as it's not *too* big, actually makes it better. More lights and more wide eyes. Snorkelers who try to dive down or those who use scooters can scare them off.

If you started diving because you wanted to feel like you were floating in space, night dives provide that feeling. But for this dive, weight yourself a bit heavy; it'll make it easier to stay put. (Don't assume that if the surf is up, boats won't go. Though usually calm, we see boats out there when the surf is high enough to make us grateful *we're* not there.) Some companies use ⅓–½ of the 50- to 60-minute dive for roaming around. Others, like Kona Coast, spend nearly all of their time with the mantas. See the chart on page 214 for a list of companies doing this dive. Note that for Manta Ray Dives (325–1687), we've received an unusual amount of *horrible* e-mails from readers about them, and our own experience concurs. So use them only as a last resort. Neptune Charlies seems to use the same phone.

Lastly, if the mantas *don't* show, the airport site is more exciting that the Sher-aton Resort site. Garden eels and other treats make a manta no-show less disappointing there.

If you've night dived before, *do this one!* If you've never night dived before, consider doing it now! Expect to spend about $99–$145 for this dive—the best money you will ever spend underwater *if they show.*

If you only want to snorkel with the mantas and don't want a long boat ride, Sea Paradise charges snorkelers a steep $79 for their 5-minute boat ride from Keauhou Bay.

EXPLORE A MILE-LONG CAVE

Several readers asked us where they could explore a relatively pristine cave on their own. This one, located off Saddle Road, is one of the newest ones on the island. Formed during the same lava flow of 1881 that threatened Hilo and created the well known, but hardly pristine, Kaumana Cave, 14 miles east, this might well be part of the same tube, though parts are blocked off. Called Emesine Cave, there are incredible formations inside, including lava stalactites, channels and shelves that look so perfect and smooth you'd swear they were man-made (though they're not), along with numerous surprises.

Although there is no one out at the cave checking, the state requests you contact them (587–0166) to get a permit before hiking it. (They say there are cave-adapted organism here, but the cave is *very* young, geologically speaking.) When we dutifully called to ask for a permit, they told us to just go ahead and hike it anyway without one. Trying to be diligent, we told them there was a sign mentioning a permit. They seemed confused and then said we could come into the Hilo office and get a piece of paper just so they can keep track of who's going there.

As a cave, this lava tube presents dangers that you need to respect. Though seemingly stable, any cave can have areas where rocks can collapse. Most of the cave is over 10 feet tall, but there are opportunities to whack your head. (Personally, when exploring caves we wear a hard hat with a head-band flashlight attached to the top.) Bring *at least* two strong flashlights. (We bring three). The stronger the light, the more enjoyable the experience. You'll miss *a lot* with a weak light and increase your chances of tripping or hitting your head. (We use a SCUBA dive light; Longs Drugs sells them the cheapest.) Getting into the cave from the entrance is a little awkward. And please make sure you don't harm any of the formations or take any souvenirs other than photos from the cave. We're making some people mad just by telling you where this cave is, so make sure you leave the cave as you found it. (Sorry to sound so preachy, but we can already hear the chorus of critics, who themselves didn't even know about this cave, saying that we shouldn't have revealed this gem.)

To get there, take Saddle Road (Hwy 200) from Kona to $\frac{4}{10}$ mile past (east of) the 22 mile marker. On the south side of the road is a short 4WD road that leads to a powerline road (see map). Take this powerline road for $2\frac{1}{2}$ miles. (The power poles are now cut down.) This lava road itself is easy walking but isn't very interesting, and Saddle Road weather may mean misty and wet. Near the cave the road passes through a lush fern area and descends to newer lava. About 200 feet after the descent ends, look to your right for the tube opening. The tunnel passes under the road, and that's the route you want. (The other way in the cave, heading uphill, is shorter, less interesting and requires ducking too much.) Because it's a single tube, you can't get lost. After a short distance it opens up to another skylight. Just keep going. Make sure to stop and marvel at the formations along the way; that's what you came for.

After about a mile the cave ends at a rock collapse. Don't try to go farther.

If you don't want to cover the same ground coming back, consider taking the longer route along the old Pu'u 'O'o Trail shown on the map.

Lava Tube Hike

200 | 22
20 Miles to Hilo →
Saddle Road | 21
Gate
Old Pu'u 'O'o Trail
4WD Road (but you'll have to walk it)
Darker colors are older forest areas
N W E S
Hill →
Lush fern area →
Cave
0   1 Mile

On the Pu'u 'O'o hike, the forest ends abruptly, bringing you face to face with the beating heart of the current eruption.

RAIN FOREST HIKE TO PU'U 'O'O VENT

One of the few laments people voice when visiting Kilauea Volcano is that they can't readily visit Pu'u 'O'o, the origin and lava source of the current eruption. Of course, you can still see lava flowing from up close (Pele permitting) during a visit to the park, but you can't see the *actual vent* where it originates. There are places where a person can get a glimpse of the vent from a distance (see page 121), but visiting it has been a problem. Unless, of course, you happen to know the way.

Unknown to the vast majority of island residents, the Ka-hau-a-Le'a Trail was cut by state workers in 1990 as the quickest and most direct route to Pu'u 'O'o. It just so happens that it passes through the healthiest, most beautiful and least-hiked rain forest on the entire island. Nowhere will you find a lovelier forest, no matter where you hike.

When we revealed this trail to readers in an earlier edition, bureaucrats at Hawai'i Volcanoes National Park fumed when they realized that we had pointed out a way to visit Pu'u 'O'o that doesn't go through their park. They even stopped selling this book in the park. Well, *that* certainly isn't going to stop us. Park bureaucrats may not *want* you on this trail because you are beyond their control, but they can't keep you off this legal *public* trail.

All told, it's a 4²/₁₀-mile hike to the edge of the forest from your car. (3²/₁₀ miles as the crow flies, but you ain't no crow.) The first half of the hike may as well be through the Garden of Eden. Tree ferns and 'ohi'a trees line the way, bursting with green, many covered with a velvety moss. Even if you're not up to the whole hike, a short trek through this forest is highly memorable. There are no big climbs, just lots of tiny hills and dips. This is the rain forest of your dreams. The second half of the forest shows some signs of wild pigs and is not *quite* as perfect. (Only 98% perfect.) When you get to "the big crack" (you'll know), you're 10 minutes away.

Soon after the crack, the lush forest gives way to small clearings. The trees are looking stressed. Suddenly the forest is dying. Trees are stripped of leaves, grasses are taking over. *Something* is killing the rain forest. Then, through the trees, you see the cause—a sight as awesome as any you've ever encountered. You race to the abrupt edge of the forest and come face to face with Pu'u 'O'o a mile away. The cone, around 500 feet high and built entirely during the current eruption, angrily spews 2,500 *tons* of sulphur dioxide per day, like a snorting exhaust pipe from the center of the Earth. You are on the upslope side, and the lava should be flowing on the opposite side, so you probably won't see that. But if the wind is blowing in the right direction (which it usually is), you will have a view of the beating heart of a volcano.

If the wind is blowing toward you (which it usually *doesn't*), you'll notice a sulphur smell. These occasional winds from the south are what's killing the forest edge. Savor this view, revel in it. But don't try to get closer. Don't try to walk up and peer into the lava lake; the risks are unacceptable. If the wind changes, it exposes you to potentially fatal concentrated fumes. If a cloud forms, the fog would disorient you to the point that you wouldn't know your way back to the forest. Plus, you might fall from the fragile land into a lava lake—a real bummer. Best to observe it from the forest edge, soaking up the sight for your memories of tomorrow.

This hike is not for everyone. It is a fairly long day hike, and conditions are often pretty muddy. This *is* after all, a *rain* forest. (The trail received rainfall of biblical proportions during one rainstorm in 2000. A frog-strangling *32 inches* fell in one day alone.) When the trail's fairly dry, it's not too difficult; when it's real muddy, it's a tiring round trip. The center section is the muddiest.

One of the times we hiked the trail we allowed a visiting friend, who'd never done it before, to lead, and we found the trail in the best shape since we started hiking it. Ironically, the next week we got an e-mail from a reader who had been dissuaded from hiking it by a park ranger who said she and a group of rangers had recently hiked it and *got lost*, requiring a guide to rescue them. If true, it may say more about the quality of some of the rangers at the park than the quality of the trail.

The trail has been groomed sporadically by state workers, but hunters and other users keep it in pretty good shape. A few hunter and pig trails veer off; your path is the most worn path. You may be only a few miles from your car, but if you are off the trail, it would be the longest

Pu'u 'O'o Hike

2,300

South Glenwood Road becomes Captain's Drive/Ala Kapena (Single lane from here.)

Ka-hau-a-le'a Trail

N
W E
S

0   1 MILE

Edge of Rain Forest

19°24.398'
155°06.939'
Big Crack

Remember where the trail exits the forest.

2,450'

19°24.116'
155°06.864'

Faint Geologist Lava Trail (Not designated for the public)

Park Boundary

Lava flow from current eruption

Pu'u 'O'o Summit Rim
19°23.416'
155°06.289'

3,100'

few miles of your life. A compass or GPS is comforting, just in case. Of course, we don't guarantee the trail's condition. In fact, we don't guarantee diddly when it comes to hiking. Nature changes quickly. A strong windstorm can return a nice trail back to jungle until workers come back to repair it. We are assuming that you will use your judgment on this. Also, guerrilla gardeners (you know...alternative farmers) sometimes tend their "crops" deep in the forest. They obviously like to stay as far from people as possible. The point is that you shouldn't stray a long distance off the trail for fear of stumbling onto their "farm" (not to mention getting lost in the rain forest).

Start *early* for this hike. You will want to be hiking by 7:30 a.m. to make *sure* you aren't on the trail when it gets dark. (Some who haven't heeded this warning, starting too late, have been caught on the trail at night and needed to be rescued.) We've run into our own readers on the trail who started at 10 or 11 a.m. and have chastised them for starting too late. Personally, we leave our home in Kona at the *indecent* hour of 4:30 a.m. in order to start hiking by 7 a.m. Time the hike to be back to your car two hours before sunset, just to be safe. It'll *probably* take 2½–4 hours each way, depending on conditions and your hiking skills. Bring plenty of water. Hiking boots (especially waterproof ones) are highly recommended, and a hiking stick (for probing mud puddles and balance) is *strongly* recommended. Most people will get their feet wet due to occasionally unavoidable puddles.

Once at Pu'u 'O'o, note where the trail ends at the edge of the forest for your return. Lastly, when Pu'u 'O'o finally stops erupting, it won't be *quite* as dramatic. But you can bet it'll still be worth it. The inherent lure of this area will be here for years to come.

To get to the trailhead, take South Glenwood Road between the 19 and 20 mile markers (close to the 20) on Hwy 11 (20 miles from Hilo, 95 miles from Kona). It's just south of the Hirano Store. The road curves to the right, then left and changes its name to Captain's Drive/Ala Kapena. From the highway it's 3½ miles *to the very end* (including the one-lane part) where you'll find the trail continuing south. Some readers have had their unattended car broken into here, so don't leave anything valuable in it.

HONOKANE NUI HIKE

At the north end of the island where Hwy 270 ends you'll find Pololu Valley. (See page 48.) Though the trek into Pololu takes only 15–20 minutes, the more adventurous might want to venture

Pololu Valley & Honokane Nui Hike

Honokane Iki Valley

Honokane Nui Valley

Pololu Valley

End of Road in North Kohala

Stay on this fork

440'   600'   400'

0   *Sloppiest part of trail*   1 MILE   *Pololu Beach*

270

© 2006 Wizard Publications, Inc.

beyond this beautiful valley to the more secluded Honokane Nui Valley and its accompanying stream. (Map is on the previous page.) From the car lookout, it takes most people 90–120 minutes each way to hike into Honokane Nui. On the far side of Pololu, the trail goes up the 600-foot-high mountain, over the ridge, then drops down into Honokane. The view of Honokane Nui from the ridge top is breathtaking. Be prepared for a wet, sloppy trail going up the ridge from Pololu if it's been raining recently. (It's drier going down into Honokane.) Horseback riders occasionally take this trail and leave a few...gifts along the way. (Technically speaking, the *riders* probably aren't leaving those gifts; their *horses* probably are.) Usually winter is wetter. In Honokane Nui the trail encounters an idyllic bamboo grove. If you're going to go beyond this valley into the next, take the fork to the right just before the bamboo and cross the stream. Otherwise, take the left fork and you will even-

tually encounter the boulder beach. There is a large deposit of black sand offshore, but it doesn't do *you* a lot of good. Stay out of the ocean here; it'll hurt you. On the far side of the valley is a nice stream and pool—a perfect place to have lunch.

All in all, this is a nice hike when conditions are good. There are some ruins in the valley from days gone by when it was populated. If you are tired, you might be tempted to skirt the water's edge back to Pololu, thereby avoiding the trip up and down the ridge. If it's calm and low tide, you *might* get away with it, or you might get slammed by a rogue wave and washed out to sea, so we don't recommend it unless you're feeling lucky.

Some of the valley trail intersections can get confusing, so be observant. Bring bug juice just in case. Hiking boots are recommended. When you cross Pololu's stream in the first valley, don't do it near the ocean, but rather at a place 100 feet or so back where you can often hop on

If you're willing to hike to it, Honokane Nui Valley is a rich reward for all your sweat.

dry rocks. (Don't cross when it's raging.) Leave for this hike early. Theoretically, you could walk all the way to Waipi'o Valley from here, but the trail disappears in spots and only those with mountain goat in their lineage will want to try it. The next valley, Honokane Iki, is accessible via the trail if you have the time. It's small but pretty.

JUMP OFF THE END OF THE WORLD

Cliff jumpers, rejoice. There's a place just past the south end of Alii Drive. Drive to the end of the road and take the lava road by foot toward the ocean, veer toward the left, and just before the road begins to ascend (next to a short paved section), take the trail to the right to the ocean. It's only a 5–10 minute walk altogether. There at the cliff you are confronted by a 35-foot drop to the water. You have your choice—there are several elevations above the water. And beneath you is clean, clear water up to 15 feet deep. If you *want* to hit bottom, you probably can if you do your best impression of a pencil; Better to spread 'em as soon as you strike water. This is your cliff-jumping opportunity, where countless locals (who named it this) have dared the ocean. Use your best judgement in deciding whether to jump. Judgement is what adventures are all about. The surf can rearrange the bottom, bringing in shallower boulders so you'll have to evaluate all conditions for yourself. And there could be a critter near the surface that you could collide with. After you've jumped, do you have a nice, easy path to climb back up? No, sorry. After you hit the water in a shockingly abrupt fashion, you'll look to the left of the cave you just plummetted in front of and begin the daunting task of climbing the cliff face so you can do it all over again. Don't like

Don't like heights or falling? Not to worry; it won't last long.

those options? Then don't jump off the end of the world.

Another popular cliff-jumping place is from the boat hoist area at South Point. See page 79 for directions to that. People jump from the metal ladder area and climb up the rocks to the right (looking from the water).

CLOSE ENCOUNTER WITH A DOLPHIN

You may have heard of this one. At the Hilton Waikoloa Village there's a program called Dolphin Quest. They have several Atlantic bottle-nosed dolphins in their lagoon where children and adults can get in the water and interact with them. (Our own local spinner dolphins need deeper water and wouldn't successfully adapt to the program.) You stand on a shallow sandy shore with three or four other folks while the dolphins come up to you. *They* decide if they like *you*. If so, you'll be treated to an experience that you will remember for life. It's hard to express the enthusiasm people have when they get up close and personal with these ocean-going mammals. But it's undeniable that the encounter is incredibly enriching. You also can't help but notice that the dolphins seem to love their contact with humans as well.

You may be thinking, "Is this program good for the dolphins?" That's a fair question and was a concern of ours. We found out that the company has a similar program in French Polynesia. There, the dolphins have been allowed out into the open ocean (where they could easily swim off at any time). They claim that the dolphins always return "home" to the program. That's a pretty good testimonial.

We're not experts, but the dolphins seem pretty happy to us. (We've seen other places where we couldn't make that claim.) The water in their lagoon is replaced with fresh seawater every few hours by massive pumps, keeping it very clean for them and you. The dolphins are very active and playful, reproduce when they get to the right age (wink, wink), and the trainers seem to show them extraordinary love and affection.

If you're interested, call them at 886–1234, ext. 1201. It's not always easy to get in on this. Kids are the most desired customer here. Personnel love to introduce kids, not only to the dolphins, but also to various issues regarding the dolphins' environment (without becoming too heavy-handed). Make reservations 60 days in advance to ensure access. Cost is $165 for kids 9 and under (around ½ hour with the dolphins, ½ hour of education camp). Adults can also schmooze with the dolphins for $190–$230. Other programs are available as well.

If you want to see dolphins *in the wild*, your best chance on the island is in Kealakekua Bay. There are quite a few spinners that live in the bay. While kayaking across to the Captain Cook Monument, you stand a good chance of seeing them. We were once able to slip into the water here when 19 dolphins, including babies, were swimming and splashing all around us. You might also see them on a snorkel trip to the bay.

HI'ILAWE FALLS

How about a hike to a waterfall almost as high as the tallest building in the world? Hi'ilawe Falls in Waipi'o Valley plunges 1,450 feet with a free fall of around 1,200 feet. Sound intriguing? Well, to get there, you first have to get into Waipi'o Valley on the northeast side of the island.

That requires either walking down the 1-mile paved road (with a 900-foot descent), driving a 4WD down, or using a company like Waipi'o Valley Shuttle. (See page 130 for location and more on how to get into Waipi'o Valley.)

Access in Waipi'o is a funny thing. Whether someone *owns* land is often unrelated to whether they are exercising some kind of *control* over it. There are several trails to Hi'ilawe Falls. Hopefully, this route will cause the least problem. We've occasionally had reports from readers saying they've been dissuaded from hiking the trail by grouchy residents *claiming* it's private property, but we haven't experienced that ourselves.

The map on page 132 also shows the trail. At the bottom, take the road to the left until *just after* it crosses *under* the first stream. You'll see a 5 MPH sign and a trail right next to it. It follows some PVC pipes to a rock wall. Turn left at the wall and take the vague trail to the stream. You'll have to cross it and walk *upstream* for about 100 feet on the left bank. (This keeps you from walking through a graveyard.) Then reaquire the trail on the left side. From here the trail is obvious until it reaches a dam. (Which is *exactly* what you'll say when you read this next part.) You may want to turn around here and lie to your friends and tell them you finished it.

Here's why. You'll need to enter the water where the trail stops and wade through the small reservoir on the left side. It's pretty deep. Once out of the water, 50 feet ahead on the left is a crude natural rock staircase climbing precariously 20 feet. On top, boulder-hop until you come to a bamboo forest and pick up the trail. The trail's fairly obvious for a while, until you have to cross again. Look for an opportunity to get on the right side. It's not obvious. It's easier to follow coming back, and you'll probably realize all the opportunities you missed to stay on the trail. Often, especially during the last third, the trail is on the far (right) side. Watch for it; trail travel is much faster than river rock walking. And remember, this is not a properly maintained trail, but rather a trail of use, so don't expect a fancy trail.

At the falls, the air is filled with the hiss of water dropping delicately into the pool, and the area abounds with broken rock from above. The view is stupendous. If you get beaned by a rock that has fallen 1,450 feet, you can count on doing your best imitation of a fence post.

Different subject, but while you're down in the valley, another waterfall drops almost into the ocean and is located to the right (east) of the end of Waipi'o Beach. Getting to it is described on page 131. Of course, it's unlikely you'd have enough steam left to do the second hike, especially if you have to walk back up Waipi'o Valley Road.

COMMAND YOUR OWN BOAT

There are lots of charter boats plying the waters off Kona. But what if you want to do things your *own* way? At press time, only one company rented power boats. Kona Boat Rentals (326–9155) at Honokohau Harbor rents 21-foot, single-hull boats. They're made using an amazingly tough material/ process called Roplene. With their 115-horsepower outboards, they'll cut through the water at 30+ MPH. Best of all, you *don't* need prior experience. (Though they will screen you to make sure you're not a moron.) Take it as far north as Kawaihae, as far south as Miloli'i. They'll outfit you with fishing or snorkel gear (SCUBA is extra). Their GPS is preprogrammed with numerous moorings, and they'll show you how to tie up to them. They'll give you some instructions, bring the boat to the harbor, and off you go.

The catch? *Price*. The half-day rental is $325; it's $450 for the day, *plus* gas. That's a big chunk of money. If you have 4 to 6 people, it's not quite as painful when you split it. Seeing the area this way is a real hoot. But nobody ever said hoots were cheap. Nevertheless, it's a great way to SCUBA, snorkel or fish *where* and *how* you want.

If you just can't stomach that much money, Captain Cruise (329–4977) has cheaper 16-foot pontoon boats for rent. They'll only go 8 or 9 MPH but you can get 'em out of Honokohau Harbor for only $69 per hour, $250 per half day which *includes* fuel.

FOUR WHEELIN' BIG ISLAND STYLE

If you rented a convertable Mustang, you can skip this part. This is for those who've rented a 4WD and are willing to violate their rental care contract (the part where they tell you to stay on *paved* roads only).

South Point

Getting to Green Sand Beach shown on page 83 requires a 4WD or a hike. Virtually everyone who visits the beach turns around. What a shame. Past Green Sand Beach the road is smoother (mostly from less use) and often during the week there won't be anybody out there.

The late afternoon sun brings a golden hue to the rolling, grassy landscape bordered by the blue ocean to your right. Take your time getting to Ka'alualu Bay 3½ miles from the beach. Stop and listen to the wind as it fills the silence. Poke around the ruins of an old Hawaiian fishing village at the bay.

Once through the first gate at Ka'alualu Bay, you'll want to stay to the left at every opportunity when you want to return. This brings you back the *much* preferred way. The hardest part is flying through sand pits that dot the road. Be careful not to get stuck. Keep your momentum when driving through them— *don't stop*—and you should be fine. Close all four gates behind you and you'll return to South Point Road just north of the wind farm. And if you should come upon any locked gates or any places where you can't or don't want to proceed any farther, we have a one word solution to your problem—backtrack.

Kilohana Hunter Reserve

Off Saddle Road between the 43 and 44 mile marker is one of the least known major unpaved roads on the island. This 35 mile dirt road links up with Mauna Kea Road (the road that leads up to the summit). Labeled as R-1 on signs (referred to as the Mauna Kea Access Road by some government agencies), this road allows you to circle Mauna Kea at a high altitude. Along the way you'll view moonscapes, volcanic pu'us (hills) and some decidedly delicious scenery. You might also see lots of game birds and possibly some goat, deer or sheep.

Early mornings are best, before the clouds roll in and start erasing your vistas. You could literally spend days exploring the different roads in this reserve.

Starting up the road, there are opportunities to venture off R-1. Just always remember how to backtrack onto the main road and watch for the one time where you need to turn right through a gate to stay on R-1. This road is relatively smooth for long stretches. You'll slow down on the short, rocky climbing areas and through a long field of 'a'a lava. Eventually you'll climb up to the 9,500 foot level and are presented with

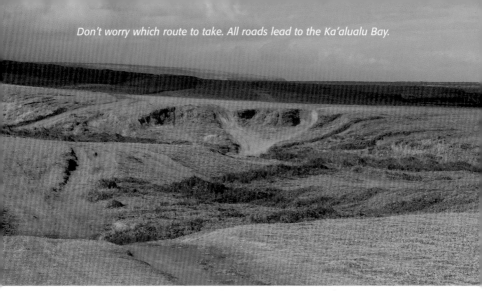

a majestic moonscape. Black sand and tephra litter the landscape and you'll want to stop and take a photo of you beside your vehicle. *No one* back home will believe you when you tell them this is Hawai'i. This was a scene of violent volcanic fountaining, and the scale is something you have to see in person.

Look for opportunities to deviate to other roads, such as the incredible R-10 (then look for a fork guarded by a simple unmarked signpole, and go to the left), which leads up to a beautiful, quiet wasteland of lava pu'us, endangered silverswords and breathless elevations of over 12,000 feet. The quiet is almost deafening as the landscape gets more and more Mars-like. The great telescopes of the summit are nowhere to be seen. This is what it looked like before astronomers ever discovered Mauna Kea. Keep track of which roads you took up here and backtrack to R-1. Watch as clouds start slithering up the valleys, worming their way to the top. Roads go off in different directions from R-10, even leading back to the saddle side of Mauna Kea. The sense of isolation and aloneness is palpable. And whatever route you take up there, it's a driving and navigational adventure.

Back on R-1, after viewing many volcanic hills below you, you'll descend to the visitors center on Mauna Kea Road. Either head to the summit for a peek, or head back. If you stay on the main road, it'll take 3–4 hours plus stopping time.

We didn't make a map of this area because we figured it would do more harm than good. It's a road-filled area and you need to discover it on your own. Besides, it would literally take us many weeks to map the area and it would ultimately end up more confusing that useful.

Mana Road

This is the 44 mile road that stretches from Waimea to Mauna Kea Road, cutting through beautiful Parker Ranch land along the way. If it's fairly dry, this is a doable trip. If it's been raining heavily, you'll want to avoid unless you have an amphibious vehicle. Because some of the puddles are *very* intimidating.

After 18 miles of reasonably smooth dirt road, the second gate ushers you into the real 4WD world. Soon you'll be driving two ruts in tall grass and hills. Alternate tracks will confront you when road conditions necessitate detours. They *should* wind around to the "main" road. At 22 miles is the fourth gate and some kind of ranger station. A couple miles ahead is a monument to David Douglas, killed at this spot. (See page 134 for more on him.)

The road's not bad after this. It's still 4WD, but it's ranchland with some rocky climbs. When you come to another ranger station, the road smooths out until you reach Mauna Kea Road. In all it should take you 4 or 5 hours (in dry conditions).

HIKE TO FLOWING LAVA

This one is difficult to describe for the simple reason that we won't know where lava is flowing at the time you read this. It may be flowing right at the end of Chain of Craters Road in Hawai'i Volcanoes National Park, making this description unnecessary. But maybe not. The lava flows change location all the time, so we'll tell you how to find out where they are and how to get there.

You can call the park at 985–6000 for an eruption update. Unfortunately, they sometimes don't say exactly *where* it's flowing, and they may have false or misleading information on the recording. You can also look at the map posted at the park visitor center.

Our web site at www.wizardpub.com has an updated lava flow map on it and a link to the official USGS lava flow status, usually updated daily. Check it before

you leave on your trip to Hawai'i. The flows should be somewhere between the end of Chain of Craters Road in the park and the end of the lava road in Kalapana. If you hike from the park, you are nearly always permitted to hike to the unsupervised flows. They may *imply* that you can't, but it is almost always permitted.

What if it's flowing *outside* the park? If you look at the map on page 100, you'll see where Hwy 130 ends and a lava road leads toward a lava-destroyed subdivision. This lava road gets you about 2 miles closer to the flows and was cut on top of the old state road out to *near* the park boundary. Until 2001, it was a junky 4WD road and access was disputed. Then the county saw a way to make money: Fix it up for regular cars and charge $5 per car to drive it. (Two weeks after it opened, lava covered it again, so the $5 seems very fair given how many times they'll have to repair it.) If lava is flowing on *this* side of the volcano, this is the road to take. If it's not flowing here, the county may not have the road open during your visit. Call the county at (808) 961–8093 for an update on the road and viewing conditions.

The general rule of thumb is that eastern flows on the county side (from Kalapana) are rigorously supervised, and you won't be able to get as close. Western flows near Chain of Craters Road are supervised by the park, and they are pretty good about letting you get close when it's safe. Flows in the park more than a mile from Chain of Craters Road are usually *unsupervised,* and only your own common sense is there to supervise you. (And maybe your smarter spouse.)

At the flows you are presented with several dangers. Lava benches form seaward of the old seacliffs. They can collapse at any time, taking viewers with them, so *don't* go on the benches below. Collapses also can hurl rocks inland. Lava tubes travel under you. Hot water can splash on you. There may be signs where the flows enter the ocean telling you to go no further. Heed them. There may be surface flows; watch for them.

Lava flows are *least* impressive between 10 a.m. and 2 p.m. (because the red lava is competing with the sun.) Don't hike here in the dark without flashlights. Our preference is to hike out in the late afternoon, so we get to see lava during the daylight and at night.

There are other dangers, as well, such as bad gases that trade winds *normally* blow to the southwest, and we are counting on your own good judgment to keep you out of trouble. We are not attempting to convey all the dangers present on this hike. You'll have to evaluate some on your own. The park has a brochure about viewing lava safely that you may want to pick up. This is a thrilling hike of a lifetime, but not for the faint-hearted, and bad decisions can result in tragedy. Contrary to what you might think, *smaller* lava flows, with less steam at the ocean, are much more dramatic than large ones since they're less likely to be completely engulfed by steam.

There's nothing but your own good judgment to keep you out of trouble—and off the lava bench on the right side—when the lava's flowing in remote places.

Your table is ready...

By their very nature, restaurant reviews are the most subjective part of any guidebook. Nothing strains the credibility of a guidebook more. No matter what we say, if you eat at enough restaurants here, you will eventually have a dining experience directly in conflict with what this book leads you to believe. All it takes is one person to wreck what is usually a good meal. Many of us have had the experience when a friend referred us to a restaurant using reverent terms, indicating that they were about to experience dining ecstasy. And, of course, when you go there, the food is awful and the waiter is a jerk. There are many variables involved in getting a good or bad meal. Is the chef new? Was the place sold last month? Was the waitress just released from prison for mauling a customer? We truly hope that our reviews match your experience. If they don't, please drop us a line. We read every restaurant comment readers send and they help us in deciding which restaurant to reevaluate on a given day.

Unlike some travel writers who announce themselves to restaurants (to cop a free meal, if the truth be told), we always review *anonymously* and only expose ourselves after a meal (not literally, of course) by phone if we need additional information. By their reviews, many guidebooks lead you to believe that every meal you eat in Hawai'i will be a feast, the best food in the free world. Frankly, that's not our style. Like anywhere else, there's ample opportunity to have lousy food served with a rotten ambiance by uncaring waiters. In the interest of space, we've left out *some* of the dives. We did, however, leave in a few of these turkeys just to demonstrate that we know we live the real world. Restaurants that stand out from the others in some way are highlighted with **ono** this symbol.

For each restaurant, we list the price *per person* you can expect to pay. It ranges from the least expensive entrées alone, to the most expensive plus a beverage and usually appetizers. You can spend more if you try, but this is a good guideline. *The price excludes alcoholic beverages since this component of a meal can be so variable.* Obviously, everyone's ordering pattern is different, but we thought that it would be easier to compare various restaurants using dollar amounts than if we used different numbers of dollar signs or drawings of forks or whatever to differentiate prices between various restaurants. All take credit cards unless otherwise noted. When we mention that prices are reasonable, please take it in context. We mean reasonable *for Hawai'i.* (We *know* you pay less back home.) Food in Hawai'i is expensive, even if it's grown here. (You probably pay less for our fruit on the mainland than *we* do here.)

When we give directions to a restaurant, *mauka side* of highway means "toward the mountain" (or away from the ocean). The shopping centers we mention are on the maps to that area.

The difference between local and Hawaiian food can be difficult to classify. Basically, local food combines Hawaiian, American, Japanese, Chinese, Filipino and several other types and is (not surprisingly) eaten mainly by locals.

Most restaurants close around 9 p.m.

Lu'aus, those giant outdoor Hawaiian parties, are described at the end.

Below are descriptions of various island foods. Not all are Hawaiian, but this might be helpful if you encounter dishes unfamiliar to you.

ISLAND FISH & SEAFOOD

If you've been fishing today and want to visit your new friend, **Marina Seafoods** (326–2117) at Honokohau Harbor sells fresh fish from the fishing boats and is often cheap.

Ahi–Tuna; raw in sashimi or poke, also seared, blackened, baked or grilled; good in fish sandwiches. Try painting ahi steaks with mayonnaise, which *completely* burns off when BBQ'd but seals in the moisture. You end up tasting only the moist ocean steak. Generally most plentiful Apr.–Sept.

Lobster–Hawaiian spiny lobster is quite good; also called "bugs" by lobster hunters. Maine lobster is revived on the Big Island, called Keahole Lobster.

Mahimahi–Deep ocean fish also known as a dolphinfish; served at luaus; very common in restaurants. Sometimes tastes fishy, which can be offset in the preparation.

Marlin–Tasty when smoked, otherwise can be tough; the Pacific Blue Marlin is available almost year round.

Monchong–Excellent tasting deepwater fish, available year round. Usually served marinated and grilled.

Onaga–Also known as a ruby snapper; excellent eating in many preparations.

Ono–(Wahoo); *awesome* eating fish and can be prepared many ways; most plentiful May through October. Ono is also the Hawaiian word for delicious.

Opah–(Moonfish); excellent eating in many different preparations; generally available April through August.

'Opakapaka–(Crimson snapper); great tasting fish generally cooked several ways. Common Oct.–Feb.

'Opihi–Limpets found on ocean rocks. Eaten raw mixed with salt. Texture is similar to clams or mussels.

Poke–Fresh raw fish or octopus (tako) mixed with seaweed (limu), sesame seed and other seasonings and oil.

Shutome–Swordfish; dense meat that can be cooked several ways. Most plentiful March through July.

LU'AU FOODS

Chicken lu'au–Chicken cooked in coconut milk and taro leaves.

Haupia–Coconut custard.

Kalua pig–Pig cooked in an underground oven called an imu, shredded and mixed with Hawaiian sea salt (outstanding!).

Laulau–Pork, beef or fish wrapped in taro and ti leaves and steamed. (You don't eat the ti leaf wrapping.)

Lomi salmon–Chilled salad consisting of raw, salted salmon, tomatoes and two kinds of onions.

Pipi kaula–Hawaiian beef jerky.

Poi–Steamed taro root pounded into a paste. It's a starch that will take on the taste of other foods mixed with it. Best eaten with kalua pig or fish. Visitors are encouraged to try it so they can badmouth it with authority.

OTHER ISLAND FOODS

Apple bananas–A smaller, denser, smoother texture than regular (Williams) bananas.

Barbecue sticks–Teriyaki-marinated pork, chicken or beef pieces barbecued and served on bamboo sticks.

Bento–Japanese box lunch.

Breadfruit–Melon-sized starchy fruit; served baked, deep fried, steamed, or boiled. Definitely an acquired taste.

Crackseed–Chinese-style, spicy preserved fruits and seeds. Li Hing Mui is one of the most popular flavors.

Guava–The inside is full of seeds, so it is rarely eaten raw. Used primarily for juice, jelly or jam.

Hawaiian supersweet corn–The finest corn you ever had, even raw. We'll lie, cheat, steal or maim to get it fresh.

Huli huli chicken–Hawaiian BBQ style.

Ka'u oranges–Locally grown. Usually, the uglier the orange, the better it tastes.

Kim chee–A Korean relish consisting of pickled cabbage, onions, radishes, garlic and chilies.

Kulolo–Steamed taro pudding.

Liliko'i–Passion fruit.

Loco moco–Rice, meat patty, egg and gravy. Specialty of Café 100 in Hilo.

Lychee–A reddish, woody peel that is discarded for the sweet, white fruit inside. Be careful of the pit. Small seed (or chicken-tongue) lychees are so good, they should be illegal.

Macadamia nut–A large, round nut grown primarily on the Big Island.

Malasada–Portuguese doughnut that is dipped in sugar.

Manapua–Steamed or baked bun filled with meat.

Mango–Bright orange fruit with yellow pink skin. Distinct, tasty flavor.

Manju–Cookie filled with a sweet center.

Musubi–Cold steamed rice, sometimes sliced spam rolled in black seaweed.

Papaya–Melon-like, pear-shaped fruit with yellow skin best eaten chilled. Good at breakfast.

Pipi Kaula–Hawaiian-style beef jerky. Excellent when dipped in poi. (Even if you don't like poi, this combo works.)

Plate lunch–An island favorite as an inexpensive, filling lunch. Consists of "two-scoop rice," a scoop of macaroni salad and some type of meat, either beef, chicken or fish. Also called a Box Lunch. Great for take-out.

Portuguese sausage–Pork sausage, highly seasoned with red pepper.

Pupu–Appetizer, finger foods or snack.

Saimin–Thin Chinese noodles cooked in a Japanese-style chicken, pork or fish broth. Word is peculiar to Hawai'i. Local Japanese say the dish comes from China. Local Chinese say it comes from Japan.

Shave ice–A block of ice is "shaved" into a ball with flavored syrup poured over the top. Best served with ice cream on the bottom. Very delicious.

Smoothie–Usually papaya, mango, frozen passion fruit and frozen banana, but almost any fruit can be used to make this milkshake-like drink. Add milk for creaminess.

Taro chips–Sliced and deep-fried taro; resembles potato chips.

KAILUA-KONA AMERICAN

Aloha Angel Café
79-7384 Mamalahoa Hwy • 322–3383

We like to stop here if we want a big breakfast on our way to the volcano. They offer good food at reasonable prices. On the lanai, the table all the way to the back has a nice view down to the coast. A few omelettes, Thick sliced French toast, and the breakfast burrito is big and hearty (though you might consider the extra meat option). Lunches are pretty good, featuring fish sandwich, 6 oz. burgers, a touch of Mexican and fish tacos. The place generally has a laid-back, funky feel. The service is either great or bad, depending on whether they remember you exist. Lots of homemade baked goods and they have a good mocha. **$9–$13** for breakfast and lunch. Located in a restored theater building on the highway in Kainaliu (just south of Kailua-Kona). For entertainment try feeding sugar or cornbread to the unusually friendly chameleons and geckos on the railing.

Bad Ass Coffee Company
75-5770 Alii Dr. • 326–4637
Mediocre coffee and day-old Costco muffins. The saving grace is their location in Waterfront Row on Alii Drive where you can take your coffee to a table overlooking the water.

Beach Tree Bar & Grill
100 Ka'upulehu Dr. • 325–8000

 Fantastic beachside setting at the Four Seasons at Hualalai 14 miles north of Kona. Mixed menu with grilled fish, pad Thai noodles, burgers and hot dogs, BBQ chicken and tuna salad sandwich. **$12–$18**. Pricey food 'cause you're at a pricey resort.

Big Jake's Island BBQ
Mamalahoa Hwy • 328–1227
It's not that we don't like the food here, it's just that you pay restaurant prices but end up eating on styrofoam plates on picnic tables outside. Food is pulled pork, ribs, brisket and other BBQ staples. **$8–$24** for lunch and early dinner. On Hwy 11 next to a fish market at the 106 mile marker.

Bubba Gump Shrimp Co.
75-5776 Alii Dr. • 331–8442
ONO Remember the 1994 movie *Forrest Gump,* when Bubba describes all the ways you can fix shrimp? Well, the owners of this small chain apparently didn't see it because most of the recipes mentioned in the movie aren't on the menu. But that's OK because this is an easy place to like. The whole restaurant is based on the movie, and the dishes are named after its characters. Though the movie novelty has worn off by now, they have friendly service and overall, it's fun. The service can seem a bit unresponsive until you realize that the ping-pong paddle on the table that says, "Stop Forrest Stop" is meant as a signal to the waiter that you want 'em. (Beats the heck out of the old eye-contact method.) The restaurant has improved in recent years and most of the food is pretty good with lots of shrimp dishes (obviously!), fish, some steak, burgers and salads. Good coconut shrimp—

Bubba would have approved. Grandma's firepot fish is very tasty. We absolutely *love* their hush pups (different from hush puppies). Their Medal of Honor Margarita is smokin' good, and the portion is hefty. Breakfasts are their weak point. Killer views, but the food's not great. And their biscuits and gravy are downright awful. (The menu says, "Momma only makes it once a week." Well, Momma, that's one day too many.) They won't take reservations (and long waits are not uncommon at night). Overall, a fun atmosphere and acceptable food make a good experience if you can tolerate the somewhat rushed and thinly stretched service. Their location is dreamy. Right on the water on Alii Drive next to Waterfront Row in downtown Kona. **$9–$15** for breakfast, **$15–$25** for lunch and dinner.

Buns in the Sun
75-5595 Palani Rd. • 326–2774
ONO The sandwiches are good and the selection quite admirable. They use really good bread (baked there). Service is often indifferent. For breakfast they have pastries, as well as egg dishes, including kalua pig and eggs with rice (a worthy choice). Avoid the biscuits and gravy; they taste like plastic. Good, flaky croissants. In the Lanihau Shopping Center off Palani Road. Breakfast is a reasonable **$5–$7**; lunch is **$7–$11**.

Coffee Shack
83-5799 Mamalahoa Hwy • 328–9555
ONO A good place to stop on your way to the volcano— they open at 7:30 a.m. Except when

we want a *big* breakfast, this is where we often stop. *Fantastic* view down the slopes of Mt. Hualalai overlooking Kealakekua and Honaunau—try to get a railing table and check out the gigantic avocado tree and the coffee trees below you. (It's nice to sit there drinking coffee grown from those very trees.) Tables are outdoors but covered, and the place is clean. Nice selection of coffee drinks, tasty homemade baked goods and breads (when fresh, which is not a certainty), a small selection of breakfast items and a good selection of sandwiches. Their home-grown coffee is usually tasty (occasionally off). Lunch brings sandwiches and pizza and can get busy; breakfast is more relaxing. **$8–$13** for breakfast and lunch. Service is often slow. On ocean side of highway in Captain Cook between the 109 and 108 mile markers.

Costco
73-5600 Maiau St. • 331–4834

You'd be surprised at how many people eat at the food stand at Costco. Their pizza is surprisingly good (they use pretty good ingredients and the crust is fresh), and it's *very* cheap. Less than **$11** for a gigantic pizza. They also serve hot dogs, salads and a few other items. In the back of the store they have tasty whole rotisserie chickens for **$5**. You need to be a Costco member to get in. We gave them an ONO because of the value—can't beat it. North Kona, see map on page 165.

Denny's
75-1027 Henry St. • 327–2184

You mean the chain? The cheap Grand Slam breakfast (which is over *$7* here)

and all that? Yeah. Nearly everyone knows what kind of food to expect at a Denny's. This one's no different. The reason we're putting 'em here is that they have an excellent view of Kailua-Kona and the ocean, and they are the first place in town to be open 24 hours. Otherwise, it's the same old Denny's. In the CrossRoads Shopping Center at Palani Road and Hwy 11.

Drysdale's Two
78-6831 Alii Dr. • 322–0070

They serve chicken, burgers, ribs, fish— you get the picture. A sports bar with food. The food is acceptable, certainly not grand (the ribs are usually decent), but the portions are on the large size. Try the ostrich or buffalo burgers. With reasonable prices, some outside tables, a casual atmosphere and a full bar, this place is popular with visitors and locals. **$8–$20** for lunch and dinner. Open later than most restaurants, in case you're hungry when the rest of Kona closes up. In the Keauhou Shopping Center off Kamehameha III in South Kona.

Durty Jakes
75-5819 Alii Dr. • 329–7366

Right next to the road on Alii Dr. That's good because of the ocean right across the street, bad because of the loud traffic noise at street level. Burgers, sandwiches and salads for lunch, bring on steak, seafood and pasta at dinner. Food is not overly impressive. They are *literally* operating in the shadow of Lulu's upstairs which does a better job with a similar menu. So if you don't mind climbing stairs, keep going up. Jakes' busy bar seems to be the center of attention. **$7–$15** for breakfast, **$9–$14** for lunch,

$14–$22 for dinner. In Coconut Grove Marketplace in downtown Kona.

Evie's Organic Café
79-7460 Mamalahoa Hwy • 322–0739
Lots of organic here. Items like wraps, sandwiches, one large salad, waffles and tofu. Darn fine smoothies. Their system is kind of strange. Pay up front but make sure you bring your receipt to the kitchen or they won't make your meal. **$11–$16** for breakfast and lunch. In Kealakekua in the Mango Court next to Subway.

Harbor House
Honokohau Small Boat Harbor
326–4166
Ask anyone who frequents Harbor House why they go, and they'll give you a one-word answer— *Schooners!* Located at Honokohau Harbor 2 miles north of Kona overlooking the water and boats, they serve the coldest beer on the island in ultra-thick, 18-ounce frosted schooners for around $3. (Oh, I almost forgot, they serve food, too.) This is a popular place to stop after a fishing or SCUBA excursion. The food consists of average fish and chips, fried calamari, burgers and assorted other fast food. We didn't give 'em an ONO *because of the food;* it's just a great place to tip a cold one and watch the tranquil harbor waters while you go over your adventures of the day. **$6–$12.** Head toward the harbor off Hwy 19 between the 97 and 98 mile markers and turn right at the buildings. Closes around 7 p.m.; the schooners aren't as cold near closing time.

Hard Rock Café
75-5815 Alii Dr. • 329–8866
After a promising start it seems to have slipped lately and is not one of the better-run Hard Rocks. The ambiance still works well. The interior is swimming with rock 'n' roll memorabilia and rock music fills the air. The best views are near the lanai, and the volume of music is softer. Their view of the ocean across the street is very nice. But service is slow and the food merely adequate. Drinks are clever but seem light on the alcohol. Burgers, sandwiches, ribs, pasta, fajitas and large salads. Appetizers are *expensive.* **$10–$25** for lunch and dinner, open till midnight. On Alii Drive in Coconut Grove Market Place in Kona.

Huggo's
75-5828 Kahakai Rd. • 329–1493
This is a very difficult restaurant to review. They have *gorgeous* open-air views adjacent to the ocean at Kailua Bay. They are so close to the water because they are grandfathered into the regulations restricting oceanside construction. The sound of the surf can get loud enough to sometimes create a sort of sound arms race among patrons, where the volume keeps escalating. The ocean proximity alone almost gets them an ONO. But execution is spotty. Food is often over or undercooked. Service can get forgetful. No doubt with their setting they have no trouble filling their tables. And the recipes are quite good, like the crab-crusted ono or the tender teri beef. Add Pasta, steak, seafood and some veggie items and you have the potential for a great meal, if all cylinders are firing. Try to get a railing table where you look down onto sand, rock and water. (Preferable over the patio tables.) The adjacent lounge is a good place to enjoy a drink at sunset. Since it's so pricey and the view so important to the experience, con-

sider them for lunch or an early dinner, because you're paying premium prices and getting a premium location with merely adequate food. **$10–$25** for lunch, **$25–$50** for dinner. Off Alii Drive, downtown Kona near Royal Kona Resort.

Island Lava Java
75-5799 Alii Dr. • 327–2161

ONO The coffee is pretty good (though sometimes not very hot), and the food is tasty and not *too* ridiculously priced for the location. (They're right across the street from the ocean with excellent views.) Good baked goods and a few breakfast items like the tasty breakfast wraps. Their cinnamon rolls are obscene and utterly massive (big enough to use as a flotation device if you fall in the water), and they taste great. An easy recommendation although the rolls don't usually come out of the oven until around 7:30 a.m. Good (though *very* pricey) fresh-squeezed pineapple juice. Get an outdoor table. Lunch is fairly well-prepared sandwiches and soups. There used to be a Cook Island pine tree out front. It fell, smiting (I always wanted to use that word) the business for six months. Alii Dr. in Kona in Alii Sunset Plaza. **$4–$10** for breakfast and lunch.

Jameson's by the Sea
77-6452 Alii Dr. • 329–3195

ONO This is the kind of restaurant that can drive a guide-book writer crazy. Sometimes so good, sometimes so bad. Sometimes we give 'em an ONO, sometimes not. Located next to White Sands Beach on Alii Drive, the setting is wonderful. Their dreamy outdoor railing tables overlook the beach and get you close to the water. (These outdoor "railing" tables are much preferred to the official "outdoor" tables whose view of the ocean is partially blocked by a wall that makes you feel like you're in a hole. Sometimes insects from the beach fly onto the tables; unavoidable, I'm afraid.) The ambiance is first rate. But the food is *soooo* variable here—sometimes great, sometimes downright terrible. Some of the dishes seem ill-conceived, others flavorful. (Flavors are not subtle here.) Steak, seafood and lobster. Entertainment is often provided, usually by some pretty bad Hawaiian lounge lizards. *Give me that crazy, kooky huki-lau, yeeeah!* The portions are too small on some items (like the baked stuffed shrimp), and the service is responsive but often snippy. Sometimes we vow not to return but usually change our minds when we want the railing table setting. Then we pay $10 for a grilled ham and cheese sandwich at lunch and mumble, until the view of White Sands Beach makes us smile again. We like to arrive for dinner about 45 minutes before sunset, though you may not see the sun from the railings. Lunch is **$10–$20**, dinner is **$25–$40**.

Java on the Rock
75-5828 Kahakai Rd. • 329–9262

ONO An espresso bar that serves a little bit of food. Only three items at breakfast. They cook their eggs using the cappuccino machine and put them in a tortilla. Is a breakfast burrito worth almost *$7?* Not anywhere else. But their location is *wonderful*. It's right next to the water in an ultra-relaxing atmosphere, so you're paying for that. They're not exactly lightning fast, but with this location you're not exactly in a hurry. Around **$10** for coffee and a breakfast entree. Next door to Huggo's off Alii Drive near the Royal Kona Resort. You can't linger past 11 a.m. That's when Huggo's takes over the spot, and it becomes Huggo's on the Rock.

Ke'ei Café
79-7511 Mamalohoa Hwy
322–9992

(ONO) Not really American, sort of a hodge-podge of items from many countries. (I guess that *is* American.) You know how you sometimes purposely get into a rut at a restaurant by ordering the same dish because you love it so much? That's how one of us is for the fresh fish (especially ono) on red Thai curry and jasmine rice; the other likes the (spicy) fajitas stuffed with chicken or tofu, salsa, black bean chili sauce and avocado. The decor is nicely appointed, but passing cars from the highway are too loud. Don't worry about it, though. The flavors are unlimited. (Try the eggplant rolls with couscous inside for an appetizer or the excellent coconut shrimp rice cakes.) Also available are rib eye steak, great pork chops and a few other items. Desserts are bread pudding, a mango crisp and more. And they make good mango martinis. Service has improved. (You used to need a flare gun to get their attention.) On Hwy 11 just south of Kona in Kainaliu between the 112 and 113 mile markers. **$15–$30** for dinner. Lunch (wraps, fish tacos, noodles and a pasta) is **$10–$13**. Reservations recommended. No credit cards.

Kimo's Family Buffet
75-5739 Alii Dr. • 329–1393
Buffets by the pool at Uncle Billy's Kona Bay Hotel in downtown Kona on Alii

Drive. **$8** for breakfast buffet, **$10** for dinner buffet. Is it the best food on the island? *Get real!* But it's cheap, cheap, cheap. Eggs and the like at breakfast, chicken, potatoes, etc., for dinner. Nothing you wouldn't expect.

Kona Beach Restaurant
75-5660 Palani Rd. • 329–2911
Located in King Kamehameha's Kona Beach Hotel, the restaurant is right next to Kamakahonu Beach and the 'Ahu'ena Heiau, so get a table next to the window, which makes a delightful way to start the day. The food is acceptable. For breakfast it's either a buffet for **$15** or off the menu. They have fairly good prime rib and seafood dinner buffets for **$32** Fri. and Sat. Otherwise, dinner is unremarkable steak, ribs and chicken. **$6–$11** for breakfast, **$17–$34** for dinner.

Kona Inn Restaurant
75-5744 Alii Dr. • 329–4455
(ONO) Mostly seafood with a little pasta and stir-fry. Nice ambiance—A good place for a sunset dinner. Just a strip of grass separates you from the ocean. Dinner includes many varieties of fish. Consider the *super*-rich but tasty stuffed local fresh fish. At dinner, avoid the uncomfortable antique chairs in favor of the high-back wicker chairs. **$8–$14** for lunch, **$20–$40** for dinner. The food and service are usually very good. Check out the ceiling fans—all interconnected by an old belt system. Some parents like to bring their keikis here where the munchkins can play on the grass while the grown-ups can dine and keep an eye on them. Located on the ocean side of Alii Drive in downtown Kona at the Kona Inn Shopping Village. Can't miss it.

Kona Style Fish & Chips
75-5693 Alii Dr. • 329-4488

They brag about their fish batter, but it tastes an awful lot like Long John Silver's to us. They also have fish sandwiches and non-seafood items like chicken and burgers. We wouldn't steer you *away* from here, but we wouldn't direct you *to* them either. It's neutral...with a fairly pleasant view of the ocean across the street. **$5–$10** for breakfast, **$8–$20** for lunch and dinner. Across from the seawall on Alii Dr.

Kona Village
Queen Ka'ahumanu Hwy • 325-5555

ONO Located at secluded Kona Village between Kona and the Kohala Resort area (see map on page 159), the food here is excellent and pricey and offered at *fixed* prices (since meals are included in the rooms). Breakfast is **$29** and lunch is a **$35** buffet outdoors at Hale Moana. The wind and birds can be a problem, but the food and oceanside view make up for it. Lots of salads, tasty fish, pork or beef and scrumptious desserts. For dinners indoors you choose from several complete meals for **$75** at Hale Moana (Pacific Rim) or **$75–$100** at Hale Samoa (which has a dress code—long pants, etc.) These complete meals include appetizers, soup, salad, entrée and dessert, featuring seafood or steak in an elegant and romantic atmosphere. Children allowed (but they pay full price) at Hale Samoa. Reservations *required* for non-guests. Ask them about the time a plane crashed into the Talk Story Bar. Kona Village is north of Kona on Hwy 19 near the 87 mile marker.

Lava Java—See *Island Lava Java.*

Lulu's
75-5819 Alii Dr. • 331-2633

ONO With their Caribbean/South Seas-type decor, ample portions, tasty food and giant margaritas, Lulu's works. Numerous sandwiches (love the Maui teriyaki chicken) and burgers, they also have a large pupu selection and some good veggie items. Nice view overlooking the water. (Just pretend you don't see the enormous power lines in the way.) On Alii Drive at Coconut Grove Market Place. (The music from Hard Rock can permeate Lulu's.) **$10–$25** for lunch and dinner. The menu lists several other Lulu's locations in the South Seas—such as Tonga—but according to a highly placed source deep within the Lulu's organization (our waitress), the only Lulu's are in Hawai'i.

O's Bistro
74-5605 Alapa St. • 327-6565

ONO Formerly called Oodles of Noodles, the menu is eclectic Pacific Rim. Items like Kona style tuna casserole (Mom never made it like this—pretty tasty), pad Thai (nice flavors), raviolis, saimin, fish tacos and pork scallopini demonstrate how unclassifiable it is. Most items are good but some, such as the summer rolls, are disappointing. The atmosphere is jazzy and relaxed, service is friendly but sketchy. Prices are high—too high—so the ONO is marginal. (Can anything justify a *$18* tuna casserole, no matter how good?) But we can't deny that the food is good. **$12–$20** for lunch, **$27–$40** for dinner. In the CrossRoads Shopping Center.

Oceans Sports Bar & Grill
75-5811 Alii Dr. • 327–9494

A sports bar with a broad selection. Lots of pupus, burgers, fajitas, pastas and ribs. With their pool tables, lots of TVs and sporty atmosphere, it would be a great place for an afternoon cocktail if it weren't for one thing: The drinks are tasty but so incredibly weak, a bottle of rum must last a *lifetime* in their bar. Stick with the beers or go elsewhere. **$9–$18** for lunch and dinner. Behind Hard Rock Cafe off Alii Dr.

Outback Steakhouse
75-58 Alii Dr. • 326–2555

Yeah, we know it's Australian, not American. But we don't *have* an Australian category and besides, it's basically steak, chicken and a little seafood. Lobster is also available. Though items have names like Jackaroo Chops or Wahalla Pasta, they merely refer to pork chops or pasta alfredo. Nonetheless, the Australian tie-in is kind of fun. Prices ain't cheap. A 9-ounce tenderloin is $26 and salads are around $11. Simple grilled chicken is the cheapest meal and it's $15. Overall, a decent, if somewhat pricey choice for ordinary food served with a somewhat funky attitude. **$17–$35** for dinner. Located behind Coconut Marketplace in downtown Kona. Access the parking from Kuakini.

Pahu I'a
100 Kaupulehu Dr. • 325–8000

(ONO) This is one of our favorite restaurants on the island. The lanai tables (which are a bit too close together) are as close to eating on the beach as you'll get; ask for them. The menu is mostly seafood, lobster and beef. Items change often but are usually utterly delicious. Flavors aren't hit-you-over-the-head knockouts, but rather super-skillful blends of subtlety. And their warm Valrhona butter chocolate cake is a fitting end to your meal. We like to arrive about 45 minutes before sunset to get a good table and to gawk at the superb beachside setting. This is a romantic place. Service is top-notch professional. They rarely do anything wrong, but, of course, you pay for that perfection and portions are scaled back as is the norm at fancy restaurants. Breakfast is **$15–$30** (with a great but pricey **$38** buffet). Dinner is **$40–$60**. Expensive, yeah. But, oh, what a meal. Reservations recommended far in advance. Resort wear required. Located at the Four Seasons at Hualalai 14 miles north of Kona on Hwy 19.

Paleo's Bar & Grill
75-5663 Palani Rd. • 329–5550

WANTED: RESTAURANT GOOD ENOUGH TO PROPERLY UTILIZE THIS CHEF. That's what it felt like to review this place. The food is good, *real* good. Well-prepared, well-conceived and the portions were generous. Plus they're across the street from the Kailua Pier with nice views of the water. It's an unusual menu of pasta, pineapple pork chops, steak Diane, stir fry and shrimp scampi. But the service is super weak and the place isn't well organized. If you don't mind putting up with that (or if they get any better) and the chef still works there and it isn't his day off, you'll have a great meal. But there are too many caveats in that recommendation to give 'em an ONO. On the corner of Alii Dr. and Palani Rd. **$20–$35** for dinner.

Peaberry & Galette
78-6831 Alii Dr. • 322–6020

Peaberry coffee is when a single bean grows in a coffee cherry, instead of the regular two. It's incredibly expensive (overly so since the flavor isn't appreciably better in our opinion). This place claims to use Kona peaberry as their main pour and a cup costs $2. They also have crêpes as their food offering, but they're pricey. Most will set you back $10 or more. In the Keauhou Shopping Center, south Kona. **$7–$15**. They open at 9:30 a.m. and close at different times.

Quinn's Almost-by-the-Sea
75-5655 Palani Rd. • 329–3822

ONO Truth in advertising. You're close to the ocean but can't really see it. Lunch offers seafood, burgers and sandwiches. The fish sandwich, especially Cajun style, is excellent, as are most seafood items. (Switch the mahi mahi sandwich for ono or ahi—it's *mo bettah*.) The clam chowder could use a little improvement. For dinner, it's the same menu plus more steak and seafood. Service is quick at lunch time. Consider the quasi-outdoor section for a nice lunch-time nautical, green ambiance. Lots of specials here. Most of the food is tastily prepared. We recommend lunch over the pricey dinner. **$9–$13** for lunch, **$9–$27** for dinner. On Palani Road across from the King Kamehameha Beach Hotel in downtown Kona. Limited parking.

Starbucks
74-5588 Palani Rd. • 329–1166

Don't need to spend a lot of page space for this. Like the Starbucks you have back home. Their baked goods are *excellent;* they get them from Mamane Bakery in Honoka'a. Surprisingly, their Kona coffee doesn't seem appreciably better enough to justify the higher prices over their other blends. In Kona Coast Shopping Center on Palani Road, Kona.

U • Top • It
75-5799 Alii Dr. • 329–0092

ONO There's nothing else like this on the island. Everything orbits their tasty taro pancrêpes. Top 'em any way you like. Add sausage, spam, fried rice and eggs and you have their Kanaka Attack. Top the pancrêpes with tomatoes, basil, pepperoni, salami and cheese and you have the Pizzaro. Or add chocolate hazelnut, raspberries and passionfruit sauce and you get Pele's Passion dessert. The topping selection is vast, so it's only your imagination that stands between you and a good meal. Be creative and enjoy the novelty. They also have burgers, pot pies, teri beef and other non-crêpe items. Good Tropical Dreams ice cream. This is a great concept—what's not to love? Hidden away behind Island Lava Java on Alii Drive. **$7–$13** for breakfast and lunch. Closed Mondays.

Wendy's
78-6831 Alii Dr. • 322–8081

We're a little embarrassed about this. Normally we wouldn't be reviewing a fast food restaurant—love 'em or hate 'em, they're pretty predictable, right? You know, Wendy's...burgers, frosties, a salad bar. Yeah, *that* Wendy's. It's not even a particularly *good* Wendy's food-wise. But this one distinguishes itself by having a million-dollar view—along with $2 hamburgers. Great place to watch the sunset from this location overlooking the ocean from up the mountain, and you may see fish or whales breaching. They even have a telescope for viewing. If you want fast food but still want to experience a touch of the exotic, give 'em a try. **$4–$8**. Located at Keauhou Shopping Center (south Kona) off Kamehameha III.

KAILUA-KONA CHINESE

Ocean Seafood
75-5626 Kuakini Hwy • 329–3055
Very clean, quite authentic. Usually well-prepared dishes, fresh ingredients and lots of attention to quality, but sometimes they drop the ball. Buffets offered most of the time—these are an *excellent* bargain. Lunch buffet for $9, dinner buffet $14–$16. Otherwise, off the menu is **$10–$20** per person. Located in the King Kamehameha Mall in Kona. See map on page 60.

KAILUA-KONA FRENCH

La Bourgogne
77-6400 Nalani St. • 329–6711
(ono) This *tiny* restaurant on Hwy 11 between Keauhou and Kona serves tasty and well-conceived dishes, including lamb, duck, venison and even veal sweetbreads. Good and reasonably priced wine list. Only dings: a bit cramped and enclosed with no view. Closed Sunday & Monday. Dinner is **$25–$40**.

KAILUA-KONA GREEK

Cassandra's Greek Taverna
75-5669 Alii Dr. • 334–1066
(ono) As close as you'll get to authentic Greek food on the Big Island (with an island twist). Lunch makes use of pitas, omelettes, gyros, plus burgers and fries. For dinner it's gyros, lamb, seafood, casseroles and pastas. Pretty good food. **$8–$12** for lunch, **$20–$30** for dinner. In the heart of Kona on Alii Drive across from the seawall.

KAILUA-KONA ITALIAN

Basils Restaurante
75-5707 Alii Dr. • 326–7836
Want the good news or the bad news first? Good news? Well, they have a large selection of pizza and pasta, with a bit of seafood. And portions are mostly generous. Bad news? The food is incredibly bland. It's as if they're *terrified* of seasonings here. Keep the salt and pepper shakers handy unless you're into hospital food. Their best asset is the hot bread they bring before dinner. **$10–$20** for lunch or dinner. On Alii Drive across from Hulihe'e Palace.

Kona Brewing Co & Brewpub
75-5629 Kuakini Hwy • 329–2739
(ono) A cool place to go for some tasty brew and a pizza or salad. 12 taps feature 8 different beers made there, as well as 4 seasonal and guest beers. They range from the mild (Lilikoi Wheat Ale) to the not-so-mild (Fire Rock Pale Ale). Their best is the Hefeweissen. Most of the pizzas (except their Hawaiian style) are delicious. *Love*

the Ka'u Pesto. If you normally sprinkle red peppers on your pizza, consider replacing the regular sauce with their Cajun sauce instead. In fact, they have 6 different sauces and *lots* of toppings so the possibilities are many. As a result, we're forced to review them often so we can evaluate all the permutations. (We do it for you, only for you. Aren't we selfless?) Their Kilauea lava flow dessert is pretty criminal, and a half portion is probably enough for two. The service could use a little improvement, and we wish they could do something about the flies and gnats at the outside tables, but overall, this is a *great* place with the best pizza on the island. On Palani and Kuakini behind Kona Business Center. $10–$20 for lunch and dinner. You may have to drive to the end of Pawai Place off Kawai St. to access it. See map on page 60.

Rocky's Pizza & BBQ
78-6831 Alii Dr. • 322–3223

If you catch 'em on a *real* good day, the pizza is average. Pizza, BBQ ribs and chicken, pasta and hot sandwiches. You can tell that they put in the effort—I mean, they *do* seem to care and we hate to beat up on them. But the food, both the pizza and the sandwiches, never rises above mediocre. In Keauhou Shopping Center off Kamehameha III. $8–$18 for lunch, dinner.

KAILUA-KONA JAPANESE

Hayashi's Sushi Take Out
75-5725 Alii Dr. • 326–1322

 Excellent and cheap. The sushi is made right before

your eyes and tastes great. Just a few outdoor tables, but this is the place to get your sushi fix. $3–$6. Kona Marketplace Shopping Center off Alii Drive, *way* in the back.

Kenichi Pacific
78-6831 Alii Dr. • 322–6400

 Very well-prepared sushi in a slightly ritzy atmosphere. In addition to the sushi, they also have other entrées under the fusion genre. Items such as steak, seafood and lamb. In fact, their mac nut encrusted lamb is absolutely wonderful, and unexpectedly unJapanese. The attention to detail is obvious. The molten cake dessert is *ultra* rich chocolate. (Oh, yeah!) It ain't cheap here, but with good service, good food and a good environment, it's easy to recommend. $15–$45 for lunch and dinner. In the Keauhou Shopping Center at the south end of Alii Dr. Open nightly, but lunch is Tues–Fri.

Sushi Shop Kyotoya
North Kona Shopping Ctr. • 987–8490

Located next to Kona Business Center in the North Kona Shopping Center, this *used* to be good sushi at a reasonable price. What happened? The sushi doesn't taste fresh anymore. Simple hole-in-the-wall (literally) walk-up window, simple outdoor tables. $5–$9 for lunch. No credit cards.

Teshima's Restaurant
79-7251 Mamalahoa Hwy • 322–9140

Clean, friendly place with simple but tasty Japanese, American and local items, such as bento, teriyaki beef and fried fish. There's something for everyone at this family-run restaurant. Our only gripe is that they have a habit of bringing all the food at once, typical of restaurants in Japan. Off Hwy 11 in Honalo, just south of Kona. Lunch is **$6–$10**, dinner is **$10–$15**. Cash only.

KAILUA-KONA LOCAL

Ba-Le
74-5588 Palani Rd. • 327–1212

 Ok, so it's not really local. It's part of a chain of Vietnamese noodle shops with French bread sandwiches. But the food is good for the price. Those who aren't fond of Vietnamese flavors will probably like the sandwiches, beef stew or the roast beef croissant. Lots of veggie items. **$4–$8** for lunch and dinner. In Kona Coast Shopping Center, Palani Road, Kona.

Kona Mixed Plate
75-5660 Kopiko St. • 329–8104

 Local-style dishes, such as chicken katsu, teri beef, shrimp tempura and bulgogi (which is avoidable). Choose your items, plus mac or tossed salad and rice. They also have burgers and sandwiches. Quality is good, but remember—whether you like it or not depends on whether you like local-style food, which tends to be fattier and saltier than you're probably used to. In Kopiko Plaza off Palani Road. Closed Sun. **$7–$13**. Cash only.

Manago
82-6155 Mamalahoa Hwy • 323–2642

 It's like eating in Grandma's kitchen. Ambiance is *so* homey. They are famous across the island for their pork chops, which, I'm happy to say, are *not* just like Mamma used to make. (Hers were always so dry.) These are moist, fatty and flavorful. (They use an ancient, cast-iron pan.) They bring your sides at the very beginning and you share them. They also have teri steak, butterfish, liver, etc. For dessert they feature...absolutely nothing. Pick up a Snickers bar in the lobby. Closed Monday. South of Kona in Captain Cook off Hwy 11 at the Manago Hotel. Can't miss it. **$3–$5** for breakfast. **$10–$14** for dinner.

KAILUA-KONA MEXICAN

Killer Tacos
74-5483 Kaiwi St. • 329–3335

 The kind of place you'd never find if someone didn't tell you about it. Tucked away in an industrial area, the name is spot on. (Well, we've never actually seen anyone drop dead here.) Killer tacos, killer burritos, killer portions and killer prices. Pretty deadly, huh? The most expensive thing is the $7 taco salad which is...well, you know. Put kalua pig or the spicy ground beef in your burrito, or bag one of the fish tacos. The only thing that needs improving is the salsa—consider substituting it for hot sauce. See Kona map, page 60. Take Kuakini Hwy, then right on Kaiwi, right on Luhia. It's on the right side. **$4–$8** for lunch and dinner.

Pancho & Lefty's
75-5719 Alii Dr. • 326–2171

We wrote this review several different

times, trying to capture our experiences of this dining establishment. We finally decided to abide by the old axiom: If you can't say something nice, don't say anything at all. With this in mind, Pancho and Lefty's is located on Alii Drive in downtown Kona. 'Nuff said.

Tres Hombres Cantina
75-5864 Walua Rd. • 329–2173

On Walua Road just off Alii Drive in Kona, the atmosphere is fine and the food has improved of late. It's a standard assortment of Mexican items, plus some seafood. But it's fairly flavorful. Don't overlook the easy-to-miss outdoor section away from Alii Dr. **$8–$15** for lunch, **$10–$20** for dinner.

KAILUA-KONA THAI

Kona Taeng-On Thai Food
75-5744 Alii Dr. • 329–1994

Sorry, but the food's not good enough to warrant the prices. Good menu but uninspiringly prepared. Service is a little cranky. **$10–$25**. Upstairs on Alii Drive across from Kona Marketplace.

Orchid Thai Cuisine
74-5563 Kaiwi St. • 327–9437

A simple, utilitarian atmosphere in an industrial area. But the food is very good and reasonably priced. *Super* good chicken saté. Typical Thai menu, less than bubbly service. But the food keeps us coming back again and again. BYOB. **$8–$16** for lunch and dinner. In Kuakini Center. Take Kuakini Highway north, right on Kaiwi Street. It's in back of the center.

Royal Thai Café
78-6831 Alii Dr. • 322–8424

A smooth-running machine that puts out good Thai food. Spotlessly clean, crisp and responsive service, and the variety of food is admirable. The red and yellow curries are delicious. (We're not as fond of their green curry.) Try the fresh basil rolls for appetizer. (Stab with fork rather than use chopsticks with this one.) Other items include Pad Thai, lots of vegetarian items and even Thai dumplings. The spicy mint noodles are fantastic. Try the Thai tea. For dessert you have a choice of ice cream…or no dessert. This is a very easy restaurant to like. Our only complaint is they'll sometimes bring all but one dish, which may come too late. In the Keauhou Shopping Center at Alii Drive and Kamehameha III Highway. **$6–$10** for lunch, **$10–$25** for dinner.

Thai Rin
75-5799 Alii Dr. • 329–2929

Good location across from the ocean. The food's fine—not bad, not great. (Orchid Thai is better.) The Pad Thai noodles are good. There are several vegetarian items. They'll turn the heat up as much as you want. Lunch is **$8–$15**, dinner is **$10–$20**. In Alii Sunset Plaza.

KAILUA-KONA TREATS

Cuz'ns
75-5744 Alii Dr. • 326–4920

Smoothies here are real variable. Sometimes fairly good, sometimes way too thin and sweet. Pricey at **$4** each. You're better off next door at **Kona Coffee Café** (329–7131) where you can grab a cold frappe. (Don't let them twist your arm into buying their overpriced bags of Kona coffee.) At the back of the Kona Inn Shopping Village.

French Bakery
74-5467 Kaiwi St. • 326–2688

This is the place to go in Kona for wicked baked goods. Croissants, muffins, danish and some sandwiches. They also make some pies, and their bread is ono. Open early and they close at 2 p.m. during the week; closed on Sundays. We often take our visitors here on their last day—a treat before the long plane trip. Also a good place for take-out sandwiches. $4–$8. Cash only. In north Kona near Hwy 19.

Kailua Candy Company
73-5612 Kauhola St. • 329–2522

Handmade chocolates are the specialty here. Expensive but delicious. Try the a'a lava (dark chocolate with coconut and mac nuts) or the turtles. They also make utterly indecent cheesecake with some world-class flavor combinations sold by the slice. They were in the process of moving at press time to the industrial area near Costco off Hwy 19 at the 96 mile marker, so call them for further directions.

Kanaka Kava
75-5803 Alii Dr. • 327–1660

Gee, we didn't know *where* to put this one. It's a kava bar. Kava (called awa in Hawai'i) is made from a root and tastes a little like woody water. It's a mild relaxant/pain killer. Polynesians have been using it for generations, and it has cultural importance here. When you get a bowl you're supposed to gulp it down

fast, don't sip. It may make your mouth tingle. Consider it once at least for the novelty. $4 for the kava. They also have some pupus to wash it down. On the backside of Coconut Grove Marketplace on Alii Drive.

Mac Pie Factory
74-5035 Queen Ka'ahumanu Hwy 329–7437

Exceptional pies made with locally grown macadamia nuts and Maui sugar. Similar to a pecan pie but with several flavors. (They're generous with the samples, too.) Between the 97 and 98 mile markers on Hwy 19 behind the Chevron Station.

Mrs. Barry's Kona Cookies
73-5563 Maiau St. • 329–6055

Unfortunately, they have good homemade cookies and a good variety as well. Try the chocolate chip/mac nut cookies. Hard to find. See map on page 165. They're on Maiau Road on the way to Costco.

Scandinavian Shave Ice
75-5699 Alii Dr. • 331–1626

They used to have great shave ice, but they've gone downhill lately. $3–$5. Next to Banyan Court on Alii Dr. You're actually better off going to **Beach Dog Computer Center** behind Cassandra's on the corner of Alii and Palani Rd. They have better shave ice and Internet access as well.

Tropical Dreams Ice Cream
Various Locations

This is the best ice cream we've ever found in Hawai'i and it's made on the island. Although they have a store in Hawi on the northern tip of the island, to get it in Kona you'll have to visit one of their resellers, such as **Daylight Donuts** in Keauhou Shopping Center, **Kailua Candy Co.**, **Thai Rin Restaurant**, **U · Top · It Restaurant** and **Rocky's Pizza**.

Tropical Island Flavor
A Kiosk in Lanihau Center

Probably the best shave ice in Kona. Good, fine ice and chilled syrups. (Necessary to avoid the dreaded *chunking* that happens if you don't chill 'em.) Add ice cream on the bottom, and for **$3** you have a *broke da mouf* experience. Next to Longs Drugs in Lanihau Center off Palani Road.

KOHALA

There are a lot of ONO symbols in the Kohala dining section. That's no accident. If you're staying in Kohala, you'll find that the food choices are outstanding. That makes it difficult for us as reviewers. Normally, if we think a place is a dump, we say it's a dump. If the food or service is lousy, we say it's lousy. Unfortunately for us, most Kohala restaurants have great food and service and excellent atmosphere. This makes it hard to review without sounding like a bootlicking commercial for Kohala restaurants. The resorts go to great lengths (and expense) to feed you and keep you eating at the resort. The downside for you is that you can pay *dearly* for those ONOs. Most of the restaurants here are pricey, and you'll find that eating in Kohala will cost you more than on any other part of the island. It wasn't our intention to gush over so many restaurants in Kohala, but we can't deny the fundamental quality of their offerings.

The restaurants at the **Four Seasons** and **Kona Village** are in the Kona dining section since they are often frequented by people staying in Kona.

If you want to cook your own meals, you'll soon learn that there are no large **grocery stores** in this area. You *will* find one, however, a few miles up the road in Waikoloa Village.

When we mention that a restaurant has lunch only, or breakfast and dinner only, you should take this with a grain of salt. Resorts are constantly rearranging these options. Also, you'll find the resorts mentioned are shown on the maps on pages 53 and 152.

For simplicity, we are *excluding* restaurants in the northernmost part of Kohala (Hawi and Kapaʻau). They are described under DINING ELSEWHERE.

KOHALA AMERICAN

The Bay Terrace
68-1400 Mauna Lani Dr. • 885–6622

At the Mauna Lani Bay Hotel, the beautiful indoor/outdoor setting and outstanding food make this a winner. The breakfast buffets (**$26**) have an excellent cross section of breakfast items and fresh fruit. Or go à la carte for **$10–$16**. Closed Tues. and Wed.

Big Island Steak House
69-250 Waikoloa Beach Dr.
886–8805

Steak, ribs, pasta and some seafood. The prices certainly aren't justified given the setting. Cheap furnishings, unkempt surroundings, the place seems in desperate need of an upgrade. The service is adequate and the food passable, but you're paying (especially at dinner) to get your socks knocked off and yet they'll stay firmly attached to your feet. *Maybe* consider breakfast or lunch, but go *anywhere* else at dinner. Breakfast and lunch are **$9–$15**, dinner is **$23–$45**. In Kings' Shops in the Waikoloa Resort area.

Brown's Beach House
1 North Kaniku Dr. • 885–2000

ono Very good outdoor setting near the beach at the Fairmont Orchid. (Sometimes it gets too breezy.) Sandwiches, salads, pizza and burgers available. At dinner the seafood is their best bet. They also have lamb and chicken. **$20–$25** for lunch, **$30–$55** for dinner.

The Canoe House
68-1400 Mauna Lani Dr. • 885–6622

ono The indoor/outdoor setting near the ocean at this Mauna Lani Bay Hotel restaurant, coupled with expertly prepared and presented food, make this a memorable choice for seafood. This is a great restaurant by anyone's definition and one we are happy to re-review any time we can. The sunsets from an outdoor railing table are smashing most of the year. Items change often, so we'll refrain from singling any out. It's hard to go wrong here, unless you forget your credit card. Expect **$35–$55**, dinner only. Reservations recommended (make them for an early dinner if you want a sunset).

Coast Grille
62-100 Kauna'oa Dr. • 880–1111

ono Located at the Hapuna Beach Prince Hotel, the setting overlooking Hapuna Beach is wonderful. They have indoor and outdoor tables, but it's the outdoor ones that give it the dreamy atmosphere. Seafood is the specialty here, and they do it well. With fish caught daily, herbs from their garden and attentive presentation, your meal here should be superb. The wine list is one of the most extensive on the island. Their oyster bar has several varieties of oysters. The mac nut crusted mahi mahi with a starter of seared ahi Summer rolls are guaranteed winners. Put this one on your list of possible sunset dinner restaurants. **$25–$55**. Reservations recommended.

The Gallery Restaurant
68-1400 Mauna Lani Dr. • 885–7777

ono This is a nice alternative to the more traditional resort restaurants. Located at the Mauna Lani Golf Clubhouse at the South Course (veer to the left from the Mauna Lani traffic circle), the atmosphere is relaxed but still nice with golf course and distant ocean views. The dinner menu is steak and seafood. Service is friendly but can be slow. Consider the "reconstructed" apple pie—very unusual but tasty. Lunch (which is hot and cold sandwiches and some specialties) is **$14–$20**, dinner is **$35–$55**.

The Grill
1 North Kaniku Dr. • 885–2000

ono *Very* expensive but excellent quality steak, seafood, lobster and chicken. Our biggest complaint is the portions. Yeah, we know all about EINSTEIN'S THEORY OF DINING RELATIVITY: In the universe of expensive restaurants, price is inversely proportional to the quantity of the food. But it seems a little extreme here. For instance, order the braised Kamuela lamb ravioli and you get *one stinkin' ravioli!* And $55 worth of lobster is likely to leave you hungry at the end. Good? Absolutely. But they need to bump the portions. (You know, it feels good to vent once in awhile.) Otherwise, the wonderful food and atmosphere make it a restaurant worth recommending as long as you remember the caveat. In the Fairmont Orchid. **$40–$60**. Reservations highly recommended.

Kamuela Provision Company
425 Waikoloa Beach Dr. • 885–1234
Steak, seafood, some pasta and a token veggie item at this Hilton Waikoloa restaurant. The views, especially from the outdoor tables, are fantastic. Inside you'll find an upscale yet casual decor. Start everything off with the appetizer platter for two, which has mac nut shrimp, seared ahi, lobster martini and crab cakes. Dinner selections seem to change often enough that we won't recommend a particular dish. The desserts are very tasty. They have one called *Message in a Bottle*. Order it 24-hours in advance and it'll include a note with any message you want. (You romantic softy, you.) You may like the elevated outdoor oceanside tables for sunsets, lively indoor tables or a cocktail at the other outdoor tables near the top of the pool waterfall. Food and service quality are high. Wine list is acceptable. **$30–$50** for dinner. Reservations *required*. Resort

wear with collared shirts required, but shorts are OK. Take the train *or boat* to the left from the lobby.

Kawaihae Harbor Grill
Kawaihae Harbor • 882–1368
Fresh fish and some veggie entrées. Only view is of harbor storage tanks and a drainage ditch, but inside the atmosphere's fine. The food is underwhelming. For instance, the fish and chips is *exceptionally* greasy. Other entrées are similarly forgettable. Dinner adds seafood curry, tortellini, and pork chops. But why would you want to pay $28 for pork chops *here*? Their sister restaurant next door, Seafood Bar, is also avoidable. Located on the highway on Kawaihae. **$10–$16** for lunch, **$23–$35** for dinner.

Kings' Shops Food Court
69-250 Waikoloa Beach Dr.
If you're going into shock over the price of food in Kohala, the Food Court at the Kings' Shops (take road at the 76 mile marker—see map on page 53) has the usual cast of characters like burger and pizza stands. The pizza stand has adequate pizza and a few other items. Try a Blizzard at DQ. There's also a Subway. Though more expensive than food courts on the mainland, it's *way* cheaper than your other choices in Kohala. You may want to take your stuff to the outdoor tables overlooking the golf course pond. **$5–$10**.

Nalu's Bar & Grill
69-275 Waikoloa Beach Dr.
886–6789
Expensive but convenient if you're lounging around at 'Anaeho'omalu Beach. **$11**

burgers, $8 hot dogs, that sort of thing. But you can enjoy the pretty view, then lazily saunter back to your beach chair to sleep off your meal. In the Marriott 5 minutes from the beach. Open 11 a.m. to 6 p.m.

Ocean Grill
68-1400 Mauna Lani Dr. • 885–6622
If you're at the beach at the Mauna Lani Bay Hotel and are looking for a quick bite, this is your best bet unless you want to venture far from the beach. $10 hot dogs, $14 burgers and $20 salads—that's the theme here. But the food's fairly tasty and—most important—it's convenient for lunch and a tropical drink. $10–$30 for lunch. Behind the blue cabanas at the Mauna Lani beach.

Ocean Terrace
62-100 Kauna'oa Dr. • 880–1111
Breakfast only at this Hapuna restaurant, which offers nice ocean views. Buffets ($24) offer a nice variety of items. À la carte menu includes three-egg omelettes for $17.50, Belgian waffles for $15, and steak and eggs for $19. Kind of pricey, huh? But the quality is good. (It *better* be.)

Orchid Café
425 Waikoloa Beach Dr. • 885–1234
Located at the Hilton Waikoloa Village, this poolside restaurant has a limited breakfast menu. Lunch features sandwiches, pasta, pizza, and some Asian dishes. Their best attribute is the soda shoppe, which serves ice cream, sundaes, cookies, banana splits—you get the picture. A great place to pick up a treat; the regular meals are adequate. $10–$15 for breakfast, $12–$25 for lunch.

Orchid Court
1 North Kaniku Dr. • 885–2000
Breakfast buffets are $27. They also have various "complete breakfasts" for $16–$19, but these seem overpriced. À la carte also available. For dinner they change their name to **Norio's**, a Japanese restaurant. Overall a nice setting and good food. In the Fairmont Orchid.

Palm Terrace
425 Waikoloa Beach Dr. • 885–1234
Palm Terrace sports a dashing atmosphere with tables near the indoor garden or outdoor near the pond and waterfall. (We prefer the latter.) This is a buffet place, and they do it well. With different themes throughout the week, dinner buffets include Polynesian, Chinese, Paniolo BBQ, Prime Rib, etc. They are usually very busy and serve a huge number of meals, but it's unlikely you'll have to wait too long. The food is usually well prepared but the price—$38—is pretty steep. À la carte items also available for those who don't want to do the buffet. As for breakfast, the buffet is $27 for cold continental items. We think the dinner is the better bargain here. Located at the Hilton Waikoloa Village. No reservations.

Pavilion at Manta Ray Point
62-100 Mauna Kea Beach Dr. 882-7222
Located at the Mauna Kea Beach Hotel, breakfasts are pricey but outstanding with a huge selection. À la carte includes smoked salmon Benedict with sauce Maltese and French asparagus, corned beef hash with poached eggs, or their delicious French toast.

Japanese items also available. Full breakfast buffets with tons of selections are $29, Continental buffets (cold items only) are $22. The breakfast view of Mauna Kea Beach is smashing. For dinner, consider the island fish, prime rib or one of their pizzas. Children's menu includes hot dogs, the ever-exotic peanut butter, etc. Expect to pay $26–$50 for dinner. Reservations required.

Starbucks
69-250 Waikoloa Beach Dr.
886–1717
At the Kings' Shops (but not in the food court). You know what to expect. The baked goods there are from Mamane, so they're good.

The Terrace
62-100 Mauna Kea Beach Dr.
882–7222
Located at the Mauna Kea Beach Hotel, they have an outdoor setting. (Railing tables to the right have better views.) Sunday brunch only, which is $42. They also have a very good **clambake** on Saturdays at the outdoor **Hau Tree** for $82, which includes lobster, crab, prime rib—even clams!

KOHALA EURO-ASIAN

Roy's Waikoloa Bar & Grill
69-250 Waikoloa Beach Dr.
886–4321
Some people are born to do certain things. Roy Yamaguchi was born to run restaurants. This growing chain rarely fails to please. The food is delicious, well-conceived and nicely presented. Dishes range from dim sum appetizers, fish and beef. Specials abound and change nightly. The atmosphere is casual and somewhat noisy. The service is efficient sometimes bordering on pestering. Prices are reasonable *for what you get.* Entrées aren't huge, so consider the delectable appetizers. Reservations strongly recommended for dinner. (Ask for a table near the glass wall overlooking the golf course pond.) Their dark chocolate soufflé is legendary. Lunch is $10–$15, dinner is $20–$35. In the Kings' Shops at the Waikoloa Resort area near Hwy 19's 76 mile marker.

KOHALA ITALIAN

Anthony's Italian & Irish Pizzeria
68-1845 Waikoloa Rd. • 883–9609
First of all, the only thing Irish about this place is the Guinness on tap. It's Italian here. And although the pizza is filling, so are styrofoam peanuts (which are actually a bit tastier). They say they only serve 12-inch pizzas, then cruelly hand you a 16-inch pizza to deal with. In short, it ain't worth leaving the comfort of a Kohala resort for your drive into Waikoloa Village. $8–$20 for lunch, $10–$30 for dinner. In the Waikoloa Village Shopping Center.

Café Pesto
Kawaihae Shopping Ctr. • 882–1071
Excellent selection of fine Italian food. Pizzas, pastas and some calzones. Pizza is light—feather-like crust, light sauce, light toppings. It's also delicious and they feature several unique combinations. 9-inch pizza OK for 1 person, 12-inch for hearty, half-starved appetites. Try the

kalua pig-and-pineapple combination. Pastas can be excellent but are sometimes disappointing. They can be fussy on substitutions. With those caveats, it's a great restaurant, and we recommend it wholeheartedly. In Kawaihae Center (Hwy 270 before 3 mile marker behind 7/11). **$10–$20** for lunch, **$12–$35** for dinner.

Donatoni's
425 Waikoloa Beach Dr. • 885–1234

You can arrive at Donatoni's by boat if you wish. As soon as you walk into the fabulously elegant setting, you know you are in for a treat. Tables are assembled in several romantic rooms, one of which has a fireplace. There are outdoor tables as well. The menu features items such as the excellent gnocchis, ossobucco, lamb, prawns, lobster, steak and fresh fish. The quality and service are excellent, even for a Kohala restaurant. The wine list is more than adequate. Recommending Donatoni's is a no-brainer. Do it if you feel like pampering yourself with excellent Italian food. Located at the Hilton Waikoloa Village. **$25–$50**, reservations required. Resort wear required.

KOHALA JAPANESE

Imari
425 Waikoloa Beach Dr. • 885–1234

Elegant black-and-copper decor with wood floors and shoji doors all around, you have your choice of three types of Japanese food. Teppan-yaki style (where food is prepared in front of you by a talented, knife-wielding chef), a sushi bar (tables near there will be quieter) or shabu-shabu (where items off the menu are served tableside). The ambiance is thick with Japanese culture and music, and the quality of the food is very good. If Japanese food is not your thing, they have steak, fish and lobster. Located at the Hilton Waikoloa Village, reservations required. Dinner is **$30–$60**. Resort wear with long pants and collared shirts required.

KOHALA MEXICAN

Tres Hombres Beach Grill
Kawaihae Shopping Ctr. • 882–1031

Here's a unique ambiance for you—South Seas Mexican. The pleasing decor features lots of personalized surfing and movie posters. The food *can be* good (the fajitas are weak, though), and the portions range from average (combos) to huge (the black bean burrito). Prices are too high, especially at dinner. I mean, $10 for nachos? $15 for a burrito? An á la carte shrimp taco for $9? *C'mon!* Anyway, at least the combos are reasonably priced. Try the *wonderfully* seasoned banderillas (fish kabobs) for an appetizer. Lunch is a little cheaper, but overall it's just too darned expensive. **$9–$18** for lunch, **$11–$23** for dinner. Nowhere near a beach, despite its name. In Kawaihae Center near the 3 mile marker on Hwy 270.

DINING IN WAIMEA

Waimea is a cool place to eat—literally. Located up at the nippier 2,500-foot level, it's a nice place to eat when you're staying in the Kohala area and want to eat away from the resorts.

Charley's Thai Cuisine
65-1158 Mamalahoa Hwy
885-5591

ono Let's face it. The name Charley isn't exactly *synonymous* with awesome Thai food. But that's exactly what you get here. Wonderfully concocted Thai food in a pleasant, Thai atmosphere. Good curries, good summer rolls. Thai-style plate lunches and lots of shrimp dishes make it a compelling experience. Lunch and dinner are **$9–$16**. In Waimea Center on Hwy 19.

Daniel Thiebaut
65-1259 Kawaihae Rd. • 887-2200

ono First thing's first. The food's great! It's French/Asian with a local twist. (Now *there's* a category.) Their menus change with the seasons. It's hard to define the food here. Their millefeuille of Waimea strawberry dessert is fantastic. Presentation here is as good as the food, and the ambiance is pleasing. This is probably the best meal in Waimea—and the most expensive. **$10–$15** for lunch, **$30–$40** for dinner. Reservations recommended. We *have* had disappointing meals here, but not often. (Avoid the stir fry.) On Waimea's Restaurant Row; see map on page 135. They have good bartending skills (consider the passionfruit mai tai or the wonderful lava flows) and their wine and spirit selection is outstanding. Speaking of spirits, if you don't like the garden lanai tables (we've seen customers ask to be switched to other tables), our waitress told us it's because a ghost walks those tables. Just thought you'd like to know.

Edelweiss
65-1299 Kawaihae Rd. • 885-6800

ono When's the last time you got your fill of fine German food? Burgers and sandwiches at lunch are complimented by bratwurst, wiener schnitzel and venison, all served with skill by Chef Hager, formerly of the Mauna Kea Resort. Dinner includes lamb, German sausage, pasta al fresco, liver—the menu is eclectic. There are more specials than printed items and they *don't* write them down, so don't hesitate to ask the server to repeat them. They have a small but smartly chosen wine list and an *excellent* Hefeweissen on tap. Expect to stay full for hours from the decidedly rich entrées. Rich and heavy works in cooler Waimea, but don't try going to the beach afterward, or you may split wide open. Service is no-nonsense, and smiles *don't* abound. Open Tues–Sat. **$8–$12** for lunch, **$25–$35** for dinner. On Waimea's Restaurant Row, see map on page 135.

Great Wall Chopsui
65-1158 Mamalahoa Hwy
885-7252

If you're looking to lose weight and want a buffet, this is the place to go. Because you won't be going back for seconds. Bland, tasteless Chinese food. **$8–$15** for lunch and dinner. In Waimea Center.

Hawaiian Style Café
64-1290 Kawaihae Rd. • 885-4295

ono Looks like a dive on the outside. (Then again, it looks a little like a dive on the inside.) But this is probably the best deal on the island when it comes to *quantity* and heartiness. Let me give you an example. Two eggs, your choice of meat, plus hash browns or rice. Then add either toast or two fluffy pancakes (the size of hub caps). All for $5.50. Now that may be obtainable back on the mainland, but it's utterly *unheard* of in Hawai'i. They're open from 7:30 a.m. to 12:30 p.m. on weekdays, closed Saturdays and open 7:30 a.m. to 10:30 on Sundays. The early lunch features thick burgers obscured by a towering mound of fries, as well as some other items. The food's not the best, but you ain't *paying* for the best. The atmosphere is laid-back with a few tables (which probably aren't cleared or cleaned as often as they should be) and a large sit-down counter. This is how Mom used to cook before she found out it was bad for you. Sometimes we miss it. **$5–$8**. On Waimea's Restaurant Row, see map on page 135.

Leilani Bakery
65-1158 Mamalahoa Hwy
885–2772
Average baked goods served without a smile. For a place that serves food, they have a weird habit of closing for lunch. In Waimea Center in Waimea.

Merriman's
65-1227 Opelo Rd. • 885–6822
(ONO) This used to be the best food in Waimea. Although that's no longer the case, it's still a good restaurant. In fact, the food is more *consistent* than our favorite—Daniel Thiebaut—but doesn't quite reach their height when they are on all cylinders. Peter Merriman is an excellent chef, and the food is usually wonderful. But service can be scattered; enough that it almost cost them their ONO. Lunch includes wok-charred ahi, salads, fish, ribs and

sandwiches. The menu seems to change, so we're nervous about recommending specific items. Dinner features steak and seafood. Try the unusual congo bar for dessert. They have a good wine list, but the mark-up seems pretty extreme. If you're in Waimea and want some tasty food, give them a try. On Waimea's Restaurant Row, see map on page 135. Reservations recommended **$10–$16** for lunch, **$25–$45** for dinner.

Paniolo Country Inn
65-1214 Lindsey Rd. • 885–4377
Breakfast is served pretty fast (if you're in a hurry). Coffee is not very good, but the price is acceptable. Lunch and dinner need help. They do a surprisingly bad job on steak; pizza is fairly tasty. They also have some Mexican items and burgers. **$4–$10** for breakfast, **$9–$25** for lunch and dinner. On Hwy 19 just north of the Hwy 190 intersection.

Waimea Ranch House
65-1144 Mamalahoa Hwy
885–2088
A small but fairly well-chosen menu of mostly Italian-inspired dishes. *Ah*, the potential. This is a restaurant that we *really* want to like, because the recipes seem so good. Items like sautéed garlic broccoli (*super* garlicky and spicy), pork loin stuffed with pancetta, fontina and brandy sauce, herb scampi with tomato basil sauce and curry butter, braised duck and fusilli with sautéed steak, sweet onions and basil. *Sounds* so good. But execution is sorely lacking. The food tends to be overcooked, or delivered cold, or takes *forever*. We've seen entrées sitting uncollected for over 15 minutes while the hungry customer simply

stairs and drools. Service seems well-meaning, but...uncalibrated. **$9–$15** for lunch, **$25–$35** for dinner.

Yong's Kalbi
65-1158 Mamalahoa Hwy
885–8440
Korean food with a local twist. Good fried mandoo (Korean dumplings). Be brave when picking some of the odder items (and avoid the chicken Katsu). **$8–$12** for lunch and dinner. Closed Sunday. In the Waimea Center.

HILO AMERICAN

Bear's Coffee
106 Keawe St. • 935–0708
If you have a bird that needs feeding, this place might do. Because their portions are about that size. Most egg items come with *one* egg. And their specialty—waffles—*do* have a fairly good flavor, but they're airy to the point of being an illusion. Get 'em with fruit if you want any chance of feeling fulfilled. For lunch they have pizza, some Mexican and salads. On Keawe between Kalakaua and Waianuenue. **$5–$10** for breakfast and lunch.

Fast Food
Hilo's fast food joints are mostly clustered around Puainako Town Center up Hwy 11 from town.

Harrington's
135 Kalanianaole Ave. • 961–4966
ONO Overlooking the Ice Pond at Reeds Bay, the setting at night is soothing and romantic. Well-prepared steak and seafood (though most of the seafood is frozen) with acceptable

service and entertainment some nights. Reservations recommended. **$20–$40** for dinner.

Hilo Bay Café
315 Makaala St. • 935–4939
ONO The best food you'll find in Hilo. Wonderfully creative dishes with quality ingredients, much of it organic. Items such as ahi and smoked bacon club on focaccia bread and gourmet salads at lunch are priced fairly reasonably. Dinner brings an equally creative flair to the menu. **$10–$15** for lunch, **$10–$30** for dinner. On Hwy 11 between Wal-Mart and Office Max.

Ken's House of Pancakes
1730 Kamehameha Ave. • 935–8711
A Hilo staple, they offer a vast breakfast selection, large portions, poor coffee and usually adequate food at reasonable prices. For quality, compare them to a Denny's—dependably mediocre. The whole menu is available 24 hours a day—unusual for a Big Island restaurant. Service is sometimes unresponsive because the place can get crowded. Breakfast and lunch **$6–$10**, dinner **$6–$15**. On Hwy 11 near Hwy 19.

Queen's Court
71 Banyan Dr. • 935–9361
Located in the Hilo Hawaiian Hotel, their buffets are well-known in Hilo. In the past they shined and we raved about them, but lately they've been short of the mark. Everything from the killer desserts to the great adult beverages seem to have slipped. Seafood Buffet Fri, Hawaiian Buffet on Sat and Sun, and crab legs and prime rib Mon–Thur. Most buffets include either beer or wine. Prices are **$28–$30**.

We wish we could say something more positive. They *know* haw to do it right, but seem to have chosen the simpler, cheaper route.

Seaside Restaurant
1790 Kalanianaole Ave. • 935–8825
Their freshwater fish is raised right there in a large, serene pond, but they seem to be gravitating more toward ocean fish lately. (We're told it's because it's "less work.") If you want the catfish, you have to order in advance because they need to go catch it. If they didn't have the view of the pond, the atmosphere would be non-existent and a bit loud. Service is friendly, but they often don't bring dinners at the same time. The freshwater fish like ahole-hole (we're not making that up) is served head and all. Avoid the lobster. For dessert you have a choice of apple pie or *no* apple pie. (Add ice cream for a little extra.) Overall, the food's good (love the butterfish) but overpriced. Outdoor tables include a show called *count how many skeeters the geckos can eat.* **$15–$30**. On Kalanianaole Avenue, east Hilo past Banyan Drive 2½ miles east of Hwy 11. Reservations recommended.

Uncle Billy's Restaurant
87 Banyan Dr. • 935–0861
Ambiance is likeable, whimsical, Polynesian cliché. Entertainment nightly—they reserve the right to drag you on stage to perform for your fellow diners. Food is fairly good but a bit overpriced. As for service, you'll either be treated like a member of the family…or like an irritating rash. **$5–$10** for breakfast, **$15–$25** for dinner, which is steak, seafood and pasta. On Banyan Drive in the Hilo Bay Hotel.

HILO ITALIAN

Café Pesto
308 Kamehameha Ave. • 969–6640
Same as the Café Pesto mentioned in Kawaihae on page 262. On Kamehameha between Mamo and Furneaux.

Pescatore
235 Keawe St. • 969–9090
This place was opened on a bet to see if Hilo could support an authentic Italian cuisine restaurant—and *you* are the winner. It's one of our favorites in Hilo with smartly conceived entrées that deviate from simple pasta and sauce. The specials are usually delicious and often come with a dessert (such as the double chocolate truffle cake, which will change your life). Try to resist filling up on the tasty rolls. The atmosphere is subdued Italian. Lunch includes a good choice of pastas and sauces, as well as lasagna or steamed veggies with pasta. This is a no-brainer for a recommendation, though sometimes the service is a tad unresponsive and the drinks need help. On the corner of Haili and Keawe. **$6–$10** for breakfast, **$8–$13** for lunch, **$20–$35** for dinner.

HILO JAPANESE

Nihon Restaurant
123 Lihiwai St. • 969–1133
The building overlooks Hilo Bay, but they don't make good use of the view. This is a good place to go to be ignored. Prices are too high given the setting and lackluster service. You can do better. Sushi bar plus

steak and seafood. **$8–$13** for lunch, **$15–$25** for dinner. Off Banyan Drive. Closed Sun.

Ocean Sushi
239 Keawe St. • 961–6625

(ONO) Sushi lovers, rejoice. You've found a sushi place that serves killer sushi for cheap, cheap. Not much of an ambiance; just close your eyes and revel in the variety and quality. Rolls are anywhere from $2–$5 and they have platters and boxes with all kinds of selections. Service is fast and efficient. If the wasabi is still stinging, try one of their ice cream pies to put out the fire. BYOB. Figure around **$10** for lunch or dinner. Their sister restaurant across the street, **Tsunami Grill**, lacks the pizzazz. Stick with Ocean Sushi.

HILO LOCAL

Café 100
969 Kilauea Ave. • 935–8683

(ONO) Possibly Hilo's most popular eating establishment. This is the most successful local restaurant on the island. For over 60 years they've served cheap, tasty, artery-clogging food and are legendary for their loco mocos. (These consist of fried eggs over rice and SPAM or a similar meat—if there *is* a similar meat—all smothered with brown gravy.) They have nearly a dozen varieties of loco moco, along with burgers, chili, stew, sandwiches and specials for as little as $1.50. We gave them an ONO because this is quintessential local food. But if you're watching your cholesterol or fat intake, it'll rock your Richter scale like no other place. Grab your food at the win-

dow and eat at one of the outdoor tables. Less than $5 for breakfast, **$3–$7** for lunch and dinner. On Kilauea near Mohouli. Closed Sun.

HILO THAI

Naumg Mai Thai Kitchen
86 Kilauea Ave. • 934–7540

(ONO) Pretty good Thai food (though much less spicy than most except for the fiery papaya salad). Lunch is plate lunch-style—charge by the number of items. Dinner is typical Thai selection of curries and fish dishes. Try the chicken rama. **$6–$8** for lunch, **$10–$20** for dinner. On Kilauea Ave. Take Haili to Kilauea.

Sombat's
88 Kanoelehua Ave. • 969–9336

(ONO) *Very* good flavors and a real treat considering the prices. Don't neglect the wonderful green curry chicken—exceptionally good and complex flavors. Or the vegetables with oyster sauce. The heat level isn't overly high, so prod them if you want them to wound you. It's BYOB and they'll even give you a nice beer glass if you bring your own. Good quality and an obvious attempt to keep things healthy. It's **$9–$18** for lunch and dinner. Next to Ken's House of Pancakes near the corner of Kamehameha and Hwy 11. Park around back.

HILO TREATS

Big Island Candies
585 Hinano St. • 935–8890

Tasty but amazingly overpriced chocolates, cakes, nuts and candies. You can also look through the glass and watch the whole process. It's a tour bus magnet, so it's either packed inside or dead, depending on your timing. On Hinano Street off Kekuanaoa, east Hilo.

Hilo Homemade Ice Cream
1477 Kalanianaole Ave. • 933–9399
Not as sweet or rich as other gourmet ice creams. Lots of exotic flavors from this quaint ice cream shop. Service is slow.

Tropical Dreams Ice Cream
174 Kamehameha Ave. • 935–9109
(ONO) Just as delicious as the Tropical Dreams ice cream in Hawi. Located in the Kress Building on Kamehameha Street.

Wilson's by the Bay
224 Kamehameha Ave. • 969–9191
(ONO) They make good and very reasonably priced shave ice. Also consider the surprisingly addictive chocolate-covered sunflower seeds.

DINING IN PAHOA

Pahoa is the main place to eat when you're in lower Puna (meaning Kapoho to Kalapana). All the restaurants are on the main (and only) road going *through* town (not on the bypass). Once in town you can't miss 'em.

Aloha Outpost Internet Café
15 Pahoa Kalapana Rd. • 965–8333
The menu is small—a few tasty sandwiches and some vegetarian items. They also serve delicious Tropical Dreams ice cream. Internet access is $6 per hour.

$5–$8 for breakfast, lunch and early dinner. Near Subway just north of the main part of Pahoa town.

Black Rock Café
15-2872 Government Main Rd.
965–1177
An interesting menu of burgers, steak, Korean BBQ ribs, fish, pizza and pasta. They even claim that you can order anything from the lunch and dinner menu at breakfast. Actually, this is the best breakfast in Pahoa—consider their reasonably good biscuits and gravy. Overall, the food is mostly fine, sometimes even good. Their pizza is the best in Pahoa. (Of course, that's akin to having the greatest Mongolian food in all Ecuador.) It varies a lot and sometimes they use *way* too much cheese, so consider asking them to go easy. The draft beer is embarrassingly cheap, and it's possible that fact colored our judgment; we almost gave 'em an ONO (but then we stopped ourselves). Their Bananas Foster is their best dessert. Service can be *slooow*. $4–$6 for breakfast, $5–$20 (though you probably won't spend $20) for lunch and dinner.

Luquin's Mexican Restaurant
15-2942 Pahoa Village Rd.
965–9990
(ONO) Standard Mexican food, plus a few specials like tofu enchiladas and tacos (ono), potato tacos, fish tacos (very popular) and taquitos (also ono), fish and shrimp. Sometimes the food is on the bland side; depends who's cooking. They also have some American items. Prices are extremely reasonable for the location. The service is friendly (but can be *oh-so-slow*), and the portions are large. You're likely, es-

pecially at dinner, to spend your evening dining with Pahoa's upper crust—complete with stinky dreadlocks and clothing that hasn't been washed since tie-dye was king. A pitcher of margaritas is $14 and beer is cheap. Desserts are reasonable but unpredictable—stick with the flan. Breakfast is **$6–$9**, lunch and dinner are **$4–$15**.

Ning's Thai Cuisine
15-2955 Pahoa Village Rd.
965–7611

Good Thai food here. The food is flavorful and they're willing to give it heat if you ask. If you want to hurt, as for "Thai hot." **$12–$20** for lunch and dinner. In downtown Pahoa; can't miss it.

Paolo's Bistro
333 Pahoa Rd. • 965–7033

In terms of ambiance and food, it's the nicest restaurant in Pahoa. The menu is pretty limited and it's BYOB, but the food quality is very good. Pastas, a fish dish and a few specials. On main road in Pahoa. **$12–$25**. Easy to recommend. Closed Monday.

DINING IN HAWI

Aunty's Place
55-3605 Akoni Pule Hwy • 889–0899
Here's a unique category. A German/pizza/local restaurant. Gotta admit, it's original. The food's pretty good. With lunch items ranging from pork schnitzel sandwiches (tasty) to lasagna (call to see if it's available), there's probably something that'll interest you. Dinner is more German and the food's heavier. **$6–$10** for

lunch, **$7–$14** for dinner. On Hwy 270, west side of Hawi.

Bamboo Restaurant
55-3415 Akone Puli Hwy • 889–5555

Located in an old, quaint dry goods building in Hawi, they have an eclectic menu with uniquely prepared foods. Try the potstickers lined with peanut butter—weird but delicious (though the portion is small). They also have fresh fish and kalua pork and cabbage. You might want to try the lilikoi margaritas. For dinner add steak, more seafood and more money. Our only complaint is the priceyness. I mean, $34 for a rack of ribs? Phew, pretty steep, we'd say. But if you can tolerate the prices you'll like the food. They have a gallery inside the building offering all kinds of nice, locally carved wood and other products. Lunch is **$10–$20**, dinner is **$15–$40** per person. Closed Sunday nights and Monday.

Hula La's Mexican Kitchen
55-3419 Akoni Pule Hwy • 889–5668
A hole in the wall in the Kohala Trade Center in Hawi (on Hwy 270). The food's fairly good. Consider the Kamehameha combo burrito—pretty hearty. They don't give any chips, and there are only a few tables, but it's not a bad choice. **$5–$9**.

Kohala Rainbow Café
54-3897 Akoni Pule Hwy • 889–0099

This is just about your last dining opportunity on the north shore before the end of the road at Pololu, and it's a *super* easy place to like. The food is healthy, fresh, tasty and reasonably priced. Nearly everything is locally-grown—much of it organic—and the greens seem so fresh, you'd think they went outside and picked them for your meal. The wraps are awesome and if you need a splash of guilt, add some chili Fritos. They also have burgers (onion rolls only), sandwiches, salads, etc. **$7–$10** for lunch. On the Hwy in Kapa'au across from the Kamehameha Statue.

Sushi Rock
55-3435 Akoni Pule Hwy • 889–5900
In the last building in Hawi inside a store called **Without Boundaries** before heading toward Kapa'au, this *tiny* operation (we're talking three tables) has very fresh and nicely conceived sushi for reasonable prices. And their homemade dark chocolate cheesecake is addictive enough that you might need a 12-step program to get off of it. **$12–$30** for lunch or dinner. Avoid the drink specials in favor of another piece of sushi.

DINING NEAR 'AKAKA FALLS

Woodshop Gallery Café
28-1692 Old Government Rd.
963–6363
There's not much to eat between Hilo and Honoka'a. In Honomu on the way to 'Akaka Falls on Hwy 220, this small café has a good ahi sandwich, a taro and a garden burger and other sandwiches. Best food in Honomu. **$4–$7**. Otherwise, **Lisa's Pizza & Deli** (963–5252) is merely adequate. **Mr. Ed's Bakery** (963–5000) has a big selection of poor-tasting baked goods. (Of course, of course.)

Before Hwy 19's 7 mile marker (before you get to 'Akaka Falls) keep an eye out on the mauka side for **Baker Tom's** (964–8444). They have lots of different types of malasadas (try the blackberry), pull-aparts and sometimes the most wonderfully sweet and impossibly small tomatoes. Very reasonable prices.

DINING IN LAUPAHOEHOE

Laupahoehoe is the tiny town north of Hilo and 'Akaka Falls but before you get to Honoka'a. **Back to the '50s Highway Fountain** (962–0808) is a friendly (albeit selectively, since we've also seen them ignore other customers to the point that they left) '50s-style diner with burgers, loco moco, tater tots, roast beef and chicken. The food is pretty basic—nothing stands out—but the atmosphere works pretty well. Enter the town of Laupahoehoe from the road that parallels the highway mauka of Hwy 19 on either side of the 25 mile marker. **$4–$8**. Closed Monday.

DINING IN HONOKA'A

Café Il Mondo
45-3626 Mamane St. • 775–7711
Pizza, calzone, lasagna, salads and hot sandwiches. Lots of different coffee drinks. The pizza is pretty good (not great) with crunchy crust. Calzones are large and tasty. Fairly good meatball sandwich. Service is slow at times. One thing that rubs us the wrong way: They don't serve alcohol and encourage you to BYOB. Then they quietly charge you $2 when you do it. Tacky. On Mamane Street (240) in Honoka'a, ocean side. **$6–$12** for lunch and dinner. Closed Sunday and Monday. No credit cards at press time.

Jolene's Kau Kau Korner
45-3625 Mamane St. • 775–9498

ⓞⓝⓞ A simple, homey, cheap atmosphere. This is a mom and pop (well, mom, at least) diner-type restaurant with cheap food and...well, that's it. Cheap food. And it ain't bad. Items like shrimp and tempura vegetables for $11 is a pretty good deal around here. Burgers for $3, plate lunches, teriyaki chicken, saimin, etc. $5–$13 for lunch.

Simply Natural
45-3625 Mamane St. • 775–0119

A health food restaurant that serves eggs and pancakes for breakfast, sandwiches and taro burgers for lunch. The taste isn't compelling, but it's not bad. $4–$7 for breakfast, $5–$8 for lunch. On Hwy 240 in Honoka'a. Cash only. Closed Sunday.

Tex Drive-In & Restaurant
45-690 Pakalana • 775–0598

ⓞⓝⓞ Every good restaurant does at least one thing well, and Tex is a perfect example. Most of the food is merely adequate fast food, such as burgers, teriyaki chicken, etc. for lunch; cheap (and it tastes that way) breakfasts. But Tex *excels* at making the best malasadas (a Portuguese doughnut dipped in sugar) on the island, served fresh and warm throughout the day. The plain ones are delicious, but now that they have them filled with Bavarian chocolate or tropical fruits, we never hesitate to stop by when we're in the neighborhood. Located on Hwy 19 near Honoka'a and the 43 mile marker. Sometimes the wait (even if nobody is ahead of you) can be long. $3–$5 for breakfast, $4–$10 for lunch and dinner.

DINING AT KILAUEA VOLCANO

Kiawe Kitchen
19-4005 Haunani Rd. • 967–7711

ⓞⓝⓞ A small but appealing menu of pizzas, salads (which, alas, are their weak point), pastas, steak and some specials at dinner. It's pizzas and sandwiches at lunch. As for those pizzas, they have *incredibly* thin crusts and are very tasty. They come with traditional red sauce, pesto sauce (yummy) or as white pies (olive oil-based). Add a pleasing, slightly jazzy atmosphere and you have an easy place to like. On the corner of Huanani and Old Volcano Road; can't miss it.

Kilauea Lodge & Restaurant
19-3948 Old Volcano Rd. 967–7366

ⓞⓝⓞ This cozy restaurant in the sometimes chilly village of Volcano serves delicious food in a warm atmosphere. The owner/chef was a make-up artist on *Magnum P.I.* when he bought this place. He went to Europe to learn how to cook and has excelled nicely. Items such as fresh fish, steak, venison, antelope, rabbit, ostrich and chicken are all expertly prepared and presented. Expensive, but *very* good food and *very* good service. One of the best restaurants on the island. We like to get a table near the "International Fireplace." Dinner is $25–$35.

Lava Rock Internet Café
19-3972 Old Volcano Rd. • 967–8526

Admirable selection of hearty burgers, sandwiches, chili, salads, chicken, fajitas (which you can avoid), fresh-tasting taco salad, stir fry and more. Many items are veggie and most cost about $6 with generous portions. (Good milkshakes.) Breakfast items include some clever omelettes and French toast with 'ohelo berry. Service is so-so. They have a computer with 'Net access for $10; hence the name. Amazingly variable. We've been there on days when we would give them an ONO in a heartbeat. Other times it's surprisingly bad. So what's a poor guidebook writer to do? We left it out, but it may be good here. $6–$9 for breakfast, $7–$11 for lunch, $10–$20 for dinner. Right in Volcano Village. Closed Sunday and Monday.

Thai Thai
19-4084 Volcano Rd. • 967-7969

Excellent menu of curries, soups, stir fry, noodle dishes and vegetarian items. They have good Pad Thai. Curries are unusual, and curry lovers (like us) will either like the novelty (we do) or dislike the flavor. (Avoid the red.) Good summer rolls. If you like heat, they'll wound you here. Thai hot means Thai hot, so go milder unless you've got an asbestos-lined tongue. Our only concern is the service can be uneven. Rushed at times, slow at others. If you catch 'em at the right pace, you'll like the place. Desserts are sparse—get the tapioca pudding. Decoration is beautiful and calming. $15–$30 for dinner. In Volcano Village.

Volcano Golf & Country Club
Pi'i Mauna Dr. • 967-8228

At the sometimes misty Volcano Golf Course just outside Volcano Village, the food is surprisingly tasty (though the portions need to be bigger). Burgers, chicken, beef—the stir-fry chicken and teriyaki beef are both good. Breakfast menu is small. The macadamia nut pie (similar to pecan pie) is great. This is an acceptable choice, though you have better options in Volcano Village. $5–$8 for breakfast, $7–$13 for lunch.

Volcano House
Hawaii Volcanoes National Park
967-7321

You won't be overwhelmed with dining selections *inside* Hawai'i Volcanoes National Park—this is it. Breakfast and lunch are buffets; dinners are from the menu. Breakfast and lunch are our favorites here, but not because of the food. The lunch food is overpriced and underwhelming, sometimes not edible. (Breakfast buffet is not too horrible.) So how could we *possibly* give them an ONO? Simple. The view is more delicious than anything the restaurant ever served. It overlooks Kilauea Crater in its entirety—a view you'll remember years after your heartburn goes away. (Though we've occasionally seen people sitting at the window by themselves, with their backs to the window—*go figure!)* Don't overlook the room to your left if all the window tables seem taken. Lunch can be a zoo with buses dropping people off by the dozens at noon—avoid until 12:30 p.m. At dinner, hotel guests and area residents create a quieter time and the food's better. Of course, the view disappears with the sun. Pasta, fish, filet mignon, scampi—most are quite well-prepared and at a more leisurely pace. $11.50 for breakfast, $14 for lunch, $17–$30 for dinner. (Reservations required for dinner.) We gave it an

ONO symbol because of the tasty *view*, not the food. (They stopped selling our book at the small shop next door because of that last comment.) In the same building is **Uncle George's**—a snack (and real) bar that sports a similar view, a lunch-time alternative to the buffet described above. Their selection dwindles when the sunlight does. **$5–$10**.

DINING NEAR SOUTH POINT

Desert Rose Café
Pohue Plaza • 939–7673

Probably the best food in this part of the island. In the Pohue Plaza in HOVE near the 77 mile marker on Hwy 11, the menu is a tad pricey but the food is very good and the prices reasonable. Sandwiches, burgers, salads and some pretty creative breakfast items. **$9–$15** for breakfast, lunch and dinner.

Ocean View Pizzeria
525 Lotus Blossom Ln. • 929–9677

Pizza, sandwiches, some baked goods and ice cream. The pizza is just OK, but your options are limited here. In the only shopping center on the mauka side before the 77 mile marker. **$5–$10**.

DINING IN NA'ALEHU

Hana Hou Bakery
95-1148 Spur Rd. • 929–9717

Na'alehu is a pretty remote place on your way to the Volcano, and it's surprising and gratifying to have great food in the middle of

nowhere. Breakfast includes different kinds of hash browns and corned beef hash, homefries with salsa, sour cream and eggs, etc. Lunch and dinner include plate lunches sandwiches and specials. Saturday is prime rib night but if they are serving their turkey dinner, don't pass it up. Consider their tasty lilikoi lemonade. And lastly, it's *mandatory* that you try their homemade pies. Better than your own grandmother's. **$7–$10** for breakfast, **$9–$15** for lunch and dinner. Look for a sign on the ocean side shoulder of the road in Na'alehu.

ISLAND NIGHTLIFE

Not in the same league as what you'll find in Honolulu or any other big city, but on the Big Island we don't exactly spend *all* our evenings watching old reruns of *Gilligan's Island*. (Well... maybe Fridays.) There *is* life after sunset here.

The liveliest is **Kona**. Every Friday the Entertainment section of the local newspaper, *West Hawai'i Today*, lists everything that's happening for the week ahead. Very handy. Much of the action takes place on Alii Drive. It's easy to walk downtown and check out what's shakin'. Directions to these places are in their reviews. For cocktails, the **Billfish Bar** at the King Kamehameha Hotel is famed for their cheap drinks. Try a frozen mai tai at **Ocean View**, usually very tasty. **Huggo's** can be very romantic, and they often have live music. Jazz on the left side and a local guitarist on the right at **Java on the Rock**. But the best place in Kona for a sunset cocktail has to be the **Verandah Lounge** at the

Outrigger Keauhou Beach Resort (322–3441) at the south end of Alii Dr. Some good tropical drinks (consider the tropical itch or the hula girl) and the location is absolutely incredible. It's surrounded on three sides by a shallow, protected lagoon that actually meanders *under* the building. Fish, eels and sometimes turtles amble about. Add a sunset and the one that you love and you'll find this place irresistible. Note that the potency of the beverages seems to vary considerably here. **Kona Brewing Co. & Brewpub** (329–2739) on Kuakini and Palani behind Kona Business Center is a good place for a cold, locally made beer. 12 different brews.

If you're interested in spectator sports, the best we can do is direct you to the **night volleyball court** next to the Coconut Grove Marketplace on Alii Drive. There are games most nights.

The **Aloha Theatre** south of Kona up in Kainaliu often has fun local plays. Call 322–9924 for more information.

Big Island Comedy Club (329–4368) is a roving comedy act (often at the **Royal Kona Resort**). Call to see where they are performing.

Moviegoers will want to call **Keauhou Cinamas** (324–7200) or **Makalapua Cinemas** (327–0444) in Kona to see what's playing.

In Kohala, nightlife is a resort affair (so to speak). Many of the mega-resorts have lounges. An example is the **Honu Bar** at the Mauna Lani Bay Hotel (885–6622). Very upscale with billiards and chess. The **Copper Bar** at the Mauna Kea has hula and live music nightly. (Check out the tree that goes through the roof.) Good places to have a drink include **Kamuela Provision Company**

at the Hilton, **Brown's Beach House, Ocean Bar** and **Polo Bar/Paniolo Lounge** at the Fairmont, and the **Beach Tree** at the Four Seasons (325–8000). The latter also has a fun Surf & Sand BBQ on Saturdays.

In Hilo, **Cronies** (935–5158) at 11 Waianuenue is a pretty good sports bar with good beers, bar games and a young, lively atmosphere. Food is adequate. **Wai'oli Lounge** (935–9361) in the Hilo Hawaiian Hotel sometimes has good local bands performing contemporary Hawaiian music. (But the drinks have been small, weak and overpriced the past few times we were in.) **Harrington's** (see review) is a very romantic spot on the water. **Uncle Billy's** (see review) has a hula show at 6 p.m. and 7:30 p.m.

LU'AUS

We've all seen them in movies. People sit at a table with a mai tai in one hand and a plate of kalua pig in another. There's always a show where a fire dancer twirls a torch lit at both ends and hula dancers bend and sway to the beat of the music. To be honest, that's not far from the truth. Lu'aus can be a blast and, if your time allows for one, they are highly recommended. The pig is baked in the ground all day creating absolutely delicious results. Shows are usually exciting and fast-paced. Although lu'aus on O'ahu can make you feel like cattle being led to slaughter, the lu'aus on the Big Island are smaller, more intimate affairs of usually 100–200 people. Most lu'aus are all you can eat and drink (including alcohol) for a set fee (except where noted below). If the punch they are serving doesn't satisfy you, they usually have an open bar to fill your needs.

Different resorts hold their lu'aus on different nights. These change with the whims of the managers, so verify the days we list before making plans. Many lu'aus advertise that they are rated number one. By whom? At any rate, this is what we thought of them.

Our hands down favorite is 10 miles outside Kona to the north. The **Kona Village Lu'au** (325–4214) on Fridays is also the most expensive lu'au. It's **$89** *plus* drinks, and the cash bar is expensive. (But heavily poured.) The grounds are absolutely beautiful. *This* is how lu'au grounds should look. Add to this the best lu'au food we've had at any lu'au *in the state* (and we've been to them all), a great and enthusiastic show and you have the ingredients for a wonderful evening. They start letting cars in at 4:45 p.m. and it's first-come-first-served seating at 5:30 p.m.

In Kona, your best bet is probably **King Kamehameha's Kona Beach Hotel** (329–2911). This is a much improved lu'au. The food is fairly good and the location overlooks a sandy cove and the Alii Drive shoreline. Their show is better than most and includes some history and more songs than some others. The free bar is open until 7:30. After the imu ceremony, a royal procession is brought ashore in canoes and walks through the grounds. Tu, W, Th, Su—**$65**. Preferred seating is an extra $10, bringing you closer to the stage and first dibs on the buffet.

Royal Kona Resort (329–3111) M, W, F—**$72**. It's $5 extra for preferred seating. This used to be our favorite in Kona, now it's our last choice. The food isn't very exciting and the buffet seems poorly managed. Items might run out before your table is even called. The show is presided over by a Hawaiian lounge lizard, creating a somewhat Vegasy experience. The location is the star here—*right* next to the water. Tables on the north (right) side are usually served last. The free bar closes around 8 p.m. One kid free per paid adult.

In Kohala, the **Mauna Kea** lu'au (882–5801) is on Tuesdays for **$82**. Ask for directions in the lobby. The grounds are superb—right near the water, and you can wander over to the manta ray area after it's over and maybe watch those leviathans do their dance. The food is excellent, making this an easy-to-recommend event. You can start eating from the moment you show up—unusual for a lu'au—and you can keep eating until the end of the show. After your one free drink, you'll have to pay and the bar closes when the show starts. The show is their weakest area with too much audience participation, but the rest of the experience makes up for it. Though not a lu'au, they also have a very good **clambake** on Saturdays at the outdoor **Hau Tree** for $82, which includes lobster, crab legs, prime rib and clams. The **Waikoloa Beach Marriott** (886–6789) has fairly good food and a mediocre show. They ask you to show up at 5 p.m. then make you wait an hour before eating with no entertainment provided during that time. Located adjacent to the fishponds at 'Anaeho'omalu. Su & W—**$75**. The **Leg-**

ends of the Pacific (885–1234, ext. 54) Polynesian show at the Hilton Waikoloa Village on Fridays is not a lu'au per se. No pig buried in the ground here. The show is pretty good and the food is tasty, but they need more Hawaiian dishes and more selections. Only one drink is included. In general, you can do better for **$78**.

DINNER CRUISES

Dinner cruises off the Kona Coast are a nice alternative. **Captain Beans' Cruises** (329–2955) is owned and operated by tour giant Roberts Hawai'i, and because of their demographics, you probably won't end up with a boat full of idiots—it's a good mix of passengers. Known locally as the classic booze cruise (though they now charge extra after your first drink), you and up to 220 other passengers (on the bottom deck) leave Kailua Pier on a 150-foot boat and head south. **$63** includes pickup in Kona, add $8–$11 for Kohala pickup. They do a surprisingly good job, with lots of interactive entertainment. (Try not to fall off the tables when you dance on them.) The food is basic but pretty tasty (though they badly need a *real* dessert). One tip: Keep your plate full; tables sometimes run out. The boat is smooth, roomy and comfortable, and with the constant entertainment it's easy to forget you are on a cruise, so walk to the railings after dinner and enjoy the coastline—watch for flying fish. All in all, it's a hoot. Most on board seem to have a good time. Best views are off the starboard side (closest to the dock when you're boarding)—you'll get sunset going out, city lights coming back in. Closed Mondays.

Sea Paradise (322–2500) has a sailboat that does dinner cruises for up to 36 people. **$95** for 2 hours, drinks are included. The food's not bad and it's a relaxing, romantic trip. No tables, you'll have to use your lap for your plate. Saturdays only at press time.

Red Sail Sports (886–2876) leaves 'Anaeho'omalu Beach in the North Kohala Resort area for a 2-hour sunset cruise. Dinner and open bar included for **$72**.

DINING BEST BETS

Best Pizza—Kona Brewing Co.
Best Malasadas—Tex Drive-In
Best Haunted Restaurant—Daniel Thiebaut
Best Use of a Pound of Sugar—One Cinnamon Roll at Lava Java
Best Meal by a Fireplace—Kilauea Lodge
Best Bargain for Food *Volume*—Hawaiian Style Café
Best Use of a Crêpe—U • Top • It
Best Addiction—Chocolate-covered Sunflower Seeds at Wilson's by the Bay
Best Mexican Food—Killer Taco
Best Use of Glassware—Schooners at Harbor House
Best Seafood—Pahu I'a at Four Seasons
Best Place to Take Your Food to Go—Sunset at Pu'uhonua o Honaunau
Best Lu'au—Kona Village
Best Sunset Cocktail—Verandah Lounge

Hotels shown in this color. Condominiums shown in this color.

Rental Agents

Abbey Vacation Rentals *(non-smoking only)*	(866) 456–4252 or (808) 331–8878
ATR Properties, Inc. *(non-smoking only)*	(888) 311–6020 or (808) 329–6020
Classic Resorts	(800) 642–6284 or (808) 885–5022
Hawaii Resort Mgmt./Kona Hawaii Vacation Rentals	(800) 622–5348 or (808) 329–3333
Hawaii's Best B&B *(Bed & Breakfast referral service)*	(800) 262–9912 or (808) 962–0100
Keauhou Property Management, Inc. *(very nice units)*	(800) 745–5662 or (808) 326–9075
Land Office, Inc.	(800) 359–6089 or (808) 939–7368
Property Network, Ltd. *(non-smoking only)*	(800) 358–7977 or (808) 329–7977
South Kohala Management	(800) 822–4252 or (808) 883–8500
SunQuest Vacations	(800) 367–5168 or (808) 329–6438
West Hawaii Property Services, Inc.	(800) 799–5662 or (808) 322–6696

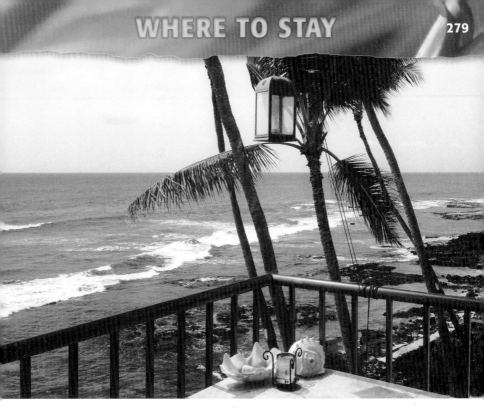

Room with a view...

Your selection of where to stay is one of the more important decisions you'll make in planning your Big Island vacation. To some, it's just a place to sleep and rather meaningless. To others, it's the difference between a good vacation and a bad one.

There are four main types of lodging on the island: hotels, condominiums, bed and breakfasts, and single family homes. The vast majority of visitors stay in one of the first two types. But B&Bs and single family homes are often overlooked and can be very good values. If your group or family is large, you should strongly consider renting a house for privacy, roominess and plain ol' value. There is a list of rental agents in the index at left, each willing and happy to send you a list of homes they represent. We also have a B&B referral service there.

Hotels usually offer more services, but smaller spaces and no kitchens. **Condominiums** usually have full kitchens, but you won't get the kind of attention you would from a hotel, including daily maid service. There are exceptions, of course, and we will point them out when they come up. You can find their locations on the various maps.

All prices given are RACK rates, meaning *without any discounts*. Tour wholesalers and travel agents can often get better rates. Most resorts offer discounts for stays of a week or more, and some will negotiate price with you. Some won't budge at all, while others told us *no one* pays RACK rates. Also, these prices are subject to taxes of over 11%.

See all Web reviews at: *www.wizardpub.com*

These are *subjective* reviews. If we say that rooms are small, we mean that we've been in them, and they feel small or cramped to us. If we say that maintenance is poor, we mean that the paint might be peeling or the carpets are dingy or it otherwise felt worn to us.

Throughout the book we talk about the positives associated with the various areas. In deciding where to stay, here are three negatives for each major location worth considering:

Kohala: Food will cost you more. You are far from the town of Kailua-Kona and its available resources. You are far from the volcano.

Kailua-Kona: Vog will be more of a nuisance in Kona. Traffic, while not *nearly* as bad as the mainland, can be troublesome at commute time. There's more noise along Alii Drive.

Hilo: Activities are less numerous. The ocean is less pleasant. Rain will probably be a companion.

The gold bar indicates that the property is exceptionally well priced for what you get.

SOLID GOLD VALUE

The gem means that this hotel or condominium offers something *particularly* special, not *necessarily* related to the price.

A REAL GEM

WHERE ARE THE REST?

You'll notice that some of the resorts listed here don't have full reviews. That's because the book has increased *36 pages* over the last two editions (to accommodate all the new stuff we've found).

Also, we wanted to include aerial photos of the resorts. After all, a picture speaks a thousand words (and a thousand

words takes too long to read, anyway).

So we had a choice. Give you less info on *all* of them or do detailed reviews on only a *portion* of them. Neither choice seemed palatable.

So we came up with a *third* way: List minimal info on all (including if they are GEMS or SOLID GOLD VALUES), print full detailed reviews on *most,* and post full reviews of *all* on our Web site at **www.wizardpub.com**. After all, most people use this section before they come to the islands. And with the Web (which has infinite space available), we could do more, like post larger aerial photos of the resorts with specific buildings labeled when appropriate, provide constant updates when necessary and put links to the various rental agents or hotels right in the review, allowing you to go to their sites and get more photos of the rooms. You should remember, however, that resorts post photos to lure you in, and some aren't above posting modified or overly flattering shots when they were new and sparkling. Our aerials don't lie and are designed to give you a feel for their ocean proximity (does oceanfront *really* mean oceanfront?), so you'll know what kind of view to expect from a given location within the resort. Resorts whose review is posted on our Web site are identified with WEB REVIEW

Please remember that all these reviews are *relative to each other*. This is important. Even staying at a dump right on the ocean is still a *golly gee!* experience. In other words, *Hey, you're on the ocean on the Big Island!* So if we sound whiny or picky when critiquing a resort, it's only because their next door neighbor might be such a better experience. It doesn't mean you'll be miserable; it just means that *compared to another resort*, you can do better.

See all Web reviews at: www.wizardpub.com

HOTELS

All hotel rooms described **(shown in this color)** have air conditioning, an activity or travel desk, telephones, lanais (verandas), cable TV and have cribs available upon request. None have room service unless otherwise noted.

CONDOS

One of the confusing aspects to renting a condo **(shown in this color)**, especially in Kona, is the fragmented nature of the market. Each unit usually has a different owner, they all use different rental agencies to manage them, and it changes all the time. (Spreadsheets, blinding headaches and blurred vision are all necessary to figure it out.) Therefore, when *we* review them, we may look at 10 units and get 10 winners. *You* may rent one and get a dump because the owner is using furniture from a landfill and carpet from the finish line at the Ironman Triathlon. You never truly know what you're going to get because condominium owners usually have complete autonomy in how they furnish their individual units. (Notice how we neatly cover our 'okoles, so that if you get a less-than-charming condo in a resort we recommend, we can always say you got one of the few duds there.)

Also remember that many condos have cleaning fees. We don't list the fees because they will vary for each unit, rental agent or owner. Expect to pay $60–$190. And beware that cleaning standards in Kona condos aren't as good as other areas around the state. The only big rental agent that will waive the cleaning fee (if you stay 6 nights or more) is Property Network.

When we describe a particular resort, we will often give the names or phone numbers of one or two companies that dominate the rental pool. But realize that this does not always do justice to the *entire* property. When we describe rates, they are for the larger rental agents. Different agents have different policies for the same complex.

Once you have decided where you want to stay, you can contact the resort. You may also want to contact some of the **rental agents** on page 278 to determine if they represent any units from the property you have chosen.

Many condos have minimum stays—usually three nights. We don't always list this because it changes with different rental companies. More and more rental agents are also requiring you to pay *all* of your condo rental costs before you arrive. It may make you nervous, but you might not have a choice if you're intent on staying at a particular place.

Three bedroom/two bath units are described as 3/2, two bedroom/one bath units are described as 2/1, etc. Differentiation between half baths and full baths is not made. The price spread for rooms of a given size is due to different views, different locations within the resort and seasonal fluctuations. So when you see that a 2/2 unit rents for $140–$180, you should figure that $180 units have a better view or are closer to the water. Also note that unlike some other Hawai'i locations, Kona condo RACK rates seem more negotiable. The terms Oceanfront, Ocean View and Garden View are used rather capriciously in Hawai'i, so you should be skeptical of them. **Unless otherwise noted**, all rooms come with telephones, complete kitchens, coffee makers, lanais (verandas), cable TV, ceiling fans, coin-op laundry rooms, free local calls and have cribs available upon request. Maid service is

See all Web reviews at: www.wizardpub.com

only when you check out and units won't have air conditioning or elevators unless otherwise noted.

BED & BREAKFASTS

Rather than describe the countless B&Bs scattered about the island, you're better off calling **Hawai'i's Best B&B** (800) 962–0100. We have lots of links to B&Bs on our web site, but it's not practical to personally review them the way we do other accommodations.

KOHALA

Kohala is famous for its **mega-resorts**. These destination resort hotels have tons to see and do on the premises, pricey restaurants offering superb atmosphere and cuisine, and almost unending sunny weather. The developers have created oases in the lava desert where lava once stretched uninterrupted for miles.

You will notice that accommodation prices are high in Kohala. These snazzy resorts don't come cheap. We leave it up to you to decide if it's in your budget. A lot of them have REAL GEM icons next to them. We like to think of ourselves as stingy with these, but facts are facts—these *are* gems. But like the genuine article, these gems come at a price.

Picking the best mega-resort in Kohala is not a straightforward process. All of them have radically different personalities, so *your* personality is key to which one you'll like best. Most of these resorts do a great job at creating an atmosphere. They question is, is it *your* atmosphere? In our view, the Mauna Lani Bay Hotel has the best exotic tropical feel. The Fairmont Orchid has the richest, most luxurious feel. The Hilton Waikoloa Village has the most jaw-drop-ping elaborate, yet family-oriented feel. The Mauna Kea has the best beach location. And 10 miles south of the main Kohala resort area, Kona Village has the most "authentic" old Hawai'i feel. The Four Seasons has some of both Mauna Lani's and the Fairmont Orchid's assets. Rich and luxurious yet also a great tropical feel. Most of these resorts are world class, and we don't say that lightly. Choosing one just depends on what you want.

If it's a cheap **condo** you're looking for, go elsewhere. Kohala only has up-scale condos for rent.

Fairmont Orchid, Hawai'i
(800) 845–9905 or (808) 885–2000
1 North Kaniku Dr.

540 rooms, 10 tennis courts (7 lighted), 24-hour room service, 4 shops, 18 con-ference rooms, ballroom, several restaurants, 2 golf courses, valet parking, pool and 2 spas, health club, business center, beauty salon, child care program ($85 per day), empty fridge available. We try not to blather on about a resort—it hurts our credibility. But when it's right, it's right. The Fairmont Orchid has an intoxicating richness that permeates everything. The lush grounds have a very sculpted and precise feel. Nothing is out of place. The inside is just as flawless. The lobby, halls and rooms are all richly furnished with lots of wood and fine car-

A REAL GEM

See all Web reviews at: www.wizardpub.com

pets—even the elevators seem affluent. The overall effect is European elegance with a tropical touch. The cleaning staff here deserves medals. The entire staff seems obsessed with pleasing you. Restaurants are what you'd expect, on the higher end with delicious results. The manmade beach is usually calm and protected. Lots of activities are available. The tennis complex is the best on the island, and the two Mauna Lani golf courses are humbling and world renowned. You can get a massage next to the ocean at the "Spa Without Walls" where the sound of the surf helps you relax. (As if you'll need any help.)

They have an optional $40 per person per activity card that'll cover snorkel gear, lounge chairs, a kayak for an hour, etc. Local calls are $1.50. Laundry is valet only.

Some of the partial ocean views will require imagination to see the ocean.

Otherwise, the Fairmont Orchid is exceptional in every way. It has become popular with business travelers, and if you're looking to be pampered, consider it. It's not the most Hawaiian resort on the island, but it might be the ritziest. Rooms (522 sq. ft.) are $329–$759. RACK rates are high—this ain't for the budget traveler—but they often have specials to ease the pain a bit. One-bedroom suites (which are *very* nice) are $959–$1,399 and are 1,050–1,477 sq. ft. Larger suites available. They also have a gold floor which has more services for more money.

Fairway Villas
(800) 688–7444 or (808) 886–0036
(866) 456–4252 or (808) 331–8878
69-200 Waikoloa Beach Dr.

WEB REVIEW

Four Seasons Resort
(800) 332–3442 or (808) 325–8000
100 Ka'upulehu Dr.

243 rooms, 8 tennis courts (4 lighted), 5 conference rooms, 4 pools, keiki (kid) pool, lava snorkel pool, 4 spas, coffee makers in rooms, free Nintendo, free Wi-Fi in lobby and other places, free valet parking, free child care, *private* golf course, health spa, 3 restaurants, business center, free laundry room, empty fridge, 24-hour room service. This resort *shines*, even among its superb competitors. 243 rooms among 37 one- and two-story bungalows in several semi-circles with 6–8 rooms per building, plus a few golf course buildings. They used a lot of local materials, giving the resort a very Hawaiian feel. All units (even golf course units) have nice ocean views. (Building 25 is closest to the water.) Second-floor rooms have better ocean views, but first-floor rooms have a pleasant garden on the other side of the bathroom glass with a second private *outdoor lava shower* ensconced in the garden where water gurgles over a short lava ledge. What a great place to have your morning shower! This makes the first floor a better value than the higher-priced second-floor rooms. Overall, rooms are of average size, nicely furnished with cool slate floors.

A REAL GEM

One feature we've never seen anywhere else is a large, lava anchialine

See all Web reviews at: www.wizardpub.com

pond with 2½ million gallons of fresh and salt water. Connected to the ocean, its level rises and falls each day with the tide. Inside are 40 species of fish, including several spotted eagle rays. You won't find a safer place to snorkel in the state. It's great to be there when they feed them.

If you bring your keikis, you'll find free licensed child care program for young'uns 5–12. (They also have a free teen center.) The resort is the only one with a *truly* private golf course. Only guests and residents of the development are allowed to play, so tee times are spaced farther apart. It's a very nice player-friendly Jack Nicklaus course for about $195. The same goes for the full spa, which offers enough luxuriating decadence to melt your toenails. The resort fronts a beach, but the swimming is poor due to a lava shelf. They do have a manmade quasi tide-pool at the shore for wading in. However, just a short stroll south is Kuki'o Beach with somewhat better swimming.

Services here are extraordinary, even for a Kohala resort. (An example: chilled towels at the pool and Evian spritz service. How's that for pampering?) The swimming pools are scattered around the resort. Some, such as the main lipless infinity pool, are cleverly constructed so that, while swimming, it seems to be part of the ocean. Most resort items, like valet parking and room safes, are free. They even have a free sunglass cleaning service. (Though, oddly, local calls are $1.) Their restaurants, such as Pahu I'a, are excellent. No surprise there. If you have kids, the Seashell is the semi-circle you want; honeymooners (or those who want the quietest region) should choose the Palm Grove. Rooms of 600–670 sq. ft. are $675–$995. Suites are $1,095–$8,350!

Hapuna Beach Prince Hotel
(800) 882–6060 or (808) 880–1111
62-100 Kauna'oa Dr.

Hilton Waikoloa Village
(800) 221–2424 or (808) 886–1234
425 Waikoloa Beach Dr.

1,240 rooms, 3 pools, 3 hot tubs, valet parking ($14.50), fitness room, health spa, beauty salon, 8 tennis courts, two golf courses, **SOLID GOLD VALUE** 24 conference rooms, business center, coin-op laundry, empty fridge, hi-speed Internet access in room, room service, 9 restaurants, tons of shops, tram and a boat service. Where do we start? How about *wow!* This is the one you've probably heard about. This resort, built in the late '80s and spread over 62 acres, is the most elaborate of them all. (By the way, despite its name, it is not located in or next to the town of Waikoloa Village.) Over a thousand rooms in three separate towers are joined by a tram and boat network right out of Disneyland. A swimming pool has a pounding waterfall and an Indiana Jones-type swinging bridge overhead. There is a dolphin pool where lucky guests can get in the water with dolphins. The whole experience is described in ADVENTURES on page 233. *$7 million* worth of artwork is spread all over the resort. Parrots are also scattered about. There are multiple concierge desks around to assist in booking activities, making reservations or pointing the way to a particular part of the resort. The one thing

See all Web reviews at: www.wizardpub.com

the Hilton doesn't have is a Mauna Kea-type beach. (They have a manmade inland lagoon beach instead.) But 'Anaeho'omalu Beach is a half-mile walk or drive south. There's a large lagoon where guests float around in kayaks, paddle boats and rafts. In terms of amenities, the Hilton Waikoloa is an excellent place for families. Kids will *never* get bored here. There's a shallow swimming pool with a sandy beach at one end, a water slide, sand volleyball court and enough activities to wear out any teen or crumb cruncher and their kid's camp is $85 per day as well as a night camp and a play hour for kids under 5. Consider a ground floor cabana room in the Lagoon Tower in front of the dolphin pool where kids can frolic on the grass.

Large groups will find the group facilities superb. From their 24 conference rooms to the ballroom the size of Waikiki to their business services area, which rents everything from computers to cell phones—if you're here for business, they can accommodate you. The restaurants here are excellent. Fine Italian, Japanese, American—even a decent ice cream soda shoppe, 8 lounges...We could go on and on, but we're running out of room.

The resort might seem overwhelming at first. It cost over a third of a *billion* dollars to construct, and a staggering 1,200 employees are needed to run it all. You won't see all of them running around, however. That's because they go from here to there via an extensive underground tunnel network. Tunnels have dashed lines separating the lanes—even shoulders—and when you're down there, you're likely to run into your chef in uniform cruising along on a three-wheeled bike.

The entire resort is oriented inward, resulting in a destination that is self-contained. Some people who visit the Hilton Waikoloa snort that it's not real. Frankly, they miss the point. It's not *supposed* to represent reality. It's fantasy, escape, a leap into never-never land. You wouldn't sniff that Disneyland is phony, would you? The designers of the Hilton Waikoloa Village did a great job of achieving their objective—making an out-of-this-world playground/fantasyland for adults and kids. If that's what you are looking for, you will find it here in abundance. If you want to experience a calm piece of authentic old Hawai'i, you've come to the wrong place.

Rates are *cheap* for Kohala (but the spread is huge). Rooms of 530 sq. ft. are $199–$589. Executive floor rooms (which includes some extra services and amenities) are $294–$639. The 55 suites range from $1,060–$6,415. They have lots of optional resort fees which cover various services.

Islands at Mauna Lani
(800) 642–6284 or (808) 885–5022
68-1375 Pauoa Rd.
 ♦

Kolea
(866) 456–4252 or (808) 331–8878
69-1000 Kolea Kai

126 units, a/c, pool, keiki pool, BBQ, Wi-Fi in some, spa, fitness room, washer/dryer in unit, private elevators, business center. It's hard to imagine being unhappy here. These are some of the

See all Web reviews at: www.wizardpub.com

most impressively appointed condos we've seen and it's the only condo complex in Waikoloa that's next to the beach. Rooms are richly furnished with high end appliances, African mahogany trim throughout, Travertine floors, granite countertops, a wall of glass that'll fold away from the 430 sq. ft. lanai (and its separate kitchen) making it part of the living space, and so much more. Even the closets light up automatically when you walk in. Although decor varies from unit to unit, we didn't see any that weren't outstanding. They have a sand bottom children's pool with its own waterfall. First floor units are the least expensive, because views might be encroached upon by a home in front of you. (Second and third floor units have better views, especially bldgs. 4–8, 10 and 12.) An easy place to love. 2/2 units (1,270–1,554 sq. ft.) are $375–$550. 3/3 units (1,716–2,147 sq. ft.) are $500–$1,050. 3-night minimum. All units are non-smoking.

A REAL GEM

Kona Village Resort
(800) 367-5290 or (808) 325-5555
Queen Ka'ahumanu Hwy

125 units, 2 pools and 2 spas, 3 lighted tennis courts, restaurants, fitness room, free child care program most months for kids 6 and up, health club, free laundry facilities with free soap, free 100% Kona coffee beans in room (don't grind too early), refrigera-

A REAL GEM

tors, free lu'au, *meals included.* This is a rather unique place on the Big Island. Located between Kona and the main Kohala resort area, this resort was built in 1965 as a place to get away from it all. (And back then it *was* away from it all.) No phones, TVs or radios—they even have their own electrical generators and wells. Nestled next to a fine salt-and-pepper beach, most rooms are charming thatched, free-standing bungalows (some are duplexes). Some are right on the beach, and a few rooms are adjacent to pockets of black sand. The layout is similar to what Gilligan's Island would have looked like with more people and more money. Nine different kinds of huts are scattered about with trees, hammocks and a large exotic fishpond filling in the scene. The rooms along the tranquil ponds *define* serenity. We like them as much as the oceanfront rooms. All 82 acres are surrounded by a fresh sea of stark black lava. Service and staff are top notch—you want it, they'll get it. They'll even pack you a lunch for your off-site excursions. You can sign for anything, so leave your wallet in the room safe. An astounding percentage of their guests are repeats. Their Friday lu'au is the best on the island, and the food at the restaurant is great. This is the sort of place you want to come to if you are burned out, want peace and relaxation, and don't plan to get out a lot. Many guests don't even rent a car. They just lounge around the well-tended grounds the whole time or get picked up for activities. Lots of resort activities are included, plus freebies such as glass bottom boat tours, kayaks, snorkel gear, etc. Check out the manta ray that sometimes hangs out near the coconut tree light at night. This is a good place for honeymooners, and they have nice wedding services. They've won

See all Web reviews at: www.wizardpub.com

plenty of travel awards—justly so. They are synonymous with perpetuating the "old Hawai'i feel."

This resort used to be super secluded. But the quiet was broken when the Four Seasons, a golf course, and a residential community moved in next door. Expect a little less peace (and isolation) than in years past. They still have the no-nonsense guards at the entrance and on the beach to keep outsiders out. The price is high here, but it *includes meals* (or at least a high food credit). There are Jacuzzi bathtubs in some rooms, but don't expect flashy rooms. Simple, small and clean with a funky hut design with tiny bathrooms in some. By the way, the golf course next door *probably* won't be available to you. (They seem to have a somewhat tense relationship with the Four Seasons.) Rates *for two* are $625–$1,130. Rooms are 336–720 sq. ft. Price rises a lot for more people since meals are included.

Mauna Kea Beach Hotel
(800) 882–6060 or (808) 882–7222
62-100 Mauna Kea Beach Dr.

310 rooms, pool, spa, 13 tennis courts, free valet parking, coin-op laundry, room service, lu'au on premises, conference room, health club, 2 golf courses, restaurants, empty fridge, hi-speed Internet access in room, Nintendo, child care service. This was the first resort to grace the Kohala lava

A REAL GEM

desert area, and a large part of their business is repeat customers. Built by Laurence Rockefeller in 1965, it set the standard for all that came afterward. The Mauna Kea has traditionally been one of the most popular resorts on the island, and it's still a grand place to stay. Though the rooms are quite small and far from elaborate, they're very comfortable, and the resort is *very* restful and pleasing. Building 2 units are a bit bigger and newer than Building 1 units. (There are lots of categories. For instance, you're better off in the upper floor Beach Front rooms for $640 than the Ocean Views for $660.) Many people like the slow pace here. They are now getting third-generation guests who often have such a family affection for the place that when the hotel tries to change things, they sometimes rebel. Like the orange towels at the pool. Repeat guests howled when they replaced them with a different color, so back came the orange. Some of the staff has been here since the opening, and the warmth is refreshing. They have the best beachside location on the island, with the marvelous Kauna'oa Beach (usually called Mauna Kea) right at its doorstep. This beach *alone* qualified it for A REAL GEM, as far as we're concerned. The lu'au has a *great* setting. While other resorts might be newer and glitzier, Mauna Kea still stands the test of time. Think of it as a time-practiced excellence. Rooms (400–545 sq. ft.) are $420–$710, suites (800 sq. ft.) are $1,050–$1,700.

Mauna Lani Bay Hotel & Bungalows
(800) 327–8585 or (808) 885–6622
68-1400 Mauna Lani Dr.

WEB REVIEW

See all Web reviews at: www.wizardpub.com

Mauna Lani Point
(800) 642–6284 or (808) 885–5022
68-1050 Mauna Lani Point Dr.

116 units, a/c, pool, BBQ, spa, washer/dryer in unit, sauna, daily maid service. The interiors have nice furnishings, huge master bathrooms, pleasing layouts, good location and relaxing views across the golf course. Compared to some of the grander resorts in the area, it's not as compelling. Some units could use refurbishing. Some have very nice ocean views. You'll have to use stairs to get to your room, either down or up. 1/2 units (1,500 sq. ft.) are $350–$495, 2/3 units (1,900 sq. ft.) are $465–$695. 3-night minimum.

Mauna Lani Terrace
(800) 822–4252 or (808) 883–8500
68-1399 Mauna Lani Dr.

80 units, a/c, pool, spa, sauna, keiki pool, washer/dryer in unit, BBQ. Most units overlook the ancient fishponds, creating an amazingly tranquil setting. Some units have ocean views, as well. Buildings J, K and L

A REAL GEM

often have nice sunset views. Most units have higher-end furnishings and they'll do your grocery shopping for you (for a fee). 2- and 3-bedroom units are the better units. Try to avoid ground units. The master bathrooms are large (but with curiously small tubs). The complex is right next to the Mauna Lani Bay Hotel with all of its services. Grounds are nicely groomed. 1/2 units (1,058–1,150 sq. ft.) are $450, 2/3 (1,407–1,481 sq. ft.) units are $625. 3-night minimum.

Shores at Waikoloa
(800) 922–7866 or (808) 886–5001
69-1035 Keana Pl.

WEB REVIEW

Vista Waikoloa
(800) 822–4252 or (808) 883–8500
(866) 456–4252 or (808) 331–8878
69-1010 Keana Pl.

122 units, a/c, pool and 2 spas, fitness room, business center, washer/dryer in unit, elevator, Wi-Fi in main office, BBQ. Considering the calibre and the fact that it's in Kohala, this is a pretty good deal. Units are large and nicely furnished, the layout is pleasing, grounds are well groomed, the bathrooms have nice, deep

SOLID GOLD VALUE

See all Web reviews at: www.wizardpub.com

tubs. Views aren't overwhelming—distant ocean with some obstruction by another resort. But if you want a condo in Kohala, this is as close as you'll come to inexpensive yet pleasant. Bldgs. E & F are the best, A & B *feel* the closest to the road. 2/2 units (1,262–1,406 sq. ft. plus huge lanais) are $260–$280. 3-night minimum. The second set of numbers has fewer but nicer units.

Waikoloa Beach Marriott
(888) 797–1907 or (808) 886–6789
69-275 Waikoloa Beach Dr.

WEB REVIEW

Waikoloa Colony Villas
(800) 922–7866 or (808) 886–8899
(866) 456–4252 or (808) 331–8878
69-555 Waikoloa Beach Dr.

162 units, 2 pools, 2 spas, fitness room, tennis court, washer/dryer in unit, a/c, BBQ. This property is very similar to the Fairway Villas. The buildings seem a bit quieter and less dense than Fairway. But Fairway is closer to the Kings' Shops and the ocean. Both were completed in 2004. Furnishings vary from unit to unit but overall are pretty good. These are 2-story townhouses in clusters of 6 with solid walls between them. The large bathrooms have very small tubs and separate showers. Some layout aspects are awk-

ward (like how you have to close the master bedroom door to get to the bathroom door). Other aspects, like the sunken living rooms, are pleasing. Pool view units are actually better than ocean views which are very distant. 2/2s and 2/3s (1,236–1,446 sq. ft.) are $395–$475. 3/3s (1,699 sq. ft.) are $470–$560. The second set of numbers has much cheaper prices (and some garages available), a 3-night minimum and their units are non-smoking. From them, it's a SOLID GOLD VALUE.

KAILUA-KONA

The resorts in Kailua-Kona and the surrounding area aren't of the same calibre as the glitzy mega-resorts of Kohala, but neither are the prices. You'll find that you can stay and eat in Kona a lot cheaper than Kohala. Condos are far more numerous here than hotels. Some condos are a downright bargain, while others can only be recommended to in-laws.

Most accommodations in Kailua-Kona are along Alii Drive. This road fronts the shoreline offering splendid ocean locations and sunsets. The penalty for staying on Alii Drive is auto noise. Cars and motorcycles scoot by, sometimes creating unpleasant reminders in *some* condos that you are still in the real world. (Other condos keep their rooms far enough from the road to keep them blissfully quiet.)

The high season in Kona is December through March, and most condos charge more at that time. Also, most condos have a minimum stay.

If you're looking for a good deal and have a little time before your trip, the classifieds in the *West Hawai'i Today* newspaper (329–9311) on the west side, or *Hawai'i Tribune-Herald* (935–6621)

See all Web reviews at: www.wizardpub.com

on the east side often have incredible deals from individual owners of condos and houses. We have links to them from our Web site at **www.wizardpub.com**. From the web you can also search for individual condo owners. If you're not a web person, from the mainland, you can buy an individual paper or get a short-term subscription. It'll cost you a few dollars, but you may save hundreds or even thousands of dollars on your accommodations. Just remember that you won't have the security of working with an established rental agent or company.

Alii Villas
(800) 367–5168 or (808) 329–6438
(888) 311–6020 or (808) 329–6020
75-6016 Alii Dr.

125 units, a/c in some (ask for one because others can get hot), washer/ dryer in unit, BBQ, pool. Units are fairly small but **SOLID GOLD VALUE** with prices starting at $99–$136 for 1/1 units (620 sq. ft.), the value can be excellent. 2/2s (with 1,050

sq. ft.) are $162–$183. The pool is away from the ocean and isn't exactly dreamy to hang around at. Shop around with different rental agents. This ain't the greatest place to stay and it's pretty institutional-feeling. But the price is pretty reasonable. 3-night minimum.

Banyan Tree
(800) 622–5348 or (808) 329–3333
(800) 367–5168 or (808) 329–6438
76-6268 Alii Dr.
WEB REVIEW

Casa de Emdeko
(888) 311–6020 or (808) 329–6020
(800) 367–5168 or (808) 329–6438
75-6082 Alii Dr.
WEB REVIEW

Country Club Villas
(800) 745–5662 or (808) 326–9075
(800) 622–5348 or (808) 329–3333
78-6920 Alii Dr.
WEB REVIEW

Hale Kona Kai
(800) 421–3696 or (808) 329–2155
(800) 367–5168 or (808) 329–6438
75-5870 Kahakai Rd.

39 units, a/c, elevator, BBQ, pool. Broken into two wings (the short wing and the long wing) with no grounds. Rooms are pleasant and clean, and the liv-**SOLID GOLD VALUE**

See all Web reviews at: www.wizardpub.com

ing rooms and the bedrooms both face the water. The pool's so close to the ocean you'll get sprayed on big surf days. Rooms ending with 07 and 08 have bedrooms that face each other, affording less privacy. The solid gold value is because of their stellar ocean proximity. 1/1s (648–696 sq. ft.) are $135–$173. ($20 gets you a pretty nice wraparound lanai.) 3- or 5-night minimum.

Hale Pohaku
(888) 311–6020 or (808) 329–6020
76-6194 Alii Dr.

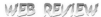 ◆

Kahalu'u Bay Villas
(800) 367–5168 or (808) 329–6438
78-6715 Alii Dr.

Kanaloa at Kona
(800) 688–7444 or (808) 322–9625
(800) 745–5662 or (808) 326–9075
78-261 Manukai St.

166 units, 3 lighted tennis courts, 3 pools, room safes, washer/dryer in unit, BBQ.

A REAL GEM

Upscale units with amenities, such as showers with two heads and large Jacuzzi bathtubs in the 2- and 3-bedroom units by the water, outdoor wet bars, Jenn-Air ranges with indoor grills in some, etc. 2/2 units are quite

large, 3/2 units simply add an open loft. Our only complaint is that they seem to nickel and dime you on the small stuff, like charging $1 to *receive* a FAX and air conditioning that is an extra $15 *per day.* For these room rates they should include these. Nice location on the shore. Overall, you should be pleased here. 1/2 units (1,200–1,336) are $239–$349, 2/2 units (1,648 sq. ft.) are $259–$429, 3/2 units (1,838 sq. ft.) are $395–$479. 2- or 3-night minimum. The second set of numbers has fewer units but cheaper prices.

Keauhou Akahi
(800) 799–5662 or (808) 322–6696
(888) 311–6020 or (808) 329–6020
78-7030 Alii Dr.

Keauhou Kona Surf & Racquet Club
(800) 799–5662 or (808) 322–6696
(800) 622–5348 or (808) 329–3333
78-6800 Alii Dr.

188 units, 3 lighted tennis courts, BBQ, pool, washer/dryer in unit. There are older townhouses and newer condos. *Huge* variation in rooms here, even among the condos. Buildings 1–5 have outstanding rooms with incredible locations. On the other hand, some of the buildings have tacky rooms with poor maintenance. The townhouse units are older and more weathered. The swimming pool is larger than most condo pools. There are several interesting archaeological sites on the grounds.

See all Web reviews at: www.wizardpub.com

Tennis is a big deal here and they have a tennis pro on site. End units (not in the townhouses) have wonderful wrap-around lanais. 2/2 units (1,175 sq. ft.) are $175–$325, 3/2 units (1,300 sq. ft.) are $$200–$355. The second set of numbers has cheaper units of lesser quality. All units are non-smoking. 3- or 4-night minimum.

Keauhou Palena
(800) 799–5662 or (808) 322–6696
78-7054 Kamehameha III Rd.

Keauhou Punahele
(800) 367–5168 or (808) 329–6438
(888) 311–6020 or (808) 329–6020
78-7070 Alii Dr.
WEB REVIEW

Keauhou Resort
(800) 367–5168 or (808) 329–6438
78-7039 Kamehameha III Rd.
WEB REVIEW

King Kamehameha's Kona Bch Hotel
(800) 367–6060 or (808) 329–2911
75-5660 Palani Rd.

460 rooms, 10 shops, 2 restaurants, 10 conference rooms, business center, coin-op laundry, empty fridges, coffee maker in room, pool and spa, lu'au. Built in the mid '70s, the King Kam (as it's known locally) is a Kona fixture. Located next to the Kailua Pier, the hotel is fronted by the tiny but calm Kamakahonu Beach. The 'Ahu'ena Heiau shown on page 58 is also on the grounds. This area was the home of King Kamehameha during his latter years, and his legacy has been adopted by the hotel. Paintings of him and other royal family members are strewn about the resort. The lobby is laid out like a mall, emphasizing the multitude of shops available. Some are worth stopping for.

This is a resort in transition. The rooms are fairly worn here, and the King Kam definitely shows its age—a once grand hotel past its prime. Until recently, there was little attempt to improve things. Zero concern, zero aloha, zero consideration. But a staff shake-up has ignited some desire to improve the hotel. Although it's obvious they aren't exactly dumping money into the place, they *are* trying and it's refreshing. Staff is better, fresh paint is showing and they are positioning themselves as a budget hotel with a central location. Parking is $9 and local calls are $1.

The hotel was for sale at press time so its condition could change. King Kam is the center of the universe every October when the Ironman Triathlon takes place. Most of the athletes stay here, as do many from the television crew, and rooms are hard to get then. Rooms are $180–$280, ridiculously priced suites are $500–$950 and it's likely that few pay full price.

Kona Alii
(800) 358–7977 or (808) 329–7977
75-5782 Kuakini Hwy.
WEB REVIEW

See all Web reviews at: www.wizardpub.com

Kona Bali Kai
(800) 367-5004 or (808) 329-9381
(800) 622-5348 or (808) 329-3333
76-6246 Alii Dr.

155 rooms, pool, small spa, washer/ dryer in oceanfront units *only* (others use coin-op laundry), BBQ, elevators. With some units on both sides of Alii Drive, the oceanfront units can be a very good deal, depending on who you rent from. The complex is run by Castle Resorts (the top phone numbers), but units rented from Hawai'i Resort Management (second set of numbers) can offer dramatically cheaper rates. Bear in mind that with the latter you won't get daily maid service. Units are smallish but the views are excellent. The pool is annoyingly located behind the main building and you probably won't want to use it. Units across the street are not worth the discount—go for oceanfront. Castle Resort prices for studios are $200–$220, 1/2s are $220–$300, 2/2s (808 sq. ft.) are $350–$360, 3/2s (1,075 sq. ft.) are $450–$460. Property Network also has units here. Castle has the most, but they're overpriced.

Kona By The Sea
(800) 922-7866 or (808) 327-2300
75-6106 Alii Dr.

86 units, central a/c, room safe, pool and spa, daily maid service, washer/ dryer in unit, elevators. Nicely furnished units, quiet, with pleasant grounds. The pool has an adjacent sandy area that's kind of nice. The oceanfront saltwater pool mentioned on page 62 is next to the grounds. It's run more like a hotel than a condo (but rooms are individually owned) and local calls are 75¢. Though some sections have 4 floors, the better views are from 2 & 3 since tree crowns can block some of the 4th floor units. This is a nice resort, but the RACK rates are *way* too steep, so try to get a package deal or a discount. 1/2 units (1,036 sq. ft.) are $280–$395, 2/2 units (1,400 sq. ft.) are $345–$460.

Kona Coast Resort
(800) 745-5662 or (808) 326-9075
(800) 799-5662 or (808) 322-6696
78-6842 Alii Dr.
WEB REVIEW

Kona Hotel
(808) 324-1155
72-65908 Mamalahoa Hwy
WEB REVIEW

Kona Islander Inn
(800) 622-5348 or (808) 329-3333
75-5776 Kuakini Hwy
WEB REVIEW

Kona Isle
(888) 311-6020 or (808) 329-6020
75-6100 Alii Dr.
WEB REVIEW

See all Web reviews at: www.wizardpub.com

Kona Magic Sands
(800) 622–5348 or (808) 329–3333
77-6452 Alii Dr.

37 rooms, pool, a/c in *some*, BBQ. You can see and hear the ocean right from your bed. Units are *very* small (450 sq. ft.)—a studio **SOLID GOLD VALUE** with a kitchenette. The bed area seems to be formed from a converted lanai in some rooms. But you can't beat the oceanside price of $105–$135. 3-night minimum. Upper floors have better views. Units ending 01–04 have extra large 250 sq. ft. lanais. Units can vary a lot, so ask for remodeled unit.

Kona Makai
(800) 358–7977 or (808) 329–7977
(800) 367–5168 or (808) 329–6438
75-6026 Alii Dr.

Kona Nalu
(800) 367–5168 or (808) 329–6438
76-6212 Alii Dr.

Kona Reef
(800) 367–5004 or (808) 329–2959
(800) 367–5168 or (808) 329–6438
75-5888 Alii Dr.
130 units, a/c, pool, spa, elevator, washer/dryer in unit, BBQs. Buildings A and D are fairly quiet, but units next to Alii Drive are noisy. The rooms are not bad, not great. If you're gonna stay here, try to get a corner unit. Although there's a/c

in most, it's not in the bedroom, and it may get hot in there (and not the way you intend). If you need a room that's elevator-accessible, get in Bldg. F. Because in a fit of goofiness, at the other buildings, the elevator only stops *between* floors. Ocean view rooms have pretty tranquil views. 1/1s (611–651 sq. ft.) are $240–$295. 2/2 units (905–1,120 sq. ft.) are $400. Their RACK rates are insane, but few pay them since discounts are as easy to get as a sunburn. SunQuest has *much* cheaper prices. 3-night minimum.

Kona Seaside Hotel
(800) 367–7000 or (808) 329–2455
75-5646 Palani Rd.
WEB REVIEW

Kona Seaspray
(808) 322–2403
78-6665 Alii Dr.
WEB REVIEW

Kona Tiki Hotel
(808) 329–1425
75-5968 Alii Dr.
15 rooms, pool, empty fridge. This small hotel, built in 1953, is an old-style Kona hotel. All rooms have incredible oceanfront views **SOLID GOLD VALUE** right next to the water. How close? The swimming pool is permanently salty from waves washing over the rock wall and is available 24 hours "if

See all Web reviews at: www.wizardpub.com

you behave." Continental breakfast is free. The guests usually end up forming a loose family of sorts. You won't find the usual array of amenities. Missing are phones, air conditioning, TV, laundry facilities—they don't even take credit cards (cash or TCs). (They *do* have a BBQ with a dynamite view for you to use.) This is the kind of place that visitors looking for a smashing oceanfront location, simple room and *very* reasonable prices will come back to over and over. Rooms are $65–$79. Kitchenettes are $88. Rates per couple. They charge an extra $6.70 per kid. 3- to 7-night minimum at times. All units are non-smoking.

Makolea
(800) 367–5168 or (808) 329–6438
(888) 311–6020 or (808) 329–6020
78-216 Makolea St.
WEB REVIEW

Manago Hotel
(808) 323–2642
82-6155 Mamalahoa Hwy (11)
WEB REVIEW

Outrigger Keauhou Beach Resort
(800) 462–6262 or (808) 322–3441
78-6740 Alii Dr.
309 rooms, 6 tennis courts (2 lighted), 4 conference rooms, 2 restaurants, 3 shops, pool, spa, keiki (children's) pool,

fitness room, Nintendo, coin-op laundry room, empty fridge, coffee makers in room. Originally built in 1970 (but completely refurbished with a bright, open feel), the hotel borders Kahalu'u Beach on one side and a tide-pool on another. Many of the rooms have nice views. The oceanfront rooms are *worth every penny*. They're the only rooms on the Big Island that are *directly* over the water. Just look down, and you may see turtles and eels swimming in the shallow tide-pool. Other rooms are nice for the money. (Although some have silly little square tubs, other have showers only.) For the location, it's a great deal. Their Verandah Lounge is a truly kickin' place to have a sunset cocktail. Rooms (420 sq. ft.) are $239–$399. (But parking is $5 and local calls are a buck.) Their one-bedroom suite (758 sq. ft.) is $499. Their "Best Value Rates" are usually available and rooms start at $149. *Wow!*

SOLID GOLD VALUE

Royal Kahili
(800) 358–7977 or (808) 329–7977
(888) 311–6020 or (808) 329–6020
78-6283 Alii Dr.
WEB REVIEW

Royal Kona Resort
(800) 222–5642 or (808) 329–3111
75-5852 Alii Dr.
WEB REVIEW

See all Web reviews at: www.wizardpub.com

Royal Sea Cliff Resort
(800) 688–7444 or (808) 329–8021
75-6040 Alii Dr.

142 units, tennis court, a/c, room safe, 2 pools (1 saltwater), spa, sauna, washer/dryer in unit, Wi-Fi resort wide, daily maid service. The resort is run similarly to a hotel (though units are individually owned) and units are fairly large. The recreation area has an outdoor kitchen and BBQs. Note from the aerial photo that the middle rooms, though called "Partial Ocean View," have very poor views. (Think of the resort as a tree and try to get a room on a branch, not the trunk.) Also, since the floors are stair-stepped, upper floor units look down on the lanais of the floors beneath them. They have lots of packages available, so you shouldn't end up paying RACK rates. Studios (500 sq. ft.) are $215–$255, 1/1 units (700–784 sq. ft.) are $249–$415, 2/2 units (950–1,430 sq. ft.) are $289–$459. Local calls are $.75. All units are non-smoking.

Sea Village
(800) 367–5168 or (808) 329–6438
(888) 311–6020 or (808) 329–6020
75-6002 Alii Dr.
WEB REVIEW

Sheraton Keauhou Bay Resort
(888) 488–3535 or (808) 930–4900
78-128 Ehukai St.

521 rooms, pool, 2 spas, 2 lighted tennis courts, fitness room, room service,

A REAL GEM

valet parking, 2 restaurants, lounge, empty fridges, 5 shops, 7 conference rooms, business center, Wi-Fi throughout resort, coin-op laundry room, coffee makers in room, free room safes, Nintendo, chapel, child care program, health spa. This resort was closed for 3 years before $80 million dollars worth of renovations ushered in the new Sheraton in 2005. It's best described as sophisticated, tropical, understated, islandy and it embraces their oceanside location. (No sand beach, however.) Their mantra (and marketing direction) is family, fitness and fun and it's reflected in their multi-level water feature with 200-foot waterslide, waterfall and pool that meanders into the lobby atrium. The fitness room (for those who can't bear to be on vacation without working out) is state of the art with a killer view of the ocean. The keiki center might just well be the best we've seen in the state, complete with foosball, PlayStation, basketball, ping pong, widescreen movie theater, craft room and more. (It's $60 for a full day which includes lunch.) Kids eat free at the Kai Restaurant with a paying adult. While we're talking about keikis, they even offer SCUBA in their pool to kids as young

See all Web reviews at: www.wizardpub.com

as 5. They have a good wedding infrustructure including a chapel and a staff member called the Director of Love. (*That* must look cool on a business card.)

Unlike most resorts, most extras are included in the room price except self-parking ($6), valet parking ($11), Internet ($10) and local calls are $1. Overall they've done a good job turning an aging resort into a modern, comfortable, family-friendly getaway. Hence, the GEM. All rooms are non-smoking. Rooms (450 sq. ft.) are $325–$425, suites (925–3,000 sq. ft.) are $850–$3,000. Their partial ocean view category is worth the upgrade over the mountain view rooms.

Uncle Billy's Kona Bay Hotel
(800) 367–5102 or (808) 329–1393
75-5739 Alii Dr.
WEB REVIEW

White Sands Village
(800) 622–5348 or (808) 329–3333
(800) 367–5168 or (808) 329–6438
77-6469 Alii Dr.
WEB REVIEW

HILO

Your choices in Hilo are much more limited than on the western side of the island. The number of overnight visitors here is a fraction of what the Kona side gets. The hotels are older here, so don't expect the swankiness of the Kohala resorts. But you shouldn't expect Kohala prices either. Hotels can be had quite cheap in Hilo, so even if you are staying on the western side, you should strongly consider staying at least a night here

when you are exploring this side or visiting the volcano. That'll keep Hilo from becoming a blur during an around-the-island driving frenzy.

Most of the hotels are located along Banyan Drive. Many have outstanding views of Hilo Bay.

Arnott's Lodge
(808) 969–7097
98 Apapane Rd.
WEB REVIEW

Country Club Hawai'i Condo Hotel
(866) 935–7171 or (808) 935–7171
121 Banyan Dr.

147 rooms, Wi-Fi available, lanais on most, microwave and empty fridge, daily maid only if you pay the daily rate. So what are they—a hotel or a condo? They are a hotel with rooms owned by individuals, so expect variations among the rooms. If you don't expect squat for service here, you won't be disappointed. Many rooms are dumpy and not worth the price. Consider the other offerings in Hilo. Rooms (around 300 sq. ft.) are $79–$99, kitchenettes (which only add a hot plate—woo-wee!) and are $79.

See all Web reviews at: www.wizardpub.com

Dolphin Bay Hotel
(877) 935–1466 or (808) 935–1466
333 Iliahi St.

16 rooms, TV, Wi-Fi in lobby and *some* rooms, coin-op laundry, no a/c, coffee makers in *some*. One of the better bargains in Hilo. **SOLID GOLD VALUE** Rooms are clean and have complete kitchens. The lack of telephones may make arranging your day awkward, but the room quality and kitchen at this price make it easy to recommend and you can always use the phone in the lobby. Located in northern Hilo. (See Hilo map, page 108.) Rooms are $89–$99 (it's worth the up-grade to Superior), 1- and 2-bedrooms units are $119 and $129. Free coffee, cakes and fruit in the morning. Good staff.

Hilo Bay Hostel
(808) 933–2771
101 Waianuenue Ave.
WEB REVIEW

Hilo Hawaiian Hotel
(800) 367–5004 or (808) 935–9361
71 Banyan Dr.
WEB REVIEW ◆

Hilo Seaside
(800) 560–5557 or (808) 935–0821
126 Banyan Way
135 rooms, pool, coin-op laundry, no elevator, empty fridge in some, coffee

Ice Pond

maker upon request, lanais on some. Clean, simple rooms across from the ice pond. Rooms (around 170 sq. ft.) are $110–$120, with kitchenettes for $130. You will usually get a discount, and if you get a room for $70 it's a SOLID GOLD VALUE. Add $30 for a car. Rooms facing the pool are preferable since they're away from the busy street.

Naniloa Volcanoes Resort
(808) 969–3333
93 Banyan Dr.
WEB REVIEW

Uncle Billy's Hilo Bay Hotel
(800) 367–5102 or (808) 935–0861
87 Banyan Dr.

Uncle Billy's

144 rooms, pool, restaurant, coin-op laundry, empty fridge, coffee makers in *some*. Owned by the same family as the Kona Bay Hotel, rooms are decent sized and clean. The lobby is funky—sort of a

'50s Hawai'i as the mainland saw it. Superior type rooms are the best value. If you go oceanfront, get a wraparound. Rooms are clean for their age, but the resort could use some renovation. Rooms are $104–$129, kitchenettes are $119–$134. Car packages are available as well as other discounts; be sure to check.

Wild Ginger Inn
(800) 882–1887 or (808) 935–5556
100 Puueo St.
WEB REVIEW

VOLCANO VILLAGE

The town of Volcano Village has a limited number of places to stay, but the choices you *do* have are superb. If you are spending a week on the Big Island, at least one night should be spent here. This is the most convenient place to stay when you explore the volcano. You can take your time and do the volcano justice. Remember, it gets chilly here at 4,000 feet, so bring something warm and waterproof. There are lots of B&Bs in Volcano Village, so check out the service listed on page 278 or check our Web site.

Inn at Volcano
(800) 937–7786 or (808) 967–7786
19-4178 Wright Rd.
6 rooms, spa. Built in 1942 but thoroughly remodeled, this inn is equivalent to

A REAL GEM

a beautiful, upscale lodge. The Continental Lace Suite is their very romantic bridal suite with double Jacuzzi bathtub in the bathroom. The Treehouse Suite is two story; a wooden spiral staircase leads to the bedroom with its dreamy view. The bathroom has a Jacuzzi bathtub, TV and a fireplace in it. The extra

touches are too numerous to mention (including marble bathrooms in some and afternoon tea in the common area which has free Internet access). The grounds are lush and tidy. All rooms have TVs and VCRs. Gourmet candlelit breakfasts included (tall people duck). Rooms are $170–$185, suites (275–500 sq. ft.) are $200–$400 (no minimum). All rooms are non-smoking. We've had a number of bad e-mails from readers but our own obsevations haven't matched them.

They also have other properties, such as a simple B&B for $65–$85 (good for families on a budget), houses and cottages off grounds, the Lokahi Lodge and more. We like the suites at the inn the best, but Lokahi is a fairly good deal at $110–$170. Call them for a complete price list of all their properties.

Kilauea Lodge
(808) 967–7366
19-3948 Old Volcano Rd.

14 rooms, coffee makers with free coffee, Wi-Fi in dining room, no TV or phones

(except in cottages), lanais on some, restaurant, centrally heated, fireplaces in

A REAL GEM

some, hot tub. Opened in 1938 as a YMCA youth camp, this quaint lodge was converted in 1986 by Albert and Lorna Jeyte. (He was a makeup artist on *Magnum P.I.*) The whole thing is very well done. There are different types of rooms, such as the Honeymoon Deluxe (very romantic), Hale Maluna building (snug rooms with fireplaces and incredible skylights in the bathrooms) and two cottages. The grounds are lush and well-tended. The staff is top-notch. Breakfast is included in the price. Rooms (225–400 sq. ft.) are $150–$165. 2/2 cottages (800–1,000 sq. ft.) are $180–$190. All rooms are non-smoking.

Volcano House
(808) 967–7321
Hawai'i Volcanoes National Park

42 units. This hotel/lodge is located on the rim of Kilauea Caldera inside Hawai'i

A REAL GEM

Volcanoes National Park. They are a protected park concessionaire and our expectations were low, but we're pleased to say that this hotel, like the park itself, is surprisingly well run. The rooms are small but clean. They have phones, but no TVs or radios. At night most people either head down to the lava flows (Pele permitting), relax at the bar, watch the movie about the volcano shown at 7:30 p.m., or just curl up by the fire in the lobby fireplace, said to have been burning continuously since 1874 (though they "move" the fire when they need to clean the fireplace). Some of the rooms (especially 30–33) have excellent crater views. No minimum stay. The lobby gets unbelievably busy at lunch but quiets down at night. The cheapest rooms are in the 'Ohi'a building (avoid the downstairs rooms if possible—they're below ground level and they may get a little buggy). The 'Ohi'a wing has a little lobby with its own fireplace (you may have to light that one—don't be shy about asking for more wood). The more desireable main Bldg. rooms (200 sq. ft.) are $170–$225, 'Ohi'a rooms (120 sq. ft.) are $95–$125. They also operate 10 cabins for $50 at Namakani Paio.

WAIMEA

Things get chilly up here at 2,500 feet, as well. You have your choice: There's the 30-room **Kamuela Inn** (800) 555–8968 or (808) 885–4243 at 65-1300 Kawaihae Road. This charming and quaint inn is smaller than the Waimea Country Lodge. It's clean and the setting is well-groomed, but the rooms are *real* variable in terms of decor. Rooms in the older section are $59–$72, kitchenettes are $89–$99, newer section is $79–$85, with suites for $185. Phones in some, continental breakfast included. The slightly better bet is the **Waimea Country Lodge** (800) 367–5004 or (808) 885–4100 at 65-1210 Lindsey Road. 21 clean, spacious rooms with high, knotty pine ceilings in the preferred 2nd floor units. Rooms are $109–$120, Kitchenettes are $129. If you don't get a kitchenette, consider getting a Superior. Good staff. Laundry on site if you wait till they're done using it.

Then there's the upscale **Jacaranda Inn** (808) 885–8813 at 65-1444 Kawai-

See all Web reviews at: www.wizardpub.com

hae Rd. Built in 1897 as a Parker Ranch manager's house, it's been converted into a charming luxury inn. This is a great place! Think of it as the kind of inn that Mark Twain would have stayed at a century ago. There are 8 different rooms and a cottage, each with its own theme in purple (the color of Jacaranda trees) and lavishly furnished. Each has a private bath and entrance. Most bathrooms have double Jacuzzi tubs. Rooms (454–665 sq. ft.) are $125–$199, 3/3 cottage with kitchen (1,695 sq. ft.) is $450. (The cottage is *nice*.) Excellent service. All rooms are non-smoking.

A REAL GEM

NORTHERN TIP OF THE ISLAND

In Hawi, the **Kohala Village Inn** (808) 889–0404 at 55-524 Hawi Road is an excellent value for someone looking to get away from it all. A quaint, simple old Hawai'i inn that's very clean. Rooms (200–400 sq. ft.) are $65–$95. Suites (420 sq. ft.) are $100–$120. Free continental breakfast and Internet access in lobby. Back building rooms are quietest. No phones but they'll take messages.

In Kapa'au, the **Kohala Club Hotel** (808) 889–6793 at 54-3793 Akoni Pule Hwy was built in the late 1800s as an English gentleman's club. Left in disrepair, it's being partially restored by its present owner. Consider this an historic experience, not a lavish one. 4 rooms (100–120 sq. ft.) are $50–$89. Cash only.

SOUTHEAST PART OF THE ISLAND

These two places are on the south side of the island, and they are a *long* way from other towns. In Na'alehu you'll find the **Shirakawa Motel** (808) 929–7462

at 95-6040 Mamalahoa Hwy. 12 rooms, full kitchens in some, hot plates in others, TVs in some, no laundry facilities. On the positive side, it's run by nice people and it's inexpensive. On the negative side, it's a dump. $43 for a single, $45 for doubles, $55 for kitchenettes, and a 1/1 for $65. Though they only have a dozen units, the room numbers go up to 38. What happened to the others?

Located near Punalu'u Beach is **Colony One at SeaMountain** (800) 359–6089 or (808) 939–7368 at 95-789 Ninole Loop Rd. 74 units, pool and spa, golf course, bbq, washer/dryer in some. This condo complex is in the heart of SeaMountain, a very remote region in the southern part of the island. This was a troubled resort in the past but they've put quite a bit of effort in lately and it shows. And the price is hard to beat. The grounds are pleasant. Think of this as an alternative place to stay if you want to explore Hawai'i Volcanos National Park (28 miles away) but still want to stay near the shoreline where it's more tropical (though the units are not beachside). It's quiet and peaceful. All units are non-smoking. Studios (475 sq. ft.) are $60–$95, 1/1 units (700 sq. ft.) are $60–$120, 2/2s (1,000 sq. ft.) are $95–$150. Vacation International (800) 444–6633 also operates some units here, but their prices are higher.

HONOKA'A

About 8 miles from Waipi'o Valley is **Hotel Honoka'a Club** (800) 808–0678 or (808) 775–0678 at 45-3480 Mamane St. 19 rooms (#10 and #16 are the best), this place is tiny, ancient and clean. Rooms (149–200 sq. ft.) $55–$75, they also have hostel beds for $28–$30 per person. All are non-smoking.

INDEX

Dining Index on page 240, Where to Stay Index on page 278.

INDEX

Dining Index on page 240, Where to Stay Index on page 278.

INDEX

Dining Index on page 240, Where to Stay Index on page 278.

INDEX

305

Dining Index on page 240, Where to Stay Index on page 278.

Dining Index on page 240, Where to Stay Index on page 278.

Dining Index on page 240, Where to Stay Index on page 278.